ENCYC...

FEM...OM

ENCYCLOPEDIA OF

FEMINISM

Lisa Tuttle

Facts On File Publications
New York, New York ● Oxford, England

Encyclopedia of Feminism

© Lisa Tuttle 1986

First published in the United States of America in 1986 by
Facts On File Publications
460 Park Avenue South
New York, New York 10016

Library of Congress Cataloging in Publication Data

Tuttle, Lisa, 1952–
Encyclopedia of feminism.

1. Feminism—Dictionaries.   2. Women's encyclopedias
and dictionaries.   I. Title.
HQ1115.T87   1986   305.4'2'0321   85-31212
ISBN 0-8160-1424-8

This book was designed and produced by
The Rainbird Publishing Group Limited
27 Wrights Lane, London W8 5TZ

Typeset by Wyvern Typesetting Ltd, Bristol
Made and printed by Cox & Wyman Ltd, Reading

For Joan Altobelli and Marsha Walker
and for Genevieve and Lindsay
with hope for a feminist future

Acknowledgments

This book is very much the product of other books, the result of work done by many writers, historians, philosophers, researchers, scientists, creators, thinkers, activists and artists, most of whom are credited within the pages that follow. I was fortunate to have had access to the Fawcett Library at the City of London Polytechnic, and I am grateful to the staff there, particularly David Doughan. The Feminist Library, in Hungerford House, was also very useful, and I appreciate the help given me by Susan Searing, Women's Studies Librarian-at-Large, when I visited the University of Wisconsin in Madison.

Candida Lacey, peerless researcher, contributed substantially, and I thank her. Without her assistance, finishing this book would have been impossible. I'm grateful also for the editing skills of Liz Blair and Gillian Bate.

Thank you to all those who read various entries, criticized, commented, advised, made suggestions, loaned me books, tracked down obscure information, and listened to me go on and on – especially Chris Atkinson, Sarah Biggs, Avedon Carol, John Clute, Leah Fritz, Gillian Hill, Rob Holdstock, Sarah Lefanu, Agnes Pivot, Linda Steele and Birgit Voss. I'm particularly grateful to Chris Atkinson and Malcolm Edwards, in whose house much of this book was written. Thanks also to Charlotte Bunch, Hal Davis, Alice Echols, Ellen Frankfort, Jo Freeman, Jeanne Gomoll, Bell Hooks, Paula Treichler, Betsy Warrior and my mother for answering my letters and sending useful information and clippings.

Last, but far from least, I'd like to thank Maxim Jakubowski for first suggesting and then commissioning an encyclopedia of feminism; and Women in Publishing for inspiring Maxim, and for encouraging, sustaining and entertaining me during the last three years.

Introduction

What is feminism? This book is an attempt to answer that question, not by offering an ideology or a list of politically correct attributes, but by including as much as possible of what has been called feminism, both now and in the past, in the hope that, from the diversity, a picture will emerge. As my starting point, I have taken the widest possible definition by assuming we may call feminist anyone who recognizes women's subordination and seeks to end it, by whatever means and on whatever grounds. This includes every shade of political thought along the scale from liberal feminists who believe their demands for equality can be met without otherwise changing the structure of society, to those lesbian feminists who propose that all power be put into the hands of women and men reduced to no more than ten per cent of the population. Anti-sexist men are included herein, revolutionaries, reactionaries, scholars, artists, activists, and even some women who say 'I'm not a feminist, but. . .'

I believe there is a need for a general reference work, accessible to both the committed feminist and the pre-feminist reader alike. Because feminism is a living, changing movement – not a theory but a world-view – not all feminist writers share the same vocabulary or common references. I have tried to include entries on all individuals, organizations, classic works and specialized terminology which might be used without explanation in some feminist texts. I have also tried, with the topic entries (on such subjects as HOUSEWORK, MARRIAGE, PORNOGRAPHY and VIOLENCE), to provide a simple (I hope not simplistic) description of some of the most important insights of feminism. The *Encyclopedia* is meant not only as a reference, but as an introduction, a way in to feminism for anyone wondering where, among all the books in print, to start. It is a book meant for browsing; words in SMALL CAPITALS within any entry are a suggestion that the reader turn to those entries and read on.

Preserving and increasing women's knowledge is a feminist priority. Dale Spender has warned, 'Unless we take preventive measures, feminist ideas which no longer have the appeal of "novelty" but which are none the less essential to our understandings and a vital part of our traditions will drift – as they have in the past – to the brink of oblivion. Unless we keep reminding each other of our heritage we endanger it, we risk losing it as we contribute to our own amnesia.' (Spender, 1985). With this in mind, I have been more interested in inclusion than exclusion. Although the emphasis may be on the major topics, events, figures and ideas of feminism through the ages, I've also been interested in rescuing as many early feminists from obscurity as I possibly could. What haunts me are those left out due to lack of time or resources; the thought of all the volumes that could yet be written. This could be a life-time's work. I dreamed of writing not only a feminist's guide to feminism, but to everything for which there is a feminist perspective, which is to say everything which affects women, which is. . . everything.

Who am I to write such a book – even a modest, scaled-down version? I'm a feminist, but not a famous one; I'm not a committee or a co-operative, not a superwoman, not even a scholar. Aware of the hubris – or at least chutzpah – inherent in such a venture, I embarked upon it anyway. I did so partly as a political act, to help in women's liberation, but mostly because I wanted an *Encyclopedia of Feminism* to exist. It was a book I needed. Rather than wait patiently (as women are supposed to do) for people better qualified than myself to produce it in the distant future, I set out to write it myself.

The ideas in this book are not my own, but the interpretations of them are. I have tried to make it clear when I am expressing my own opinion, and although I have tried to be objective, I hope the reader will remember with me that total objectivity is a myth. If you think I am wrong, you are probably right. My hope with this book is not to offer any final answers, but to contribute to the construction of feminist alternatives by encouraging more questions.

A

A Woman's Place

A WOMEN'S CENTRE started in 1977 by a group of women in a squat in London. In 1982, with funding from the Greater London Council, A Woman's Place moved to Hungerford House, Victoria Embankment, where six paid workers and a larger voluntary collective provide information and services to women both nationally and internationally. A Woman's Place provides free meeting rooms for over thirty women's groups, offers specialized contacts on many issues, including health, housing and legal rights, and includes a feminist bookshop.

ableism

Term constructed by analogy with sexism and racism (able+ism) in the early 1980s, used to mean the oppression of those with physical or mental disabilities by those who consider themselves able-bodied. Some feminists now use the term TAB or 'Temporarily Able-Bodied' to point up the fact that disabilities are an issue for everyone, not merely those who are called handicapped.

abolition movement

The American anti-slavery movement (from approximately 1830–63) is usually seen as the birthplace of the women's rights movement. Women committed to abolishing slavery were barred by their sex from joining most abolition organizations, and so had to form their own groups. The experience of political organizing and public speaking in the face of male objections and attacks paved the way for similar activities directed at winning the vote and other legal rights for themselves.

abortion

One of the most emotive issues of the modern women's movement. Although feminists of the nineteenth and early twentieth centuries were generally anti-abortion, a basic feminist tenet of the latter half of the twentieth century is that every woman has the right to control her own reproductive life.

Until the early 1800s it was a woman's choice, common law considering it a crime only after 'quickening' (stage of discernible fetal movement). Even the Catholic Church did not categorize it as murder until 1869. In the 1860s, powerful anti-abortion movements in America and Britain resulted in new legislation making it illegal.

Not all abortion law reform groups have been feminist, and

there is a division between those who favour reform (which presumes abortion must be regulated and decided on by someone other than the woman involved) and those who would repeal all legal restrictions.

In America, a statement calling for an end to laws against abortion was carried in November 1967 as part of the NOW BILL OF RIGHTS FOR WOMEN, after a lengthy and emotional debate among members.

Colorado was the first state to reform the nineteenth-century laws, in 1967, and by 1970 eleven other states had followed. Hawaii, New York and Alaska based their changes on repeal rather than reform arguments.

On 22 January 1973, the U.S. Supreme Court declared, in the case of Roe vs. Wade, 'We recognize the right of the individual, married or single, to be free from unwarranted governmental intrusion into matters so fundamentally affecting a person as the decision whether to bear or beget a child. That right necessarily includes the right of a woman to decide whether or not to terminate her pregnancy.'

In 1977, the Supreme Court upheld states' rights to withhold medical welfare funds for abortions.

In Britain, the Abortion Law Reform Association was formed in 1936 and worked towards the 1967 Abortion Act. This did not repeal previous legislation, but only outlined specific instances in which abortion was no longer considered a crime. The decision remains with the doctor, rather than with the woman concerned, with the result that many women find it difficult or impossible to get an abortion through the National Health Service.

In 1975 the feminist national abortion campaign was launched, and the ALRA changed its policies and its name to 'a woman's right to choose' (AWRC).

Abzug, Bella, 1920–
American lawyer and politician. Founder of the NATIONAL WOMEN'S POLITICAL CAUCUS and Women Strike for Peace (1961–70). Active in federal (member, House of Representatives, 1971–6) and New York State politics, and a frequent commentator on women's issues.

Adams, Abigail, 1744–1818
American. Remembered chiefly for her relationships to husband John Adams and son John Quincy Adams, and reputed to have influenced their decisions as President. Her attempt, however, to use her influence to achieve equality for women under the new American Constitution did not succeed. In one of her best-known letters to her husband, before the Constitution had been written, she implored him to 'Remember the Ladies, and be more generous and favorable to them than your ances-

tors. Do not put such unlimited power into the hands of the Husbands. Remember all Men would be tyrants if they could. If perticular care and attention is not paid to the Laidies we are determined to foment a Rebelion, and will not hold ourselves bound by any Laws in which we have no voice, or Representation.' Unfortunately, John treated her request as a joke, and she subsided without carrying out her threat of rebellion.

Addams, Jane, 1860–1935

American. One of the most widely admired American women of the twentieth century. She began her long career as a social reformer by establishing the settlement Hull House in Chicago in 1889. It was instantly successful, and from being a refuge for poor immigrants, it was soon the source of campaigns for equal rights and social justice for all Americans. Addams' emphasis on reform and fairness meant that her brand of feminism was rarely seen as threatening: her view of government as 'housekeeping on a large scale' informed her belief that women had a special contribution to make to the world, and caused her to be active in the women's suffrage movement. She served as vice-president of the National American Woman Suffrage Association from 1911–14. In 1915 she headed the Women's Peace Party and the first Women's Peace Congress at the Hague. Her PACIFISM grew directly out of her feminism, for she believed the control of VIOLENCE was essential for women to achieve equality. So long as society sanctioned violence, men would be able to physically dominate and control women. This aspect of her feminism was far less acceptable to the public, particularly after America entered World War I, and for a time her popularity was eclipsed. In 1920 she became a founder-member of the American Civil Liberties Union, and her activities on behalf of blacks, immigrants and other disadvantaged groups caused the Daughters of the American Revolution to label her 'the most dangerous woman in America today'. In 1931 she was awarded the Nobel Peace Prize. Her writings include *Newer Ideals of Peace* (1907) and *Twenty Years at Hull House* (1910).

Advocate of Moral Reform

American evangelical journal founded 1834 by the New York Female Moral Reform Society with a policy of staffing it as far as possible only with women. By the 1850s it was the most widely-read evangelical journal in the country and had become emphatically feminist, demanding higher wages and better job opportunities to enable women to be independent.

affirmative action

American term used for any institutional policy established to break down the white male monopoly in any field of employment by actively recruiting women or others customarily discriminated against and by preferential hiring practices. The term originated in President Johnson's Executive Order 11246 (amended, in October 1967, to include a ban on sexual discrimination as well, and renumbered 11375) which required that all institutions which did business with or received grants from the federal government should not only refrain from discrimination in hiring, but must 'take affirmative action to ensure that applicants are employed, and employees are treated during their employment without regard to their race, color, religion, sex or national origin.'

Although guidelines for affirmative action have been much firmer in regard to race than sex, it has been useful as a means of counteracting the unconscious bias against women (tests have shown that even when women are equally qualified, they are not perceived to be as good as men) as well as redressing the balance by which white men usually receive (unacknowledged) preferential treatment. It is seen not as a permanent reversal, but as an interim measure, a form of POSITIVE DISCRIMINATION to end all discrimination.

Against Our Will
Book, subtitled *Men, Women and Rape*, by Susan BROWNMILLER, first published in 1975. Thoroughly researched, and closely analytical, it is the definitive work on all aspects of RAPE, which it shows to be a major weapon used by men for the intimidation of all women, and therefore one of the most basic concerns of feminism.

ageism (age + ism)
Term referring to the practice of devaluing and discriminating against people because of their age. Although men may also be victims, ageism is more commonly directed at women and may be seen as another aspect of SEXISM, the inevitable response of a society which equates the value of women with their sexual attractiveness to men.

Ain't I A Woman
Subtitled *Black Women and Feminism*, this book by Bell HOOKS, first published in 1981, examines the dual oppression of racism and sexism suffered by black women in America, and shows how the largely white, middle-class women's movement has either ignored the black woman, or romanticized her as a 'strong' female not in need of liberation, or assumed her concern was only with racism. The title comes from a famous speech by Sojourner TRUTH at the second annual women's rights convention in Akron, Ohio in 1851, when she cast scorn on the white male contention that women were physically too weak to bear the burden of equal rights.

Akerman, Chantal, 1950–
Belgian film-maker. Although she
has denied the label of 'feminist
filmmaker', her films have been of
particular interest to feminists for
the way they look at women and the
way that women audiences relate to
them. Her full-length films include
*Jeanne Dielman, 23 Quai du Com-
merce, 1080 Bruxelles* (1975), *Je Tu Il
Elle* (1974), *Les Rendezvous d'Anna*
(1978) and *Toute Une Nuit* (1982).

Alcott, Louisa May, 1832–88
American author. Although best
remembered for conventional
domestic tales like *Little Women*,
and what she once described as
'moral pap for the young', Alcott
also wrote the strongly feminist,
somewhat autobiographical novel
Work (1873). She was never actively
involved in the women's movement of her day, but women's
rights were deeply important to
her, and she promoted feminist
principles through her life and her
writing. As she wrote to Lucy
Stone in 1873: 'I am so busy just
now proving "woman's right to
labor", that I have no time at all to
help prove "woman's right to
vote".'

Alcuin
Book by Charles Brockden Brown
published in 1798. Taking the form
of a dialogue between a medieval
scholar Alcuin, and an eighteenth-
century widow Mrs Carter, it
examines the oppressions suffered

by women and advocates better
education and political rights as the
remedy.

Aleramo, Sibilla (pseudonym of
Rina Faccio), 1876–1960
Italian writer. As Rina Faccio she
began writing articles on 'the
woman question' and other social
conditions in 1897, and quickly
established a national reputation. In
1899 she edited a new magazine,
L'Italia femminile (Female Italy), and
she was a member of the Unione
Femminile, which established
advice and information centres for
women. As she began to recognize
that legal and material changes
would only scratch the surface of
women's condition, her feminism
became more personal and
psychological and was expressed
almost entirely through fiction and
poetry written under the name
Sibilla Aleramo. Her autobiographical novel, *Una donna (A
Woman)* was an immediate success
on publication in 1906, and
although she wrote many other
books, none ever matched its
popularity. In the 1920s her feminism became more and more literary, as she attempted to discover a
feminine sensibility to counter the
domination of male literary forms.

Aliberty, Soteria, 1847–1929
Greek teacher and writer. Her literary works were chiefly biographical
studies of women, and she did
much to publicize women's

achievements, writing for the *Women's Newspaper* published in Athens. She founded the first Greek women's association, Ergani Athena.

'Alice Doesn't'

Strike called by the NATIONAL ORGANIZATION FOR WOMEN on 29 October 1975, named after the popular film *Alice Doesn't Live Here Any More*. Women were asked to stop their work, paid or unpaid, and spend the day demonstrating their refusal to support an oppressive, sexist system. Although 1,000 women marched in Los Angeles, 800 women demonstrated in front of the White House, and there were ZAP ACTIONS, marches and teach-ins in Honolulu, Detroit, Philadelphia and San Francisco, many parts of the country were unaffected, and for most women it was business as usual.

Allen, Grant, 1848–99

British writer. Author of *The Woman Who Did*. A believer in free love, he considered himself a feminist.

Alpert, Jane, 1947–

American. Radical activist of the late 1960s, she was the staff-member of RAT who triggered its transformation into a women's paper. In May 1970 she went underground to avoid sentencing for her role in the bombing of several buildings in New York. While living underground her attitude towards politics and the male-dominated Left changed, and she became committed to feminism. In 1973 she wrote an open letter to her 'sisters in the Weather Underground' in which she renounced her former allegiances and expressed her belief that feminist revolution should result in the formation of a new matriarchy, a theory she called 'MOTHER RIGHT'. She gave herself up in November 1974, and the women's movement was split between Leftists who denounced her as a traitor and those who supported her as a woman whose first allegiance was to other women. She served twenty-seven months in prison. In her autobiography *Growing Up Underground* (1981) she defined her current belief in feminism as a way of working for the social changes she has always cared about, but no longer as a matriarchal ideology.

Alpha Suffrage Club

The first black women's suffrage organization in America, it was founded in Chicago in 1900 by Ida WELLS-BARNETT.

Alta

American poet. One of the first, most openly political, of contemporary feminist poets, she also founded one of the first feminist presses in America, Shameless Hussy Press, in 1969. She is the author of *Letters to Women* (1970),

Burn This and Memorize Yourself
(1971), *No Visible Means of Support*
(1972), *Momma: A Start on All the
Untold Stories* (1974) and *I Am Not a
Practicing Angel* (1975).

Amatniek, Kathie
See SARACHILD, KATHIE

Amazons
Ancient race of women warriors
from the Black Sea region; possibly
also North Africa. No men were
allowed to live among them, unless
as crippled slaves, and the ancient
Greeks found them fierce enemies.
Male scholarship has generally dismissed them as myth; Merlin Stone
has suggested that tales of a fierce
warrior race may have grown out of
factual accounts of matriarchal
Goddess-worshippers struggling to
protect their temples from
patriarchal invaders. Traditions of
bands of female warriors exist in
other parts of the world. Helen
Diner calls them the 'extreme
feminist wing of a young human
race whose other extreme wing
consisted of the stringent patriarchies.' Whether myth or reality, they
have been reclaimed as a powerful,
positive image for women-centred
women today.
(*See also* LABRYS; MATRIARCHY;
UTOPIA)

Amberley, Viscountess
(Katherine Louisa Stanley),
1842–74
English. She read a paper on female
suffrage at the Mechanics Institute
in Stroud, in 1870, and although the
meeting was calm and respectable,
Fleet Street and royalty alike
expressed themselves to be
scandalized. Queen Victoria wrote
in a letter to a friend: 'The Queen is
most anxious to enlist everyone
who can speak or write or join in
checking this mad, wicked folly of
"Woman's Rights" with all its
attendant horrors, on which her
poor feeble sex is bent, forgetting
every sense of womanly feeling and
propriety. Lady Amberley ought to
get a *good whipping*.'

American Equal Rights
   Association
Organization founded in 1866 to
further the interests of blacks and
women. Led by Wendell Phillips,
Horace Greeley and other men, it
soon took the stance that now was
the 'Negro's hour', and that woman
suffrage, being of less importance,
must wait for another day. This led
directly to the founding, in 1869, of
the women-only NATIONAL WOMAN
SUFFRAGE ASSOCIATION, and the
AMERICAN WOMAN SUFFRAGE ASSOC-
IATION.

American Woman Suffrage
   Association (AWSA)
Founded in November 1869, this
was formed as a conservative alternative to the NATIONAL WOMAN SUF-
FRAGE ASSOCIATION. Membership
included both men and women and
was especially attractive to upper-
and middle-class clubwomen. It

concentrated on winning suffrage on a state-by-state basis, and the official publication, the *Woman's Journal*, steered clear of all controversial subjects in an attempt to make the idea of women's suffrage respectable. Leading members of the group included Lucy STONE, Henry BLACKWELL, Henry Ward Beecher and Julia Ward HOWE. In 1890 AWSA merged with the National Association to become the NATIONAL AMERICAN WOMAN SUFFRAGE ASSOCIATION.

American Women

Title of the report prepared by the PRESIDENT'S COMMISSION ON THE STATUS OF WOMEN, released on 11 October 1963. Although certainly not feminist in outlook or assumptions, by documenting the extent to which women were denied many basic rights and opportunities, it helped to provide the groundwork for the modern women's movement in America.

Ames, Blanche, 1878–1969

American artist and inventor. A leading botanical illustrator, and inventor of an antipollution toilet and other devices, she made her mark on the women's suffrage movement through a series of very popular pro-suffrage cartoons. Her belief in the necessity of self-determination for women led her to activism chiefly in areas concerning health and BIRTH CONTROL. She cofounded the Birth Control League

of Massachusetts in 1916 and used all her professional, social and political skills to make birth control a public issue. When all attempts to change the laws controlling birth control information failed, she declared that women must take matters into their own hands and share the information doctors would not give them. Her contribution was to publish formulae for spermicidal jellies, and illustrated methods for making diaphragms from a baby's teething ring or jam-jar rings. In 1941 she became a member of the corporation of the New England Hospital for Women and Children, founded in 1862 to train women as physicians and nurses and to provide health care entirely by and for women. In 1950 financial difficulties led to attempts to include men on the staff, but Ames objected and led a fund-raising effort which enabled the hospital to survive under its original women-only terms.

(*See also* HEALTH MOVEMENT)

Ames, Jessie Daniel, 1883–1972

American. She became involved in the struggle for women's suffrage in 1916, writing, speaking and organizing on behalf of women's rights, and helping to ensure that Texas became the first southern state to ratify the NINETEENTH AMENDMENT. In 1919 she founded the Texas League of Women Voters, and went on to become active in Democratic party politics. But she was disturbed by the contradictions of a feminist movement which excluded black women, and in 1924 she became a director for the Commission on Interracial Cooperation (CIC). Her major contribution in bringing anti-racist and women's rights interests together was as the founder of the Association of Southern Women for the Prevention of Lynching (ASWPL) in 1930. The ASWPL worked through existing women's groups to urge the wives and daughters of the men who lynched to restrain them, to bring pressure on the police to protect black prisoners and bring mob members to trial. In addition to encouraging women to learn to understand and control male VIOLENCE, Ames also challenged the common justification for lynching: that it was in defence of white womanhood. She collected statistics which revealed that only twenty-nine per cent of lynch victims had been accused of any sort of crime against women, and she urged her sisters to protest against the stereotype of the vulnerable white woman in need of male protection.

anarcha-feminism

Also called anarcho-feminism or feminist ANARCHISM, it can be traced back to anarchist women of the nineteenth and twentieth centuries such as Emma GOLDMAN and Voltairine de CLEYRE, but it was not recognized as being a development or expansion of anarchism until self-defined feminist anarchists began appearing in the 1970s. Anarcha-feminist groups and publications have been generally short-lived, but anarchist principles have always been present within the women's liberation movement and from time to time feminists will make the theoretical connection with anarchism, seeing the end to sexist oppression as necessarily linked to ending *all* forms of structured oppression and power relationships. Anarcha-feminists are opposed to all governments, hierarchies and leaders; believe in the necessity for the individual to control her own life; in the importance of spontaneous, direct action; in the revolutionary potential of women working individually and in small groups to create an alternative to the present system.

anarchism

From the Greek *anarchos*, meaning leaderless. Term for the belief, which developed into a political movement in the nineteenth century, that all government is evil and should be abolished, to be replaced by the voluntary cooperation of individuals.

In theory, anarchism is extremely compatible with feminism; both individualist anarchism which has as its highest good the freedom of the individual (regardless of sex) and social anarchism, which shares many of the goals and beliefs of radical feminism.

Many feminists agree with anarchists that hierarchies and power relationships are inherently bad: it is not enough to replace male presidents or prime ministers with female, not even politically correct, feminist females, when the system itself is wrong. Feminism does not (except as mainstream or LIBERAL FEMINISM) aim to put women into men's place, but to replace PATRIARCHY with a non-hierarchical, non-coercive, non-oppressive, non-sexist society.

Like feminists, most anarchists believe that the means and the end must be in harmony: freedom cannot be achieved for all in the future by limiting it for some in the present. Both feminists and anarchists attempt to put their beliefs into practice in the present, in their own lives, as much as possible, reflecting the understanding that 'THE PERSONAL IS POLITICAL'. Feminists and anarchists both practise DIRECT ACTION as a means of achieving their goals, and the very existence of the WOMEN'S LIBERATION MOVEMENT – a leaderless, decentralized structure – proves that the ideals of social anarchism are practical. Carol Ehrlich (1976) has suggested that 'the refining distinction from radical feminist to anarcho-feminist is largely that of making a step in self-conscious theoretical development'.

But although many women have been attracted to anarchism, they have usually found that in practice male anarchists are unwilling or unable to give up their own entrenched sexism. Early feminist anarchists such as Emma GOLDMAN and Voltairine de CLEYRE received little support from their male comrades in their struggle against specifically male power, and their view of the importance of sexual and psychological freedom was often seen as threatening by contemporary feminists. Women anarchists today tend to feel that feminist anarchism, also called ANARCHA-FEMINISM, provides the best hope for achieving both feminist and anarchist aims.

Ancient Society
See MORGAN, LEWIS HENRY

Anderson, Elizabeth Garrett, 1836–1917
English doctor. Inspired by a meeting with Elizabeth BLACKWELL, she battled against prejudice and hostility to get the necessary education (sometimes slipping through unsuspected loopholes in the law which were closed after her) and became the first English woman doctor. In 1866 she opened St Mary's Dispensary for Women, later the New Hospital for Women and Children, renamed after her death the Elizabeth Garrett Anderson Hospital.

A pioneer in opening the medical profession to women, she was also, like her sister Millicent Garrett

Fawcett, one of the leaders of the women's suffrage movement. She was on the committee which circulated the first petition for women's suffrage, which was presented to J. S. Mill in 1866. She was the first (and only) woman member of the British Medical Association from 1873–92. In 1908 she became the first woman mayor in England (of Aldeburgh).

androcentric
Male-centred. This term was introduced by Lester F. Ward in *Pure Sociology* (1903), defined by him as 'androcentric theory is the view that the male sex is primary and the female secondary'. It was taken up and popularized by Charlotte Perkins GILMAN, who used 'Our androcentric culture' as the subtitle for her 1911 book *The Man-Made World*. Since 1911, the word has been widely used by feminists to point out the male bias in almost everything. Used interchangeably with PHALLOCENTRIC and masculinist.

androgyny
Word often used to describe the feminist ideal, more frequently used in the 1960s and 1970s than in the 1980s. Composed of the Greek for male (*andro*) plus female (*gyn*) it is not used in the sense of physical hermaphroditism, but suggests a world in which SEX-ROLES are not rigidly defined, a state in which 'the man in every woman' and 'the

woman in every man' could be integrated and freely expressed. Many feminists, from Virginia WOOLF to Carolyn HEILBRUN, have written about their dreams of an androgynous future in which everyone will at last be free to be fully human. More recently, however, some feminists have expressed their uneasiness both with the concept and the term. Ours is a culture which has traditionally awarded more recognition to what are seen as male powers and virtues, so that any attempt at androgyny now is likely to be male-dominated. Some feminists also feel that the task of feminism is to question and then eradicate the false distinctions between masculine and feminine, not perpetuate the old duality in a new form. Merely to push together the attitudes and abilities we have been taught to think of as 'male' with those we call 'female' would not necessarily result in the creation of a new, non-sexist person. Janice Raymond has suggested that the feminist vision of the whole person must be rooted in GYNERGY, and suggests the term 'integrity' as better representing the aims of feminism.

Anger, Jane
Pseudonym (presumably) of the earliest known politically feminist writer in English. Her protest, entitled *Jane Anger Her Protection For Women. To Defend Them Against the Scandalous Reports Of a Late Surfeit-*

ing Lover, and All Other Like Venerians That Complain So To Be Overcloyed with Women's Kindness was published in London in 1589.

Ann Veronica
Novel by H. G. Wells first published in England in 1909. It tells the story of a determined young woman who wants more from life than her middle-class, suburban, Edwardian upbringing will allow. She runs away from home, fends off unwanted lovers, studies science, becomes involved with the SUFFRAGETTES and spends time in prison before deciding that what she wants is her married professor. She declares her passion for him, he responds, and they elope. Against all the moral standards of the day, a happy ending is allowed: in the last chapter they appear to be legally married, a baby on the way, and reconciled with Ann Veronica's relatives. Called 'a poisonous book' and banned by libraries when it first appeared, it is very tame today, chiefly interesting for the vividly drawn character of Ann Veronica, who was based on one of Wells' young lovers, Amber Reeves.

Anneke, Mathilde, 1817–84
German–American. Militant suffragist and author of tracts on women's rights, she left Germany and moved to America in 1849, where she immediately became involved in the women's movement. At conventions all over the country the passion of her speeches reportedly stirred listeners even before they were translated into English, and from her home in Milwaukee, Wisconsin, she published a monthly feminist journal in German.

Anthony Amendment
Another name for the NINETEENTH AMENDMENT to the Constitution of the United States, so called after Susan B. ANTHONY.

Anthony, Susan B., 1820–1906
American. Undoubtedly the most widely-honoured American feminist of all time, during her life she was called 'the Napoleon of the women's rights movement' and 'the Moses of her sex', while women long after her death continue to be inspired by her rallying cry 'Failure is impossible!' as well as by her example. In 1979 her profile adorned the new U.S. dollar coin.

She came to the cause of women's rights through her involvement in the temperance and ABOLITION MOVEMENTS. Most of her work – writing, speech-making, organizing, inspiring – was achieved in collaboration with her friend Elizabeth Cady STANTON, who she first met in 1851. During the 1850s Anthony worked as an agent for the American Anti-Slavery Society, demanded equal pay for teachers, and petitioned, campaigned and canvassed for the Married Women's Property Act and for woman suffrage. She travelled widely throughout the States and Territories, lecturing, fund-raising, and spreading the word about women's rights.

In 1869, with Stanton, she founded the NATIONAL WOMAN SUFFRAGE ASSOCIATION, for which she was the driving force throughout its existence. She edited and published a radical women's newspaper, THE REVOLUTION, from 1868–70, and from 1881–6 worked with Stanton and Matilda Joselyn GAGE on the HISTORY OF WOMAN SUFFRAGE.

Without ever ceasing to be active in suffrage campaigns on local, state and national levels, she became interested in the idea of an international woman's movement in the 1880s, and, in March 1888, called an international conference in Washington, D.C., at which the INTERNATIONAL COUNCIL OF WOMEN was organized. In 1904, she presided over the International Council of Women in Berlin where, with Carrie Chapman CATT, she founded the INTERNATIONAL WOMAN SUFFRAGE ALLIANCE.

anthropology

Because it is concerned with social structures and the influence of culture on human nature and relationships, the study of anthropology has contributed much to the development of feminist theory. It provides a much-needed cross-cultural perspective to western feminists, revealing that much of what we take for granted as being biologically or psychologically based is determined not by anatomy or genetics but by social conditioning: traits considered feminine in one society turn out to be masculine in another. Not only do cross-cultural studies reveal the many different ways people have found of being human, they also provide the necessary data for anyone trying to find what universals, if any, run through all human societies. Feminists have looked to anthropology, among other sciences, to try to discover the origins of PATRIARCHY. Although it can be argued, many accept Claude Lévi-Strauss' theory that there is, in all human societies, a basic need to establish the difference between the sexes, which has resulted in the social creation of GENDER. No matter how drastically they may differ from one group to another, gender differences are a basic part of life in every culture. There are no cultures which do not discriminate on the grounds of sex, and although it doesn't take the same form everywhere, and is not always perceived as oppressive, male dominance appears to be universal. No true MATRIARCHY exists, and there are no societies in which women, as a group, have more actual, material power or are considered superior to men.

Despite the fame of Ruth Benedict, Margaret MEAD, and other women in the profession, most anthropologists have been men, and until very recently most of the information gathered and theories generated by them have been biased, operating on the assumption that the male role in society is the important one, with women seen only in relation to men, if not overlooked entirely. This is something which feminist anthropologists are working to correct. For example, feminists have exposed the fallacy in the 'man the hunter' theory, that traces everything which sets us apart from other primates and makes us distinctly human, to the experience of hunting in groups. Since hunting is an activity restricted in primitive groups to males, this theory would seem to imply that humanity is itself a masculine trait, and women therefore less than human. Not only does this ANDROCENTRIC attitude fail to recognize or account for the experiences and contributions of more than half the human race, but it gives an inappropriate emphasis to the importance of hunting in what are known as hunter-gatherer societies. In remaining gathering-hunting tribes today, although meat is highly valued, the gathering activities of the women provide up to eighty per cent of the diet, and are thus far more necessary for survival. Recent evidence has shown that many tools which were once assumed to be part of a hunting technology in existence some four million years ago were actually used for cutting plant material. Rather than weapons, the earliest tools invented were probably containers for food, and some sort of sling for carrying babies, which suggests that the image of 'woman the gatherer' as our ancestor is more appropriate than 'man the hunter'.

anti-male

Term often used to object to or to attack feminists, the implication being that to disagree with or object to male dominance is unnatural, even anti-human. To say that feminists are man-hating or anti-male also serves to obscure the fact that, as Mary DALY has pointed out, all patriarchal societies are profoundly anti-female. To be 'anti-male' is usually just a matter of being positive about women.

anti-porn movement
See PORNOGRAPHY

anti-sexist men
See MEN AGAINST SEXISM; MEN'S LIBERATION MOVEMENT; EFFEMINISM

Aphra

The first modern feminist literary magazine, founded by Elizabeth Fisher in 1969 and published quarterly from New York until 1979. It was named in honour of Aphra BEHN, and in addition to fiction and poetry published provocative articles on such subjects as language, women in religion, the arts and the family.

Appeal of One-Half the Human Race, Women, Against the Pretensions of the Other Half, Men, to Retain Them in Political, and Thence in Civil and Domestic Slavery

Published in England in 1825, this book is usually considered the most significant work of feminism to appear between Mary WOLL-STONECRAFT's *Vindication of the Rights of Woman* (1792) and John Stuart MILL's *The Subjection of Women* (1869). Although not as widely read as the other two books, it was well received in Socialist, Co-operative and other radical circles of the day. It was written by William THOMPSON in collaboration with Anna WHEELER. Although his name alone appears as author, the ideas were as much hers – he called himself the 'interpreter and scribe' of Wheeler's sentiments in the dedication. The book originated as a response to James Mill's 1820 'Article on Government' which claimed women had no need of political representation, for their interests were included in those of the men they lived with. First pointing out that not all women had husbands or fathers to look after them, Thompson and Wheeler went on to argue that men's interests were very often antithetical to those of women, and presented a scathing critique of marriage as having been constructed entirely to men's advantage, with the married woman reduced to an 'involuntary breeding machine and household slave'. Nor did women choose this slavery voluntarily, for law and custom denied most women any alternative means of survival. The book ends with a call to women to raise their voices against oppression and demand their rights as human beings to equal individual liberty, equal laws, equal morals and equal education.

Armand, Inessa, 1874–1920

French-born Russian revolutionary. She developed a feminist consciousness at an early age, and her career as an activist began with a Moscow organization to aid prostitutes. Disenchanted by the futility of such charitable efforts, she became involved with the Social Democrats and worked to change society. Arrested for her part in the December Uprising of 1905, she went into European exile. From 1910 she planned and wrote for a Russian women's journal, *Rabotnitsa* (*Woman Worker*), and toured colonies of Russian émigrées giving lectures on the woman question. After the Revolution, she founded the Zhenotdel (women's bureau) and was named its first director, a post she held from 1917 until her sudden death from cholera.

Arnold, June, 1926–83

American writer. A co-founder of the feminist PUBLISHING company, Daughters, Inc. Her novels include *Applesauce* (1966), *Sister Gin* (1975)

23

and *The Cook and the Carpenter* (1973), which was written using a neuter pronoun, 'na', for all the characters, 'trusting the reader to know which character is female and which male'.

art and artists

There has been no single feminist art movement, nor even a widely accepted definition of what feminist art should be. Feminists in the arts can be divided into three different categories:

1. Artists who feel that their sex, and sexual politics, have nothing to do with their work, which they want to be judged on the same terms as that by men. Aware of sexual discrimination and prejudice within the arts establishment, they respond with demands for more opportunities and better representation for women and their work in galleries, museums, exhibitions, surveys, textbooks and classrooms. One approach is rediscovery, in which unjustly neglected female artists are reclaimed and studied, to prove that women do have a history in the arts. Books such as Germaine Greer's THE OBSTACLE RACE are a useful corrective to male-oriented texts, and all-women exhibitions can provide the information and role models that young artists need.

Protests against exhibitions in which women artists are largely ignored can be useful in focusing attention on sexism, but they can also be seen as a matter of special

pleading for inferior work, as some reviews of the 1978 HAYWARD ANNUAL II showed. It is more difficult to prove unfair discrimination in the arts than in areas in which ability can be measured against certain absolute standards: unfashionable male artists, too, are discriminated against since in the end the decisions made by gallery owners or art buyers come down to personal preference.

In 1970, only $4\frac{1}{2}$ per cent of the work in the Whitney Museum's annual survey of American art was by women. Picketing throughout the winter of 1970–1 by the Ad Hoc Women Artists' Committee calling for equal representation resulted in a rise to 22 per cent in the 1971 survey. But this was a very small and temporary gain. Although there are now more women artists than ever, the Museum of Modern Art's 1984 'International Survey of Recent Painting and Sculpture' featured work by 151 men and only 14 women.

2. Cultural feminists who reject the male-determined values of the patriarchal establishment and seek an alternative, either by redefining areas in which women have traditionally excelled – such as weaving, quilt-making and pottery – as valid art forms, or by establishing women-only schools and galleries in which students and artists can feel free to explore their own creativity without the pressure to conform to male standards. They offer a valu-

able support system, better opportunities, information traditionally denied to most women, and the freedom necessary for the personal development out of which new art comes: and yet, from another perspective, this 'woman only' art movement can look like a ghetto. No matter how radical and potentially disturbing to the status quo they may be, cultural feminists can be safely ignored by the male establishment as they perpetuate the 'separate spheres' argument and have little if any effect on the mainstream of art and public opinion.

3. Feminist artists who create their art out of an awareness of being women in a patriarchal society, yet hope to speak to both men and women. Although they don't necessarily want to be accepted by the establishment, they know they must be noticed, at least, if they are to make an impact and enlarge the accepted artistic traditions to include female as well as male visions of the world.

Judy CHICAGO said in 1974: 'My investigation of women's art has led me to conclude that what has prevented women from being really great artists is the fact that we have been unable so far to transform our circumstances into our subject matter. That is the process of transformation men have been able to make while we have been embedded in our circumstances, unable to step out of them and use them to reveal the whole nature of the human condition.'

Yet women who attempt to do just this, although they may find a response from other women, are usually ignored or ridiculed by the establishment, as reactions to Judy Chicago's THE DINNER PARTY and Mary Kelly's POST-PARTUM DOCUMENT have shown. The GATEKEEPERS of our cultural traditions continue to be male, and the feminist movement in the arts still has a long way to go.

assertiveness training
Programme designed to help women overcome early indoctrination in passive behaviour through techniques to change their attitude and behaviour. Many women have found it a useful way of refusing victimization and changing their lives and expectations. However, although it is used by feminists, it is a very limited and reformist process which does not question or try to change the system, but only teaches individual women how to make use of male strategies for their own benefit.

Astell, Mary, 1668–1731
English. An intellectual writer who contributed to many of the philosophical and theological debates of her day, she was a feminist long before that term was used, being the first to demand that women be given an education equal to that of men in her anonymously

25

published *Serious Proposal to the Ladies* (1694). She planned a course of study and attempted to found a college for women, even convincing Princess Ann to finance it. However, opposition from Bishop Burnet on religious grounds caused the Princess to donate her £10,000 elsewhere. Despite this failure, and constant ridicule from her male colleagues, Astell continued her argument against the inequities of a male-dominated society in *Some Reflections Upon Marriage Occasioned by the Duke and Duchess of Mazarine's Case* (1700). Dale Spender has suggested that Mary Astell was one of the very first to analyse the workings of what later feminists would call the patriarchy. Her writings were important to Mary HAYS, and may have influenced Mary WOLLSTONECRAFT. Lost to history until reclaimed and reprinted by feminist scholars in the late 1970s, Astell's works are still relevant, and can still be seen as radical today.

Atkinson, Ti-Grace, 1939–
American. One of the most prominent figures in the WOMEN'S LIBERATION MOVEMENT in the late 1960s and early 1970s, she was seen by the media as a feminist leader despite her activities in non-hierarchical, leaderless groups. An early member of the National Organization for Women, she resigned as President of the New York Chapter when her attempts to alter its tradi-

tional structure to that of a 'participatory democracy' failed. She joined with other radical feminists to form a group called THE FEMINISTS in October 1968, and was a cofounder of Human Rights for Women, Inc. A collection of her speeches and essays was published as *Amazon Odyssey* (1974). In 1985 she was working towards a theory of women's oppression and meeting regularly with other feminists in New York in an attempt to reestablish a strong, radical feminist presence in the United States.

Atwood, Margaret, 1939–
Canadian writer. She acquired international fame as a poet with her first collection *The Circle Game* (1966), but is now better known as a novelist. A major theme in her work is woman's quest for self-identity, and she often writes about women who learn to refuse to be victims. She is the author of *The Edible Woman* (1969), *Surfacing* (1972), *Lady Oracle* (1976), *Life Before Man* (1979), *Bodily Harm* (1982) and *The Handmaid's Tale* (1986), as well as eight volumes of poetry, short stories and works of criticism.

Auclert, Hubertine, 1849–1914
French. First working with Léon RICHER and Maria DERAISMES, she became impatient with their moderate tactics and broke away in 1878 to form her own group, Droit

de la Femme, renamed Société de Suffrage des Femmes in 1883. She attempted to break through class barriers and recruit proletarian women to a movement which was demanding the vote, equal pay for equal work, equal access to professions, and other civil rights including divorce. Her tactics were far more radical than those practised by other feminists of her day and included street demonstrations, lobbying, the attempt to vote, refusal to pay taxes, and, in 1885, a 'shadow election' in which fifteen women stood for office, providing a great deal of publicity (or at least notoriety) for the women's suffrage movement. In 1883 she attended a conference in Liverpool which laid the foundations for the INTERNATIONAL COUNCIL OF WOMEN. She founded a magazine, *La Citoyenne*, in 1881, which lasted until 1891. By the early 1900s she was ever more militant in her campaign for suffrage, but she had become almost totally isolated from the attitudes of other French suffragists. She wrote a number of books about women and politics, including *Le Droit Politique des femmes* (1878), *La vote des femmes* (1908) and *Les femmes au gouvernal* (1923).

Augspurg, Anita, 1857–1943
German. A radical feminist much inspired by the militant tactics of the British suffragettes. With Minna CAUER she co-founded the Verband fortschrittlicher Frauenvereine (Union of Progressive Women's Associations) in 1900. In 1902 she became the first President of the new Deutscher Verband für Frauenstimmrecht (German Union for Women's Suffrage). In 1904 she co-founded the INTERNATIONAL WOMAN SUFFRAGE ALLIANCE, of which she became vice-president. In 1913 she founded a militant suffrage organization, Deutscher Frauenstimmrechtsbund (German Women's Suffrage League). After suffrage had been achieved she continued to campaign for women's rights.

Aurora Leigh
Novel in verse by Elizabeth Barrett BROWNING, first published in England in 1857, which examines various forms of male dominance and feminine role-conflicts through the autobiography of a woman poet. Ellen MOERS has called it '*the* feminist poem'.

Awakening, The
Novel by Kate CHOPIN first published in 1899. It depicts the 'awakening' of Edna Pontellier, a young married woman in the Creole society of Louisiana, to sexual passion and, through that, to a sense of herself as an individual, apart from her conventional roles as wife and mother. A landmark in American literature for its realism

and sexual honesty, when originally published it was condemned by reviewers as 'poison', banned by libraries, and subsequently forgotten until a more sympathetic generation of readers in the 1970s rediscovered it. In 1981 a film version called *The End of August* was released.

axe
See LABRYS

B

Bachofen, Johann Jakob,
1815–87
Swiss scholar. Earliest proponent of the 'MOTHER RIGHT' theory. Glimpsing an actual historic struggle between the sexes hidden behind mythological accounts, Bachofen postulated that humanity had originally lived under a matriarchal system which was later overthrown by the new patriarchal order which wrote it out of history. Helen DINER and Elizabeth Gould DAVIS, among others, have built upon his theories in their rewritings of women's history.

Bajer, Fredrik, 1837–1922
Danish politician. Co-founder, with his wife Matilde Bajer, of Dansk Kvindesamfund (The Danish Women's Association). As a Member of Parliament, he was always interested in women's rights and played a role in the passage of an 1880 law giving economic independence to married women.

Bajer, Matilde, 1840–1934
Danish. Inspired by a Danish translation of John Stuart MILL's *The Subjection of Women*, she founded a small library and discussion group called the Women's Reading Society (Kvindelig Laeseforening), and, with her husband Fredrik

BAJER, organized the Danish Women's Association (Dansk Kvindesamfund). At first she concentrated on economic issues, such as better employment opportunities and financial independence for married women, but when she became involved in the drive to abolish state regulation of prostitution in the 1880s she became convinced that women would not be able to effectively change society until they had the vote. In 1886 she founded the Danish Women's Progress Association (Dansk Kvindelig Fremskridtsforening) to work for moral reform and women's suffrage. She continued to be involved in both Danish and international feminist organizations until after World War I.

Bambara, Toni Cade, 1931–
American writer. Calling herself 'Pan-Africanist-socialist-feminist', she brings together black and feminist consciousness in her work, and says, 'I work to produce stories that save our lives'. Her books include the novel *The Salt Eaters* (1980) and short story collections *Gorilla, My Love* (1972) and *The Sea Birds Are Still Alive* (1971). She has edited the anthologies *The Black Woman* (1970) and *Tales and Stories for Black Folks* (1971).

Barney, Natalie, 1876–1972
American. One of the first modern
women to live openly as a lesbian,
she was famous for her beauty, her
love affairs, and her wit. She envisioned the social transformation of
women being brought about by the
efforts of an intellectual and artistic
élite, and devoted her life to making
such an élite possible, by creating
an atmosphere conducive to
creativity. She settled in Paris in
1898 and became the centre of a
group of poets, writers and artists.
Her salon at rue Jacob was famous,
and in 1920 she responded to the
Académie française (which did not,
until very recently, admit women)
by founding her own Académie des
Femmes. She was the author of
more than twenty books, including
poetry, drama, fiction, essays and
autobiography.

Barre, François Poulain de la,
1647–1723
French philosopher. He wrote three
feminist works, *De l'Egalité des
Deux Sexes* (1673), *De l'Education
des Dames* (1674) and *De l'Excellence
des Hommes contre l'Egalité des Sexes*
(1675). In these books he refuted the
generally accepted notion of
women's intellectual inferiority,
arguing that this apparent inferiority was due to custom, tradition
and, most of all, to an inferior education. The brain was sexless, he
declared, and there were no studies
beyond women's capacity. He
believed that male jealousy, preju-

dice and man-made laws kept
women in subjection, but that this
could be changed, and must be, for
the betterment of all. Women could
and should be educated, he argued,
and once the universities had
opened their doors to women,
women would be capable of holding any position or office currently
held by a man.

battered women
'Battering' is the term commonly
used to describe a woman's physical
abuse at the hands of a man she lives
with. In the past, common law
established wife-beating as a male
prerogative (the saying 'rule of
thumb' comes from the size of the
stick a man was allowed to use to
punish his dependants) and
although this is no longer the case,
both law and public attitudes still
assume that battered women are not
deserving of the same rights held by
other assault victims. Attacks
which would, on the street, result in
conviction and serious penalties for
the attacker, are considered somehow outside the law when they take
place in the home, and the injured
woman is under pressure to
forgive, rather than prosecute, and
may even be blamed for her own
injuries.

The feminist response to the
plight of battered women comes
from three directions. Most visible
– and, so far, most effective – has
been the movement to provide
temporary refuges to allow women

and children an escape from their attackers. Another tactic has been to change laws and to ensure that existing laws are enforced, to compel the recognition and punishment of woman-battering as a serious crime. The third way is to examine the root of the problem – VIOLENCE – and to try to change the social and psychological structures which allow the perpetuation of male violence against women. This may be done through education, through publicity, and through encouraging both women and men to change. In Boston in 1977, a group called Emerge was the first to approach the problem of battered women with the idea that violence was the responsibility of the violent person, and that violent men could change themselves. There are now more than 100 American and Canadian organizations working in cooperation with women's refuges to provide counselling for men who want to understand and change their own violent behaviour.

The problem of battered women was first effectively raised as a feminist issue in the 1870s by Frances Power COBBE, whose pamphlet *Wife Torture* caused the passage in 1878 of the Matrimonial Causes Act in Britain, which gave magistrates' courts the power to grant a legal separation with right of maintenance to a wife whose husband had been convicted of aggravated assault upon her. However, by the 1920s, with the subsidence of the first wave of feminism, battered women were lost to the public eye until the re-emergence of feminism as a powerful social movement in the late 1960s.

The first refuge for battered women was Chiswick Women's Aid, established in London in 1971, and the publicity it received led to the establishment of many others. The American public was slower to accept the reality of battering as a widespread social problem. The first American shelter opened in 1974, in St Paul, Minnesota, and the publication of *Battered Wives* by Del Martin in 1976 stirred much wider interest and understanding.

Although violence is an important feminist issue, and studies have shown that the existence of a feminist movement is necessary for effective campaigns against woman-battering, these campaigns are not always feminist in nature. The feminist understanding of battering sees it as a logical outgrowth of SEXISM, an inevitable aspect of a patriarchal society which devalues women and rewards men for violent behaviour. Erin PIZZEY, the founder of Chiswick Women's Aid and the most powerful figure in the battered women movement, caused dismay in feminist circles with her contention that battering is a psychological, more than a social, problem, laying the blame on deviant men and colluding, violence-addicted women.

Baumer, Gertrud, 1873–1954
German writer. A conservative feminist, she was the president of the Bund Deutscher Frauenvereine (League of German Women's Associations) from 1910–19. This group moved to the right under her leadership, becoming both more nationalistic and less effective in the struggle for women's rights.

Beale, Dorothea, 1831–1906
English educator. With Emily DAVIES and Frances Mary Buss, one of the key figures in the British women's educational movement. She became Principal of Cheltenham Ladies College in 1858, and under her guidance it became a highly efficient, prosperous and famous school. She founded a connected teacher training college (St Hilda's) and in 1892 established St Hilda's College, Oxford. A member of the KENSINGTON SOCIETY, she also campaigned for women's suffrage.

Beard, Mary Ritter, 1876–1958
American historian. Considered by historian Gerda Lerner to be the inventor of the concept of WOMEN'S STUDIES.

Active in the women's suffrage movement from 1900 both in America and Britain, she worked with the National Women's Trade Union League to organize the New York shirtwaistmakers' strike of 1909, and edited *The Woman Voter* (published by the Woman Suffrage Party of New York) from 1910–12. A special sympathy with working women led to her involvement with the Wage Earners' League, and she was active in the CONGRESSIONAL UNION (later, the National Woman's Party) from 1913–17.

As she turned her time and attention more to scholarship and writing, one overriding concern became clear: women's history. She realized that women had always been far more influential than male-dominated histories admitted, and she was determined to make women's contributions visible.

Beginning in 1934 she struggled to establish and organize the World Center for Women's Archives, but the venture failed for lack of funds in 1940. Her 40-page critique, 'A Study of the Encyclopaedia Britannica in Relation to its Treatment of Women' was never acted upon. Among her other publications were *Women's Work in Municipalities* (1915), *On Understanding Women* and *America Through Women's Eyes* (1933), although she received more attention for the series of books on American history which she co-authored with her husband.

At the age of seventy she produced her major work, *Woman as a Force in History* (1946). Fiercely criticized by the male historical establishment when it appeared, twenty years later it was recognized by feminist scholars as a ground-breaking work.

beauty contests

A natural target for feminist protest, since they exist only to present women as sex objects. The danger of such protests is that the contestants, or uninvolved women, may perceive feminist anger as directed at *them*. Demonstrations against beauty contests are not meant to be anti-woman, but are aimed at the men and attitudes which force women into competition with each other to fulfil artificially imposed standards of femininity. The first major action of the WOMEN'S LIBERATION MOVEMENT in America – the first which received national publicity and made the public aware of the movement – was the protest in Atlantic City, New Jersey, against the Miss America Contest on 7 September 1968.

(*See also* BRA-BURNERS)

Beauvoir, Simone de, 1908–1986

French philosopher. Author of the classic text THE SECOND SEX (*Le Deuxième Sexe*, 1949) and one of the great figures of modern feminism, she contributed in the realms both of action and ideas, as well as providing a model in her own life for the liberated woman: independent, unmarried and childfree by choice, surrounded by friends of both sexes, successful and honoured in her chosen work, living out her principles of equality and freedom.

At the time of writing *The Second Sex* she declared she was not a feminist, believing the class struggle to be more important and that women's rights would come with the achievement of socialism. By 1970, however, she had come to a different conclusion, and joined the new Women's Liberation Movement. Still a socialist, she had seen that sexual inequities continued even in the most revolutionary leftist societies, and realized that if women do not fight for their rights in the present, the future will be no better.

Among her many activities in the women's movement were her participation in campaigns for the legalization of ABORTION; the founding, with Gisèle HALIMI, of Choisir, a feminist legal reform group, in 1971; editing the journal *Questions féministes*; and, from 1974, presiding over the Ligue du droit des femmes (League of Women's Rights).

Her chief involvement was with the materialist feminists of France, and she rejected any philosophies which made special claims for women's powers or essential feminine qualities. She believed foremost in equality, in human rights, and saw work as the first condition for women's independence.

Bebel, August, 1840–1913

German political leader. The first Marxist to deal comprehensively with the 'WOMAN QUESTION'. Author of *Woman and Socialism*

(1879), widely translated and highly influential in spreading socialist-feminist ideas. Although he is sometimes quoted as being sympathetic to feminism, he did not believe that a separate women's movement was necessary, but emphasized the vital importance of the female half of the labour movement. He encouraged feminists to join the proletarian movement, believing that women could not be free except in a socialist society. He thought that sexual independence would follow naturally from economic independence, and believed that MARRIAGE, like bourgeois capitalism, was on the decline and would soon disappear.

Becker, Lydia, 1827–90

English political organizer, writer and active campaigner for women's suffrage. Secretary of the Manchester National Society for Women's Suffrage, which she was instrumental in founding in 1867, she was the first woman to speak in public on the subject of women's rights in Britain (in the Assembly Room of the Free Trade Hall, Manchester on 14 April 1868). She also served as one of the first elected members of the new School Boards (1870), president of the Manchester Ladies' Literary Society, and treasurer of the Married Women's Property Committee. She founded a monthly newspaper, THE WOMEN'S SUFFRAGE JOURNAL, which she edited until her death and, with the

legal representation of Richard PANKHURST, put together a test-case through which she hoped to prove the right of women to vote on the grounds of ancient statutes. Sylvia PANKHURST said of Becker that she was 'regarded by the large public as the typical Women's Suffragist of her time', and Ray STRACHEY called her a 'pillar of the movement' whose death resulted in 'a phase of temporary discouragement' for the cause of women's suffrage.
(See also CHORLTON V. LINGS)

Beguinism

A women's movement in thirteenth-century Europe. Although religious in origin and intent, it sprang up independently, apart from the church, through the desire of working women to live together, outside men's control and traditional family life, in self-supporting celibate communities. In the fourteenth century the Beguine movement declined sharply when the church required the women to live in special Beguine houses as lay associates of the male Franciscans or Dominicans.

Behn, Aphra, 1640–89

English writer. The first English-woman to earn her living as a writer, she also led an adventurous life, astonishing for a woman of her time – or any other. She travelled to the West Indies where her experiences of a slave rebellion made her an early abolitionist, and she worked as a spy for King Charles II against the Dutch. She believed in the right of women to have education, work, and to love whomever they chose, in or out of marriage. Her plays, novels and poems were sexually candid and unusual in presenting life from a woman's point of view. Although her writings were extremely popular in her day, she obviously encountered a great deal of male hostility, for she wrote a defence not only of her own work, but of the right and ability of women to write at least as well as men. After her death, she was forgotten as a writer and remembered, if at all, chiefly as a scandalous, sexually promiscuous woman – and some 'de-biographers' argued that she had never existed at all. She is another proto-feminist who has been reclaimed by modern feminists. One of her plays, *The Lucky Chance*, was chosen by the Women's Playhouse Trust as their inaugural production in 1984.

Belmont, Alva (Mrs Oliver H. P. Belmont), 1853–1933
American. A New York society leader (her first husband was William K. Vanderbilt) and wealthy philanthropist, she became involved in the women's suffrage movement after her second husband's death in 1908, and for several years paid the major part of the NATIONAL AMERICAN WOMAN SUFFRAGE ASSOCIATION's expenses.

She was equally generous with her time and organizing abilities, and became one of the leaders of the CONGRESSIONAL UNION (later, the NATIONAL WOMAN'S PARTY). In 1920 she urged women to boycott the Presidential elections, saying, 'suffragists did not fight for your emancipation for seventy years to have you now become servants to men's parties,' and she hoped that the National Woman's Party would become a real alternative to the major political parties.

Bengis, Ingrid, 1945–
American writer. Author of *Combat in the Erogenous Zone* (1972), an autobiographical book which looked frankly at the ideas and experiences of man-hating, lesbianism, and love.

Betteshanger
Ten-minute film about an organization of miners' wives during the 1972 strike; the first film with an all-woman crew to be made in England.

Beyond God the Father
Book by Mary DALY first published in 1973. A major, radical work of feminist philosophy which locates the only hope for human evolution in SISTERHOOD, and explores 'the potential of the women's revolution to transform human consciousness'. A critique not only of church and patriarchal society, but of language itself, which Daly defines

as PHALLOCENTRIC, and therefore false or alien to the experience of women. In this book she makes a start, continued in her later work, on the process of renaming, as she attempts to look beyond phallocentric morality and towards the creation of a process of human becoming.

Beyond the Fragments

Published first as a pamphlet and then, revised and expanded, as a book in 1979. Subtitled *Feminism and the Making of Socialism*, it consists of essays by Sheila ROWBOTHAM, Lynne Segal and Hilary Wainwright, with an introduction by Hilary Wainwright. It was an attempt to forge a new unity between feminism and socialism by suggesting ways that the insights and grass-roots activism of the women's liberation movement could be applied to revitalize the overly centralized and hierarchical NEW LEFT in Britain. Response at first was promising, and in the summer of 1980 over 1,600 British militants gathered to chart a course for a newly feminist socialism. Within a year, however, the impetus for the new movement apeared to have died.
(*See also* SOCIALIST FEMINISM)

Biblioteca Femina

See SETON, GRACE GALLATIN

Big Mama Rag

Feminist periodical founded in 1972 and published eleven times a year by a collective based in Denver, Colorado, it offered extensive coverage of both national and international liberation movements and addressed itself to both the theory and the practice of women's liberation until forced by financial pressures to cease publication in 1984.

Biggs, Caroline Ashurst, 1840–89

English journalist. Active in the struggle for women's rights, she served as editor of *The English-Woman's Review*, 1870–89. Sister of Emilie Ashurst VENTURI.

Bill of Rights for Women

Drawn up by the NATIONAL ORGANIZATION FOR WOMEN (NOW) at the second national conference, Washington D.C., November 1967, then presented to all major political candidates running for national office in 1968, as follows:

I Equal Rights Constitutional Amendment.

II Enforce Law Banning Sex Discrimination in Employment.

III Maternity Leave Rights in Employment and in Social Security Benefits

IV Tax Deduction for Home and Child Care Expenses for Working Parents.

V Child Care Centers.

VI Equal and Unsegregated Education.

VII Equal Job Training Opportunities and Allowances for Women in Poverty.

VIII The Right of Women to Control Their Reproductive Lives.

WE DEMAND:

I. That the United States Congress immediately pass the Equal Rights Amendment to the Constitution to provide that 'Equality of rights under the law shall not be denied or abridged by the United States or by any State on account of sex,' and that such then be immediately ratified by the several States.

II. That equal employment opportunity be guaranteed to all women, as well as men, by insisting that the Equal Employment Opportunity Commission enforces the prohibitions against sex discrimination in employment under Title VII of the Civil Rights Act of 1964 with the same vigor as it enforces the prohibitions against racial discrimination.

III. That women be protected by law to ensure their rights to return to their jobs within a reasonable time after childbirth without loss of seniority or other accrued benefits, and be paid maternity leave as a form of social security and/or employee benefit.

IV. Immediate revision of tax laws to permit the deduction of home and child care expenses for working parents.

V. That child care facilities be established by law on the same basis as parks, libraries, and public schools, adequate to the needs of children from the pre-school years through adolescence, as a community resource to be used by all citizens from all income levels.

VI. That the right of women to be educated to their full potential equally with men be secured by Federal and State Legislation, eliminating all discrimination and segregation by sex, written and unwritten, at all levels of education, including colleges, graduate and professional schools, loans and fellowships, and Federal and State training programs such as the Job Corps.

VII. The right of women in poverty to secure job training, housing, and family allowances on equal terms with men, but without prejudice to a parent's right to remain at home to care for his or her children; revision of welfare legislation and poverty programs which deny women dignity, privacy and self-respect.

VIII. The right of women to control their own reproductive lives by removing from penal codes laws limiting access to contraceptive information and devices and laws governing abortion.

Billington-Grieg, Teresa

(Teresa Billington), 1877–1964 English. One of the earliest and most active members of the WOMEN'S SOCIAL AND POLITICAL UNION, she drafted the constitution and worked as a national organizer.

But in 1907 there was a split in the Union between the followers of the Pankhursts, and those who wanted a more democratic, and locally-based, structure. As one of the latter, she was a founding member of the WOMEN'S FREEDOM LEAGUE. Author of *Towards Women's Liberty* (1906) and many articles in *The Vote*, she was twice imprisoned for her part in protest campaigns. After 1911, although she continued to believe in women's rights, she went her own way, and wrote a book criticizing the tactics of her former comrades in the WSPU, *The Militant Suffrage Movement* (1911).

biological determinism

The concept that biology is destiny; that human nature and society are dictated largely or entirely by the demands of human physiology, and that there is an essential, unchanging difference between the masculine and the feminine. This has traditionally been an anti-feminist argument, used to restrict women's rights on the grounds that, as females, they are somewhat less than human. However, there is a strand of biological determinism in some feminist attitudes and theories, particularly in CULTURAL FEMINISM. Some examples are the idea that women are 'naturally' more peaceful than men, or that all men are rapists. This idea is sometimes referred to as BIOLOGISM or ESSENTIALISM.

biological differences

Biology has traditionally provided the strongest argument for sexism: that because men and women are biologically different, they have different needs and abilities which must be reflected in their social roles.

Biological differences between female and male would seem to be undeniable (although Monique WITTIG, for one, has questioned even this). Women, but never men, may menstruate, lactate and give birth to children. What is arguable, however, is how important this fact is, what influence such physiological traits have on human nature, and how they should be interpreted and treated by society.

Liberal feminists and socialist feminists have generally minimized the importance of biology in human life, stressing human similarities, and pointing out the role played by education and social expectations in what might appear, to be the purely physical. For example, menstrual difficulties may be caused by cultural attitudes towards MENSTRUATION; and childbirth can be experienced as a joy, or as a profoundly alienating experience. Even if it is presumed that MOTHERHOOD carries certain responsibilities, which would make it impossible for a woman to fill a 'man's job', there is no fair or logical reason to treat a childless woman as if the potential (but unproven) capacity for pregnancy made her inferior or incapable. The major achievement of what is sometimes called MAINSTREAM FEMINISM has been the promotion of the idea of equal rights and equal treatment for women – so long as they conform to the male norm.

A woman-centred society, unlike our own, would consider the potential for menstruation, pregnancy and lactation to be the norm, not aberrations or deviations from it. Instead of trying to ignore the physiological changes which make reproduction possible, or treating the natural as an illness as does patriarchal society, a truly feminist society would expect to consider childbirth and CHILDCARE as part of life. If social attitudes changed so that children were treated as integral and important members of society, and their care was recognized as the responsibility of men as much as of women, then women would not be forced to choose between having children or a well-paid job, and be punished for their choice.

Radical feminist views of biology range along a continuum from the stance represented by Shulamith FIRESTONE, that biology is a trap from which we can be freed by new reproductive technologies, to the glorification of all things female which postulates that there is a special wisdom available only to women through the physical experience of their bodies.

The argument for equal rights has relied on the idea that whatever physical differences there may be between men and women, the brain itself is essentially sexless. The anti-feminist argument has always insisted on extending the idea of biological difference to the brain, finding evidence (which has changed substantially over the years) for specifically male and female abilities and ways of thinking. But even the most apparently rational and objective of scientists are inevitably affected by unquestioned background assumptions. The very idea that there are two distinct ways of being, one called masculine and one feminine, naturally leads to the confirming discovery of 'feminine' and 'masculine' behaviour. Yet women and men both secrete what we call 'male' and 'female' hormones, and surely possess more similarities than differences. The ideology of biological differences serves a social function, reinforcing sexism by implying that it is normal, natural and inevitable.

(*See also* FEMININITY; GENDER; SEX-ROLES)

biologism
Term for the idea that biology, or anatomy, is destiny; the tendency to explain things in terms of biology. Also known as ESSENTIALISM, or BIOLOGICAL DETERMINISM.

biophilic
Life-loving. Term coined by Mary DALY in GYN/ECOLOGY (1978). The

message of PATRIARCHY is necrophilia, she says, but women are filled with the 'biophilic energy' which men lack.

Bird, Caroline

American journalist. A respected figure in the women's movement since the mid-1960s, she was the official historian of the United Nations INTERNATIONAL WOMEN'S YEAR and the NATIONAL WOMEN'S CONFERENCE in Houston. Her books include *Born Female* (1970), *Everything a Woman Needs to Know to get Paid What She's Worth* (1973), *Enterprising Women* (1976) and *What Women Want* (1979).

Birmingham

Site of the last NATIONAL WOMEN'S LIBERATION CONFERENCE in 1978.

birth control

The term 'birth control' was coined by Margaret SANGER, who declared: 'No woman can call herself free who does not own and control her body'. Mary O'Brien (1981) has suggested that the freedom of birth control for women will prove to be as fundamental an historical transformation as was the discovery of paternity.

Early (pre-1920s) feminists recognized the importance of what they called 'voluntary motherhood', but for the most part they were opposed to mechanical methods of birth control. They believed that women could refuse marriage or refuse their husband's sexual demands, and that men should learn self-restraint. Contraception was seen as a corrupting practice which would allow men to indulge their lust and would do moral damage to women. Only a very few feminists – including Harriet MARTINEAU and Anna WHEELER – opposed the conventional view of women's sexuality and advocated birth control in the nineteenth century.

To modern feminists (despite a few dissenting voices who call concern with birth control reformist and heterosexist) birth control is one of the basic rights, and a necessity for women's liberation. Among the SEVEN DEMANDS of the British women's liberation movement is 'Free contraception and abortion on demand', and the 1968 NOW BILL OF RIGHTS includes 'The right of women to control their own reproductive lives by removing from penal codes laws limiting access to contraceptive information and devices and laws governing ABORTION'.

Yet although women today do have far more freedom of choice, the available methods of birth control leave much to be desired. Because research into all areas of reproductive technology is largely in the hands of men, male desires are valued over women's safety. (*See also* HEALTH MOVEMENT; REPRODUCTIVE FREEDOM)

BITCH

'An organization which does not yet exist. The name is not an acronym,' according to Joreen (Jo FREEMAN). (*See also* 'BITCH MANIFESTO')

'Bitch Manifesto, The'

Widely-read paper by Joreen (Jo FREEMAN) first published in 1970. Examining the word 'bitch' she says, 'a popular derogation to put down uppity women that was created by man and adopted by women. Like the term "nigger", "bitch" serves the social function of isolating and discrediting a class of people who do not conform to the socially accepted patterns of behavior.'

Bitches violate the (man-made) rules. Self-determining, refusing to be passive, they are the groundbreakers, the ones who change society both for themselves and for their sisters. Yet because they are defined by that society as freaks, they may hate themselves or mistrust other women. The manifesto calls for an organization of bitches, strong women who would work together for their own liberation, teaching each other that 'Bitch is Beautiful'.

black feminism

Although it attempts to speak to the needs of all women, feminism is often, and with reason, seen as a white, middle-class movement. The term 'black feminism' may be unfortunate, both because it implies that feminism is normally white and because it ignores the many other women of colour who do not define themselves as black but feel equally alienated from white feminism. Some call it WOMANISM; others would prefer to redefine the term feminism so that it can be seen as applicable to women of all races and classes.

Black feminists have existed as long as white feminists, although they have suffered the fate of most women in being 'lost' to history. In America, the first wave of feminism emerged from the ABOLITION MOVEMENT. Many abolitionists – black and white, female or male – began to realize, as they fought against slavery, that not only were all blacks oppressed racially, but that women were also oppressed because of their sex. Paula Giddings (1984) has proposed that 'The moral urgency of their being Black and female . . . suffused Black women with a tenacious feminism, which was articulated before that of Whites like Sarah GRIMKÉ, who is credited with providing the first rationale for American women's political activism.'

Similarly, the Women's Liberation Movement was born of the Civil Rights and Black Liberation movements in America, where black women, doubly oppressed, might have been expected to take the lead in the new movement, yet they did not. Black women developed a feminist consciousness

41

just as white women did, and they faced racism, patronizing attitudes and a lack of understanding from white women. Even worse, they were often made to feel they were selling out their own people by joining a white movement. As Toni Morrison explained in an article titled 'What the Black Woman Thinks about Women's Lib' (1971), 'Too many movements and organizations have made deliberate overtures to enrol Blacks and have ended up by rolling them. They don't want to be used again to help somebody gain power – a power that is carefully kept out of their hands.' Not surprisingly, just as in the first wave of feminism, most black women decided that racial oppression took priority over sexual oppression.

Yet why should fighting oppression be a matter of priorities? How can a black woman decide whether her race or her sex is more important when both are indisputable facts of her existence? Black feminists challenge the idea that a feminism which ignores racism can be meaningful. As Bell HOOKS (1984) wrote, 'Feminist theory would have much to offer if it showed women ways in which racism and sexism are immutably connected rather than pitting one struggle against the other, or blatantly dismissing racism.'

The concept of identity politics, of organizing around one's own oppression, is vital to the idea of black feminism. 'Black feminism is not white feminism in blackface,' wrote Audre LORDE (1984). 'Black women have particular and legitimate issues which affect our lives as Black women, and addressing those issues does not make us any less Black.' In their statement on black feminism the COMBAHEE RIVER COLLECTIVE declared, 'We realize that the only people who care enough about us to work consistently for our liberation is us. Our politics evolve from a healthy love for ourselves, our sisters and our community which allows us to continue our struggle and work.'

The significance of black feminism is not limited to the lives of black women only. As the Combahee River Collective expressed it, 'If Black women were free, it would mean that everyone else would have to be free since our freedom would necessitate the destruction of all the systems of oppression.'

This statement recognizes that while all women share a common oppression as women, all women are not equally oppressed. Even while being oppressed on the grounds of sex, a white woman may use the privileges of race and class to oppress others not so privileged. Race, class, and sex oppression may be experienced separately, but because they most often experience all three simultaneously, black women are not likely to believe that a feminist revolution which defeated sexism but perpetrated racism and a class society would be a revolution worth having. Black feminists have taken on the difficult but necessary task of moving away from the ideas of social EQUALITY which have prevailed in white feminism, towards the struggle against all oppression, however it may manifest itself.

Black Friday

In protest at the impending dissolution of Parliament without consideration of the Conciliation Bill to extend the Parliamentary franchise to some women, over 300 members of the WOMEN'S SOCIAL AND POLITICAL UNION marched on the House of Commons on 18 November 1910. They were met not by the usual Westminster police, accustomed to dealing politely with the largely middle-class suffragettes, but policemen from the poorer East End districts, who may have been acting under orders from the Home Secretary, Winston Churchill, to delay or avoid arrests. For whatever reason, the police responded to the women with a violence they had never before encountered, kicking, punching and attacking them sexually. After 6 hours of struggle, 115 women and 4 men were arrested, although most charges were withdrawn the following day. Although most of the injuries were less serious than the psychological damage done, there were casualties: Cecilia Haig was sexually assaulted

and died of her injuries a few weeks later, and Henria Williams, who had a weak heart, died the following month. After this experience, many suffragettes preferred to express their militancy through window-smashing and other attacks on property which would not bring them into direct contact with the police.

Black Macho and the Myth of the Superwoman
See WALLACE, MICHELE

Blackburn, Helen, 1842–1903
Irish. Dedicated throughout her life to the cause of women's suffrage, she wrote, based on personal experience, the earliest history of the British women's movement, *Women's Suffrage: a Record of the Movement in the British Isles* (1902). Between 1874–94 she served as Secretary of the NATIONAL SOCIETY FOR WOMEN'S SUFFRAGE, and she edited *The Englishwoman's Review* from 1881–90. She was also Secretary of the West of England Suffrage Society, and, in collaboration with Jessie BOUCHERETT, wrote *The Condition of Working Women* (1896).

Blackwell, Alice Stone, 1857–1950
American. Daughter of Lucy STONE and Henry BLACKWELL, she was a child of the women's suffrage movement. Upon graduating from Boston University in 1881 she went

to work in the offices of the *Woman's Journal*, which she edited for thirty-five years. Beginning in 1887 she also edited the *Woman's Column*, a collection of suffrage news items sent free to newspapers throughout the United States. During the 1880s she brought about a truce between the rival AMERICAN WOMAN SUFFRAGE ASSOCIATION and the NATIONAL WOMAN SUFFRAGE ASSOCIATION, and when the two organizations merged in 1890 she became recording secretary of the new NATIONAL AMERICAN WOMAN SUFFRAGE ASSOCIATION, a position she held for nearly twenty years. In the 1890s her interests and affiliations widened from women's suffrage to include membership in the Women's Christian Temperance Union, the Anti-Vivisection Society, the Woman's Trade Union League, the National Association for the Advancement of Colored People and the American Peace Society. After ratification of the NINETEENTH AMENDMENT she urged women not to join the system, but to remain an autonomous political force, and she helped to start the LEAGUE OF WOMEN VOTERS for this purpose. Her biography of her mother, *Lucy Stone*, was published in 1930.

Blackwell, Elizabeth, 1821–1910 English–American doctor. The first woman to be granted an American medical degree (1849), she went on to study in Europe, where the only institution which would accept her was one for the training of midwives in Paris. While working there she caught an infection which destroyed the sight in one eye, and she gave up her hope of becoming a surgeon. In England, attending lectures at St Bartholomew's Hospital, she was approached by members of the LANGHAM PLACE GROUP, who involved her in the movement for women's rights.

Her confidence restored, she returned to America and set up practice in New York in 1851. By 1857 she was able to open a small hospital, the New York Infirmary for Indigent Women and Children, and in 1868 opened a medical college which ran until 1899, when women medical students were accepted at Cornell.

In 1858 her friends in the women's movement convinced her to return to London, where her name was placed on the 1859 Medical Register – just before the law was changed to close the loophole which had allowed holders of foreign degrees (in particular women, who were not allowed to study in England) to be registered. She gave a series of lectures on 'Medicine as a Profession for Ladies' which inspired Elizabeth Garrett ANDERSON to study medicine.

In 1869 she settled in England and founded the National Health Society of London, and helped form the London School of Medicine for Women.

Blackwell, Henry, 1825–1909
American. Brother of Elizabeth BLACKWELL; husband of Lucy STONE; father of Alice Stone BLACKWELL. A 'woman's rights man', he refused to take advantage of masculine privileges in his marriage with Lucy Stone, and he devoted his life to the cause of woman's suffrage.

Blatch, Harriot Stanton,
1856–1940
American. Daughter of Elizabeth Cady STANTON, she grew up in the women's movement, and after her marriage to an Englishman in 1882, she became involved with both the Fabian and the women's suffrage movements in Britain. Her observation of militant tactics in Britain made her particularly disappointed in the American movement, which had become stagnant and dull by the turn of the century. In response, she founded the WOMEN'S POLITICAL UNION in New York in 1907, and worked at bringing more politically aware and working women into the movement, with much success. After America entered World War I she worked for the Food Administration and the Women's Land Army and wrote *Mobilizing Woman-Power* (1918). She believed that the experience of war-time work would result in women's higher self-esteem, self-sufficiency and a better chance of winning equal rights from a grateful government. After the war she joined Alice PAUL and the NATIONAL WOMAN'S PARTY to work for the EQUAL RIGHTS AMENDMENT.

Blease, W. Lyon, 1884–1963
British. Stood for Parliament, unsuccessfully, on his feminist convictions, and wrote *The Emancipation of the Englishwoman* (1910) in which he defined feminism as 'the slow and reluctant recognition by man of the fact that woman is not merely an appendage to him but a separate individual'.

Bloomer, Amelia, 1818–94
American. A member of the 'first generation' of the American women's movement, she attended the SENECA FALLS Convention of 1848 with her friend Elizabeth Cady STANTON. Like many other early American feminists, she was active in the temperance movement, and published and edited her own temperance paper, THE LILY (1845–55). Over the years, both she and her paper became more outspokenly committed to feminism. She is best remembered for her opinions on DRESS REFORM, her name becoming attached to the pantaloon-type costume ('BLOOMERS') which she promoted. After moving to Iowa in 1855 she pioneered that state's equal rights movement, becoming president of the Iowa Woman Suffrage Society in 1871.

bloomers

1) Name used for costume invented as a revolt against the uncomfortable and restricting garments women were expected to wear in the 1850s. It consisted of a tunic loosely belted at the waist, a knee-length skirt, and long, baggy pantaloons to the ankles. Although extremely modest, it quickly gained a reputation for being indecently mannish. No one knows who originally designed it, but it was advocated by Amelia BLOOMER in her paper THE LILY, and the name stuck. The first woman to gain public attention by wearing the outfit was Elizabeth Smith MILLER, a cousin of Elizabeth Cady Stanton. Lucy Stone, Susan B. Anthony and other early feminists also adopted it, only to discover that they were reviled and insulted for doing so. Most of them soon decided that the physical freedom they gained wasn't worth the mental anguish, particularly as the public image equated equal rights for women with turning women into coarse parodies of men.

2) By association, anyone advocating equal rights for women might be called a 'bloomer'.
(*See also* DRESS REFORM)

blue-stocking

Term originated in the 1750s to refer to the men and women who attended London social gatherings where literary discussions were preferred to card playing. It referred to male casual dress, since some of the men wore their ordinary blue stockings instead of the formal black silk usually donned in the evening. By the 1790s the term was used, derogatorily, to indicate a woman with literary or intellectual interests: most late-eighteenth and early nineteenth-century feminists were given this label.

Bodichon, Barbara

(Barbara Leigh-Smith), 1827–91 English. Educated at Bedford College, her main interests throughout life were art (a student of Corot, she exhibited and sold some 200 paintings), education (she opened her own coeducational school, Portland Hall, where she tested her theories, and helped Emily DAVIES found Girton College), and women's rights. In 1854 she published *A Brief Summary in Plain Language of the Most Important Laws Concerning Women*, which led to a petition, signed by 26,000 women, presented to Parliament in 1856 where it became the basis for the Married Women's Property Bill of 1857. Also out of the petition grew the LANGHAM PLACE GROUP. In 1857 she married Eugène Bodichon, a French doctor resident in Algiers. It was apparently an extremely egalitarian marriage, for she divided her time between England and Algiers, both with and without him, and continued to be active as a teacher, an artist, a writer (many articles for the *English Woman's*

Journal) and a feminist campaigner. She was also a close friend of George Eliot, who used her as a model for *Romola*.

Body Politic, The

Edited by Michelene WANDOR and published in 1972, this was the first collection of specifically British women's liberation writings. It provides a minimal historical account of the development of the WOMEN'S LIBERATION MOVEMENT in Britain from 1969–72, as well as an introduction to the various issues and political tendencies which were emerging within the movement.

body politics

This phrase recognizes that power relationships are expressed not only through formal structures and verbal communication, but also through such personal, private, and apparently spontaneous means as body language, movement and touch. Psychologist Nancy M. Henley was the first to bring a feminist viewpoint to proxemics (the study of tactile communication) in her eye-opening book *Body Politics* (1977). She described the unspoken rules and hierarchies which govern who may touch whom, when, and on what parts of the body. She recognized that there is a connection between such masculine gallantries as physically steering an able-bodied woman to a restaurant table, 'harmless' sexual harassment, and RAPE. Women

accustomed to accepting unnecessary physical guidance from men may find it harder to resist when the contact becomes sexual or violent. As Susan BROWNMILLER commented in *Femininity* (1984): 'Fear of being judged impolite has more immediate reality for many women than the terror of physical violation.'

Boston marriage

Term used in late-nineteenth-century America to describe the relationship between two women, usually feminists and independent of men (because of career or inheritance), who shared a life together.

Boston Women's Health Book Collective

A group of women who first met at a workshop on women and their bodies at the Boston Women's Conference in 1969. The experience encouraged them to continue meeting to discuss their feelings and experiences, and to research medical topics, the eventual result of which was the publication of one of the most useful and influential books of the women's liberation movement, OUR BODIES OURSELVES.

Bostonians, The

Novel by Henry James first published in 1886. It is the story of a struggle between ardent feminist Olive Chancellor and chauvinistic Southern gentleman Basil Ransom for the possession of young Verena

Tarrant. Olive wants to turn Verena's talent as an orator to the cause of women's rights, while Basil wants to marry Verena and make her his own private property. Seen by some critics as anti-feminist, and by others as a detached, ambiguous view in which both sides are mocked, it was James' self-proclaimed attempt to deal with 'the situation of women' in his day.

Boucherett, Jessie, 1825–1905
English. The chance discovery of an issue of the *English Woman's Journal* in 1859 sent her to the magazine's London office to offer her help. There she became a member of the LANGHAM PLACE GROUP and, with Barbara BODICHON and Adelaide PROCTOR, founded the SOCIETY FOR PROMOTING THE EMPLOYMENT OF WOMEN. She was an ardent advocate of careers for women, even citing pig-farming or domestic service in the colonies as being far less degrading to single, educated women than having to depend on charity. She was a member of the KENSINGTON SOCIETY, and of the first women's suffrage committee, established in 1866 to petition to Parliament for the extension of the vote to women. She edited *The Englishwoman's Review* from 1866–71, and collaborated with Helen BLACKBURN on *The Condition of Working Women* (1896).

bourgeois feminism
Term used by Marxist and SOCIALIST FEMINISTS. From the Marxist viewpoint there are only two kinds of feminism: revolutionary feminism, grounded in the struggle of the proletariat; and bourgeois feminism, which reflects the aspirations of middle-class (bourgeois) women and which claims that women's liberation can be achieved without any basic changes to the political and economic structures of capitalist democracy. Used interchangeably with the term LIBERAL FEMINISM.

Boycott, Rosie, 1951–
British journalist. Co-founder of SPARE RIB, she also edited a feminist journal in Kuwait during the late 1970s. Her autobiography, *A Nice Girl Like Me*, was published in 1984.

bra-burners
Belittling term applied to feminists in America and Britain. It originated in the mistaken belief that feminists declared their allegiance by discarding and burning their brassières, perhaps by analogy with the male anti-war protesters who burned their draft cards and perhaps through some confusion with the 'bra-less look' then in fashion. The event which gave rise to this image was the Miss America protest in Atlantic City, New Jersey, on 7 September 1968. A 'freedom trash-can' was set up and women were asked to discard symbols of the repressive ideals of femininity, such as high-heeled shoes, curlers, gir-

dles and bras. None of these items was burned, except in the inaccurate reports of male journalists, but the idea of a burning bra blazed in the public imagination and served to make a serious political movement appear ridiculous.

Brailsford, Henry Noel,
 1873–1958
British journalist. With Henry Nevinson, he resigned from the *Daily News* in protest at that paper's support of a government which denied women the vote. Although a pacifist, he approved of the militant activities of the suffragettes.

Braun, Lily, 1865–1916
German writer and critic. Although she was a socialist, her outspoken, militant feminism – expressed both in her writings and her involvement with the German women's movement – caused her to be expelled from the Social Democratic Party in 1901. Her books include *Die Frauenfrage* (1901) and her memoirs.

Bremer, Fredrika, 1801–65
Swedish novelist. Her novels, particularly *Hertha* (1856), were highly influential in inspiring the first feminist movement in Sweden, and she was also an active campaigner for women's rights. She was involved in many charitable, educational and reform movements, and established a school for training women teachers. She travelled widely in Europe and the United States to study the organization of social work in other countries, and in 1854 she appealed to women internationally to found a peace movement. The first national women's association in Sweden, founded in 1885, was called the Fredrika Bremer Society in her honour.

Briffault, Robert, 1873–1948
British doctor and author. He developed a matriarchal theory, expressed in his three-volume study, *The Mothers* (1927), based on the idea that the mother–child relationship is the first and most powerful of all social bonds, and that a primitive MATRIARCHY had universally preceded PATRIARCHY.

Bright, Jacob, 1821–99
British politician. Liberal Member of Parliament dedicated to promoting women's suffrage. He also worked for the repeal of the Contagious Diseases Acts, and helped Lydia Becker and others to form the Manchester Women's Suffrage Committee in 1867.

Brittain, Vera, 1893–1970
British writer. A member of the SIX POINT GROUP from 1922, and a regular contributor to TIME AND TIDE, the primary motivating forces of her life were pacifism and feminism. To her, feminism always meant equal opportunities and rights for women, and through her writing she tried to change the attitudes which held women back –

male prejudice and women's own sense of inferiority – and to promote the fact that women have the same rights, needs and abilities as men. Among her many books are *Women's Work in Modern England* (1928) which she wrote to encourage women to pursue careers and to expose existing sex discrimination; *Testament of Friendship* (1940), a biography of Winifred HOLTBY which explores the power, importance and reality of friendship between women; and *Lady Into Woman* (1953), a history of women's advancement in her lifetime. As well as writing about it, she lived out her belief that marriage must be an equal partnership, and that meaningful work was as necessary to women as to men: married to George Catlin in 1925, she kept her own name and never stopped working, despite having children (one of whom is politician Shirley Williams), creating a 'semi-detached marriage' which enabled her to continue her career in London when her husband's work meant he had to live in New York.

Brown, Charles Brockden, 1771–1810

American writer. He felt the American Revolution was unfinished so long as freedom and equality applied only to white males. His ALCUIN: *A Dialogue* (1798) takes a critical, sympathetic look at the position of women and argues for legal reforms.

Brown, Rita Mae, 1944–

American novelist. She became an active member of New York NOW in 1969, but the discrimination she experienced as a lesbian caused her to resign at the beginning of 1970. She joined with other lesbian-feminists to write the classic position paper on LESBIAN-FEMINISM, 'THE WOMAN-IDENTIFIED WOMAN,' and to form RADICALESBIANS. She argued that a strong feminist movement could be built only by lesbians: that to be a lesbian meant to put women first, emotionally, personally and politically. Her first novel, *Rubyfruit Jungle* (1973), is a funny and inspiring lesbian-feminist manifesto which creates in the character of Molly Bolt a natural-born radical feminist whose strength and virtue are indivisible from her lesbianism. One of the most popular of all lesbian novels, *Rubyfruit Jungle* was the first bestseller to originate with a feminist publisher. Brown's other books include a collection of essays and speeches, *A Plain Brown Rapper* (1976), *Southern Discomfort* (1982) and *Sudden Death* (1983).

Browne, Stella, 1882–1955

English. A socialist and campaigner for sexual freedom, she became involved in the BIRTH CONTROL movement before World War I. After the war she tried to force the Communist Party to recognize the importance of birth control as an issue; failing, in 1923 she transferred her allegiance to the Labour Party. In 1936 she was a founder-member of the Abortion Law Reform Association. She was far in advance of other campaigners for birth control: in 1912 she was writing for *The Freewoman* on the rights of all women, whether married or single, to sexual pleasure, and she spoke of ABORTION as a woman's right as early as 1915.

Browning, Elizabeth Barrett, 1806–61

English poet. Like many women writers of her day, Browning was anti-suffrage, believing Victorian women were not yet ready to cope with political equality; despite this belief, she had feminist sympathies as seen in her long, triumphant poem about an independent-minded female poet, AURORA LEIGH.

Brownmiller, Susan, 1935–

American journalist. A founder-member of the NEW YORK RADICAL FEMINISTS in 1969, her most important contribution to feminist theory is undoubtedly her book AGAINST OUR WILL (1975), an exhaustive analysis of RAPE which identifies it as the major weapon used by men in the oppression of women. She is also the author of *Femininity* (1984) as well as many articles and essays.

Bunch, Charlotte, 1944–

American. Involved in the Women's Liberation Movement since the late 1960s, she was a founder of THE FURIES, a lesbian feminist newspaper, and QUEST: *A Feminist Quarterly*, where she remains a contributing editor. She has edited a number of feminist anthologies and written for many magazines. An activist, editor, writer, teacher, speaker and organizer, she has been influential as a theorist, involved in developing a definition and theory of feminism which will transcend established labels and single issues. She believes that our future depends on the expansion and clarification of feminism, which she has defined as 'transformational politics . . . a perspective on life that can transform the next century . . . a perspective on the world that grows out of women's oppression'. She is currently active on issues of concern to women globally, following her work as a consultant to the United Nations Secretariat for the World Conference of the United Nations Decade for Women.

(*See also* NONALIGNED FEMINISM)

'Burial of Traditional Woman-hood, The'

Held in the midst of an anti-war demonstration in Washington, D.C. in January 1968, this was the first public CONSCIOUSNESS-RAISING action taken by radical women in America. They hoped to convince women who were protesting against the Vietnam War that until they dealt with their own oppression they would be helpless to solve other problems of society. The slogan 'SISTERHOOD IS POWERFUL' made its first appearance here.

Burning Questions
Novel by Alix Kates SHULMAN first published in 1978, it examines the modern feminist experience through the story of Zane IndiAnna. In the form of a fictional autobiography, it traces Zane's life from a conventional midwestern childhood, through beatnik glory in Greenwich Village, to marriage and motherhood, culminating in her discovery of the women's liberation movement in 1968. After that her life is transformed through CONSCIOUSNESS-RAISING, SISTERHOOD, divorce, love affairs with women and men, and radical political action. The book ends on a positive, self-affirming note.

Burning Times, the
Term used by Mary DALY to refer to the period of the European witchhunts in the fifteenth, sixteenth and seventeenth centuries, but also to 'the perpetual witchcraze which is the entire period of patriarchal rule'.

Burns, Lucy, 1879–1966
American. During a trip to Britain in 1908 she met leaders of the militant suffrage movement and was inspired to abandon a brilliant scholarly career to devote herself to political activism. She campaigned in England and Scotland for the WOMEN'S SOCIAL AND POLITICAL UNION, serving as a salaried organizer in Edinburgh from 1910–12. She was arrested several times and took part in prison hunger strikes, receiving a special medal of valour from the WSPU. During this time she met another young American fighting for suffrage, Alice PAUL, and when she returned to the United States in 1912 they worked together on the committee of the NATIONAL AMERICAN WOMAN SUFFRAGE ASSOCIATION. Believing that suffrage could be attained more quickly through a constitutional amendment rather than the state-by-state campaigns of NAWSA, they formed the CONGRESSIONAL UNION FOR WOMAN SUFFRAGE in April 1913. With Alice Paul, Lucy Burns shaped the major policies of the Congressional Union, as well as those of its successor, the NATIONAL WOMAN'S PARTY. She also edited the Congressional Union's newspaper, The Suffragist, from 1915–16. Her courage and resolute militancy were legendary, and by 1916 she had spent more time in jail than any other American suffragist. Following the passage of the suffrage amendment in June 1919, she declared herself physically exhausted, and retired to private life.

Butler, Josephine, 1828–1906
English. Although she was an early member of the LANGHAM PLACE GROUP, and was involved in the education struggle in her capacity as

President of the North of England Council for the Higher Education of Women from 1868–73, for the most part her commitment to a militant campaign against the CONTAGIOUS DISEASES ACTS has caused her to be seen as an outsider to the women's movement of her day. Many working for better education, career opportunities and votes for women were afraid their cause would be tarnished by association with a battle and a subject – PROSTITUTION – which Victorian ladies were not allowed to acknowledge. Yet Butler herself, braving physical and verbal abuse, saw her struggle as very much a part of the movement for equality. In 1873 she said, 'If I were not working for Repeal, I would throw my whole force into getting the suffrage. I feel more keenly than I ever did the great importance of our having votes *as a means* of self-preservation.'

As Dale Spender and Jennifer Uglow have pointed out, Butler was radical in her feminism in that she made the link between economics and sexuality, recognizing that it was the male division of women into two separate classes which would perpetuate the subordination of women despite token advances.

In 1886 Butler's campaign achieved repeal of the Acts, and she moved to other fronts of the same battle, investigating and exposing child prostitution, and expanded her campaigns to the Continent. She was a founder-member of the National Vigilance Association, and published many books and articles.

C

Caird, Mona, ?1855–1932
English poet and novelist. Most of her novels were published under the pseudonym G. Noel Hatton, but she was also a feminist theorist, author of many essays on women's situation, some of which were collected as *The Morality of Marriage and Other Essays on the Status of Women* (1897).

Califia

1) Fictional Queen of the AMAZONS, heroine of the sixteenth-century romance *Amadis de Gaule*. California was named in her honour by Spanish explorers who hoped they had found the home of the Amazons.

2) Feminist educational programme founded in Los Angeles in 1976.

Camera Obscura

Journal of FILM theory and critical analysis written from a feminist and socialist perspective, founded in 1976 and published three times a year by a collective based in California. Frequently technical and abstract, the journal uses semiology, textual analysis, Marxist theory and psychoanalytic theory to examine how patriarchal ideology is reproduced by film.

Campbell, Beatrix, 1947–
British journalist. She joined the women's liberation movement in 1970, and has worked for SOCIALIST FEMINISM ever since as a writer, speaker and organizer. A founder of RED RAG and co-author, with Anna COOTE, of SWEET FREEDOM: *The Struggle for Women's Liberation* (1982). Her feminism is integrated into all her writing, whether or not it is specifically about 'women's interests'. As she wrote in her book *Wigan Pier Revisited* (1984): 'Orwell wrote his experiences of the working class by reference only to men. Men still do this – they talk of men's struggles, movements and characteristics as if they were writing about the whole class. As a feminist I didn't invert their bad habits by only talking to women – this book is about women *and* men, though it takes the standpoint of women as its reference point.'
(*See also* WOMAN-CENTREDNESS)

Capetillo, Luisa, 1880–1922
Puerto Rican journalist. A factory worker from girlhood, she was one of the first to speak out against U.S. exploitation of island labour, and became a reporter for the labour newspaper, *Workers' Union*. In 1910 she founded a feminist magazine, *La Mujer*, and caused a local sensa-

tion by wearing trousers in public. She is the author of *My Opinion on the Liberties, Rights, and Obligations of the Puerto Rican Woman* (1911).

capitalism
Socialist feminists and Marxist-feminists, while not agreeing with traditional Marxists in identifying capitalism as the cause of women's oppression, do recognize the ways in which the capitalist system benefits from and perpetuates sexism. To them, as to most radical feminists, the overthrow of PATRIARCHY will also require the abolition of capitalism. LIBERAL FEMINISM does not challenge capitalism, assuming that its goal – the full equality of women – can be accommodated within a capitalist framework. Some even assume that capitalism is a system which can be used against patriarchy, through the development of women's networks and women-run businesses. In practice, however, feminist businesses, whether bookshops, publishing houses or record companies, have discovered that high political ideals do not help in running a successful business. The collective process preferred by feminists is slow and inefficient by capitalist standards, and overheads are higher for alternative businesses which have fewer customers. Although they may survive, feminist enterprises tend to be marginal, presenting an alternative to some, but no real challenge to the existing patriarchal, capitalist

economy.
(*See also* MARXIST-FEMINISM)

Career feminism
Term used by Myra Marx Ferree and Beth B. Hess in *Controversy and Coalition: The New Feminist Movement* (1985) to delineate that aspect of the modern women's movement which emphasizes the achievement of personal goals, the importance of women forming networks and acting assertively, and women's right to any sort of job in society. This is a type of feminism usually acceptable to women who say 'I'M NOT A FEMINIST, BUT . . .' and is perhaps more widely known, particularly in America, by the term MAINSTREAM FEMINISM.
(*See also* ASSERTIVENESS TRAINING; EQUAL PAY FOR EQUAL WORK)

Carter, Angela, 1940–
English writer. Her novels and short stories are often concerned with female sexuality, power relationships between men and women, and other subjects on which a feminist sensibility is focused through the lens of the fantastic. Her books include the novels *The Infernal Desire Machines of Doctor Hoffman* (1972), *The Passion of New Eve* (1977) and *Nights at the Circus* (1984); a collection of journalism and criticism, *Nothing Sacred* (1982); *The Bloody Chamber* (1979); and *The Sadeian Woman* (1979).

Cary, Mary Ann Shadd,
1823–1893
American teacher, journalist and lawyer. She became famous in the 1850s as a leader of the black emigration movement to Canada which followed the passage of the Fugitive Slave Act in 1850. In 1853, she helped found the *Provincial Freeman*, a non-partisan weekly newspaper devoted to the interests of blacks in Canada, and was acclaimed as the first black woman to establish and edit a newspaper in North America. After the Civil War (during which she helped recruit black soldiers in Indiana) she moved to Washington, D.C., taught in public schools, and began to study law at Howard University. After attending the Woman Suffrage Convention in Washington in 1870 she was inspired to write a statement to the Judiciary Committee of the House of Representatives, claiming her right as a taxpayer and citizen to vote, and in 1871 she was one of a very few women who did actually register to vote. Throughout her life she was active in the struggle for women's suffrage, and she gave a stirring speech at the 1878 National Woman's Suffrage Association convention. In 1880 she organized the Colored Women's Progressive Association, and in 1883 she was at last awarded her law degree. Paula Giddings (1984) has suggested that Cary not only initiated the trend towards the involvement of more black women in the struggle for women's suffrage, but helped to create a new feminism which addressed the specific needs of black women.
(*See also* BLACK FEMINISM)

Cat and Mouse Act
The popular name for The Prisoners' Temporary Discharge for Ill-Health Act, passed by the British Parliament on 25 April 1913. The Act was in direct response to the SUFFRAGETTE tactic of hunger-striking in protest at not being treated as political prisoners. Forced feeding had been resorted to, but this caused such a public outcry and sympathy for the brutalized women, that a Bill was introduced in which prisoners who had damaged their health by their own conduct (i.e. hunger-striking) might be released to recover, and then imprisoned again, with the time spent outside prison not counted as part of the sentence. Lord Robert Cecil referred to this as 'what is commonly called a cat-and-mouse proposal, namely, catching the women, then letting them go again; then catching them again.' The Act was unsuccessful, however, for the freed suffragettes used their freedom for more militant actions and evaded re-arrest, so that by October of the same year, forced feeding was once more resorted to by prison officials rather than let their prisoners go.

Catalyst

American non-profit-making organization founded in 1961, dedicated to expanding women's career options. It publishes a series of low-cost self-guidance pamphlets for women entering the labour force for the first time or returning to careers after an absence; a list of local resource centres which offer counselling, job referrals, and placement services; and a National Roster, issued monthly, listing college-educated women who are seeking administrative, technical, managerial or professional positions. In 1980 it established the Career and Family Center to conduct surveys exploring corporate attitudes and practices as they affected dual-career couples, and to develop a prototype college course to help students plan realistically for a life in which both partners will be employed.

Catt, Carrie Chapman,
1859–1947

American. After working as a teacher, school administrator and journalist in her home state of Iowa, in 1890 she brought her genius for organization to the woman suffrage movement, literally transforming it with definite plans of action on a state level, a membership system, study courses and a manual of organization. In 1900 she succeeded Susan B. Anthony as President of the NATIONAL AMERICAN WOMAN SUFFRAGE ALLIANCE (NAWSA), resigning in 1903 due to her husband's illness. After his death in 1904, she became President of the INTERNATIONAL WOMEN'S SUFFRAGE ALLIANCE, and also turned her attention to winning the vote on the state level, leading major campaigns in New York from 1912.

In 1916, under pressure from a membership which saw her as the only hope to free the national movement from stagnation, she resumed the presidency of NAWSA. Under her direction there was an immediate change for the better: a new determination and professionalism sparked the movement, resulting in the passage of the NINETEENTH AMENDMENT in 1920.

Suffrage achieved, Mrs Catt then founded the LEAGUE OF WOMEN VOTERS and – always a pacifist – became involved in the peace movement. She also found time to write several books, including *Woman Suffrage and Politics* (1933).

Cauer, Minna, 1841–1922

German. Active in the German women's movement from the 1880s, in 1900 she co-founded, with Anita AUGSPURG, the Union of Progressive Women's Associations (Verband fortschrittlicher Frauenvereine). She also co-founded the German Union for Women's Suffrage (Deutscher Verband für Frauenstimmrecht) in 1902, and was a member of the INTERNATIONAL ALLIANCE OF WOMEN from 1904. She was a radical, militant feminist who campaigned against state regulation of prostitution, tried to interest working women in the movement, and organized public street demonstrations for women's suffrage.

Cause, The

1) A short history of the women's movement in Great Britain written by Ray STRACHEY, published in 1928. At that time an organized women's movement scarcely existed any more, so this book not only informed younger women about their history, it inspired pride and kept the feminist tradition alive.

2) Term used to refer to the struggle, whether militant or constitutional, for women's suffrage in Britain (c. 1864–1918) and, by logical extension, to the larger cause of women's freedom.

celibacy

Unmarried state; to live without sexual relationships. For early feminists, given the difficulties of birth control, celibacy was one sure way of maintaining a single life, ensuring the possibility of self-definition and a life devoted to work or friendship or a cause not dictated by a connection to one man. During the second wave of feminism, the modern view of sexuality meant that celibacy was usually perceived as a denial of needs or the refusal to accept lesbianism. But by the mid-1970s celibacy began to be seen once again as a meaningful option for the feminist who felt no sexual desire for women yet wished to detach herself from men and devote her energies and emotions to women.

Cell 16

One of the first women's liberation groups in America, it was founded in Boston in the summer of 1968 by Roxanne DUNBAR, who placed an ad. for members in an underground newspaper. They published A JOURNAL OF FEMALE LIBERATION (No More Fun and Games), and influenced many other groups.

Chace, Elizabeth Buffum, 1806–99

American. One of the organizers of the first national women's rights convention in 1850, she was active in the anti-slavery, temperance, peace, child welfare and prison reform movements. She founded the Rhode Island Woman Suffrage Association and presided over it until her death.

Chancellor, Olive

Fictional character, the strong-willed feminist protagonist of THE BOSTONIANS by Henry James.

Changer and the Changed, The

See WILLIAMSON, CRIS

Charnas, Suzy McKee, 1939–

American writer. Her first novel, Walk to the End of the World (1974) uses SCIENCE FICTION to explore how a sexist culture deforms humanity and destroys the possibility of love, by taking our male-dominant culture and carrying it to what can be seen as its logical, horrifying conclusion. In the sequel, *Motherlines* (1978) she offers an alternative, women-only society, creating a convincing and scientifically plausible race of AMAZONS.

Chernyshevsky, Nikolai, 1828–89

Russian. He is remembered chiefly for his only novel, WHAT IS TO BE DONE? (1864) which he wrote while in prison for his revolutionary activities, and which provided advanced Russian women with a doctrine of sexual freedom and personal emancipation.

Chesler, Phyllis, 1940–

American academic and writer. Her first book, WOMEN AND MADNESS (1972) was an extremely influential work of feminist theory, developing the thesis that PSYCHOLOGY (in particular, psychiatry) is one of the most powerful of modern weapons used to oppress women. Her other books include *Women, Money and Power* (1976) written with Emily Jane Goodman; *About Men* (1978); and a journal of her experiences of pregnancy and MOTHERHOOD, *With Child* (1979).

Chew, Ada Nield, 1870–1945

English. Working-class campaigner and union organizer, she came to public attention in 1894 with a series of letters exposing the exploitative conditions in the clothing factory where she worked, published in the *Crewe Chronicle* over the signature 'A Crewe Factory Girl'. A member of the Independent Labour Party, she worked in the Women's Trade Union League until 1908, when she devoted herself to the campaign for women's suffrage. Her articles and short stories were published in many papers, including the *Freewoman*, and emphasized the importance for women to be economically independent of their husbands and involved in the political process at all levels. In 1982 a collection of her writings was published, edited and with a biographical remembrance by her daughter, Doris Nield Chew.

Chicago, Judy, 1939–

American artist. By 1970 she had realized her art was not being appreciated or understood in the male-dominated art world and committed herself to developing an alternative community for women artists. With Miriam SCHAPIRO she set up the Feminist Art Program at the California Institute of the Arts, and she helped open the Women's Building in Los Angeles among other feminist projects. In 1975 her autobiography, *Through the Flower*, was published. In 1974 she began work on the massive, multi-media artwork, THE DINNER PARTY, com-

CHILDCARE

pleted in 1979.
(*See also* ARTS AND ARTISTS)

childcare

From the very start of the women's liberation movement, childcare has been a major concern. As a 1970 NOW press release titled 'Why Feminists Want Childcare' put it: 'A basic cause of the second-class status of women in America and the world for thousands of years has been the notion that . . . because women bear children, it is primarily their responsibility to care for them . . . Women will never have full opportunities to participate in our economic, political, cultural life as long as they bear this responsibility almost entirely alone . . . We reject the idea that mothers have a special childcare role that is not to be shared equally by fathers.'

Despite continued pressure from women (a demand for federally funded, non-sexist childcare centres was made at the Congress to Unite Women in 1969, and again at the government-sponsored women's conference in Houston, Texas, in 1977) the Nixon, Ford, Carter and Reagan administrations have all taken the position that childcare is 'family business'. And in Britain, although the state offers more family services than in the U.S., most women are forced to take the primary responsibility for child-rearing, or paying another woman to do so for them, as they are caught between the economic necessity of

working and the hypocritical public attitude which implies that mothers should stay at home with their children. Many feminists have organized nurseries, playgroups and babysitting circles on a self-help basis, and in July 1980 a number of groups from all over Britain united to form the National Child Care Campaign.

If publicly-funded, community-controlled, quality childcare were available, women would not be forced into MARRIAGE for economic reasons, nor into choosing between MOTHERHOOD and career. It would also demonstrate that childcare is 'real work' which people of both sexes can be trained and paid to do, and it would begin to break down the public life/private life dichotomy which is such a basic part of the structure of patriarchy.

Another important aspect of childcare is, of course, the impact and influence it has on the child. Dorothy Dinnerstein, in *The Mermaid and the Minotaur* (1976), traces the roots of sexism (and other human neuroses) to the fact that the first and major relationship the child has is almost always with a woman. Nancy CHODOROW, in *The Reproduction of Mothering* (1978), argues that the psychological and social inequality between men and women is perpetuated by the different character structure imposed on boy and girl children by the fact that their primary caretaker is – and is always expected to be – a woman.

Boys learn to separate themselves from others, while girls grow up learning to be emotionally vulnerable, and they repeat the traditional division of labour when raising their own families. Both Chodorow and Dinnerstein, as well as others, have strongly suggested that until men take an equal role with women in the care and raising of infants and children, the construction of GENDER differences will not be changed.

childfree
Word preferred to 'childless' by those who have chosen not to have children, since '-less' may imply a lack. However, some consider 'childfree' to be insulting to children, implying they are a burden an adult might be glad to be 'free' of. There are, unfortunately, not enough positive terms yet for women who oppose patriarchal stereotypes.
(*See also* NAMING)

Children's Liberation
The idea that children, like the women with whom they are usually linked, are an oppressed class, was voiced by some feminists from the beginning of the women's liberation movement. The basic concept was expressed in the slogan 'Children are People', and various organizations and publications have promoted the idea that children are not the property of their parents, but have rights of their own. Yet

Shulamith FIRESTONE was one of the very few feminists to take the idea of children's rights to its ultimate conclusion, and to see in the oppression of childhood the model for the oppression of women. In THE DIALECTIC OF SEX (1970), she argued that the institution of childhood was a social invention which must be abolished if both women and children were to be, finally, free. She suggested that, just as in the past women had been assumed to be helpless and in need of male protection, so the apparent helplessness of children today was also socially imposed. This radical vision of childhood has not caught on widely among parents, although it has been explored in some works of SCIENCE FICTION, including THE FEMALE MAN by Joanna Russ and WOMAN ON THE EDGE OF TIME by Marge Piercy.

Chisholm, Shirley, 1924–
American politician. First black woman elected to Congress (from the 12th District, Brooklyn, in 1968), in 1972 she ran for Democratic nomination for President. She has always been a strong and active campaigner for the rights of women and of racial minorities.

Ch'iu Chin *See* JIU JIN.

Chodorow, Nancy, 1944–
American sociologist. Her involvement in the women's liberation movement led her to question

'what it meant that women parented women'. To answer that question, she wrote *The Reproduction of Mothering: Psychoanalysis and the Sociology of Gender* (1978), one of the most influential theoretical works on the topics of SEX-ROLES, GENDER, and the institution of MOTHERHOOD. Rejecting the idea that women's universally primary role in CHILDCARE could be explained by biology or by a patriarchal society which made other roles prohibited to women, Chodorow declared 'Women's mothering perpetuates itself through social-structurally induced psychological mechanisms. . . Women come to mother because they have been mothered by women. By contrast, that men are mothered by women reduces their parenting capacities.' She looked to psychoanalysis for the explanation of how predominantly single-sex parenting could cause the development of a different personality structure in girls and boys. Her conclusion was that sexual division of labour produced not merely different sex roles, but unequal ones. Women's exclusive mothering, she wrote, 'creates a psychology of male dominance and fear of women in men. It forms a basis for the division of the social world into unequally valued domestic and public spheres, each the province of people of a different gender.' To achieve women's liberation, therefore, the family must be reorganized so that women and men share parenting responsibilities equally, and children grow up dependent upon people of both genders from their earliest days.

Chopin, Kate, 1850–1904

American writer. Once considered a minor regional writer remembered for her short stories depicting Creole life, Chopin has finally been recognized as a pioneer of female realism. Throughout her work runs the theme of woman's spiritual and sensual emancipation, and she was able to surpass contemporaries like Stephen Crane and Frank Norris in her ability to depict realistically the sexual feelings of both men and women. Her third and finest novel, THE AWAKENING (1899) was condemned by reviewers and banned by libraries for immorality. Disapproval of the work extended to the author who was insulted, refused admittance to circles where she had once been welcomed, and shunned by former friends. Deeply hurt by this response, Chopin found it impossible to continue writing.

Chorlton v. Lings

Case heard before the Court of Common Pleas, 7 November 1868, which attempted to prove that certain women had the right to vote on the basis of ancient English statutes, and under Lord Brougham's Act of 1850 which declared 'that in all acts words importing the masculine gender shall be deemed and taken to include females'. Dr Richard PANKHURST assisted Sir J. D. Coleridge in presenting the case of the women, who had been organized by Lydia BECKER. The court ruled that the usage of centuries – the fact that women had not generally been permitted to vote – had more weight than the statutes cited, a ruling which made it clear to suffragists that new parliamentary legislation was their only hope.

Christian, Meg

American musician. She began her musical career as a performer in 1969, singing in clubs in the Washington, D.C. area. At the same time she was discovering feminism, and writing songs about women's lives and her own experiences. She soon gave up more traditional work to concentrate on performing music by and for women, becoming part of the emerging WOMANCULTURE and the mother, many would say, of women's music. She co-founded OLIVIA RECORDS in 1973, and their first release was her album *I Know You Know* (1975). Subsequent albums include *Face the Music* (1977), *Turning it Over* (1981) and *From the Heart* (1984).

Christian feminists

Like all patriarchal religions, Christianity has been instrumental in creating, perpetuating, and justifying women's oppression. Yet although the Christian church has been for many centuries the most oppressive institution, forcing women to submit to the rule of their fathers and husbands as stand-ins for God, this oppression is not necessarily inherent in the religion, and many women have found in it spiritual liberation and truth. Christian teachings may be emphasized and interpreted in varied and quite contradictory ways, as proven by Elizabeth Cady STANTON and her co-authors in THE WOMAN'S BIBLE (1895–8), and modern scholars have re-examined the New Testament to argue that despite later interpretations, Jesus was free from sexual prejudice.

During the puritan revolution of the mid-seventeenth century the entrenched sexism of the church was challenged as the concept that all human souls are equal in the sight of God gathered force. The more radical puritan sects took the idea of spiritual equality to its logical conclusion, accepting the authority of the spirit over that of church or state, even if that spirit happened to be manifested in a woman or a child. Although not widespread, and soon subdued, the very existence of this idea allowed feminist theory to develop within women who still defined themselves as Christian.

The discrepancy between Christian ideals and the actual treatment of women within the church began to attract more attention in the 1960s and 1970s as more and more women were influenced by feminist ideas. Individual instances of injustice began to be seen as part of a pattern of sexism. But as women began making demands of their churches they encountered a deep, often hostile, resistance to change, and were forced to ask historical and theological questions of Christianity in a search for the roots of its sexism.

In *A Map of the New Country: Women and Christianity* (1983) Sara MAITLAND argues that the root of the problem lies in the ancient heresy of dualism: the idea that the wholeness of God's creation can be divided into two and labelled 'good' (spirit) or 'bad' (flesh). According to Maitland: 'Dualism is a fundamental *ground* of oppression – the ability to assert that me and mine are better than that which is Other, and justifying this by making God, the ultimate Other, over in one's own image . . . Feminist theology perceives that dualistic splits are the cause not just of sexism, but of racism, classism, and ecological destruction.'

How far feminist theology may depart from accepted doctrine and still be considered Christian is a problem faced by feminists struggling to reconcile their spiritual with their political feelings. Some Christian feminist groups are church-linked, others are inter-denominational, and others have moved, like philosopher Mary DALY, once a respected Catholic theologian, now declaring herself 'unconfined by the teachings of church or man', into the new realm of SPIRITUAL FEMINISM.

In Britain, the Christian Feminist Movement began in 1978 as an active group concerned with examining feminist issues from a Christian viewpoint, and challenging sexism both within and outside the church. They are separate from, but closely involved with, the CHRISTIAN WOMEN'S INFORMATION AND RESOURCE SERVICE (C.W.I.R.E.S.), a network linking people working to change the position of women in the church.

Christian Women's Information and Resource Service (C.W.I.R.E.S.)

An umbrella organization linking various groups working for change in the position of women in the church, established in Oxford in 1979. It has built up a library to provide an information service for the general reader, study groups and researchers in the following areas: images of women in the church and Christian history; language and imagery in worship; women's organizations in the churches; doctrines, ethics and the religious experience from the woman's point of view; women in Third World churches; theology and sexuality; women's spirituality; and feminist theology.

(See also CHRISTIAN FEMINISM; SPIRITUAL FEMINISM)

CLAFLIN, TENNESSEE

Churchill, Caryl, 1938–

English playwright. She began writing plays for stage and radio in the 1950s. *Light Shining in Buckinghamshire* (1976) was her first play to win her attention as a feminist writer for although only five of the twenty-five characters in this seventeenth-century historical play are women, there is great emphasis in the text on the political and sexual oppression of women. Some of her plays have been scripted collectively, in collaboration with theatre companies such as Joint Stock and Monstrous Regiment. *Vinegar Tom* draws connections between the medieval attitude towards witches and the continuing masculine view of women. *Top Girls* (1982) mixes historical figures and contemporary characters, all of them women.

Cinema of Women (COW Films)

First British feminist film/video distribution collective, founded in 1979 in the belief that distribution was as important as production, and that feminist FILMS should not be distributed simply as films within the male-defined system, but as a part of feminist practice, to reach a non-cinema-going audience and be an integral part of the Women's Liberation Movement.

civil rights movement

In America, the women who started the WOMEN'S LIBERATION MOVEMENT in 1967 first made contact with each other and became more radical through their experience in the NEW LEFT, chiefly in the anti-war and civil rights movements. The way that the civil rights movement developed into the Black Power movement also provided an example for the new feminists to follow: just as blacks were refusing to allow whites to define the terms of their struggle, so women realized they could not allow men to dictate their issues, methods or goals.

Cixous, Hélène, 1938–

French writer and academic. Author of more than twenty books, she has written novels, plays, critical essays and articles, and is particularly concerned with deconstructing classical and psychoanalytical thought as she works towards a theory of women's oppression. She founded a research group on the theory of femininity at the University of Paris, and has taught in the United States and Canada as well as in France.

Claflin, Tennessee, 1846–1923

American. Sister of Victoria WOODHULL with whom she shared her career on stage (as mind-reader and lecturer), in finance (they were the first women stockbrokers in America) and journalism, publishing *Woodhull and Claflin's Weekly* which promoted, among other causes, women's rights, spiritualism and free love, and cost them a

65

prison sentence on obscenity charges. Although less well-known than her sister, she was involved in the women's movement both in America and, after 1877, in Britain.

Cleyre, Voltairine de, 1866–1912

American. Described by her friend Emma GOLDMAN as 'the poet-rebel, the liberty-loving artist, the greatest woman anarchist in America', de Cleyre was a prolific writer and popular speaker who shrank from notoriety. Although raised a Catholic, she learned to speak and write in Yiddish and became the apostle of ANARCHISM to the Jewish immigrants of Philadelphia. Women's emancipation and social oppression were the issues which dominated her life and her writings. Her career began in 1886, as the editor of a free thought paper in Michigan, *The Progressive Age*. In 1888 she became an anarchist and began to travel more widely, lecturing on social oppression, anarchism, and women's freedom. She translated *Moribund Society and Anarchy* by Jean Grave and *The Modern School* by Francisco Ferrer into English. She lectured on behalf of the Women's National Liberal Union, and in 1892 helped establish the Ladies' Liberal League. Her published writings include a volume of poems, *The Worm Turns* (1900), and lectures including *In Defense of Emma Goldman and the Right of Expropriation* (1894), *Crime and Punishment* (1903), *Anarchism and American Traditions* (1909) and *Direct Action* (1912). Alexander Berkman edited a volume of her *Selected Works* two years after her death, in 1914.

click!

Shorthand term for the moment of truth, the times in a woman's life when she suddenly recognizes her oppression and refuses to go along with it. Used by Jane O'Reilly in her article 'The Housewife's Moment of Truth' published in the first issue of *Ms.* (Spring 1972), and, in subsequent years, by many others writing to *Ms.* about their personal experiences. Defined by O'Reilly as 'the click! of recognition, that parenthesis of truth around a little thing that completes the puzzle of reality in women's minds – the moment that brings a gleam to our eyes and means the revolution has begun.'

Clisby, Harriet, 1830–1931

Australian journalist and doctor. In 1861 she worked with Caroline DEXTER on *The Interpreter*, the first Australian journal published by women. Inspired by the example of Elizabeth BLACKWELL, she decided to train as a doctor, and graduated from the New York Medical College for Women in 1865. She founded the Women's Educational and Industrial Union in Boston in 1871, and was involved with other feminist groups for many years. Towards the end of her life she retired to Geneva, where she founded L'Union des Femmes.

Clough, Anne Jemima, 1820–92
English. A teacher, she became involved in the movement for higher education for women in the 1860s. With Josephine BUTLER she organized a travelling lecture series for women, and in 1867 became secretary of the North of England Council for Promoting the Higher Education of Women. In 1871 she moved to Cambridge to supervise the residential house for women students which became Newnham College in 1880, where she served as principal until her death.

Cobbe, Frances Power,
1822–1904
Irish. An outspoken reformer involved in the movements for higher education, for the care of working girls, anti-vivisectionism, and women's suffrage. In her many articles and pamphlets she publicized the inequities of laws made by men for men, bringing to light the terrible true stories of women who suffered from the cruelties of violent husbands without legal recourse or shelter.

Combahee River Collective
Black feminist group founded in Boston in 1974. They named themselves after 'the only military campaign in American history planned and led by a woman' – a guerrilla action which freed more than 750 slaves, led by Harriet Tubman on 2 June 1863, in South Carolina. In 1979 the collective produced 'A Black Feminist Statement' to explain their political beliefs, the genesis of contemporary BLACK FEMINISM, the problems in organizing black feminists, and black feminist issues and practice.

Common Cause, The
Weekly paper of the NATIONAL UNION OF WOMEN'S SUFFRAGE SOCIETIES (NUWSS), first issue 15 April 1909; first editor Helen SWANWICK. In 1920, it became *The Woman's Leader*.

compulsory heterosexuality
Viewed by some – particularly radical and lesbian – feminists as being at the core of women's oppression, and named a crime against women by the Brussels Tribunal on Crimes Against Women in 1976. Heterosexuality is usually presented either as natural (so that any deviation is a sickness) or as a choice; the understanding behind the phrase 'compulsory heterosexuality' is that women do not have the freedom to choose. Women's SEXUALITY has been defined and developed for men's pleasure. If heterosexuality were no longer compulsory, then GENDER identity, sexuality, the structure of the unconscious as well as the structure of society would be vastly different – presumably non-sexist. Adrienne RICH and Charlotte BUNCH are

among those who have written on this subject.

Conditions

Twice yearly magazine of women's writing founded in 1976. Based in New York, it is consciously multi-racial and multi-ethnic and places an emphasis on writings by lesbians.

Condorcet, Jean, Marquis de, 1743–94

French philosopher, mathematician and politician, and an early supporter of the revolutionary liberal doctrine of equal rights for women. In an essay, *Sur l'admission des femmes au droit de Cité* (1790) he wrote: 'Either no member of the human race has real rights, or else all have the same; he who votes against the rights of another, whatever his religion, colour or sex, thereby abjures his own.' He also argued that any apparent inferiorities of women were due to deficiencies in education, or to social conditioning, pointing out that it would be impossible to judge the true capacities of either sex until they could be seen against a background of equal opportunities and experience. By 1793, the feminist movement in France had been crushed, but Condorcet continued to write on the subject of equal rights for women until his death in prison.

Congress to Unite Women

First major attempt to create an organized, unified structure for the women's liberation movement in America. It was held on 21–3 November 1969, in New York City, attended by over 500 women from the northeastern region. The whole spectrum of feminist organizations, from moderate to radical, including the NATIONAL ORGANIZATION FOR WOMEN (NOW), New Yorkers for Abortion Law Repeal, DAUGHTERS OF BILITIS and REDSTOCKINGS, was represented, yet there was no divisiveness, and general agreement on all issues. Among the resolutions passed were demands for total repeal of all abortion laws, the passage of the EQUAL RIGHTS AMENDMENT, and free, nationwide, twenty-four-hour childcare centres. At the end of the congress a press conference was held to 'announce women's unity', and a Continuing Committee was established to build a coalition of women's groups. But a unified, structured movement did not come into being, and the second Congress to Unite Women, on 1–3 May 1970, was much less successful, splits developing over questions of policy and tactics.

Congressional Union for Woman Suffrage (CU)

Founded by Alice PAUL and Lucy BURNS in April 1913, as an auxiliary to the NATIONAL AMERICAN WOMAN SUFFRAGE ASSOCIATION, with the sole aim of working for a federal suffrage amendment. By February

1914 it had become a separate organization. It was a small but dedicated group of young women who used publicity stunts, marches and demonstrations, automobile tours, motion pictures and magic lantern shows, petitions, press releases and a weekly newspaper (*The Suffragist*) to restore the languishing campaign for a federal amendment to new and powerful life. Following the precedent set by the Women's Social and Political Union in Britain (where Paul and Burns had met), the CU held 'the party in power' in America responsible for the failure to pass a women's suffrage amendment, despite the fact that they had supporters, and enemies, in both parties. By campaigning against the Democrats, they aimed to prove to the lawmakers that the lack of a federal amendment would cost them votes in the states where women had the vote. To this end, the CU organized the Woman's Party to be active in those twelve states in 1916. In 1917 the Congressional Union merged with the Woman's Party under the name the NATIONAL WOMAN'S PARTY.

consciousness-raising (CR)

The most important educational process, and probably the form in which the women's liberation movement is best known. A method of group discussion with similarities to the revolutionary Chinese practice called 'speaking bitterness', CR evolved out of 'rap sessions' among RADICAL WOMEN in New York in the late 1960s, and gradually became structured and formalized as it was recognized by radical feminists as the necessary first step on the path towards an analysis of women's oppression and action to end it. CR broke down the psychological isolation suffered by women in Western society and created the understanding that the PERSONAL IS POLITICAL. It made possible a meaningful analysis of woman's situation, based not on abstract ideas, but on shared experiences.

Usually the CR group consists of between five and fifteen women who meet weekly for a specified period which may be between six months and two years (absences are excused only for genuine emergencies). Discussions may be helped by a facilitator, or the women may take it in turns to lead. Topics – for example, childhood experiences, mother–daughter relationships, marriage, sexuality, images of femininity – are usually decided in advance, and all the women are expected to speak from their own experience. Understanding rather than advice or criticism is the aim, and every woman's experience is equally valid and important.

In form it may appear to be (and has been criticized as being) a kind of therapy, but CR is totally different from therapy in its aims. The ultimate goal of CR is highly political: to achieve fundamental changes in society, and not merely to help individuals to adjust. CR does not seek individual solutions, but works to relate the personal to the societal.

Although originally developed by radical feminists, CR soon spread to all parts of the women's movement. Even women who would not feel comfortable defining themselves as feminists have had valuable experiences with CR groups.

conservative feminists
Term sometimes applied to liberal feminists by radical feminists, and may also refer to those Zillah EISENSTEIN has called revisionist feminists.
(*See also* LIBERAL FEMINISM; CAREER FEMINISM; BOURGEOIS FEMINISM; MAINSTREAM FEMINISM; REVISIONIST FEMINISM)

Constantia
Pen-name used by Judith Sargent MURRAY for her feminist essays and stories.

Contagious Diseases Acts
Passed in England in 1864, 1866 and 1869, they gave the police authority to arrest any woman they suspected of prostitution and order her to submit to a medical examination. If she refused, she could be imprisoned. If found to be diseased, she could be confined to hospital for three or more months. Because these acts so clearly emphasized the double standard (additional provisions to arrest or hold the clients, pimps and procurers were always defeated) and increased male control of women, feminists immediately responded by calling for repeal, and many women were made more political by the experience of protest. Some suffragists were unwilling to risk reflecting scandal on their cause at a time when 'ladies' were expected to be ignorant of the existence of prostitutes, but more radical and broadly-based feminists perceived the root of women's oppression in the male-imposed division between 'good' wives and 'bad' prostitutes, both existing only for the comfort of men. The campaign for repeal, led by Josephine BUTLER and The Ladies National Association for the Repeal of the Contagious Diseases Acts, was successful in 1886.

Convert, The
Novelization, by Elizabeth ROBINS, of her own play, VOTES FOR WOMEN!, published in 1907. A witty, dramatic plea for women's suffrage, it betrays its origins through over-reliance on dialogue, long speeches and lack of non-visual action. Reprinted by THE WOMEN'S PRESS and THE FEMINIST PRESS in 1980, it is chiefly of interest today as a documentary, for in writing it Robins drew heavily on her own experience of the women's suffrage movement in Britain, and

many of the characters were taken from life (Ernestine Blunt is Christabel Pankhurst, Keir Hardie appears as Lothian Scott, etc.). When it first appeared, male reviewers complained it was propaganda, but there was an audience eager for just such propaganda, and the book was a commercial success.

Cooley, Winnifred Harper, ?1875–?1956

American journalist. Following in the footsteps of her mother, Ida Husted HARPER, she wrote and lectured on a variety of subjects, with particular emphasis on women's issues. She is the author of *The New Womanhood* (1904), a survey of the historical roots of women's personal freedom covering such topics as marriage, divorce, cooperative housekeeping, and access to paid employment.

Cooper, Anna Julia Haywood, ?1859–1964

Black American scholar, writer and educator. An activist for higher education and civil rights, she took a special interest in the rights and experiences of black women. Her first book, *A Voice From the South by a Black Woman of the South* (1892), was one of the first feminist discussions of the social status and problems of black women. Male resentment dogged her career: in 1901 she became principal at M Street High School in Washington, D.C. where she developed a college

preparatory programme and raised academic standards, yet her very success led to her being dropped from the staff in 1906. In 1925, despite obstacles placed in her way by American school authorities, she finished her thesis, in French, and received her Ph.D. from the Sorbonne. After her retirement from teaching in 1930, she continued to write. Her last book was *The Grimké Family* (1951), and she edited the diaries of her close friend, Charlotte Grimké.

Coote, Anna, 1947–

British journalist. Active in the women's liberation movement from 1971, when she helped found the Women's Report Collective. In 1972 she helped set up the women's rights group of the National Council for Civil Liberties. Co-author of three editions of *Women's Rights: A Practical Guide* and, with Beatrix CAMPBELL, SWEET FREEDOM: *The Struggle for Women's Liberation* (1982).

Courtney, Leonard, 1832–1918

English politician. Women's suffrage was his major political interest, and his continued devotion to it in the face of Gladstone's opposition in 1884, lost him the chance of rising higher in the Liberal Party.

Cousins, Margaret, 1878–1954

Irish teacher and writer. Active in the women's suffrage movement, she became treasurer of the Irish

Women's Franchise League in 1908. In 1915 she moved to India, where she became the first non-Indian member of the Indian Women's University, and helped found the Indian Women's Association in 1917. She later became the first woman magistrate in India, and, near the end of her life, received recognition for her contributions to the struggle for a free India.

coverture

A basic principle of English common law which presumed that husband and wife were one person, and that person the husband: the legal existence of the woman was incorporated into that of her husband, and her interests were supposed to be the same as his. Early feminists were faced with the choice of refusing MARRIAGE (difficult at a time when it was effectively a woman's only trade) or of becoming a non-person and attempting to reform a legal system which would not recognize them. Most chose the latter course, promoting the idea that marriage should be an equal partnership, and that women had rights regardless of their marital status, just as men did. The concept of coverture was challenged with the passage of the first Married Women's Property Acts: in 1839 in the United States, and in 1857 in Britain. Although it has long since ceased to be a meaningful legal principle, the effects of coverture linger on in many tax and property laws which presume the husband's dominance in marital partnerships.

COYOTE (Call Off Your Old Tired Ethics)

Advocacy group founded in 1973 in San Francisco by Margo St James, dedicated to decriminalizing PROSTITUTION. Although its long-term goal is to eliminate all laws regulating prostitution, it is also committed to changing the immediate conditions suffered by prostitutes, by informing them of their rights, by providing adequate legal counsel, arranging for bail, helping develop job opportunities for women wishing to leave the profession, etc. Other similar organizations were formed in other cities under other names, following the example of COYOTE, and the group has received widespread support from other feminist organizations.

CR *See* CONSCIOUSNESS RAISING.

Craig, Isa (Mrs Knox), 1831–1903 Scottish poet. In 1857 she moved to London to accept the post of Assistant-Secretary to the Social Science Association, which came under a great deal of fire for appointing a woman. However, she resigned after a year to marry her cousin, John Knox. But she remained a committed feminist, and was on the committee of the Ladies' Sanitary Association, working to educate women about the necessity of hygiene and health care. She was also a member of the LANGHAM PLACE GROUP.

Crocker, Hannah Mather,
1752–1829
American. She published a pamphlet on the rights of women in 1818, and worked for the advancement of women's education in Massachusetts, hoping to found a system of Masonic lodges which would provide the same support and advancement for women as the Freemasons did for men.

crone
Word for an old woman, reclaimed by Mary DALY in GYN/ECOLOGY as a proud descriptive. Suggesting an etymological link with the Greek *chronios* (long-lasting), she defines crones as 'the long-lasting ones . . . the Survivors of the perpetual witchcraze of patriarchy.' Yet the status of the crone is not chronological age, but the result of an interior voyage: 'A woman becomes a Crone as a result of Surviving early stages of the Otherworld Journey and therefore having discovered depths of courage, strength, and wisdom in her Self.'

Cross, Amanda
See HEILBRUN, CAROLYN G.

cultural feminism
Sometimes confusingly called RADICAL FEMINISM, this is a basically non-political attitude which concentrates on the development of a separate female counter-culture, or WOMANCULTURE. The term was first used by SOCIALIST FEMINISTS around 1972 as a critical way of referring to non-political radical feminists. It was identified as a tendency quite separate from radical feminism by the REDSTOCKINGS in 1975. Cultural feminism emphasizes the importance of a woman-identified life style and is usually unconcerned with mass reforms or public changes, preferring to concentrate on individual solutions and the creation of alternatives to the mainstream of society. Far from denying the importance of biological differences, or seeing in them the cause of women's oppression, cultural feminists tend to glorify the differences between the sexes, to imply that they are unchangeable, and to accept the idea that women are by nature less violent, more cooperative, more caring, etc. than men. The same idea also lies behind the women's PEACE MOVEMENT. Some of the major theorists of cultural feminism are Mary DALY, Adrienne RICH and Susan GRIFFIN.

cultural sadism
Term used by Kathleen Barry (1979), defined by her as 'a form of sexual violence against women that is built into the structure of societies and the lifestyles of people . . . a distinct social form that consists of practices which encourage and support sexual violence, defining it into normal behaviour.'
(*See also* PORNOGRAPHY)

D

Daly, Mary, 1928–
American philosopher. With the publication of her first book, *The Church and the Second Sex* (1968), which examined the history of misogyny in the Catholic Church, Daly was fired from her teaching position in the theology department of the Jesuit-run Boston College. After three months of protest, petitions, and a student march in her support, she was rehired with promotion and tenure. Her second book, BEYOND GOD THE FATHER: *Towards a Philosophy of Women's Liberation* (1973) moved further into radical feminism – Adrienne RICH called it 'the first philosophy of feminism' – with a rejection of patriarchal RELIGION. The purpose of this book was to show that 'the women's revolution. . .is an ontological, spiritual revolution. . .it has everything to do with the search for ultimate meaning and reality, which some would call God.' Her next book, GYN/ECOLOGY (1978), was revolutionary in form, content and impact. It was a journey into a new, metaphysical, SPIRITUAL FEMINISM. Men were depicted as evil and death-loving, parasitical on the energies of good, life-loving women. Defining RADICAL FEMINISM as 'the journey of women becoming', Daly encouraged women to withdraw from men to create a new, woman-centred universe, and led the way with her creation of a new philosophy, a new theology, and even a new LANGUAGE in which to express it. She continued the journey in *Pure Lust: Elemental Feminist Philosophy* (1984), the title of which refers to the female lust for change.

daughter-right
Term used by Janice Raymond (1975) and Mary DALY (1978) to express the need for female bonding. Mary Daly describes in GYN/ECOLOGY how mothers and daughters are divided by PATRIARCHY and manipulated into betraying each other. Yet if motherhood is a role, daughterhood is a reality shared by all women, and a recognition of this shared daughterhood can bring mothers and daughters together as sisters in the same struggle.

Daughters of Bilitis
Predating the formation of the GAY LIBERATION FRONT, this lesbian organization was founded in San Francisco in 1955. It began publishing a national magazine, *The Ladder*, in October 1956.
(*See also* LESBIANISM)

Davies, Emily, 1830–1921
English. Her chief interest and achievements were in opening higher education to women in England. In 1866 she founded the London Schoolmistresses' Association and began promoting her idea for a woman's university. In 1869 she opened her college with five pupils. She moved it to Cambridge in 1873, and it became Girton College in 1874. A member of the KENSINGTON SOCIETY, she started the Northumberland and Durham branch of the SOCIETY FOR PROMOTING THE EMPLOYMENT OF WOMEN, and was an editor of the ENGLISH WOMAN'S JOURNAL. She was, with Barbara BODICHON and Elizabeth Garrett ANDERSON, one of the organizers of the first petition for women's suffrage, which was presented to John Stuart MILL in 1866, and in 1906 she led a deputation to Parliament to demand the vote.

Davis, Elizabeth Gould, 1910–74
American librarian. Best known as the author of THE FIRST SEX (1971), an inspiring, if arguable, attempt to prove women are physically, morally and intellectually superior to men.

Davis, Paulina Wright, 1813–76
American reformer. One of the earliest leaders of the first American women's movement, she worked with Ernestine ROSE in the 1830s, petitioning the New York State legislature for a married women's property act; in 1850 she organized and presided over the first national Women's Rights Convention in Worcester, Massachusetts; and between 1853–6 she financed, edited and published THE UNA, a monthly journal devoted to the cause of women's rights. She was also a temperance worker, an advocate of dress reform, and lectured to women's groups on health and physiology.

Davison, Emily Wilding, 1872–1913
English. The martyr of the British SUFFRAGETTES, she gave her life for the cause. A teacher with degrees from Oxford and London Universities, she joined the WOMEN'S SOCIAL AND POLITICAL UNION (WSPU) in 1906 and proved to be an ardent militant, throwing stones, breaking windows, heckling politicians, and setting off the bomb which destroyed a country house Lloyd George had under construction. She was considered reckless and self-dramatizing, and not all her activities were sanctioned by the WSPU – as when, in 1911, she set three pillar-boxes on fire. She often spoke of the possibility that some woman might give her life in order that the suffering of all the militants might end in victory, and in 1912, during a hunger strike at Holloway Prison, she tried to kill herself by leaping over a stair-railing. In June 1913, she attended the

Derby at Epsom with the WSPU flag sewn into her coat, having told her flatmate of her plan to disrupt the race by waving the green, white and purple flags before the horses at Tattenham Corner. Instead, she leaped onto the course herself, directly in front of the King's horse, Anmer, who ran her down. Her skull was fractured and she died five days later. Her death did not achieve the victory she had imagined, but it did attract even more public attention, and sympathy, for the suffragettes. Davison's coffin, draped in purple, white and green, was escorted by over 2,000 uniformed suffragettes from Victoria Station, through streets thronged with spectators, to St George's Church in Bloomsbury. There, Emmeline PANKHURST was arrested, but pledged to 'carry on our Holy War for the emancipation of our sex'. Davison was buried near her mother's home in Morpeth, Northumberland. Inscribed on her gravestone: 'DEEDS, NOT WORDS.'

Declaration of Rights for Women

Document read out by Susan B. ANTHONY and distributed, printed as a broadside, at the first Centennial exhibition in Philadelphia, on 4 July 1876, in defiance of the fact that no women had been permitted to speak to the gathering. Reprinted in full in the Stanton, Anthony, Gage and Harper HISTORY OF WOMAN SUF-FRAGE, the conclusion is as follows: 'We ask of our rulers, at this hour, no special favors, no special privileges, no special legislation. We ask justice, we ask equality, we ask that all the civil and political rights that belong to citizens of the United States, be guaranteed to us and our daughters forever.'

Declaration of Sentiments

One of the most important documents in the history of American feminism, it was formulated by Elizabeth Cady STANTON, closely modelled on the Declaration of Independence, and presented and approved at the SENECA FALLS Convention in July 1848. The complete text is as follows:

'When, in the course of human events, it becomes necessary for one portion of the family of man to assume among the people of the earth a position different from that which they have hitherto occupied, but one to which the laws of nature and of nature's God entitle them, a decent respect to the opinions of mankind requires that they should declare the causes that impel them to such a course.

'We hold these truths to be self-evident: that all men and women are created equal; that they are endowed by their Creator with certain inalienable rights; that among these are life, liberty, and the pursuit of happiness; that to secure these rights governments are instituted, deriving their just powers from the consent of the governed. Whenever any form of government becomes destructive of these ends, it is the right of those who suffer from it to refuse allegiance to it, and to insist upon the institution of a new government, laying its foundations upon such principles, and organizing its powers in such form, as to them shall seem most likely to effect their safety and happiness. Prudence, indeed, will dictate that governments long established should not be changed for light and transient causes; and accordingly all experience hath shown that mankind are more disposed to suffer, while evils are sufferable, than to right themselves by abolishing the forms to which they are accustomed. But when a long train of abuses and usurpations, pursuing invariably the same object, evinces a design to reduce them under absolute despotism, it is their duty to throw off such government, and to provide new guards for their future security. Such has been the patient sufferance of the women under this government, and such is now the necessity which constrains them to demand the equal station to which they are entitled.

'The history of mankind is a history of repeated injuries and usurpations on the part of man toward woman, having in direct object the establishment of an absolute tyranny over her. To prove this, let facts be submitted to a candid world.

'He has never permitted her to exercise her inalienable right to the elective franchise.

'He has compelled her to submit to laws, in the formation of which she had no voice.

'He has withheld from her rights which are given to the most ignorant and degraded men – both natives and foreigners.

'Having deprived her of this first right of a citizen, the elective franchise, thereby leaving her without representation in the halls of legislation, he has oppressed her on all sides.

'He has made her, if married, in the eye of the law, civilly dead.

'He has taken from her all right in property, even to the wages she earns.

'He has made her, morally, an irresponsible being, as she can commit many crimes with impunity, provided they be done in the presence of her husband. In the covenant of marriage, she is compelled to promise obedience to her husband, he becoming, to all intents and purposes, her master – the law giving him power to deprive her of her liberty, and to administer chastisement.

'He has so framed the laws of divorce, as to what shall be the proper causes, and in case of separation, to whom the guardianship of the children shall be given, as to be wholly regardless of the happiness of women – the law, in all cases, going upon the false supposition of the supremacy of man, and giving all power into his hands.

'After depriving her of all rights as a married woman, if single, and the owner of property, he has taxed her to support a government which recognizes her only when her property can be made profitable to it.

'He has monopolized nearly all the profitable employments, and from those she is permitted to follow, she receives but a scanty remuneration. He closes against her all the avenues to wealth and distinction which he considers most honorable to himself. As a teacher of theology, medicine, or law, she is not known.

'He has denied her the facilities for obtaining a thorough education, all colleges being closed against her.

'He allows her in Church, as well as State, but a subordinate position, claiming Apostolic authority for her exclusion from the ministry, and, with some exceptions, from any public participation in the affairs of the Church.

'He has created a false public sentiment by giving to the world a different code of morals for men and women, by which moral delinquencies which exclude women from society, are not only tolerated, but deemed of little account in man.

'He has usurped the prerogative of Jehovah himself, claiming it as his right to assign for her a sphere of action, when that belongs to her conscience and to her God.

'He has endeavored, in every way that he could, to destroy her confidence in her own powers, to lessen her self-respect, and to make her willing to lead a dependent and abject life.

'Now, in view of this entire disfranchisement of one-half the people of this country, their social and religious degradation – in view of the unjust laws above mentioned, and because women do feel themselves aggrieved, oppressed, and fraudulently deprived of their most sacred rights, we insist that they have immediate admission to all the rights and privileges which belong to them as citizens of the United States.

'In entering upon the great work before us, we anticipate no small amount of misconception, misrepresentation, and ridicule; but we shall use every instrumentality within our power to effect our object. We shall employ agents, circulate tracts, petition the State and National legislatures, and endeavor to enlist the pulpit and the press in our behalf. We hope this Convention will be followed by a series of Conventions embracing every part of the country.

Resolutions

'Whereas, The great precept of nature is conceded to be, that "man shall pursue his own true and substantial happiness". Blackstone in his Commentaries remarks, that this law of Nature being coeval with mankind, and dictated by God himself, is of course superior in obligation to any other. It is binding over all the globe, in all countries and at all times; no human laws are of any validity if contrary to this, and such of them as are valid, derive all their force, and all their validity, and all their authority, mediately and immediately, from this original; therefore,

'*Resolved* That such laws as conflict, in any way, with the true and substantial happiness of woman, are contrary to the great precept of nature and of no validity, for this is "superior in obligation to any other".

'*Resolved* That all laws which prevent woman from occupying such a station in society as her conscience shall dictate, or which place her in a position inferior to that of man, are contrary to the great precept of nature, and therefore of no force or authority.

'*Resolved* That woman is man's equal – was intended to be so by the Creator, and the highest good of the race demands that she should be recognized as such.

'*Resolved* That the women of this country ought to be enlightened in regard to the laws under which they live, that they may no longer publish their degradation by declaring themselves satisfied with their present position, nor their ignorance, by asserting that they have all the rights they want.

'*Resolved* That inasmuch as man,

while claiming for himself intellectual superiority, does accord to woman moral superiority, it is preeminently his duty to encourage her to speak and teach, as she has an opportunity, in all religious assemblies.

'*Resolved* That the same amount of virtue, delicacy and refinement of behavior that is required of woman in the social state, should also be required of man, and the same transgressions should be visited with equal severity on both man and woman.

'*Resolved* That the objection of indelicacy and impropriety, which is so often brought against woman when she addresses a public audience, comes with a very ill-grace from those who encourage, by their attendance, her appearance on the stage, in the concert, or in feats of the circus.

'*Resolved* That woman has too long rested satisfied in the circumscribed limits which corrupt customs and a perverted application of the Scriptures have marked out for her, and that it is time she should move in the enlarged sphere which her great Creator has assigned her.

'*Resolved* That it is the duty of the women of this country to secure to themselves their sacred right to the elective franchise.

'*Resolved* That the equality of human rights results necessarily from the fact of the identity of the race in capabilities and responsibilities.

'*Resolved, therefore,* That, being invested by the Creator with the same capabilities, and the same consciousness of responsibility for their exercise, it is demonstrably the right and duty of woman, equally with man, to promote every righteous cause by every righteous means; and especially in regard to the great subjects of morals and religion, it is self-evidently her right to participate with her brother in teaching them, both in private and in public, by writing and by speaking, by any instrumentalities proper to be used, and in any assemblies proper to be held; and this being a self-evident truth growing out of the divinely implanted principles of human nature, any custom or authority adverse to it, whether modern or wearing the hoary sanction of antiquity, is to be regarded as a self-evident falsehood, and at war with mankind.

'*Resolved* That the speedy success of our cause depends upon the zealous and untiring efforts of both men and women, for the overthrow of the monopoly of the pulpit, and for the securing to woman an equal participation with men in the various trades, professions, and commerce.'

DeCrow, Karen, 1937–
American journalist and lawyer. President of the NATIONAL ORGANIZATION FOR WOMEN from 1974–6.

'Deeds, not words'
Slogan of the WOMEN'S SOCIAL AND POLITICAL UNION, it is inscribed upon the gravestone of the British women's suffrage movement's first martyr, Emily Wilding DAVISON.

Dell, Floyd, 1887–1969
American writer. Author of *Women as World Builders* (1913) and *Love in the Machine Age* (1930), an attack on patriarchal capitalism. Although he argued for women's rights, his chief interest, like that of many male feminists, seemed to be that the emancipated woman would be a better companion for man.

Delphy, Christine, 1941–
French sociologist. An editor of the journal *Nouvelles Questions Féministes*, she has contributed both theory and action to the women's liberation movement since it began in France. A materialist feminist, she argues that men and women are made, not born, and there are no essential differences between the sexes. She believes that women's oppression can only be explored, understood and changed from within an autonomous women's movement.

demands
See FOUR DEMANDS; SEVEN DEMANDS

Deming, Barbara, 1917–84
American writer. A peace activist from the 1950s, she was also a long-time advocate of civil rights and

sexual freedom, publicly declaring herself a lesbian as early as 1953. Her non-violent protests against the Vietnam War in the 1960s brought her into contact with the women's liberation movement, with which she was soon passionately involved. Her writings include poetry, short stories and personal essays, well represented in the 1984 collection, *The Barbara Deming Reader*, and two books on the women's movement, *We Cannot Live Without Our Lives* (1974) and *Remembering Who We Are* (1981).

Deraismes, Maria, 1828–94

French writer. Well known in the 1860s as an anticlerical and feminist writer and lecturer. In 1866, with Paule MINK and Louise Michel, she founded the first French feminist organization, Société pour la Revendication des Droits de la Femme (Society for the Demand for Women's Rights). With Léon RICHER in 1870 she founded the Société pour l'Amélioration du Sort de la Femme (Society for the Improvement of Women's Lot). Many of their shared goals had been at least partially achieved by the 1880s, as a system of secondary education and teacher training colleges for women was established, various laws were changed and divorce was legalized, and in 1882 Deraismes split with Richer as she decided to support women's suffrage. That same year she became the first woman freemason.

Deroin, Jeanne, 1810?–94

French. A pioneering socialist feminist. Upon her marriage in 1832 she refused to change her name. During the 1840s she edited a socialist women's paper, *L'Opinion des femmes*, struggled on despite lack of support from her male radical colleagues, and wrote *Cours de droit social pour les femmes* (1848), a bitter outcry against the social and mental enslavement of women. She was the first woman to stand as a candidate for election to the National Assembly, in 1849, arguing that a men-only organization was incompetent to make decisions on behalf of a sexually mixed society. In 1852 she was exiled to London, where she continued to write and publish works including *Almanack des femmes* (1854) and *Lettre aux travailleurs* (1856).

Despard, Charlotte French, 1844–1939

British social worker and political campaigner. After the death of her husband in 1890, she devoted herself to helping the poor, opening one of the first child welfare centres in London, founding a working men's club and speaking for the Independent Labour Party. She joined the WOMEN'S SOCIAL AND POLITICAL UNION at the age of sixty-two and was made honorary secretary in 1906. But she disliked the autocratic rule of Emmeline PANKHURST, and in 1907 broke away with other women to form the democratically run WOMEN'S FREE-DOM LEAGUE, of which she was elected President. She was a striking figure with white hair, upright bearing and a costume which usually included a black lace mantilla and sandals, and was widely idolized, a fact which led to accusations that she was steering the WFL down the wrong paths, towards her personal passions of Communism and pacifism. She left the WFL in 1918, to devote herself to the Women's Peace Crusade. She continued to demand equal suffrage even after the vote had been granted to some women, and she was one of eight women to stand for Parliament the first year they were eligible: the Labour candidate for Battersea, she lost. In 1921 she moved to Ireland to work for Sinn Fein, and became president of the Women's Prisoners' Defence League.

Dexter, Caroline Harper,
1819–84

English-born Australian writer. Active in DRESS REFORM campaigns in Melbourne. In 1861 she collaborated with Harriet CLISBY on *The Interpreter*, the first Australian journal published by women.

d'Hericourt, Jenny, b. 1850?

Nineteenth-century French doctor. A reformer and an intellectual, she was a member of a Saint-Simonian group in Paris and the author of the influential book *La femme affranchie*

(1880) which vigorously defended women against the attacks made by Michelet and Proudhon. Her friendship with Mariya TRUBNIKOVA has been credited with inspiring the beginnings of the women's movement in Russia. In 1857 she advised Trubnikova to 'surround yourself with women' but not to meddle in politics: 'Let the exclusively masculine régime vanish by itself. If you start to attack it, it is so powerful in Russia that it will crush you.'

Dialectic of Sex, The

A major work of RADICAL FEMINIST theory by Shulamith FIRESTONE, subtitled *The Case for Feminist Revolution*, first published in the United States in 1970. It offers 'a materialist view of history based on sex itself'. Using the methods of Marx and Engels, Firestone demonstrates that they never looked deep enough, never saw beneath economics to the root of all class conflict in the sex class system. The cause of women's oppression she locates in biology, in unfair, painful, 'barbaric' pregnancy which has always been the lot of females. In the past a feminist revolution has been impossible, true equality of the sexes a hopeless dream. But now that we can control reproduction, and are on the brink of breakthroughs which could free women from the necessity of physically reproducing the race (pregnancy replaced by cloning or artificial wombs) she argues that women can finally achieve fully human status. It is not enough to eliminate male privilege – sexual distinctions must be made irrelevant, and women must take control of reproductive technology for our own ends, to result in an androgynous, classless, society. CHILDREN'S LIBERATION must take place at the same time, with the end of the traditional, closed family, and the basis for racism would also fade away with the end of sexism. This book was, and still is, highly controversial. Although influential, and useful for its bold and original analysis, it is not accepted by many radical feminists today. The book's conclusions alienated many feminists who are unwilling to locate the cause of women's oppression in anything inherent in women; and there is also an unwillingness to rely on technology – for so long used by men against women – to provide the means of liberation.

Dilke, Emily (Francis Strong; Lady Dilke), 1840–1904
English writer, art critic and trade unionist. A radical, an intellectual and a suffragist, she may have been the model for Dorothea in George Eliot's *Middlemarch*. An advocate of technical education for women, she became involved with the Women's Trade Union League in 1876, and became its president in 1902, having spent many years organizing textile workers, arguing for equal pay and defending the interests of women workers at Trades Union Congress meetings.

Diner, Helen (pseudonym of Bertha Eckstein-Diner), 1874–1948
German sociologist and writer. She is best known as the author of *Mothers and Amazons: The First Feminine History of Culture* (1932), in which she argued that the patriarchal family was a relatively recent development, and sought to uncover evidence for the existence of a pre-historic MATRIARCHY. Although her theory, based on the works of J. J. BACHOFEN and Robert BRIFFAULT, and on her own interpretation of classical accounts of AMAZONS, has been attacked for being one-sided, she announced her intention at the beginning of being so, since 'the other side is fairly well known'. Even if her conclusions are not accepted, she raised many questions of particular interest to feminists, and offered an alternative to male-centred history. She also wrote novels under the pseudonym 'Sir Galahad'.

'Dinner Party, The'
Multi-media artwork created by Judy CHICAGO with the help of some four hundred co-workers from 1974–9. The work consists of a triangular table, measuring $46\frac{1}{2}$ feet on each side, bearing thirty-nine individually designed place settings, each one representing an

important woman from myth or history – Sappho, Elizabeth I, Ishtar, Susan B. Anthony, Emily Dickinson, etc. Beneath the table is a porcelain-tiled floor inscribed with the names of 999 more women who left some mark on history. Along with explanatory texts, videotapes, films and photographs of the project, this celebration of women's art and history was first exhibited at the San Francisco Museum of Modern Art in the spring of 1979, and has since been displayed in other cities.

direct action

Action taken regardless of legal constraints to bring about a political objective. Direct actions include demonstrations, strikes, the destruction of property, heckling speakers, spray-painting slogans, civil disobedience such as refusing to pay taxes or occupying a building, and other such acts of usually non-violent rebellion. Although violent terrorism is a form of direct action, it is not one favoured by many feminists. Direct action has always been important to feminist activists: because laws have been framed by and for men, women have often lacked the power to change them legally. The long struggle for women's suffrage was made longer by women's patient belief that men would be reasonable and give them the vote. Seeing the folly in this, the MILITANT SUFFRAGISTS attempted to develop their

own power, and force men to change the laws, through a militant campaign of direct action. Although women now have the right to vote, run for office, and otherwise work from within the legal framework, direct action remains a major part of the WOMEN'S LIBERATION MOVEMENT. Sometimes it is used in addition to legal action, and sometimes because a change in the law might be counter-productive, or at best useless. This is particularly notable in feminist campaigns against PORNOGRAPHY and male VIOLENCE against women. While some feminists wish to enforce new legislation to define and outlaw pornography, others consider that such laws could be turned against women, and prefer to fight it on a local level by raising the public awareness through picketing cinemas and 'adult' bookshops, and embarrassing the customers into leaving.

disabled women

With the publication in 1983 of an essay by Michelle Fine and Adrienne Asch entitled 'Disabled Women: Sexism Without the Pedestal', the connection between feminism and disability was clearly articulated and analysed, and finally began to be widely discussed. Women with disabilities have discovered that they are even more oppressed by the stereotypes of femininity than are their temporarily able-bodied sisters, because their survival sometimes depends on conformity to those stereotypes when interacting with other people or patriarchal institutions. The term 'temporarily able-bodied' or TAB is sometimes used to indicate that 'disabilities' are defined by society and are an issue for everyone. During the 1980s, more and more feminists became aware of the connection between SEXISM and ABLEISM, recognizing the same destructive myth of the 'perfect' and 'normal' person at the root of social oppression, and began to confront the unconscious ableism within the women's movement.

discrimination

To treat groups or people differently for irrelevant reasons; for example, privileging someone not on the basis of need or merit but because of their race, sex or age.

(*See also* SEXUAL DISCRIMINATION; SEXISM; AGEISM)

displaced homemaker

American term for an individual who has done unpaid labour in the home and been dependent on the income of another family member, now no longer available. These individuals are usually women who have devoted their lives to raising children and keeping house until 'displaced' by divorce or the death of their husband. Without skills or training paid employment is difficult if not impossible to come by; changes in divorce laws mean that many receive no alimony; if widowed they are not eligible for Social Security until the age of sixty. In the mid-1970s, Representatives Bella ABZUG and Barbara Jordan tried, without success, to introduce legislation which would value the homemaker's contribution as much as that of a wage-earner. At the same time homemakers (some of them previously mistrustful of feminists) were joining feminist groups – the NOW Task Force on Older Women was particularly active in the Alliance for Displaced Homemakers – to force public recognition of a problem faced by an estimated 3.3 million women. In response, in 1975 the State of California established the first Displaced Homemaker Center, in Oakland. This provided individual and group counselling, training courses in various skills, and financial and legal guidance for women facing the necessity of finding employment for the first time. Other states followed with their own centers, and in 1978 there was a national victory for the displaced homemakers campaign, with Title III of the Comprehensive Employment and Training Act stating that the Secretary of Labor 'shall make available financial assistance to conduct programs to provide employment opportunities and appropriate training and support services to displaced homemakers.' Funding for this provision, however, has been seriously threatened by the Reagan

administration.
(*See also* HOUSEWORK; WAGES FOR HOUSEWORK)

Dohm, Hedwig, 1833–1919

German writer. She was the first woman in Germany to demand women's suffrage, calling for the vote in *Der Jesuitismus im Hausstande* (1873), a book in which she attacked the male DOUBLE STANDARD. She was a prolific writer, producing theoretical treatises, novels, plays, pamphlets and book reviews, and all her work displayed a breadth of scholarship and the influence of other feminist writers as she wrote about the sexual, material and psychological oppression which she considered to be the fundamental reasons for women's subordination. She derided the idea that women were intellectually inferior to men, or that they possessed maternal or any other specifically female instincts. She argued that women had been so educated and conditioned into believing they could not think for themselves that they let men think for them, and, having nothing to sell but their bodies, were forced into SEXUAL SLAVERY. Her works include *Die Wissenschaffliche der Frau* (1874), *Der Frauen Natur und Recht, Eigenschaften und Stimmrecht der Frauen* (1876), *Die Antifeministen* (1902) and *Die Mutter* (1903).

Doll's House, A

Play by Henrik IBSEN, written in 1879, it reveals the hypocrisy and role-playing in a supposedly happy, middle-class marriage, showing through the character of Nora the conflict between the ideals of femininity and what it means to be fully adult. In the famous ending, Nora refuses to play the child-wife any longer, and leaves her husband and children, slamming the door behind her. In his notes for the play Ibsen wrote, 'A woman cannot be herself in today's society, which is an exclusively male society, with laws written by men and with prosecutor and judge who judge women's conduct from a male point-of-view.' Like Olive Schreiner's *The Story of an African Farm, A Doll's House* helped many women become aware of their oppression as it both encouraged and reflected the growing spirit of feminism.

domestic feminists

Term sometimes applied to individuals, chiefly in the nineteenth century, who wished to raise women's status through education and law not out of any belief that women's lot was unfair, but in order to improve their value to (male) society as wives and mothers. Like the term EUGENIC FEMINISM, this is a misnomer for an essentially anti-feminist movement.

double shift

Also called the double load or double day. Term developed by modern feminists to point out that for most women their working day involves one shift in the public realm, for pay, and another in the home, unpaid. This is an act of naming which recognizes HOUSEWORK and CHILDCARE as necessary and valuable work, unlike a term such as 'working woman' with its implication that only those who are paid are really working.

double standard

Patriarchal moral code which sets different rules for behaviour according to gender. Under the double standard, behaviour condemned in a woman (for example, the expression of aggressive sexuality) is accepted or even applauded in a man. What is being judged by this is not human morality, but adherence to established SEX-ROLES. As Frances HARPER wrote in a poem called 'The Double Standard' (undated; late nineteenth century), it 'excuses all in the male and accuses all in the female'. One of the aims of feminism is to abolish the double standard – which is simply another means of oppressing women – and replace it with a new single standard which would judge behaviour according to human values, not in regard to sex, age, race or class.

drama

See THEATRE

Dreier, Mary Elisabeth,
1875–1963
American. Despite a middle-class upbringing, she won the trust of working women, whose lives she always worked to improve. She led the New York Women's Trade Union League from 1906–14, organizing unskilled women into unions, and fighting for legislation to curb abuses. From 1911–15 she was the only female member of the New York State Factory Investigating Commission, which worked on the most comprehensive study of American industrial conditions up to that time. She said later that it was the attitude of male trade unionists towards their working sisters which caused her to become 'a rabid supporter of women', and she turned her energies to the struggle for women's suffrage, chairing the New York City Woman Suffrage party, and becoming involved in state and national politics. She continued all her life to serve on many government boards and private organizations concerned with women and labour. Later she worked for the cause of international peace and as an anti-nuclear campaigner, and still found time to write – an unpublished novel about the relationship between working-class and middle-class women, *Barbara Richards*, and a biography of her sister, Margaret Dreier ROBINS, published in 1950.

dress reform

In the nineteenth century women's clothing, like the feminine role itself, was restrictive, stifling and unhealthy: heavy, trailing skirts limited movement, and tightly-laced corsets made breathing difficult. Not surprisingly, women who wanted more opportunities and freedom usually felt that not only laws, but also social customs and clothing, must be changed. Although dress reform never attracted the numbers or the passionate adherence that other aspects of the women's movement did, it was a theme that ran throughout the FIRST WAVE OF FEMINISM. The height of the dress reform movement occurred in the 1850s in America, and centred on what was known as the bloomer costume, or 'BLOOMERS'.

Abolitionist Gerrit Smith, who had announced himself all in favour of women's emancipation, declared his belief that 'were women to throw off the dress' that man 'would confess her transmutation into his equal' and the days of women's subordination would be at an end. His daughter, Elizabeth Smith MILLER, was the first to wear the new costume, which consisted of a short dress over loose 'Turkish-style' trousers, in 1852. Her cousin, Elizabeth Cady STANTON, was so impressed by the 'incredible freedom' of these clothes, that she promptly made herself a similar costume, and she was followed by others who included Paulina Wright DAVIS, Lucy STONE, Susan B. ANTHONY, Sarah and Angelina GRIMKÉ.

But although they found that the bloomer costume made their lives more comfortable and efficient physically, the women who wore this sensible and modest new outfit faced so much hostility that most of them abandoned the experiment in dress reform within less than two years. Ridiculed in newspapers, shouted at by little boys and jeered at by men on the street, they grew weary of constantly defending their decision and of having their serious concern with women's rights reduced to an argument about fashion. Despite Gerrit Smith's claim that women would be accepted by men as equals if they only dressed more sensibly, the women who had tried it knew from experience that they could not change their place in society simply by changing their clothes. Dress reform was needed, but it would have to accompany or follow other needed reforms in education and law.

Drummond, Flora, 1869–1949
Scottish. Dubbed 'General Drummond' in 1908, when she led the members of the WOMEN'S SOCIAL AND POLITICAL UNION on their march to the big Hyde Park demonstration for women's suffrage. She was a lively speaker who handled hecklers with ease, and a vigorous campaigner for women's rights whose exploits resulted in her imprisonment on nine occasions. A socialist when young, she became more conservative during World

War I, eventually joining the extremely right-wing Empire League (which opposed communism and strikes), where she became Commander-in-Chief of the Women's Guild in 1928.

Dugdale, Henrietta, 1826–1918
English-born Australian. As President, from 1884, of the first Women's Suffrage Society in Victoria, she was one of the leaders of the Australian women's movement. She campaigned not only for the vote and better education and employment opportunities for women, but also for DRESS REFORM, BIRTH CONTROL, and against sexual violence. A talented speaker and writer, she believed women's worst enemies were male ignorance and hypocrisy.

Dunbar, Roxanne, 1939–
American. She came to the Women's Liberation Movement from the civil rights movement. In 1968 she founded the influential radical feminist group CELL 16 in Boston. Later she moved to New Orleans where she founded the Southern Female Rights Union.

Durand, Marguerite, 1865–1936
French actress and journalist. She became a feminist in the 1890s and was soon elected Vice-President of La Ligue Française pour le Droit des Femmes. In 1897, she established the world's first women's daily

newspaper, *La fronde*, which was entirely staffed and published by women on a daily basis until 1903, and then monthly until 1905. Besides actively campaigning for women's suffrage, she was also involved in the temperance and social purity movements. She was a candidate for the National Assembly in 1910, and during World War I she founded a women's driving organization for transporting the wounded. In 1931 she donated her collection of feminist archives to the city of Paris; this became the Bibliothèque Marguerite Durand.

Duras, Marguerite (pseudonym of Marguerite Donnadieu), 1914–
French writer and filmmaker. Women and their experience have always been at the centre of her work, and she is emotionally and intellectually a part of the women's liberation movement in France. Her films, made on low budgets and experimental in technique, include *Nathalie Granger* (1973), *Baxter, Vera Baxter* (1977) and *Agatha* (1981).

Dworkin, Andrea, 1946–
American writer. A radical feminist since the early 1970s, she is best known for her writings on male dominance, particularly as expressed through sex, violence against women, and PORNOGRAPHY. She is

the author of *Woman Hating* (1974), *Our Blood* (1976), *Pornography: Men Possessing Women* (1981), *Right-Wing Women* (1983), a collection of short stories, *The New Womans Broken Heart* (1979) and a novel, *Ice* *and Fire* (1986). With Catharine MacKinnon she co-authored a model antipornography law, the first to oppose pornography on the grounds that it violates the civil rights of women.

E

East, Rachel
Pen-name used occasionally, early in her career, for her more radical feminist writings by Cicily Fairfield, more commonly known as Rebecca WEST.

Eastman, Crystal, 1881–1928
American sociologist and lawyer. A socialist who believed revolution should be a peaceful process rather than a violent event, she worked all her life – campaigning, lecturing, organizing, and writing – for women's equality, workers' rights and peace. She helped Alice PAUL launch the CONGRESSIONAL UNION and the Woman's Party, and founded the Woman's Peace Party (which became the Women's International League for Peace and Freedom) in 1914. On the premise that 'equal means the same', she advocated not only absolute legal equality for women, but also believed that physical and moral standards should be the same for men and women. In 1909, with champion swimmer Annette Kellerman, she attempted to devise a programme to increase women's strength, and told audiences that women would become stronger and braver when they were expected to be. She also pointed out that equality did not work only in one direction: not only must women become self-supporting and independent, but men must 'know how to cook and sew and clean and take care of yourself in the ordinary exigencies of life.'

ecology
The idea of the interconnectedness of human and non-human nature is recognized by most modern feminists. For some this is a spiritual value, arising from the personal experience of a mystical communion with nature, and some SPIRITUAL and CULTURAL FEMINISTS suggest that women have a particular affinity with all of life which men lack or have lost. Other feminists stress that there is nothing mystical in the practical recognition that the stakes are too high now for humankind to go on being reckless with our environment, since we are dependent upon it for life. Women have often been connected with nature, seen in opposition to the pairing of man and civilization, and just as feminism has pointed up the limitations of this sort of patriarchal thought, so has the ecology movement recognized the danger for humanity in constructing such dichotomies as 'Man vs. Nature'. Shulamith FIRESTONE suggested, in *The Dialectic of Sex* (1970), that the

women's liberation movement and
the ecology movement emerged at
the same time as part of the common need to find social solutions to
the same basic problems. Françoise
d'Eaubonne started an 'Ecologie-
Féminisme' movement in France in
1972, declaring that the destruction
of our planet was inevitable if
power remained in male hands, and
Mary DALY made a similar connection in *Gyn/Ecology* (1978). But
although feminists have recognized
the claims of the ecology movement, the male-led ecology movement itself has too often cut itself off
from the women's movement by
insisting that women subordinate
their interests to that of a greater
cause, whether it be saving whales
or rainforests.

education
Demands for more and better education for women have been an
integral part of every feminist
movement. If biology is not
accepted as the determinant of
women's fate, then the answer for
women's subordination to men
must be found in some other area.
For a long time education was considered the key to success and pro-
sperity for men, but until the last
quarter of the nineteenth century,
formal education of any kind for
girls was rare. When it did exist, it
tended to be superficial, designed
only to help the middle-class
woman attract a suitable husband.
Men often argued that women

didn't need the education their
brothers did, since their role in life
was to marry and have children; or
they argued that women's brains
were too small or their constitu-
tions too delicate to bear the burden
of intellectual strain. Yet Mary
ASTELL, Mary WOLLSTONECRAFT,
John Stuart MILL, Elizabeth Cady
STANTON and many others
recognized that the refusal to educate women was one sure way of
keeping women oppressed. It
seemed obvious, not only to feminists, but also to those who fought so
fearfully to 'protect' women from
men's knowledge, that as long as
women remained uneducated, educated men would face no real pressure to treat women as their equals.
A major achievement, therefore, of
the FIRST WAVE OF FEMINISM in England, the United States and
throughout Europe, leading the
way to the achievement of more
legal rights, was the opening of
many schools, colleges and universities to women.

Yet despite many changes and
substantial improvements in
women's lot, winning the right to
an equal education with men has
not resulted in the end of women's
oppression as the early, reform-
minded feminists seemed so certain
it would. The reason for this lies in
the dual nature of formal education.

The whole system of higher education was developed by men, for
men, out of men's discoveries and
ideas about what was important, to

prepare men to take up roles of power in an ANDROCENTRIC society. Some women are allowed into this world, as tokens; others are discouraged, or taught the conflicting lesson that their role as women is incompatible with too much learning. Ann OAKLEY (1981) has written: 'The belief that women can escape a feminine destiny by taking education as the golden pathway to uncountable opportunities has been one of the most subversive elements in the hidden educational curriculum . . . since women first gained access to education in the nineteenth century. . . . Women's formal education mirrors, rather than determines, their position in society.'

The term 'hidden curriculum' is used by sociologists to refer to those aspects of learning in schools which are undeclared, unofficial, or unintentional results of how the teaching is organized. The official curriculum may be history or cooking, but the student will also be learning from how the teacher and other students respond to her, from the language used, from the way classes are structured according to age and sex, from the way the same behaviour in boys and girls will evoke different responses, even from the architecture of the building. Schools teach not only facts and skills; they are also socializing institutions, like the family, and they reinforce and reproduce the ideology of PATRIARCHY even when

the subject matter in the classroom is equal rights.

Recognizing this, the feminist response has been the development of WOMEN'S STUDIES. And growing out of women's studies in the 1970s and 1980s there has been a tentative and still experimental start at creating feminist education.

Charlotte BUNCH and Sandra Pollack (1983) have defined three interrelated aspects of feminist education:

1. the teaching of specific skills and information to help women survive in the existing culture while working to change it.

2. the development of feminist consciousness through educating women about women's achievements and feminist theories.

3. the creation of space, provision of tools and encouragement to enable women to develop their own ideas, art, theories, research and plans to expand feminist knowledge and action.

effeminism

Term chosen by Steven Dansky, John Knoebel and Kenneth Pitchford as being more appropriate to describe the politics of the anti-sexist man than 'feminist', which should be reserved for women. In New York City on 1 January 1973, these three announced their 'Declaration of Independence from Gay Liberation and all other Male Ideologies', and invited all other like-minded men to become

'traitors to the class of men by uniting in a movement of Revolutionary Effeminism'. In their manifesto, and in issues of *Double-F: A Magazine of Effeminism*, they declared themselves to be enemies of the PATRIARCHY who believed 'that women will seize power from the patriarchy and, thereby, totally change life on this planet as we know it . . . Exactly how women will go about seizing power is no business of ours, being men. But as effeminate men oppressed by masculinist standards, we ourselves have a stake in the destruction of the patriarchy, and thus we *must* struggle with the dilemma of being partisans – as effeminists – of a revolution opposed to us – as men. To conceal our partisanship and remain inactive for fear of offending would be despicable; to act independently of women's leadership or to tamper with questions which women will decide would be no less despicable. Therefore, we have a duty to take sides, to struggle to change ourselves – but also, necessarily, to act.'
(*See also* MAN'S LIBERATION MOVEMENT)

Eisenstein, Zillah R., 1948–
American political scientist. Author of *The Radical Future of Liberal Feminism* (1981) and *Feminism and Sexual Equality: Crisis in Liberal America* (1984), she argues that all feminism is liberal at root, but that even the most LIBERAL FEMINISM has a radical potential inherent in its commitment to the concept of sexual equality. She sees the feminist revolution endangered not only by anti-feminist forces, but also by those feminists who emphasize the importance of sexual differences, rather than human similarities, in their quest to change society.
(*See also* REVISIONIST FEMINISM)

El Saadawi, Nawal, 1930–
Egyptian doctor and writer. Her outspoken opinions on women's position in Arab society and the need for revolutionary change caused her to lose her job in the Egyptian Ministry of Health in 1972. Since then, remaining controversial, she has become famous world-wide for her writings, which include the non-fiction *Women and Sex* (1972) and *The Hidden Face of Eve: Women in the Arab World* (1979), as well as short stories and novels expressing her feminist convictions. Her best-known novel, the award-winning *Woman at Point Zero* (Beirut, 1978; English translation published in 1983) is the story of a woman imprisoned in the notorious Qanatir Prison and condemned to death for killing a pimp. The book was banned in Egypt, and in 1981, when she was arrested for her writings, Nawal El Saadawi was imprisoned in Qanatir herself for several months. In 1982 she formed a pan-Arab women's rights organization, based in Egypt despite the refusal of the Egyptian

government to give it formal recognition.

Elgin, Suzette Haden, 1936–
American linguist and SCIENCE FICTION writer. Her science fiction novels are often concerned with the horrors of sexism, while in her non-fiction she is particularly interested in the subject of LANGUAGE and women. She combined the two in her 1984 novel *Native Tongue*, which is about a group of women who change their repressive society by developing a language capable of expressing women's experiences and perceptions. While writing the book, Elgin actually constructed a language for women, called LÁADAN. Her other novels include *The Communipaths* (1970) and *At the Seventh Level* (1972).

Ellmann, Mary, 1921–
American literary critic. Author of THINKING ABOUT WOMEN (1968), an influential study of how women are written about and perceived as writers under the dominance of PHALLIC CRITICISM.

Engels, Friedrich, 1820–95
German socialist philosopher. Lifelong collaborator and posthumous editor of Karl Marx, he was a major contributor to the development of Marxist theory. Marx himself gave little attention to 'the Woman Question', so it is

Engels' work – chiefly, THE ORIGIN OF THE FAMILY, PRIVATE PROPERTY AND THE STATE (1884) – which provides the starting point for most Marxist and much socialist feminist theory about the origins of women's oppression. Engels saw monogamous MARRIAGE as the equivalent of capitalism, and sex as the equivalent of class, declaring that within the family (which was founded on domestic slavery of the wife) the husband was the bourgeois and the wife the proletarian. Women had first been forced into a subordinate position by men's desire to be certain of paternity, in order to pass on property to their own heirs. Engels believed that the collapse of PATRIARCHY would accompany the destruction of the capitalist state. When women became paid, public workers and economic dependence played no part in sexual relations, men and women could meet as equals, and male domination would disappear.

English Woman's Journal
First feminist periodical in Britain, published from 1858–64. In 1858, inspired by a suggestion from author Anna JAMESON, Bessie Rayner PARKES began the journal to serve as a forum and a centre for the nascent women's movement. Other contributors included Isa CRAIG, Emily DAVIES, Jessie BOUCHERETT and Christina Rossetti.

In 1866 it re-emerged as the *English-woman's Review*.
(*See also* LANGHAM PLACE GROUP)

Enoki, Miswo, 1939–

Japanese. Leader of the Pink Panthers, the most radical organization in the Japanese women's movement of the 1970s. She also formed the Japan Woman's Party in the 1977 general elections.

Equal Pay for Equal Work

One of the most basic and widely agreed demands of the modern feminist movement has been that men and women should receive the same wages for the same work. This is so self-evidently fair that even many anti-feminists agree to it in theory, and Equal Pay Acts were passed by Congress in the U.S. in 1963, and by Parliament in Britain in 1970. Yet in spite of the law the average working woman in both Britain and the U.S. today earns only three-fifths of the average working man's salary. One reason for this is that women are frequently restricted – whether by custom, law, social expectations or education and training – to certain jobs which are defined (by reason of being 'women's work') as less valuable than similar tasks performed by men. Far more is involved in the idea of equal pay for women than the simple exchange of money for goods or services. As well as calling for a redefinition of work, some

feminists now demand equal pay for comparable work.
(*See also* WAGES FOR HOUSEWORK)

equal rights

One major aspect of feminism has always been the struggle by women to achieve legal, social and political rights equal to those of men. This is not, however, the same thing as women's liberation, and the fact that MAINSTREAM FEMINISM is often defined as being entirely about equal rights reveals its limitations, and provides an understanding of why it is dismissed by some as BOURGEOIS FEMINISM or IMPERIAL FEMINISM. As Bell HOOKS pointed out in *Feminist Theory: From Margin to Center* (1984), all men are not equal in a racist, capitalist, patriarchal class structure. Some women aspire to share the status of white, middle-class men, but poor, lower-class and non-white women have seen that the men in their groups lack social, political and economic power, and realize that mere EQUALITY with men is not enough. Historian Carroll Smith-Rosenberg (1985) has made the distinction between feminist goals by saying that feminists can demand equality with men, or they can work for women's rights.

Equal Rights Amendment
(ERA)

Proposed amendment to the Constitution of the United States which would have made any legal discrimination on grounds of sex unconstitutional. Employment legislation, marriage laws, conscription, and admission to publicly funded schools or programmes would have been required to apply equally to men and women.

Originally drafted by Alice PAUL and introduced into Congress in 1923, the wording was changed slightly in 1944. The complete text is:

Section I. Equality of rights under the law shall not be denied or abridged by the United States or by any State on account of sex.

Section II. The Congress shall have the power to enforce, by appropriate legislation, the provisions of this article.

Section III. This amendment shall take effect two years after the date of ratification.

During all the years without an active women's movement there was little public interest in such an amendment, and the ERA was kept alive only by the persistence of the NATIONAL WOMAN'S PARTY. Finally, in 1972, the ERA made it to the floor of Congress, and on 22 March 1972, it was sent to the States for ratification.

Hawaii was the first State to ratify, followed closely by Nebraska. By the end of 1973, thirty States had passed the amendment, and only five more were required to make it part of the Constitution. At this point a well-organized, well-financed opposition, representing some of the most conservative forces in America, halted the progress of the ERA. Playing on sexual conservatism and fears of homosexuality, women being drafted to fight, and integrated toilets, the opposition even inspired several State legislatures to withdraw their original ratification.

The well-established liberal concept of EQUALITY suddenly took on a radical tinge. Feminists who had previously seen the ERA as a low-priority issue, of less importance than changing social structures and attitudes, began to see the passage of the ERA as a supremely important symbolic victory. The NATIONAL ORGANIZATION FOR WOMEN and other groups concentrated all their energies on achieving passage of the ERA in the late 1970s, sometimes to the exclusion of all else. The ERA became the single, unifying issue for American feminists, with much the same power that the vote had had for the earlier women's movement. And as more women became determined to have the principle of equal rights enshrined in the Constitution, the male backlash grew stronger. Although traditionally the Republican Party had been in favour of an equal rights amendment, in 1980 Ronald Reagan declared himself and his party to be opposed to the ERA.

The extension period for ratification expired on 30 June 1982, and the chance for an equal rights amendment died.

Equality League of Self-Supporting Women
See WOMEN'S POLITICAL UNION

equality
The idea of equality is a fundamental liberal value which can be traced as far back as Aristotle, who argued that no distinction should be made between men equal in all relevant respects. For most of recorded history 'men' has been the operative word, with sex considered a relevant distinction. The emergence of feminism can be recognized in history wherever the demand arose for women to be treated on an equal basis with men, whether that equality was seen as pertaining to matters spiritual, material, economic, sexual or political.

Although the concept of equality as a social good is widely accepted, and a major force of this century has been the various struggles and movements to make it a political reality, feminists are not agreed on how it can best be realized. Because no two individuals are alike, equality will always be relative rather than absolute, and equal rights without equal opportunities to use those rights can be a mockery.

Liberal Feminists have traditionally promoted the concept of full equality under the law and opposed all sex-based discrimination, including protective legislation for women, arguing that the same standards of safety and health should apply to everyone. Yet CAPITALISM itself is based on inequality, and although the rich and the poor may have equal rights under the law, they do not have equal power to make use of those rights. Socialist feminists have pointed out that it is not enough to outlaw discrimination – certain material preconditions must be met for genuine equality of rights. For example, without public childcare facilities, the availability of birth control information, health care and abortion, the 'right' to an education or a job on the same terms as a man is useless to many women.

One problem which both feminists and antifeminists have had with the concept is that equality is presumed to mean 'the same,' which women and men clearly are not. The traditional feminist argument has usually been to minimize the differences and to point out, justly, that BIOLOGICAL DIFFERENCES should not be taken into consideration in areas where they do not apply. Women's capacity for childbearing was once considered to disqualify her from education, political power, and any but the most ill-paid work, yet why, if a man's sexuality or potential for fatherhood is not considered a relevant distinction, should a woman's limit her rights? This has been an effective argument for many years, but more and more modern feminists have recognized its limitations. Sexual differences do exist, and they cannot – always – be ignored. Men and women have a different relation to REPRODUCTION, and although pregnancy may take up an increasingly short span of women's lives, the experience of MOTHERHOOD is very different from that of fatherhood. Zillah EISENSTEIN (1984) has written on the need for feminists to develop a theory of sexual equality which does not ignore sex as an irrelevant distinction, but rather focuses on the biological reality of the female. Men and women should have an equal share in the power relations of society, not in an identical way, but in a way that would 'equalize the different sexual relations they have to the activity of childbearing'.

Other approaches to equality which refuse the ANDROCENTRIC notion of the male as norm have come from BLACK FEMINISM, which emphasizes the power of diversity, demanding equal rights but rejecting integration with the white majority. From RADICAL FEMINISM has come the concept of WOMAN-CENTREDNESS, in which women and their needs are perceived as the norm, and men, rather than women, are expected to change.

ERA
See EQUAL RIGHTS AMENDMENT

essentialism
The belief in a uniquely feminine essence, existing above and beyond cultural conditioning; a feminist version of the old-fashioned 'eternal female' and, as such, a kind of reverse sexism, the mirror image of the BIOLOGISM which for centuries justified the oppression of women by proclaiming the natural superiority of men.

Ethelmer, Ellis
Pen-name used by Elizabeth Wolstenholme-Elmy.

eugenic feminism
Term used by the eugenics movement in Britain in the nineteenth century to describe their programme for improving the race. In actuality the eugenics movement was deeply anti-feminist, opposing any real independence for women as a threat to motherhood.

F

Fairbairns, Zoë, 1948–
British writer. Although she has also written journalism and poetry, she is best known as a novelist who has written about feminist issues within the context of genre novels. *Benefits* (1979) explores the possible results of a successful WAGES FOR HOUSEWORK campaign; *Stand We at Last* (1983) may be the first feminist family saga; and *Here Today* (1984) won the FAWCETT SOCIETY's annual book award.

Faithfull, Emily, 1835–95
English printer. Secretary of the SOCIETY FOR PROMOTING THE EMPLOYMENT OF WOMEN, with its backing she founded the VICTORIA PRESS in 1860. In 1862 she earned the title of Printer and Publisher in Ordinary to the Queen. She gave lectures and dramatic readings in London and on tour in the United States, and also wrote poetry, prose, and one novel.

false consciousness
Concept adopted from Marxism, used chiefly by Marxist and other socialist feminists, it refers to any erroneous belief which keeps a woman from becoming aware of her own oppression in a sexist society. Through CONSCIOUSNESS-RAISING, false consciousness may be replaced by feminist consciousness.

false universalism
See UNIVERSALISM

family
As the major institution for perpetuating PATRIARCHY and women's oppression, the family has been, inevitably, an important consideration for all feminists. A great deal has been written about the links between sexism and family structure, and feminists are as often accused of being 'anti-family' as of being 'anti-men'. Yet even the most radical feminists do not deny the human need for family ties; the family they object to is the rigidly defined nuclear family consisting of one man (the head), one woman (his wife) and their children. The word family comes from the Latin *famulus*, meaning servant, and as Casey Miller and Kate Swift pointed out in *Words and Women* (1976), the implication of this is that the members of the household, whether women, children or servants, were considered to be the property of the man who was its head.

In SEXUAL POLITICS (1971) Kate MILLETT called the family 'a patriarchal unit within a patriarchal whole' and argued that the family served as an agent for the larger society, ensuring conformity where political, religious and other outside forces could not. The modern feminist slogan 'THE PERSONAL IS POLITICAL' reflects the awareness that private and public life are not the separate spheres that patriarchal tradition decrees, and that it will never be enough for women to achieve economic and political equality if that equality is not reflected within the very structure of the family.

(*See also* MOTHERHOOD; CHILDCARE; MARRIAGE; CHILDREN'S LIBERATION)

Fanny Wrightists

Abusive term for feminists, from the 1830s in America. Derived from the name of Frances WRIGHT, the implication was that advocates of women's rights were also atheists and believers in free love.

Farrell, Warren T.

American sociologist. Author of *The Liberated Man*, he was promoted by the media as 'the foremost spokesperson for MEN'S LIBERATION' throughout the 1970s. As the only man to be elected three times to the Board of Directors of NOW, and the NOW Task Force Leader on the Masculine Mystique, he was visible as a token male feminist in the American women's liberation movement.

Fawcett Library

Britain's main resource for women's history. It began as the library of the London Society for Women's Suffrage (which became the Fawcett Society in 1953) under the guidance of Vera Douie, librarian from 1926–67. In 1977, due to financial problems, the Society placed the Library in the care of the City of London Polytechnic, where it is now housed and operates on a subscription basis. It holds about 45,000 books, pamphlets and leaflets; over 700 periodical titles; and press cuttings, photographs, letters and papers of many feminists.

Fawcett, Millicent Garrett, 1847–1929

English. She claimed to have been a suffragist 'from my cradle', and an apocryphal story has been told of a childhood discussion with her older sister Elizabeth Garrett (ANDERSON) and her friend Emily DAVIES in which Emily assigned different areas of the women's rights they were all interested in. She announced that she would devote herself to securing higher education, Elizabeth must open up the medical profession, and Millicent could work on getting the vote.

Her political career began with her marriage, aged twenty, to liberal politician Henry Fawcett. As he was blind, she had to read and write for him, but in addition to becoming known as his political secretary, she was active in her own right, working for the Married Woman's Property Act and joining the first women's suffrage committee in 1867.

After Lydia BECKER's death in 1890 Millicent Garrett Fawcett emerged as the leader of the women's suffrage movement. She was elected president of the NATIONAL UNION OF WOMEN'S SUFFRAGE SOCIETIES, a post she held until her retirement in 1919.

She disapproved of militant tactics and didn't want a revolution or a sex-war: women's emancipation was, in her often-repeated view, for the good of all society: 'We believe that men cannot be truly free so long as women are held in political subjection.'

Among the books she wrote were two histories of the movement: *Women's Suffrage* (1912) and *Women's Victory and After* (1919). After her death she was described as 'the Mother of Women's Suffrage', and her memorial in Westminster Abbey says she 'won citizenship for women'.

Fawcett Society

Originally the London Society for Women's Suffrage, founded 1866, it took its present name in 1953, in honour of Millicent Garrett FAWCETT. A predominantly middle-class, professional organization admitting both men and women as members, it stands for 'equal rights in law and custom between men and women'. To this end it attempts to educate public opinion to accept equal status and equal responsibilities for both sexes,

attempts to influence Parliament, keeps a watch on the media to pinpoint sexual discrimination, and holds conferences and seminars on issues of importance in the campaign for full sexual equality. It also established, and is closely involved in running, the FAWCETT LIBRARY.

Fell, Alison, 1944–

Scottish writer. Involved with the WOMEN'S LIBERATION MOVEMENT since 1969, in 1970 she moved to London where she co-founded the Women's Street Theatre Group. She was a member of the SPARE RIB collective for several years from 1975, and her poetry has appeared in many collections. Her first novel, *Every Move You Make*, about a feminist-poet – 'urban nomad' in 1970s London, was published by VIRAGO in 1984.

Female Eunuch, The

Book by Germaine GREER published in 1970. Although it was widely read and made a great popular impact when it first appeared, because of its emphasis on sexuality and on women's individual responsibility for rejecting social conditioning, the book now appears something of an oddity, still very readable and full of energy, but not connected to any of the major strands of feminist theory which developed in the 1970s. The basic premise of the book is that women have been turned into passive, sexless eunuchs by men; specifically, by such patriarchal structures as MARRIAGE and the family. The true nature of women is unknown and can scarcely even be imagined, but in order to discover it, women must refuse to perpetuate their own oppression. They must refuse to marry, refuse to function as the unpaid labourers and good consumers required by capitalism, and must learn to question even the most basic assumptions about feminine normality. By discovering the truth about their own sexuality, women will recover the energy and possibilities that have been denied them, and lead the way to a new, more joyous, way of life.

female future

Some feminists believe that mere equality will never be enough, and that women's liberation requires a change to woman-centred values and the substitution of female for male authority in all things. They are working, therefore, for what Sally Miller GEARHART has named the female future.

According to Gearhart, the female future challenges the concept of hierarchy, replacing the vertical system with a horizontal pattern of relationships which would not permit the idea of power or authority as being anywhere but within the whole group. A female future would affirm – in all people – the characteristics historically considered feminine. Above all, a female future would acknowledge femaleness as positive, primary, and the source of all life, recognizing that the female encompasses the male and can exist without the male.

There is a strong element of ESSENTIALISM to Gearhart's ideas, for although she admits that the qualities considered feminine may be culturally acquired, and can be cultivated by men as well as by women, she believes that women have, by their physical nature, a different relationship to and understanding of life than that possessed by men. Her vision of what the world might be like if women were no longer oppressed is expressed in THE WANDERGROUND (1978), and in an essay entitled 'The Future – If There Is One – Is Female', she argued that the whole world is heading for destruction unless women take control. To achieve survival, and human liberation, she said that three steps must be taken:

1. Every culture must begin to affirm a female future.
2. Species responsibility must be returned to women in every culture.
3. The proportion of men must be reduced to and maintained at approximately 10 per cent of the human race.

Her last proposal is understandably the most controversial; however, she has specified that male reduction should not be achieved through the loss of any present human life, but through women's own decision to bear more female than male children, and through new reproductive techniques such as ovular merging.

Gearhart argues that although we don't know that a female future could save the world, we have nothing to lose by acting as if it would, and that although we don't yet know the origins of VIOLENCE, we have nothing to lose by approaching the problem as if it were caused by the overabundance of males within the human species. The female future, to her, is the power of women which has been denied, trivialized, hidden and violently suppressed by the male-dominated past and present.

Female Man, The
Novel by Joanna RUSS, first published in 1975 (written 1969–71). Angry, funny and experimental, it escapes the limited options offered to women in mundane fiction, and also the difficulties inherent in trying to express a feminist vision in a form which calls for an individual solution, by using the devices of SCIENCE FICTION to create four separate characters who are all the same woman. Together, they form a collective protagonist. Individually, they are: Jeannine, traditionally helpless and feminine from an alternate world very similar to our own; Joanna, recognizably a contemporary (1969) New York academic; Jael, a professional assassin from a future

in which the sex war is a literal, bloody fact; Janet, from WHILE-AWAY, a potential future Earth without men, a whole human being, unscarred by sexism. Their personalities, their problems and worlds, and their coming together, comprise the story.

female supremacism
Another type of SEXISM, sometimes called feminism. This is based on the belief in the existence of a female principle, or uniquely feminine essence, which is the source of all good and of true morality. This belief holds that feminist revolution would bring about not EQUALITY, but the reversal of the present power structure, resulting in women's dominance over men.
(*See also* ESSENTIALISM; GYNARCHY; ROLE REVERSAL)

Feminine Mystique, The
Book by Betty FRIEDAN, first published in America in 1963. A bestseller when it came out, it is one of the classic texts of the women's liberation movement.

In it, Friedan defines the 'PROBLEM THAT HAS NO NAME', locating the source of discontent felt by so many American women in trying to live up to the 'feminine mystique', which depicts women only in relation to men, as passive, childlike creatures who desire no lives of their own. Analysing how the feminine mystique was perpetuated through sex-directed education (cooking for girls, science for boys), through women's magazines and advertising techniques directed at creating the ideal consumer, through popular culture and psychoanalysis influenced by Freudian theories (anatomy is destiny), Friedan then shows the sterility and dangers of this myth of feminine nature.

Her conclusion: 'It is still very difficult, even for the most advanced psychological theorist, to see woman as a separate self, a human being who, in that respect, is no different in her need to grow than is a man. Most of the conventional theories about women, as well as the feminine mystique, are based on this "difference". But the actual basis for this "difference" is the fact that the possibility for true self-realization has not existed for women until now . . . only the shadow of the past enshrined in the mystique of feminine fulfilment keeps women from finding their road.'

The road out, Friedan suggests, is through education. Women, like men, can find fulfilment only through a life plan of meaningful work.

Although later seen to be narrow in viewpoint in its focus on middle-class women and the redemptive power of having a career, as well as overly optimistic about the ease with which women could end their oppression, the book remains important and well worth reading.

If any one book could be held responsible for the SECOND WAVE OF FEMINISM in America, this is it, since it was the response she received from readers which led Betty Friedan to found the NATIONAL ORGANIZATION FOR WOMEN (NOW).

feminine mystique

Term used by Betty FRIEDAN to describe the oppressive, limited image of womanhood sold to and impressed upon Americans in the 1950s. A combination of Freudian psychology, an expanding capitalism's need for more consumers, and male selfishness and fears resulted in a cultural brainwashing which promoted the sexy, childlike, mindlessly obsessive housewife as the ideal. Women with careers, too much education or any sort of interest outside home and family were said to be unsexed and unnatural, while the truly feminine woman found happiness, creativity and sexual fulfilment through housecleaning, cooking, sewing, and living vicariously through husband and children.

femininism

Term applied to that strand within modern feminist thought which presumes female superiority and celebrates FEMININITY; a brand of female ESSENTIALISM which is usually associated with CULTURAL FEMINISM and which Monique WITTIG has labelled the ideology of 'Woman is wonderful'.

femininity

The socially determined expression of what are considered to be innately female attributes, virtues and deficiencies, as displayed through costume, speech, posture, behaviour, bodily adornments and attitude. Although it is presumed to have a biological basis, the fact that femininity is imposed rather than natural is obvious by the way that young women must be taught how to behave, and are punished if they fail to appear properly feminine. The assumption that femininity is a separate-but-equal counterpart to masculinity is also false. Those traits considered masculine (courage, strength, self-confidence, etc.) are for the most part desirable in any human being, whereas femininity consists of characteristics designed solely to make women pleasing to men. According to the RADICALESBIANS, femininity is 'the slave status which makes us legitimate in the eyes of the society in which we live'. Janet Radcliffe Richards (1980) has defined the essence of femininity as 'the limiting of all endeavour and activity to a confined end' – that end being what men find useful, pleasant and non-threatening.

Femininity is often referred to as 'SEX-ROLE stereotyping' and recognized as a psychological structure to keep women oppressed. One of the earliest and most consistent aims of the WOMEN'S LIBERATION MOVEMENT has been to abolish sex-roles. Particularly in the early 1970s, many feminists envisioned an androgynous future in which distinctions between 'masculine' and 'feminine' behaviour would be meaningless. If femininity consists of attributes and behaviour designed to perpetuate women's inferior status, clearly it must be abolished; but by the mid-1970s more feminists were questioning this interpretation, as well as the usefulness of the concept of ANDROGYNY. Some began to look at femininity in a new light, searching for evidence of a distinctively female culture, and for what might be superior feminine attributes which would be unfortunately lost in the attainment of mere equality with men. Psychologist Jean Baker Miller is among whose who have suggested that such 'feminine' traits as emotionalism, vulnerability and intuition are not the weaknesses our patriarchal culture has defined them, but are the very strengths which may be essential to the development of a new and better society. In this view, femininity is something which men would be advised to develop and accept in themselves.

Femininity is also the term used to represent 'THE OTHER' where masculinity or maleness is seen as the norm. Because our culture (all patriarchal cultures) is male-centred, women are the outsiders, and femininity is in opposition to whatever is considered to be important to civilization. Julia KRISTEVA has defined femininity as marginality to the symbolic order (masculinity, by contrast, is fully integrated into the symbolic order), yet makes the point that femininity is not biologically or anatomically determined. From her point of view, such modernist writers as Mallarmé and Lautréamont, although they were men, were every bit as feminine as Virginia WOOLF because of their marginal relationship to the prevailing, masculine culture.

(*See also* GENDER)

feminism

This term, from the Latin (*femina*=woman), originally meant 'having the qualities of females'. It began to be used in reference to the theory of sexual equality and the movement for women's rights, replacing WOMANISM, in the 1890s. Alice ROSSI has traced the first usage in print to a book review published in *The Athenaeum*, 27 April 1895. Not until the turn of the century, however, was the term widely used and recognized.

In the present, there are many individual definitions of feminism, and its fundamental meaning is in dispute. Dictionaries usually define it as the advocacy of women's rights based on a belief in the equality of the sexes, and in its broadest use the word refers to everyone who is aware of and seeking to end women's subordination in any way

and for any reason. Bell HOOKS (1984) objects to this 'anything goes' approach, saying it has made the term practically meaningless because 'any woman who wants social equality with men regardless of her political perspective (she can be a conservative right-winger or a nationalist communist) can label herself feminist.' Yet Alison Jaggar (1983) has argued that to deny the label to some on ideological grounds while granting it to others 'is not only sectarian but misleads us about history. Just as an inadequate theory of justice is still a conception of justice, so I would say that an inadequate feminist theory is still a conception of feminism.'

According to Donna Hawxhurst and Sue Morrow (1984), 'Feminism has only working definitions since it is a dynamic, constantly changing ideology with many aspects including the personal, the political and the philosophical. . .Feminism is a call to action. It can never be simply a belief system. Without action, feminism is merely empty rhetoric which cancels itself out.'

Feminism originates in the perception that there is something wrong with society's treatment of women; it attempts to analyse the reasons for and dimensions of women's oppression, and to achieve women's liberation. To some, liberation is defined as social EQUALITY with men, while others feel that this narrow definition reflects the class bias of what is described variously as BOURGEOIS FEM-INISM, CAREER FEMINISM, MAINSTREAM FEMINISM or LIBERAL FEMINISM. Yet Hester Eisenstein (1984), writing about the distinctive, original and revolutionary character of modern feminism, asks, 'Ought one to castigate feminism because it is insufficiently revolutionary and geared to the concerns of the working class? Or ought one to take a longer view, and ask, what would become of present social arrangements, in the capitalist West and indeed, in most societies, capitalist and communist, if all the demands of the women's movement were met with respect to all women?'

Charlotte BUNCH (1981) has pointed out that feminism is not about 'adding in' women's rights, but about transforming society, so that feminism may be called 'transformational politics'. Because everything affects women, every issue is a women's issue, and there is a feminist perspective on every subject. Feminism is a movement which seeks, as Teresa BILLINGTON-GRIEG wrote in 1911, 'the reorganization of the world'.

(See also ANARCHA-FEMINISM; CULTURAL FEMINISM; BLACK FEMINISM; HUMANIST FEMINISM; GYNOCENTRIC FEMINISM; LESBIAN-FEMINISM; MARXIST-FEMINISM; RADICAL FEMINISM; REVOLUTIONARY FEMINISM; SOCIALIST FEMINISM; WOMEN'S LIBERATION MOVEMENT; and all other entries in this book)

Feminist International Network of Resistance to Reproductive and Genetic Engineering (FINRRAGE)

At the Second Interdisciplinary Congress on Women in Groningen, the Netherlands, in 1984, 500 women from twelve countries formed the Feminist International Network on the New Reproductive Technologies (FINNRET) and agreed to hold an Emergency Conference in Sweden, in July 1985.

In Sweden, the seventy-four conference participants voted to change the group's name to FINRRAGE to acknowledge the interrelationship between reproductive and genetic technologies, and their opposition to these developments.

They passed a resolution which declared, in part, that 'the female body, with its unique capacity for creating human life is being expropriated and dissected as raw material for the technological production of human beings. For us women, for nature, and for the exploited peoples of the world, this development is a declaration of war. Genetic and reproductive engineering is another attempt to end self-determination over our bodies.

'We know that technology cannot solve problems created by exploitative conditions. We do not need to transform our biology, we need to abolish patriarchal social, political, and economic conditions.

'We shall resist the development and application of genetic and reproductive engineering.

'We want to maintain the integrity and embodiment of women's procreativity. Externalization of conception and gestation facilitates manipulation and eugenic control . . .

'We support the exclusive rights of all women to decide whether or not to bear children, without coercion from any man, medical practitioner, government or religion . . .

'We support the recovery by women of knowledge, skill, and power that gives childbirth, fertility and all women's health care back into the hands of women.

'We seek a different kind of science and technology that respects the dignity of womankind and of all life on earth. We call upon women and men to break the fatal link between mechanistic science and vested industrial interests and to take part with us in the development of a new unity of knowledge and life.'

The aims of FINRRAGE, which has national contacts in Australia, Bangladesh, Brazil, Canada, Chile, Denmark, France, Britain, India, Ireland, Israel, Japan, the Netherlands, New Zealand, Norway, Spain, Sweden, Switzerland, the United States and West Germany, are to monitor international developments in the areas of reproductive and genetic engineering; to

assess the implications of these developments for the future socio-economic position and well-being of women internationally; to provide information on social responses to reproductive and genetic engineering; and to inform women about feminist resistance.

(*See also* REPRODUCTIVE FREEDOM)

Feminist Press, The

One of the longest-established feminist PUBLISHING companies, it was founded by Florence Howe in New York in 1970 as an educational organization committed to restoring the lost heritage of women's words, lives and history. They have published books by Charlotte Perkins GILMAN, Rebecca Harding Davis, Zora Neale Hurston and others. In 1985 they announced the intention to publish more international work, including bilingual editions of work from other countries, and cross-cultural studies. In 1986 they became affiliated with The City University of New York.

Feminist Review

Socialist feminist journal founded in 1979, edited by a collective based in London, and published three times a year. Its aim, stated in the first issue, is 'To develop the theory of Women's Liberation and debate the political perspectives and strategy of the movement. To be a forum for work in progress and current research and debates in Women's Studies.'

feminist spirituality
See SPIRITUAL FEMINISM

Feminist Studies
American women's studies journal published three times a year, combining rigorous scholarship with political commitment. Founded in 1972 by Ann Calderwood, it entered a hiatus in 1976, then resumed publication in 1978 with funding from the University of Maryland, edited by a collective. In addition to scholarly and critical work – analytical responses to feminist issues – it also publishes creative writing and reports from the women's movement.

Feministo
British women's 'postal art event' started in 1975 when Sally Gollop, on the Isle of Wight, and Kate Walker in London began mailing each other images which expressed their feelings as artists confined by domestic responsibilities. They involved more of their friends, and more women came to hear about it, each replying to the artwork she received with an image or small object of her own. Rozsika Parker has suggested that both the form and the content of Feministo are a challenge to the (male) art establishment by undermining the concept of the artist as isolated genius, and

by breaking down the division between artist and audience. Not all of the women involved wanted to risk showing the work publicly, but they finally decided it was politically important to do so. The first exhibitions were in Birmingham, Liverpool and Coventry. In 1977, it was shown as part of an international celebration of women's art in Berlin, and in Australia.
(*See also* ART AND ARTISTS)

Feminists, The
Small, short-lived, but very influential radical feminist group founded in New York City on 17 October 1968 (and so referred to as the October 17th Movement until June 1969) by nine former members of the NATIONAL ORGANIZATION FOR WOMEN (NOW) and several radical women.

Rejecting the CONSCIOUSNESS-RAISING approach of the REDSTOCK-INGS and the hierarchical structure of NOW, The Feminists defined themselves as a theory-action group with the dual objectives of developing a rigorous theoretical analysis of the situation of women, and of working out in practice a new and non-oppressive form of organization. In both theory and structure they led the way for many of the radical feminist groups which came later.

In their analysis, the oppression of women is the result of the SEX-ROLE system, and the task of radical feminism must be to annihilate sex roles. To bring their theory to the public, they first demonstrated in January 1969 at the trial of an abortionist, demanding an end to all abortion laws. In September 1969 the group picketed the New York City Municipal Building Marriage License Bureau and distributed a leaflet calling for the destruction of the institution of marriage.

Committed to breaking down traditional class and power systems, the group remained leaderless but had a clearly defined structure. The division of tasks into the categories of creative and menial, and a lot system, ensured that no one always did the same type of job, and that everyone had to develop a variety of skills. A 'disc system' in which members were allotted a number of discs which they had to 'spend' whenever they spoke, ensured that no one could monopolize discussions.

During the summer of 1969 new rules were passed demanding absolute and primary commitment to the group. Because radical feminists had to reject marriage in practice as well as theory, no more than one-third of the membership would be allowed to live with a man. Alliances with any other groups or individuals were frowned on, and attendance at meetings was mandatory. Ti-Grace ATKINSON, one of the original founders of the group, was accused of being a 'star' because she was often quoted and described as a feminist leader by the media. She left the group in 1970. By that time, membership and influence of The Feminists had fallen, and although they continued to exist, they no longer contributed very much to the women's movement.

fetal identification syndrome
Identified by Mary DALY as the reason some men feel so threatened by the idea of abortion. Sensing their own condition to be that of possessors or inhabitors of women, they cannot accept woman's right to control her own body, since they might themselves be similarly rejected.

fiction
See NOVELS AND NOVELISTS

Field, Sara Bard, 1882–1974
American poet. She became involved in the women's suffrage movement in 1910, and organized the state suffrage campaign which won women the vote in Oregon by 1912. In 1914 she turned her energies to the national movement, becoming a member of the CONGRESSIONAL UNION FOR WOMAN SUFFRAGE. In 1915 she carried a petition in favour of a woman suffrage amendment, signed by 500,000 people, across the continent by automobile and presented it to President Woodrow Wilson in Washington, D.C., on 6 December 1915. She was a founder-member of the NATIONAL WOMAN'S PARTY, as

well as a pacifist. A nervous break-down in 1918, following the death of her son, brought a halt to her political activism, and although she was known until the end of her life for her support of various radical political causes, she devoted more time to her career as a poet.

Figes, Eva, 1932–

German-born British writer. Author of *Patriarchal Attitudes* (1970), an examination of the fact and ideology of women's oppression which provided one of the theoretical bases for the emerging women's liberation movement in Britain. She also wrote a study of the lives of British writers called *Sex and Subterfuge: Women Novelists to 1850* (1981) as well as other non-fiction titles, novels and children's books.

film

One of the major concerns of the contemporary feminist movement has been with how women are represented in the media and popular culture. Film attracted attention on various grounds: critics analysed the images of women in films past and present; historians uncovered women's lost contributions; festivals highlighting the work of women filmmakers were held; collectives, such as the London Women's Film Group, founded in 1971, were formed to help women acquire the skills to make their own films; filmmakers found their lives

and work changed by the impact of the women's liberation movement.

The first feminist films were low-budget, independently produced documentaries. Realism was the dominant mode, and there was a strong urge to tell the truth about women's lives (as Hollywood did not) and to offer more varied, positive and realistic images of women. Early documentaries, tackling women's issues, revealed women's oppression and at the same time demonstrated that women had the ability to fight against that oppression. The film portrait, whether biographical or autobiographical, was also very popular in the early 1970s. These early films include *Women Talking* by Midge Mackenzie (UK, 1970), *The Woman's Film* by the San Francisco Newsreel Group (USA, 1971), *Three Lives* by Kate MILLETT (USA, 1971), JANIE'S JANIE by Geri Ashur and Peter Barton (USA, 1971), and *Joyce at 34* by Joyce Chopra and Claudia Weill (USA, 1972). By the mid-1970s, the women's movement had started to make an impact on Hollywood, resulting in films about strong yet 'ordinary' women such as *Alice Doesn't Live Here Any More* (1975) and *An Unmarried Woman* (1977).

The sociological approach – comparing the roles of women in film with lived experience – was the first form of feminist film criticism, and it continues to be important. But the semiological approach is now more common. This is concerned with the science of signs, the question of how meaning is produced in a film, how images are constructed and understood by the viewer. It draws upon linguistic theory, semiotics, PSYCHOANALYSIS, and the ideas of Roland Barthes, Jacques Lacan, Michel Foucault, and the French theorists of L'ÉCRITURE FÉMININE – Hélène CIXOUS, Julia KRISTEVA, Luce IRIGARAY and others. As represented in CAMERA OBSCURA and other journals, contemporary feminist film criticism is written for a small audience in difficult, esoteric language. It begins from the theory that under PATRIARCHY women are alienated from the culturally dominant forms of expression, with no LANGUAGE of their own. It is the view of the outsider, concerned with making visible the invisible structures of representation.

Critics and filmmakers challenging the dominant modes of representation may do so by 'deconstruction' – questioning and breaking down the culturally dominant 'privileged' forms of expression – or by attempting to establish a radically different, new mode; a specifically feminine form. The question of what this feminine form would be, or where it should come from has not been answered, although some avant-garde feminist filmmakers have tried. Looking at Laura Mulvey and Peter Wollen's 1976 film RIDDLES OF THE SPHINX and

Daughter-Rite (1978) by Michelle Citron, critic E. Ann Kaplan suggested that the subject of MOTHERHOOD – repressed and ignored by the patriarchy – might be one point of entry for women to introduce change, ask questions, and begin to formulate a new reality. Other feminist filmmakers working today include Sally Potter, Lizzie Borden, Margarethe VON TROTTA and Chantal AKERMAN.

(*See also* DURAS, MARGUERITE; SANDER, HELKE; QUESTION OF SILENCE, A; VARDA, AGNES)

Filosofova, Anna, 1837–1912
Russian. With her friends Mariya TRUBNIKOVA and Nadezhda STASOVA she formed the 'Triumvirate' of early Russian feminism. Their work was philanthropic rather than political, and aimed to improve the financial situation of unmarried women by forming cooperatives to provide cheap lodgings and useful employment. She was also involved in the campaign to make higher education available to women. Somewhat more radical in her ideas than her two friends, in the 1890s she became involved in the international women's suffrage movement.

Firestone, Shulamith, 1945–
Canadian. One of the most influential early organizers of the WOMEN'S LIBERATION MOVEMENT in America, she became radicalized during student political activities in Chi-

cago. In October 1967 she went to New York City where, with Pam Allen, she organized that city's first women's group, RADICAL WOMEN. Co-founder, with Ellen Willis, of REDSTOCKINGS, and co-founder and editor, with Anne KOEDT, of *Notes from the First Year* (1968). With Anne Koedt, in December 1969, she wrote a Manifesto ('POLITICS OF THE EGO') and set of Organizing Principles for a mass-based, radical feminist movement which would combine CONSCIOUSNESS-RAISING, theory, and action, and presented them to a group of about forty women who became known as the NEW YORK RADICAL FEMINISTS. In 1970 she became nationally famous with the publication of THE DIALECTIC OF SEX, in which she presented a radical analysis of the sex class system and the case for feminist revolution.

First Sex, The
Book by Elizabeth Gould DAVIS, first published in America in 1971, which attempts to prove that, biologically and historically, women are superior to men. Seeing the male Y chromosome as a 'deformed and broken X chromosome', Davis declares 'the male sex represents a degeneration and deformity of the female', concluding that women were not only the creators of civilization, but were actually the original, and only necessary, human beings. Although both facts and conclusions are arguable, the book offers a fascinating tour through history, archaeology, art, mythology and science from an original point of view, and is a refreshing alternative to the usual masculine bias.

first wave feminism
Term used for the earlier women's movement (approximately 1860–1920) to differentiate it from the 'second wave' emerging in the 1960s.
(*See also* WOMEN'S SUFFRAGE MOVEMENT)

First World Women
Term used instead of 'Third World Women' by members of the NATIONAL BLACK FEMINIST ORGANIZATION (from 1973) after questioning the right of anyone else to call them 'third', and as 'an affirmation of ourselves as non-white women choosing our own definitions'.

Flexner, Eleanor, 1908–
American. She was the author of, among other books, one of the first, best and most comprehensive books about the first women's movements in America *Century of Struggle* (1959).

Flynn, Elizabeth Gurley,
1890–1964
American radical and labour organizer. Her mother was an Irish feminist who encouraged her daughter in whatever she felt she must do; her career as a public speaker began at the age of sixteen

with a speech to the Harlem Socialist Club on 'The Subjection of Women under Socialism'. She joined the Communist Party in 1936 and wrote a regular column for the *Daily Worker*, covering political, social and economic issues from a feminist viewpoint. In 1942 she ran for Congress, campaigning on women's issues: she advocated equal opportunities and equal pay, but also special protective legislation for women workers. She received 50,000 votes. During World War II she publicized women's contributions to the war effort and advocated unionization of war workers, public day care centres, and the drafting of women. After the war she was a member of the American delegation to the Women's Congress in Paris. She was arrested in 1951 for conspiring to advocate the overthrow of the American government and imprisoned for three years, but after her release she continued to work for the Communist Party. In March 1961 she became the first woman selected as its National Chairman.

Four Demands, The

Formulated by the WOMEN'S NATIONAL COORDINATING COMMITTEE in 1970 less as a formal statement of the politics of the British women's liberation movement than as a banner under which many women could unite and demonstrate. They were the basis of the first national marches in Britain, on INTERNATIONAL WOMEN'S DAY in 1971, and although they later evolved into the SEVEN DEMANDS, the first four have remained as:

1. Equal pay.
2. Equal opportunities and education.
3. Free contraception and abortion on demand.
4. Free 24-hour nurseries.

Fourier, François Marie Charles, 1772–1837

Utopian socialist who inspired Frances WRIGHT and other early feminists. He believed that the 'thirteen passions' of humanity, repressed by civilization, must be released for natural harmony to prevail. To this end he proposed communities known as phalanxes (*phalanstères*) composed of 1,800 women and men who had been scientifically selected to allow individuals to express their desires by working at what they enjoyed. Unlike many male utopians, he did not ignore housework or assume it was naturally the sphere of women. Among other things he suggested that children, who enjoy getting dirty, could be the rubbish collectors.

Fourth World Manifesto

Statement by Barbara Burris, in agreement with Kathleen Barry, Terry Moon, Joann DeLor, Joann Parent and Cate Stadelman, written in 1971 in response to attempts by the male-dominated Left to co-opt the Women's Liberation Movement for its own ends. Arguing against the prevailing attitude that women's liberation was trivial and unimportant compared to the struggles against racism, imperialism, etc, it declared: 'Women, set apart by physical differences between them and men, were the first colonized group. And this territory colonized was and remains our women's bodies. . . . The female culture is the Fourth World.'

Frankfort, Ellen, 1936–
American journalist. Her health column for *The Village Voice* (1968–73) stemmed from her political activism centring on women's right to control their own bodies and resulted in VAGINAL POLITICS (1972), a book which was influential in promoting the women's HEALTH MOVEMENT. She was a founding member of the New York chapter of the Feminist Writers' Guild, which began a feminist literary supplement (now published by OFF OUR BACKS) called *The Feminist Review*. Her articles have appeared in *Ms.*, the *Washington Post*, and the *Feminist Review*, and her other books include *Rosie: An Investigation of a Wrongful Death* (1980) and *Kathy Boudin and the Dance of Death* (1983).

Freeman, Jo, 1945–
American lawyer and political scientist. An early and influential participant who continues to be active in the SECOND WAVE OF FEMINISM, she founded the first independent women's liberation group in America, in Chicago in 1967, and the movement's first national newsletter, VOICE OF THE WOMEN'S LIBERATION MOVEMENT, which she edited from 1968–9. More than any other individual, she was responsible for promoting the use of the term WOMEN'S LIBERATION MOVEMENT. The other terms in use in the late 1960s were radical women's movement, which implied ties with the New Left, and women's movement, which she felt was inappropriate because the movement was not about women *per se*, but about women's liberation. Well known as a lecturer and the author of many articles and essays, her most influential work was probably that which was published under her pen-name Joreen, and which includes 'THE BITCH MANIFESTO' (1970) and 'The Tyranny of Structurelessness' (1971). Publications under her own name include the books *The Politics of Women's Liberation: A Case Study of an Emerging Social Movement and Its Relation to the Policy Process* (1975); *Women: A Feminist Perspective* (1975) and *Social Movements of the Sixties and Seventies* (1983).

Freewoman, The
Radical feminist review published weekly in England from November 1911–October 1912. Established by Dòra MARSDEN and Mary GAW-

THORPE as a forum for revolutionary ideas and discussions about women, marriage, prostitution, politics, sexual relations, and anything else concerning women's oppression and how it could be ended. Banned by booksellers and disliked by many suffragists for its critical stance on their obsession ('feminism is the whole issue, political enfranchisement a branch issue'), it attracted such writers as Rebecca WEST, H. G. Wells, Edward Carpenter, Havelock Ellis, Teresa BILLINGTON-GRIEG and Ada Nield CHEW, who raised questions in its pages which are still being argued today.

In 1913 it resurfaced briefly as *The New Freewoman: An Individualist Review*, taking a 'humanist' stance and moving away from radicalism. In 1914 its name was changed to *The Egoist*, and Dora Marsden handed over editorship to Harriet Shaw Weaver, who ran it as a literary review with little or no feminist content.

French, Marilyn, 1929–
American writer. She became famous as the author of THE WOMEN'S ROOM (1977), the best-known novel of the women's liberation movement, and followed it with a second novel, *The Bleeding Heart* (1980). Her most ambitious work, *Beyond Power: On Women, Men and Morals* (1985), contains the argument that natural human social organization developed along matricentric lines, but was corrupted by PATRIARCHY, which is dedicated to power above all. She writes: '. . . it is possible to live with an eye to delight rather than domination. And this is the feminist morality.' Her conclusion is that we are doomed to ultimate annihilation unless feminism is able to fulfil its aim of transforming society.

Freud, Sigmund, 1856–1939
Austrian founder of PSYCHO-ANALYSIS. His theories, including subsequent popularizations, developments and distortions by others, are referred to as Freudianism. At the beginning of the women's liberation movement in the 1960s, Freud and Freudianism were identified as the great enemy of women's potential, a force used to keep women psychologically oppressed at a time when many of the old physical and legal restraints lacked their former power.

Shulamith FIRESTONE argued in *The Dialectic of Sex* (1970) that Freudianism and feminism had emerged from the same historical circumstances and dealt with the same explosive material, but that Freudianism, being less threatening than feminism because it did not attack the status quo, had subsumed feminism.

Betty FRIEDAN, Kate MILLETT and Naomi Weisstein were among those who accused the Freudians of constructing an ideology of sex roles, a set of prescriptions for the normal woman with the punishment for any woman who deviated of being labelled abnormal, sick, or even mad and in need of being restrained.

By the mid-1970s, however, more and more feminists were turning back to Freud in an attempt to understand how GENDER was constructed, and the reasons for male dominance. Despite the fact that Freud was himself an anti-feminist, and firmly entrenched in patriarchal culture, he did not create SEX-ROLES, but only described how they might begin. Although it has been used against women, psychoanalysis is a tool now used by many feminists, who would agree with Juliet MITCHELL's argument in *Psychoanalysis and Feminism* (1974) that 'a rejection of psychoanalysis and of Freud's works is fatal for feminism'.

Friedan, Betty, 1921–

American. Author of one of the earliest and most influential books on the WOMEN'S LIBERATION MOVEMENT, THE FEMININE MYSTIQUE (1963) she is popularly regarded as the founder of the modern women's movement. For her, feminism has always been a theory of human rights, and because of this her brand of individualistic, liberal feminism, or as she calls it 'mainstream feminism', has found acceptance with many – perhaps even the majority of – American women.

She founded the NATIONAL ORGANIZATION FOR WOMEN (NOW) in 1966 and served as its first president until 1970. She helped found the National Women's Political Caucus in 1971, the First Women's Bank in 1973, and called the International Feminist Congress in 1973 as well as leading the National Women's Strike for Equality. Since the late 1970s her emphasis has been increasingly on changes in law, and she has been particularly active in the struggle for the EQUAL RIGHTS AMENDMENT.

In her first book Friedan called upon women to reject the FEMININE MYSTIQUE which restricted them to the roles of wife and mother, and to develop themselves as full human beings through education and work. But by *The Second Stage* (1981) she seemed to reverse herself, now blaming the new 'feminist mystique' for crippling women by denying them the right to be different from men by having children. In a sense her concerns remain the same – individual freedom of choice for women – but by presenting it entirely as a matter of individual freedom, and not considering the lack of true freedom of choice in a society where motherhood is valued less than paid work, Friedan has moved away from feminist theory – even to seeing radical feminists as the enemy – to become what Zillah R. Eisenstein has defined as a 'revisionist liberal feminist' or a 'neoconservative feminist'.

Fritz, Leah, 1931–
American. A pacifist already involved in the civil rights and anti-war movements of the day, she joined the Women's Liberation Movement by participating in the protest against the Miss America contest in Atlantic City in 1968. She is the author of a number of articles and essays, some of them collected as *Thinking Like a Woman* (1975), and of a personal history and critique of the modern American women's movement, *Dreamers and Dealers* (1979).

Fuller, Margaret, 1810–50
American. One of the New England Transcendentalists, she conducted a series of women-only 'Conversations' to discuss such topics as art, education, philosophy, history and women's rights, and made a great impression as both brilliant thinker and passionate speaker. She was equally influential in her roles as editor, critic and writer. Her most important book, WOMAN IN THE NINETEENTH CENTURY (1848), is, with Wollstonecraft's *Vindication of the Rights of Woman* and Grimké's *Letters on The Equality of the Sexes*, one of the classic early feminist texts, and it provided some of the inspiration for the American women's movement.

Furies, The
LESBIAN-FEMINIST political collective based in Washington, D.C. from 1971–4. Their aim was to develop a lesbian/feminist/separatist theory as the basis for the liberation of women, and this theory, as presented in their newspaper *The Furies* as well as in pamphlet form, had a profound impact on radical feminism in America. The group took their name from the triple Fate-Goddesses (also known as the Erinyes) who dealt out punishment to those who trespassed against the social good.
(*See also* SEPARATISM; BUNCH, CHARLOTTE)

G

Gage, Matilda Joslyn, 1826–98
American. With Elizabeth Cady
STANTON and Susan B. ANTHONY
she formed the triumvirate which
launched and guided the FIRST WAVE
OF FEMINISM in America. The most
radical of the three, she is today the
least remembered.

Writer, theoretician, historian
and grass-roots activist, Gage
devoted much of her energy to
achieving women's suffrage, but
never thought that the vote could or
should be an end in itself. Beginning with her first public speech, at
the national convention in Syracuse, New York, in 1852, her major
concern was to discover and publicize the achievements of women.
She believed that an original matri-
archate, or matriarchy, had been
overthrown by the patriarchate,
and that the combined force of
Church and State ensured that
women of the nineteenth century
were even more oppressed than
women of earlier times. Her argument, most fully expressed in her
major work, *Woman, Church and
State* (1893), was that men had collaborated to systematically deprive
women of their power and
energies, and that Christianity was
one of the most dangerous structures ever invented to justify male
enslavement of women.

In 1878 Gage began editing and
publishing *The National Citizen and
Ballot Box* as the official paper of the
National Woman Suffrage Association, giving it up in 1881 to join
with Anthony and Stanton in
working on the HISTORY OF WOMAN
SUFFRAGE. She made a major contribution to that book, yet received
less credit than Anthony or
Stanton.

In 1890, Gage was one of the few
feminists still radical enough to
object to the union between the
NWSA and the conservative
American Woman Suffrage Association, with its strong ties to the
WOMEN'S CHRISTIAN TEMPERANCE
UNION. In response, she broke away
to form the Woman's National
Liberal Union, which blamed
women's oppression on church as
well as state, called for an end to
prayer in public schools, backed
labour reforms, opposed the
government's cruel treatment of
Native Americans, and in general
demanded a much wider system of
reforms than any other suffrage
organization.

Other suffragists, even the anti-
Church Stanton, considered that
Gage had seceded from the
women's suffrage movement, and

despite all her earlier contributions to it, she was after that effectively written out of its history.

Gardner, Kay

Contemporary American composer. Music director and principal conductor of the New England Women's Symphony in Boston. Her own recorded works include *Mooncircles*, *Emerging* and *A Rainbow Path*. She combines her interests in music and spirituality by leading Music and Healing workshops at various American colleges. She has written and spoken about her theory that there may be a musical form quite different from the male-defined forms which predominate, and that the growth of the women's music movement may help in its development.
(*See also* MUSIC AND MUSICIANS)

Garrett, Elizabeth
See ANDERSON, ELIZABETH GARRETT

gatekeepers

Term first used by Dale SPENDER for 'the people who set the standards, produce the social knowledge, monitor what is admitted to the system of distribution, and decree the innovations in thought, or knowledge, or values. . . . They are in a position to determine what gets published and what does not, and most of them are men.'

gatekeeping theory

Named by Dale SPENDER (although expressed by other feminist theor-

ists before and after), the idea is simply that under patriarchy the judges or GATEKEEPERS who decide what is or is not important, valuable and true in the realm of art and ideas are always men, with the result that ours is a male culture which we have been taught, falsely, is fully human, and that it is this – and not some mysterious biological lack – which accounts for so few women artists, philosophers, writers, etc. being admitted to the ranks of the 'great'.

Gauthier, Xavière, 1942–
French author and academic. Editor of the literary review *Sorcières*, founded in 1976 and devoted to exploring women's creativity and women's LANGUAGE. Author of a number of books including a collaboration with Marguerite DURAS, *Les parleuses* (1974), and *Dire nos sexualités – contre la sexologie* (1977).

Gawthorpe, Mary, 1881–1960
English. Reading of the arrest of Annie KENNEY and Christabel PANKHURST in 1905, she was so moved that she at once joined the Leeds Branch of the National Union of Women's Suffrage Societies, and wrote a letter offering to go to prison herself. By 1906 she was an active organizer for the WOMEN'S SOCIAL AND POLITICAL UNION (WSPU) and had been imprisoned for her militant activities. In 1911 she edited THE FREEWOMAN. She was one of the most

popular speakers the WSPU ever had – permanently damaging her voice in the cause of women's suffrage – and inspired many young women, including Rebecca WEST, with feminist ideals.

Gay Liberation Front (GLF)

Movement for the rights of homosexuals, born out of the Stonewall Riots in resistance to police raids on gay bars in New York in June 1969. It shares a common goal with the Women's Liberation Movement of creating a society which does not categorize and oppress people on the basis of their sex or their sexual preference. The GLF analysis of society's treatment of homosexuality draws on a feminist analysis of the family and the effect of SEX-ROLES, and recognizes that a feminist revolution would bring about gay liberation as well. However, lesbians who have been involved in the movement for gay rights have often found the behaviour and attitudes of gay men to be every bit as sexist and oppressive as that of heterosexual men. After years of being involved in the gay movement, Liz Stanley (1982) concluded she could no longer work with gay men: 'There is no way, absolutely no way, in which our interests can be said to be the same. Gay men, perhaps more than any other men, ally themselves with the activities and products of sexism. More than any other men they choose to act and construe themselves, and each other, in ways dominated by phallocentric ideologies and activities . . .a feminist society, even a non-sexist one, would be one in which the essentials of phallocentrism are challenged and dismantled. Its achievement would entail the end of the lifestyle of the average, sexist, phallocentric gay man. . .And so they resist it.'
(*See also* LESBIANISM)

gayness
See LESBIANISM

gay/straight split

Common term for the division between heterosexual and lesbian feminists which became a major crisis in the American women's liberation movement between 1970–2. Early on in the movement there was some pressure on lesbians to keep their sexual preference private rather than making it a political issue. Some rights-oriented heterosexuals like Betty FRIEDAN considered lesbianism a 'lavender herring' distracting attention from more important things, while others were afraid the movement would be discredited. Feeling as oppressed within the women's movement as anywhere else, many lesbian feminists broke away to form their own groups and took the position that no woman who had sexual relations with a man could be a true feminist. At the same time, many feminists realized that to allow men to divide women according to sexual availability, or to be intimidated by the label 'lesbian', was profoundly oppressive, and that all feminists had a common goal of eliminating the sex-role system.

(*See also* LAVENDER MENACE, RADICALESBIANS)

Gearhart, Sally Miller, 1931–
American academic and writer. A militant lesbian-feminist since 1970, she is also active in the animal rights movement, and works with the Women's Studies Program at San Francisco State University, where she is Chair of the Speech and Communications Department. Author of *A Feminist Tarot* (with Susan Rennie, 1976) and THE WANDERGROUND: *Stories of the Hill Women* (1978).

Gems, Pam, 1925–
British playwright. Although she has rejected the label of feminist writer, her plays have presented a strong, feminist vision. They include *Dusa, Fish, Stas and Vi* (1977), *Queen Christina* (1977) and *Piaf* (1979).

gender
Term for the socially imposed division between the sexes. Whereas *sex* refers to the biological, anatomical differences between male and female, gender refers to the emotional and psychological attributes which a given culture expects to coincide with physical maleness or femaleness. 'Masculine' and 'feminine' are gender terms, and although individuals born male are expected to develop a masculine gender-identity as the natural course of events, it is widely recognized that sex and gender may not always coincide. Although a baby's sex is (usually) obvious at birth, an individual's sense of self as a sexual being must be acquired. According to researchers Robert Stoller and John Money, the 'core gender identity' is acquired before the age of two years, the result of the baby's interaction with caretakers and other aspects of environment. The usual explanation given for cases of TRANSSEXUALISM is a mismatch between a person's physical sex and gender identity.

Out of the awareness of the difference between sex and gender comes one of the most important concepts in feminist theory: that although a human being is born male or female, women and men are created by society rather than nature. Some feminists have declared that gender must be destroyed if a sexually egalitarian society is ever to become reality. In this sense, gender is used as a term synonymous with SEX-ROLE, and is usually considered to have developed out of the awareness of obvious sexual differences and to have led to the creation of an increasingly rigid definition of masculine and feminine resulting in PATRIARCHY. But Christine DELPHY has suggested that 'the sexual roles which we call gender' followed rather than preceded the hierarchical division of labour, and transformed previously socially irrelevant anatomical differences into 'a relevant distinction for social practice'.

Gender may be as inevitable and necessary a part of human identity as sexuality; differences between people need not be hierarchical, or reasons for oppression. Not all feminists envision a future genderless or UNISEX society. How gender is formed, what it means to us, whether and how it can be altered: all need to be studied. Ever since Freud, psychologists have suggested that the formation of gender identity is necessarily a different task for boys and girls, since girls relate first to a same-sex caretaker, and boys to a different-sex caretaker. Nancy CHODOROW and Dorothy Dinnerstein are among those who have theorized that women's oppression may be traced to the universal restriction of mothering to women. To abolish sexism, therefore, would require that childcare be shared equally between the sexes, to enable male and female infants to develop primary relationships with both same-sex and different-sex caretakers.

gender gap

American term for the difference in voting patterns between men and women which first appeared in the presidential election of 1980. One of the fears prior to the granting of women's suffrage was that women would vote as a bloc, cutting across the usual racial, class and economic barriers, but this did not happen; for sixty years women voted just as men did. Then suddenly in 1980 a 'gender gap', comparable to the generation gap of the previous decade, appeared: women had moved measurably and consistently to the left of men.

The term was first used in a NOW leaflet, *Women Can Make the Difference* (1981), picked up by *Washington Post* columnist Judy Mann in October 1981, and swiftly became a part of the American political vocabulary.

In the spring of 1984, MS. Magazine commissioned Louis Harris and Associates to design and administer a nationwide, representative poll of both women and men, to measure the gender gap nationally. Their findings: that the gender gap existed and was increasing; that general issues of sexual equality were becoming equally or more important to women than those relating to discrimination based on other factors, and equally or more important than generalized issues of peace, foreign policy and economic progress. On specific issues, women outstripped men on support for equal pay (by 74 to 63 per cent), on support for the EQUAL

RIGHTS AMENDMENT (ERA) (by 64 to 56 per cent), on favouring strict enforcement of air and water pollution controls (by 89 to 87 per cent) and as being critical of current foreign policy (by 61 to 59 per cent).

This change has happened only in America; European voting patterns have shown women to be slightly more conservative than men, with that gap narrowing in recent years.

Some observers have suggested that the women's liberation movement was responsible, but it seems more likely that the awareness of oppression which created the women's movement in the late 1960s has now resulted in the gender gap. According to sociologist Cynthia Fuchs Epstein, women's experience of sexual discrimination may 'create a consciousness of being outsiders, and from that consciousness, some women go on to develop a conscience about many issues.'

geography

The idea of a 'gendered geography' emerged in the 1980s as a growing body of feminist geographers pointed out how geography both reflects and reinforces the gender assumptions of society. Feminist geographers demand that gender be included – with categories such as status, class, power and race, already accepted by most geographers – as one of the important influences on the relationship between individuals and their environment. In their work, some feminist geographers concentrate on the 'Geography of women' – women's worlds as distinct from those of men – while others overlap somewhat with the work of feminist architects as they examine the disadvantages to women of living in a world designed for and by patriarchy.

Gerin-Lajoie, Marie Lacoste, 1867–1945

French-Canadian. As the daughter of a leading politician and the daughter-in-law of a famous journalist, she used her influential position well in the campaign for women's suffrage in Quebec. The author of *La femme et le code civil* (1929).

Gibbons, Abigail Hopper, 1801–93

American. Active in the social purity movement, she was head of the New York Committee for the Prevention of State Regulation of Vice and opposed all measures which would regulate (and therefore perpetuate) prostitution. She had a lifelong interest in the care and rehabilitation of female prisoners, and her years of lobbying for special treatment of women were rewarded when, at the age of ninety-one, she appeared before the New York State legislature to speak in favour of the creation of a women's reformatory, and subsequently a bill was passed.

GILLIGAN, CAROL

Gilligan, Carol, 1936–
American. Author of *In a Different Voice* (1982), a study of contrasting ways of defining and developing morality. She suggests that men tend to see the world in terms of their autonomy, and are threatened by intimacy, whereas women tend to see the world in terms of connectedness and are threatened by isolation. All psychological theories of human development have been biased, with the male view depicted as the 'normal' or even the correct one, so that women have been seen as abnormal or underdeveloped because of their different perceptions – if they have not been ignored entirely. Gilligan suggests that the female experience should be studied, and might provide new and more appropriate ways of moral development. In 1984, MS. Magazine recognized the importance of her work and named her 'Woman of the Year'.

Gilman, Charlotte Perkins
(Charlotte Stetson), 1860–1935
American writer. Called by Aileen Kraditor 'the most influential woman thinker in the pre-World War I generation in the United States', Charlotte Perkins Gilman combined socialism and feminism to provide a coherent theory of women's oppression, and offered intellectual backing for the movement for women's rights. She did not call herself a feminist; being concerned with the future of

humanity, she preferred to call herself a humanist.

Her writing and theories came directly out of her own experiences. From a child, when her father deserted the family, she saw the inequity of a system which made one half of the human race economically dependent on the other. Married to Charles Stetson in 1884, she found the strain of being a wife and mother led to a nervous breakdown, an experience she fictionalized in 'THE YELLOW WALLPAPER' (1892), but an amicable divorce, and a demanding career as public lecturer and writer, provided a cure.

Out of her lectures came the book *Women and Economics* (1898) which made her famous almost overnight. 'Until we can see what we are, we cannot take steps to become what we should be,' she wrote. Her theory was that, in the distant past, women had been denied their share of human activities by men, forced to lead restricted lives and become 'over-sexed', since their whole existence depended on attracting and keeping a man.

Recognizing that inequality begins in the home, she proposed ending the division between 'men's work' and 'women's work' by abolishing HOUSEWORK. Such jobs as cooking, laundry and childcare would be communal, public work, engaged in by men and women just as they might take any other job, and the home would be a place for rest and play in private. Woman suffrage she saw as one necessary step towards making women economically independent and thus assisting in the progress of the whole human race.

Her other books include *Concerning Children* (1900), *The Home* (1903), *Human Work* (1904), *Man-Made World* (1911), *His Religion and Hers: A Study of the Faith of Our Fathers and the Work of Our Mothers* (1923). From 1909–16 she published a magazine, *The Forerunner*, written almost entirely by herself. In it she published her short stories and utopian novels, including HERLAND, which suggested answers to some of women's problems and offered a glimpse of a non-sexist society. Her autobiography, *The Living of Charlotte Perkins Gilman*, was published after her suicide in 1935. Aware that she was dying of cancer, she chose a quick and easy death over the slow, horrible one offered by nature.

girl

Term which originally meant a child or young person of either sex, gradually came to be applied only to female children, and then by extension to any woman considered young, sexually available, dependent or inferior in status. Just as black men had earlier objected to being called 'boy', women in the 1970s protested that 'girl' was equally demeaning. In 1980s America, this protest appears to have made some impact and the use of 'girl' to refer to an adult is less common; but in Britain men still speak unselfconsciously of the 'girls' who work for or with them.

Goddess

When feminists speak of the Goddess they may mean that they believe in a divine, female being whose presence can be experienced through prayer and ritual; they may be speaking of a symbol of natural forces (birth, life and death); they may be invoking a symbol of female power; or all three. As the feminist priestess Starhawk has said: 'When I feel weak, She is someone who can help and protect me. When I feel strong, She is the symbol of my own power. At other times I feel Her as the natural energy in my body and the world.'

Although the major RELIGIONS of today are male-dominated and offer women a minor role, it was not always so. In *The Paradise Papers* (1976) Merlin Stone uncovered the ancient history of Goddess-worship and showed how it was repressed (but never entirely destroyed) by emerging patriarchal religions. Subsequently she published a two-volume work titled *Ancient Mirrors of Womanhood* (1979) in which she gathered together a body of information about Goddesses worshipped under many names in cultures from all over the world. The Goddess is most frequently associated with fertility, creation, birth and death. Often she appears in the triple aspect of maiden, mother and crone – or youth, creativity, and wisdom. Among the many names given to her are Ashtoreth, Au Set, Anat, Brigit, Coatlicue, Chicomecoatl, Danu, Devi, Hecate, Hera, Innana, Ishtar, Jezanna, Kunapipi, Kybele, Mawu, Mboze, Nu Kwa, Rhea, and Yemanja.

Ancient beliefs and traditions about the Goddess are filtered through the understanding and experiences of modern women to be adapted, accepted or discarded according to their need. Some women have found that Goddess symbols have emerged spontaneously in their dreams and fantasies; others have explored their own heritage to discover alternatives to the usual stereotypes about women.

According to Charlene Spretnak, the most basic meaning of the Goddess is the acknowledgment of the legitimacy of female power. Religions which concentrate on exclusively male images of divinity deny female power, or give the impression that female power is not legitimate. In order to believe that she has been created 'in the image' of the Judaeo Christian God, a woman must deny her own sexual identity. When God is a woman, women can find Her within themselves.

(*See also* WITCHES; SPIRITUAL FEMINISM)

Goegg, Marie, 1826–?1904

Swiss. Early and influential activist for women's rights in Europe, she was the founder and first president of the INTERNATIONAL ASSOCIATION OF WOMEN, in 1868. She founded the bi-monthly *Journal des femmes* in 1870, but it collapsed for lack of popular support after only a few months. After the governmental suppression of the International Association of Women in 1871, Marie Goegg was involved in its reformation under the name *Solidarité* in June 1872. She was elected president in 1875, and re-elected annually until 1880. During her five years as president she published a quarterly newsletter, *Le bulletin de la Solidarité*. For financial reasons, both the organization and the newsletter ceased to exist in 1880. Among her achievements, in 1868 she convinced the International League of Peace and Liberty to admit women members, and in 1872 she presented a petition to the Grand Council of Geneva, asking that women be admitted to the University of Geneva on the same terms as men. Her petition was granted, and in 1876 the first female student enrolled.

Golden Notebook, The

Novel by Doris LESSING first published in 1962. Complex, monumental work about the experiences of Anna Wulf, an intellectual and 'free woman' trying to live a life undefined by men.

Elizabeth Hardwick had said of it that it 'left its mark upon the ideas and feelings of a whole generation of young women.' Although Lessing has objected to it being read *only* as a novel about the sex war, it remains one of the most ambitious and influential novels of the modern women's movement – which in fact it preceded and to some extent predicted.

Goldman, Emma, 1869–1940
Russian-American. Outspoken, frequently arrested anarchist. From 1906 she edited the monthly *Mother Earth*, including in it topics male anarchists had given little attention to, like child-rearing and birth control. Because she was opposed to the current doctrines of social purity and considered women's suffrage just another step towards conformity, feminists of her own time denounced her. Yet she infused ideas of feminism into ANARCHISM, and believed that women must make their own revolution, and seize responsibility for their own lives, as she had done, instead of asking men to make laws to set them free.

Goldstein, Vida, 1869–1949
Australian. A campaigner against social injustice from an early age, during her twenties she studied sociology and economics to try to find the causes of poverty and women's oppression, and from then on she dedicated herself to women's interests. In 1899, she founded a monthly paper, *The Australian Woman's Sphere*, which covered not only local issues, but reprinted articles from women's papers in England and America to keep Australian women in touch with the international women's movement. She became leader of the United Council for Women's Suffrage in 1899, and in 1901 travelled to Washington, D.C. to represent Australia and New Zealand at a women's suffrage conference. Back in Australia, she founded the Women's Federal Political Association in 1903, and stood for the Australian Senate as a feminist opposed to 'narrow and selfish party interests'. Although she won over 50,000 votes, she was not elected, and she attracted a great deal of hostility. However, she continued to stand – always on an independent, feminist platform – three more times before 1917. In 1909 she launched a new paper, *The Woman Voter*. She travelled to England on a speaking tour in 1911, and aided the Women's Social and Political Union, then toured Europe working for the peace campaign. She withdrew from politics only in the last twenty years of her life.

'Goodbye to All That'
Essay by Robin MORGAN, published in the first issue of the women's RAT, 26 January 1970. In precise and angry terms it reveals the sexism prevalent in the NEW LEFT and

explains her reasons for having nothing more to do with any male-dominated movements. It became an instant classic, was widely reprinted, imitated and quoted throughout the women's movement in America.

Gouges, Olympe de
(Marie Gouze), 1748–93

French writer and revolutionary. After an early marriage, she ran away from her husband and children to live by her wits in Paris, where she was soon famous as the author of several successful comedies. Although only semi-literate, she dictated plays and revolutionary pamphlets. A fierce Republican, she founded several women's organizations during the Revolution, including the Club des Tricoteuses. Her *Déclaration des droits de la femme et de la citoyenne*, 1791 (*Declaration of the Rights of Women and Citizens*), modelled on the major document of the French Revolution, roused anti-feminist sentiments against her, and in 1793 she was sent to the guillotine for 'having forgotten the virtues which belong to her sex'.

Gourd, Emilie, 1879–1946

Swiss. Editor of *Le mouvement féministe*, a newspaper which campaigned for better education, legal rights and suffrage for women, as well as a change in public attitudes. She also wrote a biography of Susan B. ANTHONY, and edited a year-book of notable Swiss women.

President of the Swiss Women's Association (1914–28), she was elected Secretary of the International Alliance of Women for Suffrage and Equal Citizenship in 1923.

Gournay, Marie le Jars de, 1566–1645

French writer. Adopted daughter of Montaigne and editor of the definitive edition of his essays, she was also one of the first successful professional women writers. Although ridiculed for being 'unfeminine', her works sold well and were widely read. Among the writings, in which she expressed her idea that the apparent inferiority of women was solely due to the limited education available to girls, were *L'Egalité des hommes et des femmes* (*On the Equality of Men and Women*, 1622) and *Le grief des dames* (*Complaints of the Ladies*, 1626).

Grahn, Judy, 1940–

American poet. The content and style of her poetry were formed by her experience as a lesbian and in the women's movement in the Bay Area of California. She began writing her 'Common Woman' poems in 1969 after joining a consciousness-raising group, and found her own audience without a publisher, by giving the poems to ordinary women and asking for their response. Also in 1969 she was a founding member of The Women's Press Collective, publishing what had previously been considered unpublishable. She has been called the quintessential feminist writer, and her poems explore such basic feminist themes as the issues of power and powerlessness, the meaning of love, and the transformation of language. Her books include *Edward the Dyke* (1971), *The Common Woman Poems* (1974), *A Woman is Talking to Death* (1974), and *The Queen of Wands* (1982). In 1984 *Another Mother Tongue: Gay Words, Gay Worlds* was published, presenting her theory that 'What Americans called Gayness not only has distinct cultural characteristics, its participants have long held positions of social power in history and ritual among people all over the globe.'

Grand, Sarah (pseudonym of Frances McFall), 1854–1943

British novelist. In 1888, with the publication of her first novel, she left her husband and child to move to London, where she became involved in the women's movement of that time. This exposure to feminist friends and ideas led her to write *The Heavenly Twins* (1893), a heartfelt cry for the emancipation of women which became an immediate bestseller. Another novel, *The Beth Book* (1897), is semi-autobiographical, the portrait of the writer as a young woman.

Graves, Robert, 1895–1985

British poet. He tended to worship woman as a superior OTHER, an attitude many would consider distinctly anti-feminist, but some of his writings, particularly *The White Goddess* (1948), are valuable contributions to matriarchal history.

Gray Panthers

American activist organization founded by Maggie Kuhn in Philadelphia in 1972 as a network for the concerns of older people and with the specific aim of eliminating AGEISM. They provide education and action on such issues as media representation of the elderly, a national health service, and nursing home reform. Their slogan is 'Out of the rocking chair, into the street.' (*See also* OLDER WOMEN'S LIBERATION)

Greenham

The term 'Greenham' is sometimes used to mean the women's PEACE MOVEMENT, sometimes, rather vaguely, to mean an emerging women's culture, and sometimes specifically to mean the Women's Peace Camp on Greenham Common, outside the gates of the United States Air Force Base near Newbury, England. It was established in September 1981, the outcome of a 'Women for Life on Earth' march from Cardiff which included a few men as well as about forty women. The camp was established as a public protest and permanent picket against the proposed siting (later accomplished despite massive protests from the public) of the Cruise missile, and it became a woman-only camp after a few weeks, partly a tactical decision and partly a gut reaction on the part of those involved. The women at Greenham Common are probably the most visible and famous aspect of the women's movement in Britain today. Whether Greenham is feminist has been argued, some radical feminists objecting that it is a single-issue struggle which, like similar campaigns in the past, diverts energy from other tasks of immediate importance to women. Some feminists have also objected that Greenham represents the acceptable face of women-only actions, and that once again women are performing their traditional role as the peaceful, emotional (and basically ineffective) caretakers of the whole human race, rather than fighting on their own behalf. Yet many, perhaps most, of the Greenham women would call themselves feminists, and the existence of Greenham provides an inspiring example of women's power, as well as being a way in to the broader women's movement for many. (*See also* PACIFISM)

Greer, Germaine, 1939–
Australian critic, writer and lecturer. The publication of her first book, THE FEMALE EUNUCH (1970) made her internationally famous, and she has been much in the public eye ever since. Yet although the media marked her as a leader of the Women's Liberation Movement, she has never made this claim for herself, and her individual style and penchant for outrageous statements have caused controversy within as well as outside feminist circles. *The Female Eunuch* was a call for a revolution to reclaim women's energy, and although many women have found it inspiring, it is far from being a blue-print for revolution. It does not call upon women to unite, but rather to use their own originality and independence to devise individual forms of revolt. Some considered her later book *Sex and Destiny: The Politics of Human Fertility* (1984) to contradict her earlier ideas of the importance of sexual freedom, but Greer herself has said that the changes in her ideas have been developments rather than changes in direction, many of them coming out of her experience of life in other cultures. She is also the author of a major study of women as artists, THE OBSTACLE RACE (1979).

Griffin, Susan, 1943–
American poet and philosopher. Although she won the Ina Coobbrith Award for poetry in 1963, she remained unpublished until she was able to reach her audience through the establishment of women's presses. Her first collection of poetry was *Dear Sky*, published by Shameless Hussy Press in 1971. In addition to poetry and plays, Griffin has also written non-fiction, and has

become known as a feminist philosopher, author of such books as *Woman and Nature: The Roaring Inside Her* (1978), *Rape, The Power of Consciousness* (1979) and *Pornography and Silence* (1981), which combine her poetic consciousness and use of language with a close examination of our culture. What has emerged from her writings is a mystical, feminist vision, an alternative to the way we traditionally think about nature and human experience. A LESBIAN-FEMINIST, she does not write only for women, and has said that she does not intend to exclude men by her use of the word 'woman', but to invite them to include themselves, since 'it is men who separate themselves from woman and nature'. She sees a particular necessity for reclaiming and uniting the parts of ourselves which are customarily seen as opposed: intellect and emotion, the mind and the body, male and female.

Grimké, Angelina, 1805–79
American. With her sister Sarah GRIMKÉ she was the first woman lecturer for the American Anti-Slavery Society, and raised questions of women's rights in her writings on abolition, which were for the most part directed to women, and included *Appeal to the Christian Women of the South* (1836) and *Appeal to Women of the Nominally Free States* (1837).

Grimké, Sarah, 1792–1873
American. Born and raised in the South, her hatred of slavery caused her to move to Philadelphia in 1821, where she became involved in the abolition movement. Speaking first to all-women sewing circles and then to larger, mixed groups, she and her sister Angelina GRIMKÉ were the first women lecturers for the American Anti-Slavery Society, and as such roused much controversy. Having always felt deeply her oppression as a woman, and believing (unlike most abolitionists) that freedom was as important for women as for men, she wrote LETTERS ON THE EQUALITY OF THE SEXES AND THE CONDITION OF WOMEN (1838), the first sustained argument for women's rights written by an American woman.

Grog, Gina, 1847–1916
Norwegian. Founder of the moderate Norwegian women's movement from 1884, in 1885 she presided over the Kvinnestemmeretsforeningen (Women's Suffrage Society) which had a brief life. In 1895 a new National Women's Suffrage Association (Landekvinnestemmeretsforeningen) was founded, and she led that, too, always from a position of gradual reform. She represented Norway at the first international women's congresses.

Guérillères, Les
Novel by Monique WITTIG published in 1969, it was the first

literary manifestation of the women's liberation movement in France. An English translation was published in 1971. It is an epic celebration of language and the female body which depicts the battle between the sexes in terms of physical warfare, creating a race of Amazons dedicated to ending women's oppression by men. An original and successful combination of poetry and polemic, it was widely praised, and not only in feminist circles. Mary McCarthy called it 'the only work of beauty to come out of Women's Lib'.

gynaesthesia
Word invented by Mary DALY (1978) to mean 'women's synaesthesia' which she defines as 'a complex way of perceiving the interrelatedness of seemingly disparate phenomena . . . a pattern-detecting power which may be named positive paranoia.'

gynarchism
The belief that women will seize power from the PATRIARCHY, establishing a GYNARCHY and thus totally changing all human life for the better.
(*See also* EFFEMINISM)

gynarchy
Government by women, or woman-centred government. A concept similar to MATRIARCHY, and a dream rather than a reality.

Charlotte Perkins GILMAN used the term gynaecocracy. Many feminists dislike such terms, however, feeling that their structure implies hierarchy and the sort of governmental control peculiar to male-dominated institutions. The feminist goal of smashing PATRIARCHY does not include the intention of replacing male dominance with female dominance, as is sometimes imagined by anti-feminists.

gyn ecology
Term 'wrenched back' and re-created from the patriarchal term gynecology (that branch of medicine concerned with diseases in women) by Mary DALY (1978). From gynaeco (relating to women)+ecology (study of relations between living organisms and their environment). In Daly's definition, the new term is used freely 'to describe the science, that is the process of know-ing, of "loose" women who choose to be subjects and not mere objects of enquiry.' Similar to the French term *eco-féminisme*, coined in 1974 by Françoise d'Eaubonne.

Gyn/Ecology
Book, subtitled *The Metaethics of Radical Feminism*, by Mary DALY, first published in America in 1978. Far too complex to be simply summarized or even defined, this is a work combining poetry, mysticism, scholarship, history, religion,

philosophy, anger, outrage and joy, all written in an evolving, GYNO-CENTRIC language in which old words are reclaimed and new words invented to create an alternative to what Daly reveals to have been a very one-sided, PHALLOCENTRIC world-view. The style and language of the book have probably made as great an impact as the content. The author herself calls the book a journey, and says that it is 'about the journey of women becoming, that is, radical feminism'. The implication is that readers of the book can, by taking this journey, free themselves from patriarchal traps and oppression.

Although widely recognized as one of the most original and powerful statements of modern radical feminism, the book has also been criticized for abandoning a real-world struggle with sexism in favour of individual, inner changes, and also (by Audre Lorde) for racism.

gynergy

Term coined by Emily Culpepper (1975) to refer to a new, specifically female spirit or power being developed by the WOMAN-IDENTI-FIED WOMEN.

gynocentric

Woman-centred. Antidote to miso-gynistic (woman-hating) and andro-centric (man-centred) attitudes entrenched in our culture.

gynocentric feminism

Term used by Iris Young (1985) to name what she sees as a relatively new and growing form of femin-ism, in opposition to HUMANIST FEMINISM. It is a critique of the dominant, ANDROCENTRIC culture which questions traditional male values, finding a source of more positive values in women's bodies, traditional activities, and femininity. Young calls Susan GRIF-FIN's *Woman and Nature* (1978) 'one of the first written statements of a gynocentric feminism in the second wave', and also sees the work of Mary DALY and Carol GILLIGAN as contributing to the development of this new, woman-centred analysis. Whereas humanist feminism opposes the idea of GENDER distinc-tion as oppressive and claims the importance of our common humanity, gynocentric feminism asserts that there is a basic difference between male and female and that women have been oppressed because their femininity has been denied. This type of thought has also been called FEMININISM, ESSEN-TIALISM, and CULTURAL FEMINISM.

gynocritics

(from French *la gynocritique*)
Term coined in 1978 by Elaine SHOWALTER to identify the type of feminist criticism concerned with the woman as writer; with the his-tory, psychology, structure, langu-age and meaning of literature written by women.

H

Hagan, Ellen, 1873–1958
Swedish journalist. A committed
feminist all her life, in 1903 she
founded the Uppsala Suffrage
Society, and was a member of the
Central Board of the Federation for
Women's Suffrage until 1922. She
edited the women's magazine
Tiderarvet.

Hainisch, Marianne, 1839–1936
Austrian writer and educator. From
the 1860s she devoted her life to
improving the material situation
and legal rights of women, at first
concentrating chiefly on the cause
of higher education and women's
need to be financially self-supporting, founding her own public
school and writing books on the
subject. President of the General
Austrian Women's Association
(Allgemeiner Osterreichischer
Frauenverein) from 1899, she led
campaigns to reform marriage
laws, abolish legal prostitution, and
win the vote. She combined her
feminism with pacifism, and
campaigned against World War I.
Author of several books about
women, she also contributed to
many feminist journals.

Hale, Sarah Josepha, 1788–1879
American journalist. A cautious,
conservative feminist, she exhorted
women to improve themselves and
campaigned for better education,
but did not believe women should
compete with men in the political
arena. Her influence as writer, educator and philanthropist was most
strongly felt through her role as
editor of the *Ladies' Magazine* from
1828, in which she continued when
it became *Godey's Lady's Book* in
1837. She was also the author of a
compilation of over 1,000 biographies of women called *Women's
Record: or Sketches of all distinguished
Women, from the Creation to AD 1654*
(1855).

Halimi, Gisèle, 1927–
French lawyer. Co-founder, with
Simone DE BEAUVOIR, of Choisir, a
feminist legal reform group created
in 1971 to protect women who
admitted to having had illegal abortions, and committed to changing
abortion laws. Author of *La cause
des femmes* (1973) and a contributor
to *Le programme commun des femmes*
(1978), which listed women's chief
legal, medical, educational and professional needs and suggested solutions, she has frequently acted as
counsel in cases related to women's
issues. In 1981 she was elected to the
National Assembly as an Independent Socialist.

Hallinan, Hazel Hunkins,
  1890–1982
American. Became a convert to feminism in 1916, when she founded a branch of the NATIONAL WOMAN'S PARTY in Billings, Montana, and travelled to take part in demonstrations for women's suffrage throughout the United States. In 1920 she moved to London, where she became a member of the SIX POINT GROUP, and worked as a determined campaigner for women's rights until the end of her life.

Hamer, Fannie Lou, 1918–77
American. She became involved as a political activist through the Student Non-Violent Co-ordinating Committee in 1961, and from then until the end of her life she was an influential organizer and protester in the civil rights movement and a powerful inspiration to the burgeoning women's liberation movement. She ran for Congress in 1964, and in 1971 she was elected to the Central Committee of the National Women's Political Caucus.

Hamilton, Cicely, 1872–1952
British writer. Founder, with Bessie Hatton, of the Women Writers' Suffrage League in 1908. A frequent contributor to TIME AND TIDE and a playwright as well as, briefly, an actress, she is best remembered for her book *Marriage as a Trade* (1909) which expressed her view that most women married not for love but because it was the only career they were allowed; and that men have denied women autonomy in order to make themselves necessary to women.

Harper, Frances Watkins,
  1825–1911
American. The first Afro-American woman novelist, and the most popular woman poet of her day, she was an activist within the abolition, temperance and women's rights movements. She gave her first speech in New Bedford, Massachusetts in 1854, on the subject of 'The Education and Elevation of the Colored Race', and after that was always in demand as a lecturer. After the Civil War, she travelled around the southern States, holding meetings exclusively for black women, whom she recognized as the most oppressed of all groups. Her poems are highly emotional and political, frequently treating the experience of slavery from the woman's point of view. They were collected as *Forest Leaves* (1854), *Poems on Miscellaneous Subjects* (1854) and *The Martyr of Alabama and other poems* (1894). She wrote the first novel to depict life during Reconstruction, *Iola Leroy; or, Shadows Uplifted* (1892), as well as *Sketches of Southern Life* (1872).

Harper, Ida Husted, 1851–1931
American journalist. Best known as the biographer of Susan B.

ANTHONY, and editor of the final three volumes of the HISTORY OF WOMAN SUFFRAGE, she was a highly praised journalist and speaker, active in the women's movement for most of her life. She began her journalistic career in secret from a disapproving husband, for twelve years writing a weekly column entitled 'A Woman's Opinions' under a pseudonym in the *Terre Haute Saturday Evening Mail*. When her marriage ended in divorce in 1890, she accepted the position of editor-in-chief on the *Terre Haute Daily News*, and later joined the staff of the *Indianapolis News*. From 1887 she was the secretary of the Indiana state suffrage society, and in 1896 was selected by Susan B. Anthony to handle press relations during the campaign for California state suffrage. In 1897 she moved into Susan B. Anthony's home in Rochester, New York, to collaborate with her on the fourth volume of the *History of Woman Suffrage*, and began work on *Life and Work of Susan B. Anthony*, published in two volumes in 1898, with a third volume added in 1908. From 1899–1903 she edited a woman's column in the New York *Sunday Sun*, and from 1909–13 a woman's page in *Harper's Bazaar*. She was in charge of national publicity during the final stages of the National American Woman Suffrage Association's successful campaign for passage of a woman suffrage amendment, 1916–18. In the last years of her life she was active in the American Association of University Women, as well as completing the official record of the woman suffrage movement.

Hays, Mary, 1760–1843

English writer. A radical free-thinker, she was a close friend and feminist contemporary of Mary Wollstonecraft. Her novels, *The Memoirs of Emma Courtney* (1796) and *Victim of Prejudice* (1799), explored the horrors faced by women unprotected by wealth or status, and the difficulties even an educated woman faced if she wanted economic independence. Her *Appeal to the Men of Great Britain on Behalf of the Women* (1798) followed Wollstonecraft's VINDICATION as an argument for freedom and equality between the sexes, and she published a six-volume *Dictionary of Female Biography* (1803).

Hayward Annual II

Exhibition of contemporary British art held 23 August–8 October 1978 in the Hayward Gallery, London. It was the first event sponsored by the Arts Council of Great Britain that was organized and selected by an all-woman panel, and although it was not an all-woman or overtly feminist show, the intent behind it was to establish a positive precedent for the future. By admitting a bias towards women (the panel chose work by sixteen women and seven men) they hoped to reveal the far more common, but unexpressed, bias behind all previous exhibitions: for example, the all-male jury for the first Hayward Annual chose twenty-nine men and only one woman.

Selectors, who also exhibited, were Rita Donagh, Tess Jaray, Liliane Lijn, Gillian Wise Ciobotaru and Kim Lim. The other artists were Sandra Blow, Sue Beere, Pamela Burns, Marc Camille Chaimowicz, Stephen Cox, Susan Derges, Elisabeth Frink, Julia Farrer, Steve Furlonger, Alexis Hunter, Susan HILLER, Mary KELLY, Edwina Leapman, Leopoldo Maler, Adrian Morris, Terry Pope, Deanna Petherbridge, Michael Sandle and Wendy Taylor.

(*See also* ART AND ARTISTS)

health movement

Although there have always been women who struggled against male authority to keep women informed about their own bodies and health, and to offer some alternative to traditional medical practice (many of the women called WITCHES were healers and midwives), this did not become an actual movement until the late 1960s, when it began gathering force in the United States.

The women's health movement is international in scope, but far from being a monolithic organization, it is a diverse movement composed of many thousands of small, local groups and many tens of thousands more individuals, sharing feminist aims and committed to changing the way sickness and health are regarded and managed. The work done by participants in the movement falls into three basic categories: changing consciousness through education and the spread of information; providing health-related services to women; and struggling in a variety of ways to change established health institutions. Some will concentrate on one area – for example, meeting as a study and discussion group to learn about women's health, or publishing a book such as OUR BODIES, OUR SELVES – while larger organizations might publish a newsletter, provide birth control and pregnancy-testing services, and lobby for changes in laws affecting health-care, thus working on all fronts.

Some of the major issues of the Women's Liberation Movement, such as REPRODUCTIVE FREEDOM and the related issues of ABORTION and BIRTH CONTROL, are concerned not only with legal rights, but also with women's health, and the way women's lives have been dictated and prescribed by the male-run medical establishment. As feminists in the late 1960s and early 1970s organized around campaigns to reform or abolish abortion legislation and discovered through consciousness-raising sessions that personal gynaecological horror stories were part of a larger pattern, it was inevitable that health came to be seen as one of the most important issues of women's liberation. Barbara Ehrenreich and Deirdre English have written extensively on 'the sexual politics of sickness', pointing out that, as the guardian of reproductive technology, birth control, abortion and the means for safer childbirth, the medical establishment is central to women's oppression.

An early milestone of the women's health movement which might be seen as its birth as a revolutionary movement, was the 'invention' of self-help gynaecology. Feminists in Los Angeles had been meeting for some months to discuss health issues when on 7 April 1971, Carol Downer transformed theoretical discussion to empirical observation by inserting a speculum into her vagina and inviting the other women to examine her cervix. By using a speculum and a mirror, women could examine their own sexual organs, and the results were almost overwhelming. Seeing their vaginas for the first time, women felt a new sense of wholeness and power, having reclaimed a part of their anatomy which had previously seemed reserved for male observation. They could also learn to recognize early symptoms and take preventive measures against common infections, instead of having to rely on the judgments of male experts. Self-examination was demonstrated in September 1971, at the national meeting of NOW, and Carol Downer, Lorraine Rothman and Coleen Wilson travelled throughout the country to demonstrate. Their work was publicized in VAGINAL POLITICS (1972) by Ellen FRANKFORT, and the self-help aspect of the women's health movement spread rapidly to other countries. By 1975, self-examination had been demonstrated in Belgium, Canada, Denmark, England, France, Germany, Italy, Mexico, New Zealand and Northern Ireland.

That the feminist attitude towards health and medicine had a truly revolutionary potential is clear not only from the personal experiences of the women involved, but from the reaction of legal and medical authorities who recognized the threat posed by the women's health movement.

In Los Angeles, the Feminist Women's Health Center was put under police surveillance early in 1972, and on 20 September 1972, ten police officers entered the center with search warrants and arrested Carol Downer and Coleen Wilson. Downer was charged with practising medicine without a licence, for the specific crime of helping another woman apply yoghurt to her cervix as a cure for monilia. Downer's trial roused the emotions and support of feminists from all over the country. On 5 December 1972, she was acquitted by a jury of eight men and four women, but, as Jeanne Hirsch wrote afterwards in THE MONTHLY EXTRACT: 'What man would be put under police surveillance for six months for looking at his penis? What man would have to spend $20,000 and two months in court for looking at the penis of his brother? This case is a clear-cut version of the position of women in America . . .'

The situation in Britain is somewhat different, both because there are no laws to stop women helping or treating each other (except in the case of dangerous drugs or abortion) and because the existence of the National Health Service means that poor women do not face discrimination and lack of care as they do in the United States. But women in Britain face the same problems created by a male-controlled medical establishment which is organized towards treatment instead of prevention, and which prefers to keep patients in a position of docile ignorance. The vast majority of health workers in Britain are women, and women are also in the majority of those who use health care facilities, but their role within the system is one of service, not power. Everywhere that it exists, the women's health movement has the purpose of empowering women by making them more knowledgeable about their bodies, and giving them the ability to use that knowledge not only to make their own lives better, but also to change society.

Heilbrun, Carolyn G., 1926–
American. Professor of English Literature and author, under the pseudonym Amanda Cross, of witty novels about the exploits of professor/detective Kate Fansler. She contributed substantially to the creation of a feminist ideal of ANDROGYNY with her book *Toward a Recognition of Androgyny* (1973).

he/man language
Term used to describe the most obvious and pervasive instance of sexism in LANGUAGE: the use of the masculine PRONOUN (he, him) as a generic, and the use of the words MAN or mankind for the whole human race.

Henry, Alice, 1857–1943
Australian. From the mid-1880s, she became one of Australia's leading journalists. An active campaigner and lecturer on behalf of women's trade union movements and women's suffrage, she was also involved in many charitable projects, as well as radical women writers' clubs. In 1905 she moved to the United States where she was prominent in the women's movement, particularly in trade unions, and she continued to write articles and books for many years, finally returning to Australia in 1933.

Heresies
New York-based, quarterly periodical founded in 1977, devoted to

the examination of art and politics from a feminist perspective.

Herland
Novel by Charlotte Perkins GIL-MAN, first published in 1915, it takes a positive, humorous look at an all-female UTOPIA. By the end of the book, the three American men who stumble upon Herland have learned to perceive women as people first of all, and not simply as females.

Hernandez, Aileen, 1926–
American urban consultant. Long involved in civil rights and labour movements, she was appointed the head of the Equal Opportunity Commission by Lyndon Johnson in 1965, but soon resigned, frustrated by the bureaucracy and lack of progress. She was one of the original founders of the NATIONAL ORGANIZATION FOR WOMEN (NOW) and was elected its president in 1970. She was concerned, during her time in office, to change NOW's image as an elitist, middle-class organization and make it more relevant to the needs of working-class women. In 1973 she founded Black Women for Action, an organization which has filed suits in sex-discrimination cases and formed a feminist credit union.

Herschberger, Ruth, 1917–
American. A feminist at a time when there was no active women's movement, she wrote *Adam's Rib* (1948), a witty protest against sexual stereotyping.

herstory
Term used – sometimes seriously, sometimes jokingly – for women's history, and to point up the fact that what is presented as our history is all too often simply 'his story'. This, although a valid and witty comment, is sometimes perceived as an etymological misunderstanding, since the word history is derived from the Latin *historia* and has no connection at all with the English word 'his'. Mary DALY, who frequently uses word-play to make serious points herself, believes this term fails because it sounds like an imitation and has 'an "odor" of mere reactive manoeuvering, which is humiliating to women.' The word was first used in print by Robin MORGAN in January 1970 when, in the by-line to her article 'GOODBYE TO ALL THAT', she identified herself as a member of WITCH or 'Women Inspired to Commit Herstory'.

Heterodoxy
Discussion group and luncheon club for feminists in New York between 1912 and 1940. Members included Elizabeth Gurley FLYNN, Crystal EASTMAN and Inez IRWIN. It was founded by suffragist Marie Jenney Howe to enable 'unorthodox' women to meet and discuss their views on a variety of topics.

heterosexism
Term which followed the widespread use of SEXISM, it refers to

prejudice against or ignorance of an alternative to heterosexuality and the prevailing heterosexual life style; often revealed in unconscious assumptions made by individuals who would not consciously discriminate against homosexuals. For example, many historians are aware that sexist attitudes have distorted our perception of history. They have attempted to put it right by exploring and including the different experiences of women and by not assuming that male experiences and values stand for all human ones. Even a non-sexist history may be heterosexist, however, in its unquestioned, underlying assumptions; for example, that all women are motivated by an innate desire for men and marriage.

(*See also* COMPULSORY HETERO-SEXUALITY)

heterosexuality

The idea that heterosexuality is a social institution used, like MAR-RIAGE and the family, as an instrument to keep women oppressed, and not simply a natural impulse or matter of choice, was introduced in the mid-1970s in the writings of lesbian feminists including Charlotte BUNCH and Rita Mae BROWN. In *Compulsory Heterosexuality and Lesbian Existence* (1980), Adrienne RICH argued that for feminists to fail to examine heterosexuality as an institution is 'like failing to admit that the economic system called capitalism or the caste system of racism is maintained by a variety of forces, including both physical violence and false consciousness.'

For the most part, theoretical considerations of heterosexuality as an oppressive institution have been written by lesbian feminists, with the conclusion, either implied or stated, that heterosexual relationships should be rejected on a personal level. One of the most famous statements of this kind was a paper by the Leeds Revolutionary Feminists, published in LOVE YOUR ENEMY? (1981). Their 'Case Against Heterosexuality' defined heterosexuality as the fundamental means by which male domination over women was maintained, and declared that heterosexual women, even heterosexual feminists, were collaborators who undermined their own feminist activities by giving energy and support to the enemy: men. They called upon all women to give up heterosexual relationships and become POLITICAL LESBIANS.

Although many feminists, both lesbian and heterosexual, objected to the position taken by the Leeds Revolutionary Feminists, no one (as Paula Jennings pointed out in *Love Your Enemy?*) responded by attempting to refute the theory that heterosexuality was the cornerstone of male supremacy. No counter-theory was offered to describe how emotional/sexual relationships with men might contribute to feminist revolution.

Not all feminists do accept the idea that men are the enemy and that heterosexual sex (specifically, penetration) is both symbolic and actual oppression of women. For those who consider feminism a movement to end SEXISM and thus transform society so as to eradicate all forms of group oppression, men can be seen as at least potentially comrades in the struggle. Women unwilling or unable to envision SEPARATISM as a desirable goal usually consider it worthwhile trying to change men on an individual basis, and to fight to change patterns of sexual oppression in the bedroom as well as in society at large by working with and loving men.

Many heterosexual feminists, perhaps because of the conflict between personal desires and political beliefs, prefer to consider their sexuality either as an unquestioned given, or as a personal choice which does not affect the rest of their lives. Of course, this contradicts the most basic feminist insight that the PERSONAL IS POLITICAL. Christine DELPHY (1984) has written that only someone who 'sees a split between what goes on inside and outside people's heads' could imagine that interpersonal relationships are unaffected by social determinants, solely a matter of feelings, and yet 'It is not surprising that we frequently come across such idealist and individualistic arguments, since

these are the dominant ideologies of our society.'

In constructing an analysis of male domination, feminists cannot afford to leave anything unquestioned, no matter how difficult. Bell HOOKS (1984) has warned feminists to 'take care that our legitimate critiques of HETEROSEXISM are not attacks on heterosexual *practice*,' pointing out that feminism will never appeal to a mass-based group of women if they feel they are looked down on for their sexual preference, and to succeed, feminism *must* be a mass movement. Heterosexuality should not be proscribed as politically incorrect, but it must, always, be questioned and criticized. Adrienne Rich has pointed the way in her examination of another institution which oppresses women, yet which many women consider to be a personal choice: MOTHERHOOD. Just as it is possible to differentiate between the institution of motherhood, created by the PATRIARCHY to oppress women, and the experience, which many women find creative, fulfilling and joyful, so it should be possible to criticize the institution of heterosexuality without banning the enjoyment of it.

(*See also* COMPULSORY HETEROSEXUALITY; LESBIAN FEMINISM; SEXUALITY)

Heymann, Lida Gustava,
1868–1943

German. During the 1890s she was

active in voluntary social work, using her inherited fortune to found a progressive kindergarten, a school to train women as clerks, and various societies for women, including a lunch club for single women, and clubs for actresses and office workers. In 1898 she led a campaign against the state regulation of prostitution. From 1902 to the end of her life her career in feminism was closely linked with that of Anita AUGSPURG and Minna CAUER. With them and others she founded the Deutscher Verband für Frauenstimmrecht (German Union for Women's Suffrage), and became a member of the International Woman Suffrage Alliance in 1904. Always a pacifist, she attended the first International Women's Congress at the Hague in 1915. Her activities in the peace movement caused her trouble during World War I: she was officially expelled from Bavaria in 1917, and had to go into hiding. In 1919 she became vice-president of the League for Peace and Freedom. Although her radicalism isolated her from the majority of the German women's movement, with Cauer and Augspurg she continued to work with the international women's movement until her death.

Higginson, Thomas Wentworth, 1823–1911

American journalist. Abolitionist and activist for women's rights who gave stirring speeches at many American women's rights conventions. Author of *Woman and Her Wishes* (1851) and *Women and Men* (1888).

Hiller, Susan, 1940–

American-born artist resident in England since 1967. Trained as an anthropologist, she is a visual artist who has worked in a variety of media, including slides and video, both alone and in groups for performed art events. Her 'Fragments' (shown in the HAYWARD ANNUAL II) focused attention on broken pieces of pottery made by Pueblo Indian women, with the implication that (male) anthropologists had underestimated the contributions of women to culture. She has often expressed her feelings of being 'marginal' as a woman in a male-dominated society which lacks a specifically female language, and she considers art one way of finding that language to express the perceptions of more than half the population.

Hippel, Theodor Gottlieb von, 1741–96

Prussian civic administrator and author of *Über die bürgerliche Verbesserung der Weiber* (*On Improving the Status of Women*), published in 1792, which is regarded as beginning the feminist debate in Germany. In an earlier book, *Über die Ehe* (*On Marriage*), published first in 1774, Hippel expressed the view that women belonged to a separate sphere as wives and mothers. However, his own legal experience showed him how women were discriminated against, and, under the influence of the French novelist and historian Louise Keralio, and the philosophical writings of David Hume and his friend Immanuel Kant, Hippel gradually became convinced that women had been wronged, and changed his argument in subsequent editions of *Über die Ehe*. In *Über die bürgerliche Verbesserung der Weiber* Hippel called for full political, educational and professional employment opportunities for women: 'Why should not women be persons? Why should not a woman pronounce the word I?'

history

History as we know it was defined and written by men, based on the unspoken, unquestioned assumption that what men do is more significant than the activities or experiences of women. Traditional history might as well be called 'men's history', for in it only the very exceptional or deviant woman ever appears except in the role of wife or mother, and the male experience is presumed to be the human norm. This attitude has been questioned in the past, and women's constant contribution to history written about by Matilda Joslyn GAGE, Mary Ritter BEARD and others, but not until the rise of the women's liberation movement in the late 1960s did the idea that

women had a history – and that it might be completely different from that of men – really take hold.

The first effort of the new feminist historians was to discover the women who were missing from history. This search often led to women who had been famous or influential in their own time although they were obscured, misrepresented or simply ignored by male historians. But simply fitting women into a male-defined framework is not sufficient to develop the field of women's history. The attempt to fit women in led to an awareness of the limitations of the traditional questions asked of history, and therefore to a search for new questions, new concepts, and a new framework which would reveal not women's place in men's history, but women's own history.

Some of the traditions of men's history may distort that of women. For example, the division of history into periods based on political changes, revolutions, war or conquests, while it may reflect meaningful changes in the lives of men, may be meaningless in the lives of women. Eras remembered as particularly progressive may have been so for men, but repressive for women. For example, the Renaissance provided new opportunities and knowledge for men, but recent studies have shown that women were under greater restraints and restrictions at this time than they had been in earlier centuries. A woman's renaissance would look very different and might not be recognized unless new questions – such as questions about the links between sexuality and reproduction, between child-bearing and child-rearing – never asked of men, became a standard part of the historical approach.

Gerda LERNER, who has been working since the early 1960s to legitimize the concept of women's history, has said that women's history is not simply a field of study, but is also a methodology, a strategy for offsetting the usual male bias, a world-view and 'an angle of vision which permits us to see that women live and have lived in a world defined by men and most frequently dominated by men and yet have shaped and influenced that world and all human events'.

Women's history cannot be written as the history of a minority and then added on to men's history to create a whole, human history, for the simple fact that women are not a minority, and no single methodology will fit the historical experience of all women. Women throughout history have been oppressed, but they have also been oppressors, members of every class, race and ethnic group. As Gerda Lerner has said, 'The key to understanding women's history is in accepting – painful though it may be – that it is the history of the *majority* of humankind.'

History of Woman Suffrage

Six-volume compilation of reports, speeches, arguments, newspaper articles, letters and personal recollections; the classic reference work on the women's suffrage movement in the United States, 1848–1920. Volume One (1848–61) by Elizabeth Cady STANTON, Susan B. ANTHONY and Matilda Joslyn GAGE was published in 1881; Volume Two (1861–76) followed in 1882; Volume Three (1876–85) by Susan B. Anthony was published in 1887; Volume Four (1885–1900) by Susan B. Anthony and Ida Husted HARPER, was published in 1902; and Volumes Five and Six (1900–20) by Ida Husted Harper, were published in 1922.

The chief inspiration, financial support and moving force behind the whole project was Susan B. Anthony. From the beginning a collector of documents relating to the women's movement, in 1876 she proposed to Elizabeth Cady Stanton and Matilda Joslyn Gage that they compile a 'small volume' to preserve the historical record as an inspiration and guide for subsequent generations of feminists. Their work, which soon expanded beyond such modest confines, was to be presented as a gift to as many libraries, universities, schools and women's organizations as possible. Anthony poured all her own savings into the project, and in 1886 received a bequest of $25,000 which enabled her to continue the work.

The early volumes mingle the personal with the political, presenting character studies of the women's rights pioneers as well as reporting on their activities, but the later volumes, organized by professional researchers, minimized the personal to report almost entirely on tactics, strategies and campaigns used to win the vote.

Although still of great interest today, the *History* does not present a totally accurate picture of the American women's suffrage movement. It is biased and, despite its length, incomplete. The split in 1869 which resulted in the formation of two rival organizations, the NATIONAL WOMAN SUFFRAGE ASSOCIATION and the AMERICAN WOMAN SUFFRAGE ASSOCIATION, was practically ignored, and the activities of Anthony's own National Woman Suffrage Association represented as if it were the women's movement in its entirety.

Holloway Brooch

Badge of honour designed by Sylvia PANKHURST in 1909 as an award to be given to members of the WOMEN'S SOCIAL AND POLITICAL UNION who had been imprisoned for the cause. It consisted of an arrow-shape (like those on prisoners' clothes) in WSPU colours of purple, white and green, mounted on a portcullis ending in five toothed projections, with silver chains hanging down either side.

Holtby, Winifred, 1898–1935

English writer. Author of seven novels (the most popular, *South Riding*, was published posthumously in 1936), as well as short stories, poetry and criticism, she also wrote an analysis of women's position in contemporary society, *Women and a Changing Civilization* (1934). A prolific journalist, she wrote for many papers and magazines, including *Time and Tide*, of which she became a director in 1926. The subjects closest to her heart were feminism, pacifism, and inter-race relationships. In an article for the *Yorkshire Post* she wrote, 'I am a feminist because I dislike everything that feminism implies. I desire an end of the whole business . . . but while the inequality exists, while injustice is done and opportunity denied to the great majority of women, I shall have to be a feminist with the motto Equality First.' Her lifelong friend Vera Brittain wrote of her, 'Never having found it a disadvantage to be a woman, she brought to the service of women ideas which were positive and constructive.'

Holyoake, George Jacob, 1817–1906

British. A follower of Robert Owen, friend to the LANGHAM PLACE GROUP and author of many articles taking a feminist stance, he considered himself a spiritual father of the women's movement.

homosexuality
See LESBIANISM

Hooks, Bell (pseudonym of Gloria Watkins), 1952–
American academic. An advocate of anti-racist, anti-sexist, anti-capitalist politics, she is the author of two important theoretical works: AIN'T I A WOMAN: *Black Women and Feminism* (1981) and *Feminist Theory: From Margin to Center* (1984). In the latter book she contends that feminist theory lacks adequate class and race analysis since most of it has been written by middle-class whites 'at the center' who are unaware of the reality of life on the 'margins'. She attempts to create a new feminist paradigm which would recognize sexism as part of a larger problem, with domination in all its forms (whether sexual, racial, by class or by age) seen as the root of all oppression.
(*See also* BLACK FEMINISM)

Hot Wire
Subtitled *Journal of Women's Music and Culture*, this American magazine was founded in 1984 by a feminist organization called NOT JUST A STAGE and is published three times a year. Its aims are to focus on women's culture and women's creativity, to circulate information, to provide access to print for women writers, artists and photographers, and to inspire and 'work within the woman-identified women-in-print movement,

choosing women to do the work every step of the way.'

housewives
See DISPLACED HOMEMAKERS; HOUSEWORK

housework
Often perceived as trivial, housework has been recognized by feminists as a key theoretical problem, one which must be solved if equality between women and men is ever to be possible. It should be defined, as Christine DELPHY has explained, as a work relationship rather than as a set of particular tasks. The individual tasks – cooking, cleaning, laundry, CHILDCARE, etc. – are jobs which people are paid for; doing those things for oneself is also valued if otherwise one would have to pay someone else for the service. Housework, therefore, can be defined as any and all work done, unpaid, for others within a household.

This is, traditionally, 'woman's work', and changing that situation may prove to be more difficult, and more revolutionary, than to break down the barriers that have in the past kept women out of 'men's work'.

It is one of the underpinnings of the capitalist system: women as an unpaid labour force function to maintain the paid labour force, and thus keep wages down and profits up since otherwise society would have to provide these services.

Marxists have usually assumed that, after the revolution, the family would wither away along with other capitalist institutions – that change at the point of production would be followed by change at the point of reproduction – but there is no evidence that this is the case. In Russia, just as in America, working woman have felt the burden of the 'DOUBLE-SHIFT', by which they are expected to take all or most of the responsibility for cooking, cleaning and other household tasks.

One way of abolishing housework is to take it out of the private sphere by making it communal. This has been tried to a certain extent in China, and has long been a theme in theoretical and utopian writings. Many people in our society react against the idea of public dining-rooms or child-care centres because institutions like the army, orphanages and state schools have demonstrated group living at its most unpleasant. But if affectionate cooperation – love, rather than money – was behind the industrialization of housework, just as it is meant to be in the private home, then community dining-halls and child-care centres could be far more efficient, attractive and comfortable than the situation found in most nuclear families.

Moving from theory into immediate action, there have been campaigns such as WAGES FOR HOUSEWORK which attempt to ensure that women will be compensated for their time and effort, and at the same time, by validating housework as 'real work', would raise the status and self-esteem of homemakers.

Individually, many women have fought against the FEMININE MYSTIQUE or the superwoman complex in order to gain a more realistic set of expectations. The idea of contracts for housework became popular in the late 1960s: the tasks necessary to keep a household going were listed on a daily, weekly or monthly basis and then divided between partners or among all the members of a household. As Pat Mainardi pointed out in her paper 'The Politics of Housework' (1970), most men will resist such a contract, which means a loss in leisure time for them, either openly, by declaring women are better at housework, like it more, have higher standards etc., or more subtly, by doing only the tasks they prefer, or promising to 'help' but insisting housework is too trivial and boring to talk about or keep records of. This is the sort of psychological pressure and social attitude which keeps housework invisible and contributes to women's oppression.

(*See also* DISPLACED HOMEMAKERS; GILMAN, CHARLOTTE P; OAKLEY, ANN)

Housman, Laurence, 1865–1959 British author. Pacifist and adherent of the New Humanism, he believed that a change in the relations between men and women was essential to improve the world and fulfil women's potential. Wrote a one-act suffrage play called *Alice in Ganderland*.

Houston
See NATIONAL WOMEN'S CONFERENCE

Howe, Julia Ward, 1819–1910
American. The author of 'The Battle Hymn of the Republic' was also a greatly admired and respected feminist who worked for women's suffrage from the 1860s. She believed that if women freed themselves from male domination they could use their greater moral strength to achieve world peace. Her 'Appeal to Womanhood Throughout the World' was translated into five languages, and resulted in the formation of a World's Congress of Women.

How-Martyn, Edith, 1880–1954
English. Secretary of the WOMEN'S SOCIAL AND POLITICAL UNION until she left with Charlotte DESPARD and Teresa BILLINGTON-GRIEG in 1907 to found the WOMEN'S FREEDOM LEAGUE. After the vote had been won she stood for Parliament and lost, then in 1919 became the first woman member of the Middlesex County Council. She was the Honorary Director of the Birth Control International Information Centre, travelled all over the world lecturing on the subject, and wrote *The Birth Control Movement in England* (1931). She moved to Australia in 1939 where she continued to work for and lecture on women's rights.

humanist feminism
Term used by Iris Young (1985) for the type of feminism which 'defines women's oppression as the inhibition and distortion of women's human potential by a society that allows the self-development of men.' This type of feminism – the dominant type until very recently – she describes as favouring a sexual EQUALITY which would judge men and women by a single standard: the standard men have established to judge each other. Humanist feminism rejects FEMININITY and considers GENDER difference 'accidental to humanity'. In opposition to it is GYNOCENTRIC FEMINISM. She sees these two types of feminism as cutting across the more traditional divisions of feminism into RADICAL FEMINISM, SOCIALIST FEMINISM and LIBERAL FEMINISM.

hunger strikes
A form of protest taken by the militant SUFFRAGETTES in Britain when imprisoned for their activities. Forcible feedings outraged the public and attracted much sympathy for the victims, winning funds and converts to the cause of women's suffrage. In response the government passed the CAT AND MOUSE ACT.

Hunt, Harriot, 1805–75
American doctor. Long a campaigner for women's rights to education and careers and for racial equality, she protested against her lack of the vote every time she paid her taxes. In 1843 she organized a Ladies' Physiological Society in Boston, and she tried to help women develop more self-esteem as a means of conquering nervous illnesses. She had been a practising physician for eighteen years when the Female Medical College of Pennsylvania awarded her an honorary MD in 1853.

I

Ibsen, Henrik, 1828–1906
Norwegian dramatist. His 'problem plays' were serious, searching examinations of the problems of the individual confronted by the restrictions of society, and he had a particular sympathy for women trapped by marriage and the conventions of a man-made world. His A DOLL'S HOUSE (1879) in particular awakened many women to recognize themselves in Nora's plight.

Ichikawa, Fusae, 1893–
Japanese politician. Founded the Association of New Women in 1919 to work for women's labour unions and equal legal and political rights for women. While studying in the United States she met American feminists including Carrie Chapman CATT and Alice PAUL, and upon her return to Japan in 1924 she founded the Women's Suffrage Alliance. Despite failure to achieve suffrage in the 1920s, she continued to campaign for women's issues throughout the 1930s. In 1946 she founded the Women's Suffrage Centre and was elected head of the New Japan Women's League. In 1952 she was elected to the Upper House of Councillors in the Japanese Diet, and served for eighteen years. In 1974 she was returned with the support of women's groups, and was re-elected in 1980 with more votes than any other candidate.

Ignota
Pen-name used by Sylvia PANK-HURST for her articles on women's affairs appearing in the *Westminster Review*, 1906–7.

'I'm not a feminist but. . .' syndrome
Mental state of women who have become aware that SEXISM exists, that they suffer from it, and that feminism – or something exactly like it but preferably with a different name – must be necessary, yet are afraid of being mistaken for one of the ugly, humourless, dogmatic, man-hating lesbians who are labelled feminists.

imperial feminism
Term used by Valerie Amos and Pratibha Parmar in their article, 'Challenging Imperial Feminism', in *Feminist Review* 17 (1984) to identify white, Eurocentric, MAINSTREAM FEMINISM. The word 'imperial' invokes 'imperialism' to stress that this sort of feminism, which presents itself as the only feminism, has emerged from imperialist nations and retains im-

perialist, racist traditions which alienate and oppress non-white and Third World women.

(*See also* BLACK FEMINISM)

In a Different Voice
See GILLIGAN, CAROL

IndiAnna, Zane
Fictional character, the revolutionary feminist who tells her life story in BURNING QUESTIONS, a novel by Alix Kates Shulman published in 1978.

individualist feminism
A form of LIBERAL FEMINISM also referred to (negatively) as BOURGEOIS FEMINISM or (positively, in America) as MAINSTREAM FEMINISM. Its basic value is freedom: the capacity of individuals, given equal political and civil rights, to make their own choices and shape their own futures. A middle-class, reformist position, it does not question the status quo, but accepts the values and goals of privileged, white males as being desirable for women. Betty FRIEDAN's writings provide a good example of modern individualist feminist thought.

International Alliance of Women for Suffrage and Equal Citizenship
See INTERNATIONAL WOMAN SUFFRAGE ALLIANCE

International Association of Women (Association Internationale des Femmes)
Founded by Marie GOEGG in 1868 and based in Geneva. Fifteen different associations, from Switzerland, England, America, Germany, France, Italy and Portugal, were represented at its first congress, held in March 1870. It had the support of many prominent feminists throughout the world, including Elizabeth Cady STANTON in America and Luise OTTO-PETERS in Germany. Among its activities the Association petitioned the Spanish government for women's suffrage; cooperated with Josephine BUTLER in opposing the CONTAGIOUS DISEASES ACTS in Britain; and campaigned in Italy for education to be provided for girls. The International Association of Women was destroyed in 1871 by the international police repression resulting from the revolutionary uprising of the Paris Commune in 1871 – at this time, any voluntary associations with the word 'International' in their titles were considered dangerous.

International Council of Women (ICW)
An international, non-governmental body comprised of National Councils of Women of all nations, which has the aim of helping to make women aware of their rights as well as of their civic, social and political responsibilities. It was founded in March 1888, in Washington, D.C., in an attempt to pull together the many different strands of the women's movement.

Susan B. ANTHONY chaired the first gathering of forty-nine delegates representing England, France, Denmark, Norway, Finland, India, Canada and the United States. The Council declared itself in favour of opening all institutions of learning to women; for equal pay for equal work; and for an identical standard of purity and morality for both sexes.

International Feminist Network (IFN)

Originated at the INTERNATIONAL TRIBUNAL ON CRIMES AGAINST WOMEN in Brussels, March 1976, as a means of mobilizing the support and solidarity of women around the world when needed. Initial funding came from the royalties of *Crimes Against Women*, edited by Diana Russell and Nicole Van de Ven, and it was coordinated by ISIS (today, jointly, by ISIS INTERNATIONAL and ISIS-WICCA). Appeals for support are passed through the Isis groups to contact women in various countries, who may respond by sending telegrams or organizing letter-writing campaigns. IFN has responded to women suffering imprisonment, persecution or repression because of activities for reproductive freedom, women's rights, and the peace movement. The philosophy behind the network is that, 'Even a few letters of support or protest from women in several different countries can make a tremendous impact – giving other women courage and moral support and putting those who are committing injustices against women on notice that women are not alone, that international attention and publicity is focused on what is happening.'

International Tribunal on Crimes Against Women

Held in Brussels, 4–8 March 1976, and attended by over 2,000 women from forty countries. Reports were made on slavery, polygamy, clitoridectomy, RAPE, PROSTITUTION, discrimination against lesbians, torture, and many other violent crimes against women. The proceedings of the Tribunal were published as *Crimes Against Women*, edited by Diana E. H. Russell and Nicole Van de Ven, in 1976.

International Woman Suffrage Alliance (IWSA)

International organization which developed from a division in the INTERNATIONAL COUNCIL OF WOMEN at their 1904 Congress in Berlin. There, the 'radicals' who considered women's suffrage a priority, formed the IWSA as a group dedicated to achieving votes for women on the grounds that 'the ballot is the only legal and permanent means of defending' women's rights and happiness.

Led by Carrie Chapman Catt until 1923 (in 1918 it was renamed the International Alliance of Women for Suffrage and Equal

Citizenship), it was dominated by the Americans, but had, from the start, member suffrage societies in America, Canada, Britain, Germany, the Netherlands, Norway and Sweden. In subsequent years societies from Hungary, Italy, Russia, Bulgaria, Denmark, Finland, South Africa, Switzerland, Belgium, France, Serbia, Iceland, Galicia, Austria, Bohemia, Romania and Portugal also joined.

Although bolder and more dynamic than the ICW, with yearly congresses, the IWSA suffered internal problems: many member countries had more than one suffrage society who could not agree to unite; and there was always a division between those who wanted universal suffrage, and those who thought the vote should remain a class privilege extended only to qualified women.

International Women's Day

Observed by feminists all over the world on 8 March, but an official holiday only in China and the USSR. It originated in 1908 in the United States when, in response to women's demands, the Socialist Party recommended that the last Sunday in February be set aside for the purpose of demonstrations for women's suffrage. This American Women's Day (28 February 1909) caught the attention of feminists and socialists worldwide and, in 1910, at the Second Conference of Socialist Women in Copenhagen,

Clara ZETKIN proposed to internationalize the American experiment, and called for 8 March to become International Women's Day, with the slogan of 'universal suffrage'. From 1911 until it was brought to a halt in 1915 by World War I, women's parades and demonstrations were organized in many European cities. The Russian Revolution began on International Women's Day (8 March 1917 – or, by the old calendar, 23 February) with mass demonstrations and food protests launched by women and children. In Britain it did not become an annual event until after World War II. Americans did not recognize the new date and international status of the day until 1916; it was celebrated only sporadically, and died out altogether by the end of the 1930s. However, the birth of the WOMEN'S LIBERATION MOVEMENT in the late 1960s revived interest, and in the 1970s International Women's Day was celebrated more widely than ever before. In 1978 it was included in a list of holidays officially recognized by the United Nations.

International Women's Year (IWY)

In 1972 the male-dominated United Nations declared 1975 the official International Year of the Woman, an announcement heard with distrust by women all over the world. Not only was it a superficial gesture (was the problem of women to be settled in one year so the U.N. could consider only men in the years to come?) but it could actually harm the ongoing women's movement by diverting energy, funding and talents, and it could be used as a front for other undesirable goals. (The French women's liberation movement made accusations that the promotion of women's rights was a cover for a U.S. plan to limit population growth and control economic development in third world countries.)

Each member country was expected to research the current condition of women and draw up a plan for equalizing their status. Findings were to be discussed at the Conference held in Mexico City from 19 June–2 July 1975. This was attended by government-appointed delegates, and motivated by so little feminist consciousness that a man was chosen to chair the Conference, which was dominated by the usual arguments on the usual subjects (Zionism, imperialism, racism etc.), showing no understanding of how these problems might also be of particular concern to women. The World Plan of Action adopted at the end did contain some suggestions for improving the condition of women – possibly because the Conference ran out of time before they could be edited out.

At the same time, in another part of Mexico City, an unofficial Tribunal was held, attended by 7,000 women. Although it was pla-

gued by disruptions and sabotage, and the official Conference refused to consider its suggestions because it did not recognize it as an official body, this unofficial Tribunal provided an opportunity for women from many countries to make connections, communicate, and begin to explore their shared problems.

Irigaray, Luce, 1939–
French psychoanalyst. Author of *Le Langage des déments* (1973), *Speculum de l'autre femme* (1974) and *Ce sexe qui n'en est pas un* (1977). Her work has focused specifically on questions of FEMININITY and LANGUAGE, much of it amounting to a critique of Lacan's interpretation of the connection between language and SEXUALITY. She asserts that not only is women's unique sexuality denied and repressed when women are judged according to male theories of sexuality, but that women also have a language of their own, related to their sexuality, and that under PATRIARCHY this language has been denied existence.

Iron, Ralph
Pseudonym under which Olive SCHREINER'S THE STORY OF AN AFRICAN FARM was first published in 1883.

Irwin, Inez Haynes Gillmore,
  1873–1970
American writer. Co-founder, with Maud Wood PARK, of the College Equal Suffrage League, which

was an influential, national organization of undergraduates and graduates from 1900–16. Active throughout her life in the women's movement, and a member of the National Advisory Council of the NATIONAL WOMAN'S PARTY, she contributed most effectively as a feminist historian, author of *Story of the Woman's Party* (1921) and *Angels and Amazons: A Hundred Years of American Women* (1933). She wrote many novels, some of which reflect her feminism, but the books she wrote for children, especially the 'Maida' series based on her own childhood, were her most popular. She also worked for the World Center for Women's Archives, organized in 1936 by Mary BEARD, until lack of funding forced it to close in 1940.

ISIS

Non-profit-making, international women's information and communication service founded in 1974 to promote international contact and understanding among women through headquarters in Geneva and Rome. In 1984 it evolved into two organizations: ISIS INTERNATIONAL, which carried on the original purpose from Rome, and ISIS-WICCA which ran a cross-cultural exchange programme from the Geneva headquarters.

Isis International

International women's information and communication service founded in 1974 as ISIS, a non-profit-making, non-governmental group to promote communication among women throughout the world. In January 1984, ISIS became two sister organizations: ISIS-WICCA, based in Geneva, and the Rome-based Isis International, which at the same time opened a second office in Chile. The office in Rome has magazines, journals, papers and studies on women from all over the world which are available on request to women doing research. With contacts in 130 countries, Isis International is able to provide women's groups with technical assistance and training in communication skills and information management, help in organizing workshops and conferences, and in using audiovisual resources, and also publishes the *Isis Women's International Journal* twice a year, plus a twice-yearly supplement, in English and Spanish editions. Isis International is based at via Santa Maria Dell'Anima, 00186 Rome, Italy.

Isis-WICCA (Women's International Cross Cultural Exchange)

Sister-organization of ISIS INTERNATIONAL, founded in 1984 and based in Geneva. Its purpose is 'to provide an opportunity for women active in women's organizations and projects to spend time in another cultural context, with a group involved in similar work'. After a month's orientation in Geneva, twelve women are sent to 'receiving groups' in different countries, to live and work there for three months. Reports on their experiences and news about the programme are published quarterly in *Women's World*. Applications for women's groups wishing to take part are available from Isis-WICCA, P.O. Box 2471, 1211 Geneva 2, Switzerland.

Islam
See MUSLIM FEMINISTS

J

Jacobi, Mary Putnam, 1842–1906
American doctor. In 1872 she founded the Association for the Advancement of the Medical Education of Women. Well known for her teaching and research as well as her abilities as a doctor, she believed that many of the illnesses middle-class women suffered from, including menstrual pain, were caused by boredom, celibacy and the lack of meaningful work in their lives. She wrote *Common Sense Applied to Woman Suffrage* (1894), several stories, and nearly 100 medical articles. In 1880 she became the first woman to be elected to the New York Academy of Medicine.

Jacobs, Aletta, 1851–1929
Dutch doctor. One of the first women to attend a Dutch university, in 1874, she became the first qualified woman doctor. In 1882 she started the world's first BIRTH CONTROL clinic in Amsterdam, and was active in campaigns to abolish regulated prostitution, reform marriage laws, and increase knowledge about venereal disease and sexuality. A suffragist since student days, in 1894 she founded the Dutch Association for Women's Suffrage, becoming its president in 1903. She was also active in the international suffrage movement, and after women's suffrage was granted in the Netherlands in 1919 she devoted much of her energies to working for the INTERNATIONAL ALLIANCE OF WOMEN.

James, Selma, 1930–
American-born British resident. A leading activist in movements for the rights of women, immigrants and black people, she has always been particularly interested in the international dimensions of the women's movement, and in making it more broadly based. She is the author of a number of works on women's issues, the most famous of which is *The Power of Women and the Subversion of the Community* (1972), a major contribution to the debate on HOUSEWORK. In 1970, after hearing three housewives speak at a women's conference in Oxford, she founded the WAGES FOR HOUSEWORK Campaign. In 1975 she set up the English Collective of Prostitutes, and helped to found WOMEN AGAINST RAPE in 1976.

Jameson, Anna (Brownell Murphy) 1794–1860
Irish author. Trapped in an unhappy marriage, she escaped through writing, eventually the career by which she supported herself, her mother, sisters and niece.

Her feminist beliefs are not always obvious in her published writings; however, her drawing-room lectures on such subjects as social work and the employment of women caused great intellectual excitement among her listeners. Her friends included Elizabeth Barrett BROWNING, Fanny Kemble, Lady Noel Byron, and the LANGHAM PLACE GROUP, to whom she was a constant inspiration. It was at her suggestion that Bessie Rayner PARKES began to publish the ENGLISH WOMAN'S JOURNAL.

Janeway, Elizabeth, 1913–
American writer and critic. Known as a novelist (her first novel, *The Walsh Girls*, was published in 1943), she became an influential feminist theorist with the publication of MAN'S WORLD, WOMAN'S PLACE in 1971. In her view, it was the association of women with the domestic sphere that led to their oppression, and she traced the history of the family to show that the very idea of the home and nuclear family were fairly recent historical developments. Coining the phrase SOCIAL MYTHOLOGY to describe the SEX-ROLE system which makes PATRIARCHY possible, she suggested that women had unconsciously colluded in their own oppression by agreeing that men should rule in the public sphere in exchange for being allowed to keep their power in the private sphere. She also felt that infantile experience of the self as weak and the mother as all-powerful was at the heart of the anger men demonstrate towards women in adult life. She went on to expand these ideas in *Between Myth and Morning* (1974) and *Powers of the Weak* (1980).

Janie's Janie

A thirty-minute documentary FILM by Geri Ashur and Peter Barton, it is about a white, working-class welfare mother in New Jersey. Released in 1971, it established the film portrait as the archetypal form for feminist filmmakers, and remains one of the best known of early feminist films.

Jewish feminists

Traditionally, Jewish women have been subordinate to men and forced to lead restricted lives, but with the growth of feminism in the secular world, this began to be challenged. In the nineteenth century leaders of the Reform movement in Central Europe and the *Haskalan* (Enlightenment) in Eastern Europe questioned traditional male and female roles and rejected women's subordinate position. At the same time Jewish feminists in the United States and Europe formed organizations to improve the lot of Jewish women and to demand full suffrage in communal affairs: the Judischer Frauenbund directed by Bertha PAPPENHEIM is perhaps the best known of these.

Earlier Jewish feminists often felt they could achieve liberation only by rejecting their heritage, but the second wave of Jewish feminism, beginning in the late 1960s, has called for changes within Judaism, and emphasized the desire of women to be accepted as fully participating members of the Jewish community.

In 1971 Ezrat Nashim was formed, a group which continues to function today to promote education and consciousness-raising among Jewish women. At around the same time many Jewish organizations created task groups to study and improve the situation of women in Jewish communities, and throughout the United States and many parts of Europe groups of women gathered together to celebrate Rosh Hodesh, which had been referred to in early Jewish sources as a woman's holiday. Throughout the 1970s new women's rituals were created and practised, and in 1976 *Siddur Nashim*, a prayer-book with non-sexist language and some new women's prayers, was published. Also in 1976, LILITH, the first Jewish feminist journal, was published.

Equality of women in the synagogue has always been a major issue. In 1972 Hebrew Union College (the seminary of the Reform movement) ordained Sally Priesand the first woman rabbi, and in 1974 the Reconstructionist Fellowship ordained the first woman rabbi and granted full equality to women with men in all matters of ritual. By the mid-1970s, Orthodox communities began to discuss the use of the *mehitzah*, the curtain separating women and men during prayers, and the Reform movement began a campaign to excise sexism from liturgy, organization and community life. But women rabbis encounter prejudice, and there is a strong anti-feminist response within the Jewish community, with opponents accusing feminists of threatening the stability of the family, the masculinity of Jewish men, and of destroying Jewish principles and practices.

In the 1980s, feminists have moved on from the criticism of specific traditions to examine the fuller picture which emerges when connections are made among the various issues and seen in the context of Jewish history. A new feminist theology of Judaism is being developed which questions such basic issues as the understanding of God as King and Father, the conception of the Jewish people and community; and seeks to reinterpret both legends and teachings in order to base the religion within women's own experience.

(*See also* GODDESS; SPIRITUAL FEMINISM; SHIFRA; RELIGION; THEALOGY)

Jex-Blake, Sophia, 1840–1912
English doctor. Leader of the campaign to open the British medical profession to women. A contemporary of Elizabeth Garrett ANDERSON, her methods were different: she was aggressively direct,

rather than masking her determination with charm, and as a result faced even more male hostility. In 1874 she founded the London School of Medicine for Women. In 1878, as the first woman doctor in Scotland, she opened a dispensary which became the Edinburgh Hospital for Women and Children in 1886. In 1888 she opened a medical school for women which closed in 1894, no longer needed since she had persuaded the Edinburgh Medical School to admit female students.

Jiu Jin (Ch'iu Chin), 1875–1907
Chinese revolutionary and poet. She became involved in the opposition to the Manchu rulers which followed the Boxer Rebellion of 1900. In 1904 she left her husband and two children to travel to Japan, where she studied political science. There she founded a revolutionary society among the women students, and became the first woman member of Sun Yat-sen's Revolutionary Alliance. In 1906 she returned to China and founded a woman's magazine, then took up a post as principal of Tautung College of Physical Culture in Zhejiang, where she raised funds and founded a separate women's army. Her feminism evolved out of her personal struggles, and grew as strong as her enthusiasm for a revolution in China. She often used the name 'Qinxiong', meaning 'compete with men', and believed that women, because they had not, like men, been politically conditioned for centuries, could lead the way to reform and revolution. Much of her poetry, including one poem called 'Women's Rights', combined her patriotic feelings for China with an equally revolutionary feminism, calling upon women to save themselves and their country. After her execution in 1907 she became a martyr of the revolutionary cause, and is still so honoured today.

Joan of Arc (Jeanne d'Arc; St Joan)
?1412–31
French. Although she fought for God and France rather than for the rights of women, and although she died long before the ideals of feminism were articulated, she is a feminist heroine, providing an image of female power and heroism. Told in a vision by Saints Michael, Catherine and Margaret that her mission in life was to free France from the English and ensure the coronation of the dauphin Charles, she set out to do just that. Leading an army of 6,000 men, she won the battle of Orleans and saw Charles crowned, but was subsequently captured and sold to the English. After a long and brutal trial on seventy charges, including witchcraft, heresy and fraud, she was eventually convicted only of wearing men's clothing – a crime against the church – and was burned at the stake. In 1456 an ecclesiastical com-

mission reversed the judgment against her and her legend and popularity continued to grow as the years passed. She was canonized in 1920.

Johnson, Adelaide, 1859–1955
American sculptor. Perceiving feminism to be 'the mightiest thing in the evolution of humanity', she early considered it her life's mission to record and immortalize the history of the women's movement. Her exhibition at the Woman's Pavilion of the World's Columbian Exposition in Chicago in 1893 included busts of Lucretia MOTT, Elizabeth Cady STANTON and Susan B. ANTHONY. 'THE WOMAN MOVEMENT', her seven-ton sculpture of white Carrara marble, was presented to the nation on behalf of American women by the NATIONAL WOMAN'S PARTY (which had financed the work) on Susan B. Anthony's birthday, 15 February 1921. The reception given for Johnson that day was the first ever given for a woman in the Capitol building. The sculpture still stands in the United States Capitol, the only national monument to the women's movement.

Johnston, Jill, 1930–
American writer. Publicly proclaiming her LESBIANISM on her mother's birthday in 1970, she became one of the most visible and colourful proponents of LESBIAN-FEMINISM and SEPARATISM as political strategy. Yet Johnston is an artist rather than a political theorist. All her writings are autobiographical and highly idiosyncratic. Her best-known book, LESBIAN NATION (1973), has been an inspiration to many, but is hardly a practical guide to feminist revolution.

Jong, Erica, 1942–
American poet and novelist. She had a growing reputation as a feminist poet (her first collection, *Fruits & Vegetables*, was published in 1971) when her first novel, FEAR OF FLYING (1973), made her famous overnight. As an attractive, lustily heterosexual woman who had written a daring (and apparently autobiographical) novel about a modern woman's sexual fantasies and adventures, Erica Jong was widely promoted in the media as the archetypal liberated woman. Among her other books are two sequels to the first, *How to Save Your Own Life* (1975) and *Parachutes and Kisses* (1984), and the non-fictional *Witches* (1981).

Jordan, June, 1936–
American poet. An activist in the civil rights and black liberation movements, she is also a teacher and the author of many books of essays, non-fiction, poetry and fiction. Titles include *Some Changes* (1971), *Things that I do in the Dark* (1977), *Passion: New Poems, 1977–1980* (1980), and *Civil Wars* (1981).

Joreen
See FREEMAN, JO

Journal of Female Liberation, A
Also known as *No More Fun and Games*, this was the first distinctly radical feminist journal published in America. It was published by CELL 16 of Boston, beginning in 1968. In 1970, the Young Socialist Alliance (YSA, the youth affiliate of the Socialist Workers Party) infiltrated and attempted (unsuccessfully) to take over the funds, files and mailing list of the *Journal*. It came out sporadically until the mid-1970s, publishing works of radical feminist theory by Dana Densmore, Roxanne DUNBAR, Betsy WARRIOR and others.

journalism
Defining the word feminist in this instance as 'having the characteristics of females', Dr Donna Allen, editor of *Media Report to Women*, presented the Principles of Feminist Journalism in January 1976. They are a new set of standards which the WOMEN'S INSTITUTE FOR FREEDOM OF THE PRESS would like to see replace existing male journalism as being 'more respectful of people'. They follow, with brief rationale:

1. No attacks on people. ('We . . . know that media characterizations of people can be inhibiting and restrictive – both to the person characterized and to those among the public who may wish to pick up on an idea or take an action . . . public news media, we believe, should work to *widen* the social, political, or economic options for people, not inhibit them.')

2. More factual information. ('Priority is given to facts over opinion . . . Conclusions without facts keep us apathetic, powerless to act, and dependent upon the decision-making of others.')

3. People should speak for themselves. ('We believe that the surest way to dispel stereotypes, to achieve accuracy, and to add more, new factual information, is for people to make their own case directly to the public and thus to define themselves.')

Judge, The
Novel by Rebecca WEST, first published in 1922. A powerful work dealing with the relationships between the sexes and the generations, as epitomized in the epigraph: 'Every mother is a judge who sentences the children for the sins of the father.' Unusually for its period, it treats the situation of an unmarried mother with great seriousness, and the young heroine, Ellen Melville, is an attractive, ardent suffragette.

Justitia
Pseudonym of Mrs Henry Davis Pochin under which a pamphlet 'The Right of Women to Exercise the Elective Franchise' was first published in England in 1855. When it was reprinted in 1873 by the Manchester Women's Suffrage Society it carried the author's name.

K

Kautsky, Luise, 1864–1944
Austrian. Active in the socialist movement, she collaborated with her husband Karl Kautsky in writing theoretical Marxist works, but had a particular interest in women's issues, and was a leader in the women's suffrage movement from 1910.

Kelley, Florence, 1859–1932
American lawyer and reformer. Studied law in Zurich, where she met many exiled radicals and joined the Socialist Party. She wrote the first English translation of Engels' *The Condition of the Working Class in England in 1844* (1887). After her return to America, she worked at Hull House in Chicago. In 1893 she became the first woman Chief Inspector of Factories in Illinois, and pushed an anti-sweatshop bill through the state legislature. In 1899 she became the secretary of the National Consumers' League and campaigned for protective legislation for women and children. She was also active in the fight for women's suffrage, believing that women could not effectively lobby for reforms until they had the power of the vote. She served as vice-president of the NATIONAL AMERICAN WOMAN SUFFRAGE ASSOCIATION (1905–9). In 1919 she was a delegate to the International Congress of Women for Permanent Peace in Zurich.

Kelly, Mary, 1941–
American resident in Britain. Artist and lecturer on art and women's studies. Her work is radically feminist, challenging established notions of what may be considered 'art'. In her best-known work, POST PARTUM DOCUMENT, she confronts the supposed dichotomy between the masculine and the feminine by turning her own experiences as a mother into the material of her art. Her intent is to contribute not only to art, but to feminism, by examining woman's place in patriarchal society.

Kenney, Annie, 1879–1953
English. A mill-worker from the age of ten, she organized a union and became the first woman in textile unions elected to a District Committee. In 1905 she became a speaker for the WOMEN'S SOCIAL AND POLITICAL UNION (WSPU) and, with Christabel PANKHURST, was the first woman in the suffrage campaign to be sentenced to prison for militant activities. A vigorous and persuasive speaker, she was arrested many more times as she organized for the WSPU in London and the

West Country. In 1912, while the Pankhursts and Emmeline PETHICK-LAWRENCE were imprisoned, she took over leadership of the WSPU. In 1921, the vote for women won, she married, and retired from public life.

Kensington Society, The

Also known as the Kensington Ladies' Discussion Group, an English women's political and literary organization started in 1865 by a group of women who had in common an interest in higher education and better employment opportunities for women, and a direct precursor of the suffrage societies which began forming in 1867. After a meeting devoted to the question of women's suffrage, several members drafted a petition – the first of its kind in Britain – calling for the enfranchisement of 'all householders, without distinction of sex', gathered 1,499 signatures for it in less than two weeks, and gave it to John Stuart MILL for presentation in the House of Commons on 7 June 1866.

Members of the Society included Barbara Leigh-Smith (BODICHON), Frances Mary Buss, Dorothea BEALE, Jessie BOUCHERETT, Emily DAVIES, Elizabeth WOLSTENHOLME (Elmy), Elizabeth Garrett (ANDERSON), Bessie Rayner PARKES, and Helen Taylor.

Key, Ellen, 1849–1926

Swedish social reformer. Internationally famous as a lecturer and the author of more than thirty books, she campaigned for women's sexual emancipation and the glorification of motherhood. She believed that women must have complete legal and economic equality with men, because motherhood was the source of all social virtue, and therefore must be recognized as woman's highest calling. Because both unhappy marriages and outside employment could put stress on the mother's relationship with her children, Key believed that women should not be forced to marry or to take jobs simply in order to survive, and advocated State payment of mothers. Her most famous book was *Barnhets ahrundrade* (1900; translated as *The Century of the Child*).

Koedt, Anne

American artist. One of the founders of the WOMEN'S LIBERATION MOVEMENT in America in the late 1960s, she was a member of New York Radical Women, THE FEMINISTS, and the NEW YORK RADICAL FEMINISTS. With Shulamith FIRESTONE she edited the earliest compilation of movement writings, *Notes from the First Year* (1968), and *Notes from the Second Year* (1970) and *Notes from the Third Year* (1971). She is the author of what Leah FRITZ called 'the *feminist* shot heard round the world', 'THE MYTH OF THE VAGINAL ORGASM', among other influential papers.

Kollontai, Alexandra, 1872–1952
Russian revolutionary, politician,
diplomat and writer. A visit to a
factory in 1896 and a glimpse of the
workers' lives there convinced her
that reform was not enough, and
she became committed to revolution, leaving her husband soon after
because he did not share her politics. 'Women and their fate have
occupied my whole life. It was their
lot which pushed me into socialism,' she wrote later in life. She
devoted herself to organizing proletarian women from at least 1905.
At the same time, she was actively
opposed to BOURGEOIS FEMINISM,
considering the classless, woman-
only movement a threat to the possibility of a socialist society. She
declared that there could be no separate woman question while more
general social problems remained
unsolved, but she did not, like some
socialists, believe that women
should wait for their rights. Instead,
she combined socialism and feminism, urging women to become
active revolutionaries and trying to
bring about both immediate and
future changes in women's lives.
Elected Commisar for Public Welfare in 1917, she was the only
woman in the first Bolshevik
government. In 1918 she organized
the first All-Russian Congress of
Working and Peasant Women. And
she was alone among Russian
socialists in giving serious thought
to, and writing about, such controversial issues as sexual love, marriage and morality. She believed
(and lived her belief) in free love,
but recognized its dangers for
women. She was opposed to any
union based on money, be it MAR-
RIAGE or PROSTITUTION, and felt that
women and men must always meet
as equals, whether their relationship
was based on a short-lived physical
attraction, or life-long companionship. But this would be possible
only if motherhood was sanctified,
and children provided for by
society; and if a new type of woman
developed. For the new woman,
love would be a joyous and life-
enriching experience, but it would
not consume her life or absorb her
personality as romantic love was
meant to do. Her writings include
*The Social Basis of the Woman Ques-
tion* (1908), *Society and Motherhood*
(1916), *The New Morality and the
Working Class* (1918), *Communism
and the Family* (1920), her *Autobiography* (1926) and some short
works of fiction which explored, on
a personal level, theories about love
relationships.

Konradi, Evgenia, 1838–98
Russian journalist. The editor of a
progressive journal, in 1868 she was
inspired by the opening of Vassar
College in the United States to
launch a campaign for the creation
of a women's university in Russia.
The early philanthropic Russian
feminists such as Mariya
TRUBNIKOVA and Nadezhda
STASOVA were attracted to this

movement, as were many nihilists and radicals, and their pressure eventually led to the establishment of a series of higher courses for women in St Petersburg and in Moscow. By 1880, the Russian women's movement could be seen to be leading the rest of European feminism as far as education was concerned: in quality and range of women's higher education, only America was farther ahead, and Russia produced more women doctors than any other country at that time.

Kristeva, Julia, 1941–
French philosopher and critic. Her works on LANGUAGE, literature and cultural history have been influential to the development of some strands of feminist theory, although in 1983 she specifically rejected feminism along with other political movements. Following Lacan, she asserts that FEMININITY is constructed by the mode of entry into the symbolic order (civilization and the world of language), but she does not consider this to be biologically determined. The child of either sex may choose to take either the male

position (fully integrated into the symbolic order), or the female (marginal or in opposition to that order), and only our patriarchal culture makes the false, and oppressive, connection between femininity and the female sex. She is the author of many books; available in English are *About Chinese Women* (1977) and a collection of essays, *Desire in Language* (1981).

Kuhn, Maggie
See GRAY PANTHERS

Kulisciov, Anna, 1854–1925
Italian. Active in Italian politics from 1878, in 1890 she organized a conference in Milan to question women's economic and social subordination. She split with Anna MOZZONI and other feminists of the time because of her commitment to socialism, but her insistence that women's rights including the vote must be part of the Socialist Party's platform put her in opposition to most other socialists. In 1912 she founded the Unione Femminile Nazionale Socialista and edited *La digesa delle lavoratrici*, a journal for working-class women.

L

Láadan
Language for women constructed by linguist Suzette Haden Elgin beginning on 28 June 1982, partly as background to her science fiction novel about the creation of a woman's LANGUAGE (*Native Tongue*, published in 1984) and partly in response to the hypothesis that existing human languages are inadequate to express the perceptions and experiences of women. If women had an adequate language it might reflect a very different reality from that perceived by men. A *First Dictionary and Grammar of Láadan* was published in Madison, Wisconsin in 1985, by the Society for the Furtherance and Study of Fantasy and Science Fiction, Inc.

labrys
Double-bladed axe, the traditional weapon of the AMAZONS, and the central religious icon of ancient Crete, appearing always in connection with the GODDESS and female powers. Mary DALY uses it as the symbol for the 'A-mazing Female Mind . . . that cuts through the double binds and doublebinding words that block our breakthrough to understanding radical feminist friendship and sisterhood.'

Lacombe, Claire, 1765–?
French actress and revolutionary. Founder and chief supporter of the Republican Revolutionary Society in 1793, a working women's club which took part in Revolutionary campaigns and petitioned for the rights of women. Attacked for its feminism, it was suppressed by the end of 1793. She was arrested in 1794.

LaFollette, Suzanne, 1893–
American journalist. Author of *Concerning Women* (1926), in which she argued that women who relied on legal guarantees of their rights were 'leaning on a broken reed', and that real equality between the sexes would not be achieved until women had full economic independence and personal autonomy.

Lange, Helene, 1848–1930
German. A conservative feminist, she became active in the General German Women's Association in the 1880s, and campaigned vigorously for better education on the grounds that it would help women to be better wives and mothers. In 1889 she founded the German Women Teachers' Association. In 1894 she founded the Berlin Women's Association. With

the assistance of Gertrud BAUMER, she led the moderate branch of the German women's movement throughout the 1890s, and worked on *Die Frau*, the movement's main journal.

Langham Place group

Circle of friends devoted to improving the lot of women through employment, education and changes in the law, called after the address of their regular meeting place. The house at 19 Langham Place, in London, was large enough to provide a club room, a reading room, a luncheon room, as well as offices, where members throughout the late 1850s and early 1860s ran the SOCIETY FOR PROMOTING THE EMPLOYMENT OF WOMEN, founded the Society of Female Artists, edited the ENGLISH WOMAN'S JOURNAL, held discussions and provided each other with a network of support. Members of the group included Adelaide PROCTOR, Barbara BODICHON, Anna JAMESON, Bessie Rayner PARKES, Isa CRAIG, Josephine BUTLER, and Jessie BOUCHERETT. Some members went on to found the KENSINGTON SOCIETY in 1865.

language

Language is crucial to human society and, as such, important to feminists not only as a means of communication, but as a subject to be studied for an understanding of how SEXISM is constructed and maintained, as well as a potential means for eliminating sexism.

Some theorists assume that language reflects reality; others, that language is the major source constructing our reality. If it only reflects, then trying to eliminate HE/MAN LANGUAGE may be useless until people actually think and behave in such a way that sexist language would never occur to them. If language plays a shaping role, however, feminists are right to be concerned.

In the early days of the women's liberation movement, feminists were particularly interested in the representation of women throughout all aspects of our culture. They examined language to discover the ways in which women were limited, denigrated, and even denied existence through the use of ANDROCENTRIC words and speaking practices. Studies revealed that some words had different meanings according to whether they were applied to men or women; that language use and conversational style were different between the sexes; that women were pre-judged and oppressed again and again in ways that men were not.

There is a long and continuing feminist campaign for the elimination of sexist language. This may take the form of using POSITIVE LANGUAGE (using 'she' for the not-so-generic 'he'), or encouraging more thoughtful, precise language use from students and writers, and retiring words which make unnecessary sexual distinctions,

LANGUAGE

such as poetess and chairman. Handbooks of non-sexist writing, such as the one by Casey Miller and Kate Swift (1981) have been published, and many people have become sensitized to the way gender distinctions and value judgments are constantly being made in supposedly neutral language.

Through CONSCIOUSNESS-RAISING and SISTERHOOD, feminists discovered how important it was to be able to speak of their experiences, and learned the power of NAMING. By the mid-1970s, the idea that women were alienated from and silenced by 'the oppressor's language' had become a recurrent theme. Language was seen as a trap, constructed by men for their own purposes. To find freedom, women had to discover or create their own language. Their ways of doing this have varied widely. Some, like Mary DALY, have been interested in reclaiming the language, giving positive definitions to words such as hag, CRONE and SPINSTER which men have used to devalue women. Others, like Hélène CIXOUS, have called upon women to 'write their bodies', and attempted to discover a specifically female, feminine, or feminist style of writing. For some theorists of L'ÉCRITURE FÉMININE a truly feminine style of writing is intimately connected with physical and biological femaleness, while others, like Julia KRISTEVA, see feminine writing as being whatever is outside or in opposition to the dominant language. Some feminists celebrate what they believe are particularly female styles of conversation or language use in contrast to 'correct' male discourse. Suzette Haden ELGIN has even created a separate women's language, called LÁADAN.

What is meant by 'women's language' varies so much, and the term 'language' is used so generally in much feminist writing that it is not really possible to piece together one coherent, feminist theory. Poets and theorists may write about language metaphorically or literally; 'language' may be used to refer to the entire realm of the symbolic which is culture, or be limited to verbal communication; it may conflate written and spoken language as if they were the same; it may refer to particular words and vocabulary, to what is said and not said, to differences in grammar, conversational style, subject matter and body language between men and women. Three general areas/theories from which feminists write about the difference between women's language and men's language might be defined as the GENDER theory, the hierarchical theory, and the theory of l'écriture féminine. The first considers that the observable differences in male and female speech are a function of the different roles men and women have in society, those roles being determined by the SEX/GENDER SYSTEM. The second theory argues that the differences have nothing to do with sexuality, but everything to do with women's subordinate status, so that powerless men also use what might be considered 'female' language. L'écriture féminine is an idea developed by French feminists influenced by psychoanalytic and semiological theories and is chiefly concerned with language as it is expressed in writing, rather than in conversational styles. It considers language to be powerfully connected to the body and SEXUALITY and believes that women have the potential (as yet chiefly unrealized) to express experiences which male language cannot.

Among those who have written about language from a feminist point of view are Adrienne RICH, Dale SPENDER, Cheris Kramarae and Paula Treichler (who edit a journal called *Women and Language*), Robin Lakoff, and linguist Deborah Cameron.

Lansbury, George, 1859–1940
British socialist politician, a supporter of the Women's Social and Political Union from its earliest days, and an outspoken proponent of women's suffrage in the House of Commons from 1910. In October 1912 he announced that he would vote against the Government on every issue until women were granted the vote. Although it was in favour of women's suffrage, the Labour Party was not willing to go

so far, and Lansbury was told to follow the party line or leave. He resigned his seat and sought re-election as an Independent Labour candidate for Bromley and Bow. He was the first Parliamentary candidate to elevate women's suffrage to a main campaign issue, and he was also the first, and only, candidate to receive the full support of the WSPU. When he was defeated, the WSPU's patience with constitutional methods for change ended and a new phase of militancy began. Lansbury's support of suffrage, and his pacifism in the war years, kept him out of Parliament until 1922. He edited the *Daily Herald*, 1919–23, and after returning to active politics, led the Labour Party from 1932–5.

Laskaridou, Aikaterini, 1842–1916
Greek. She devoted her life and her considerable personal fortune to improving the education of Greek women. She opened the first nursery schools in Greece and trained teachers for them, created workshops where poor women could receive basic training, and wrote many treatises on child rearing and education.

Laughlin, Gail, 1868–1952
American lawyer and politician. At the age of twelve she vowed 'to study law and dedicate my entire life to the freeing of women and establishing their proper place in

this "man's world".' In 1899 she passed the New York bar examination and began to practise law. In 1900 she was appointed as an expert agent for the United States Industrial Commission, and it was her research into domestic service, uncovering the low wages and working conditions faced by rural, immigrant and black women as servants in private homes, which led her to devote herself full-time to women's rights. From 1902–1906 she travelled the country campaigning for the NATIONAL AMERICAN WOMAN SUFFRAGE ASSOCIATION. In 1908 she opened a law office in Denver, choosing that location because Colorado women had the vote. Moving to San Francisco in 1914, she opened another law office, served as a judge, and founded the California branch of the National League for Women's Services. She drafted and successfully lobbied for the passage of a law permitting women to serve on California juries. In 1919 she was unanimously elected the first president of the National Federation of Business and Professional Women, an organization which had as its goal 'the absolute elimination of the consideration of the sex of the person in occupation or opportunity or remuneration'.

As a member of the NATIONAL WOMAN'S PARTY, she worked for the EQUAL RIGHTS AMENDMENT, and in July 1927 she led a 200-car motorcade across five states to confront President Calvin Coolidge, vacationing in South Dakota, to demand his support in passing the ERA.

In 1924 she moved to Maine and accepted the challenge of local clubwomen to run for state legislature. She won easily in 1929, and went on to serve three terms, moving up to the state senate in 1935 where she served until 1941. Many of the bills she submitted were concerned with increasing women's rights and improving the quality of their lives. Among those which became law was one designed to prevent the commitment of women to mental institutions solely on their husband's word. She also travelled to other states to help women who had been convicted by all-male juries.

Lavender Jane Loves Women
Record album released in 1973. The first professionally woman-produced recording, it is a classic in the field of woman-identified music, and is considered – with the founding of OLIVIA RECORDS that same year – to mark the emergence of the concept of women's music. The Lavender Jane group consisted of Alix Dobkin, Kay GARDNER and Patches Attom.
(*See also* MUSIC AND MUSICIANS)

Lavender Menace
First used as a term by Betty FRIEDAN, then president of the NATIONAL ORGANIZATION FOR

WOMEN (NOW), in 1969 to refer to lesbians, whom she saw as a threat to the image and political success of the women's movement. In response, some twenty lesbian feminists formed a group called the Lavender Menace and wrote a position paper, 'THE WOMAN-IDENTIFIED WOMAN'. In May 1970, they made a surprise appearance (wearing 'Lavender Menace' T-shirts) at the Second CONGRESS TO UNITE WOMEN, charged the women's movement with heterosexism and discrimination against lesbian sisters, and forced the issue to be publicly recognized and discussed. Afterwards Lavender Menace continued to meet under the name RADICALESBIANS.

(*See also* GAY/STRAIGHT SPLIT)

Lawson, Louisa, 1848–1902
Australian. After leaving her husband in 1883 she became involved in radical and feminist politics. She founded the Dawn Club in Sydney in 1888 in order to pursue her interests in health, temperance, social purity, dress reform and women's suffrage. She edited the newspaper *The Dawn* from 1889–1906, insisting – despite union opposition – that it should be produced entirely by women. Among her other activities, she founded the Darlinghurst Hostel for Working Girls.

Le Guin, Ursula Kroeber, 1929–
American writer. Much of her work has been in the SCIENCE FIC-

TION and fantasy genre, where she is one of the most critically-acclaimed and widely read of contemporary authors. The alternative societies she creates in her science fiction are very much concerned with the balancing of masculine and feminine values: her 1974 novel *The Dispossessed* does away with sexist restrictions, allowing women and men to meet on an egalitarian basis in an anarchic 'ambiguous utopia', and her 1969 novel THE LEFT HAND OF DARKNESS is a 'thought-experiment' which questions the importance of gender roles by depicting a society of hermaphrodites for whom gender is a temporary and changeable affair.

leaders

The WOMEN'S LIBERATION MOVEMENT has been a leaderless movement by design. Although many reform-oriented and liberal feminist organizations such as the NATIONAL ORGANIZATION FOR WOMEN are organized on traditional hierarchical lines, more radical feminists attempt to create pre-figurative structures – that is, to produce among themselves a model of the co-operative, leaderless, non-oppressive society they are struggling to bring about. As the REDSTOCKINGS declared in their 1969 manifesto: 'We are committed to achieving internal democracy. We will do whatever is necessary to ensure that every woman in our movement has an equal chance to participate, assume responsibility, and develop her political potential.' Although few go as far as THE FEMINISTS with their rigidly controlled lot system, most feminists believe in co-operative and collective systems for sharing power. Women within the movement who are perceived as assuming leadership are subject to TRASHING and other forms of criticism or ostracism. Most feminist 'leaders' have been designated as such neither by themselves nor by other feminists, but by the media.

League of Women Voters
American organization which evolved out of the NATIONAL AMERICAN WOMAN SUFFRAGE ASSOCIATION in 1919. It had only a fraction of the membership of NAWSA, and no feminist consciousness, believing that the fight for women's rights had been won with the vote. It was opposed to the EQUAL RIGHTS AMENDMENT from the beginning, but in the 1970s joined with most other women's organizations to lobby for its passage.

l'écriture féminine
Term used by some French feminists for women's writing, used in English to refer to the theory expressed by Hélène CIXOUS in *The Laugh of the Medusa* (*La rire de la méduse*, 1975) that women must learn to 'write their bodies'. This theory holds that language and sexuality are intimately connected, and that women have been alienated and oppressed by a male LANGUAGE falsely represented as universal. This is connected with the concept of FEMININITY (*féminité*) as a challenge to the PHALLOCENTRIC universe. Cixous defines writing as 'the very possibility of change' and declares that if women dare to write directly out of their bodily, sexual, unconscious experiences – unique to them as women – the result will be not only personally liberating, but will have the power to smash the very structure of PATRIARCHY. Other French theorists connected with *l'écriture féminine* include Luce IRIGARAY and Julia KRISTEVA. One of the best explanations of this theory for the English reader is given by Ann Rosalind Jones in 'Writing the Body: Toward an Understanding of l'Écriture féminine' (1981).

Leeds Revolutionary Feminists
See LOVE YOUR ENEMY?

Left Hand of Darkness, The
Science fiction novel by Ursula LE GUIN published in 1969 to great critical and popular acclaim (it won both the Hugo Award from the fans and the Nebula Award from her fellow writers as best novel of the year). In an article entitled 'Is Gender Necessary?' (1976), Le Guin said the book was a 'thought-experiment' written to discover what would be left if GENDER could be eliminated: 'Whatever was left would be, presumably, simply human.'

The story is told through a (male) observer on the planet Gethen to observe the natives. The Gethenians are human, with one important difference. For most of their lives they are effectively sexless, taking on male or female characteristics only for a few days of each month as part of the oestrus cycle. They can never know in advance whether they will be male or female, and any individual might be a father one year and pregnant the next, with the result that in their society sex-class distinctions are impossible.

It is a daring, moving, original and well-written novel, but in later years feminist critics objected that as a thought-experiment it does not go far enough, that both the author and the narrator are still too gender-bound to present Gethenian society as it really would be. Because the Gethenians are always referred to as 'he' and shown in contexts or attitudes perceived as masculine, with the important areas of family structure and child-rearing left unexplored, Gethen seems a world more of men than of true hermaphrodites. Le Guin responded to some of this criticism in a 1980 interview by saying, 'The real subject of the book is not feminism or sex or gender . . . it is a book about betrayal and fidelity.'

No matter what her intention, or how critically the result is judged, *The Left Hand of Darkness* is one of the very few novels to confront

seriously one of the most profound questions of feminism.

legal prostitution
Definition of MARRIAGE recognized by feminists as early as Mary Wollstonecraft (1792), the point being that it is morally no better for a woman to sell herself to one man in exchange for lifelong economic support than to sell herself on an hourly basis to strangers. As Olive Schreiner wrote in *The Story of an African Farm* (1883): '. . . a woman who has sold herself, even for a ring and a new name, need hold her skirt aside for no creature in the street. They both earn their bread in one way.' Despite all the changes in law giving women more rights since then, the idea that a husband has certain property rights in his wife remains enshrined in a legal system which does not recognize the possibility of RAPE within a marriage.

Leigh-Smith, Barbara
See BODICHON, BARBARA.

Léon, Pauline, 1758–?
French revolutionary. In 1791 she spoke before the National Assembly, declaring that women were as vital as men to the defence of the Revolution, and calling for a women's militia. In 1793 she became President of the Republican Revolutionary Society, a working women's club founded by Claire LACOMBE. Little is known of her after 1794.

Lerner, Gerda, 1920–
American historian. Following the path marked by Mary BEARD, she has challenged the ANDROCENTRIC bias of traditional HISTORY and attempted to change it by exploring and publicizing the role of women in history. Since the early 1960s she has dedicated her career to developing the new study of Women's History, which she sees as necessary to correct the distorted picture offered by traditional history, and a step towards a truly universal history which would reflect the experience of both women and men. Her books include *The Woman in American History* (1971), *Black Women in White America: A Documentary History* (1972), *The Female Experience: An American Documentary* (1977), and *The Majority Finds Its Past: Placing Women in History* (1979).

lesbian baiting
The practice of scaring women away from feminism by equating it with LESBIANISM; the use of the label 'lesbian' for any woman who dares to demand her rights or identify herself apart from men. Feminists have found the most effective response is solidarity, in accepting the label with pride rather than arguing about their actual sexual preference.

lesbian continuum
Term used by Adrienne RICH for the 'range – throughout each woman's life and throughout history – of woman-identified experience; not simply the fact that a woman has had or consciously desired genital sexual experience with another woman. If we expand it to embrace many more forms of primary intensity between and among women, including the sharing of a rich inner life, the bonding against male tyranny, the giving and receiving of practical and political support . . . we begin to grasp breadths of female history and psychology which have lain out of reach as a consequence of limited, mostly clinical, definitions of "lesbianism".' (From 'Compulsory Heterosexuality and Lesbian Existence', 1980)

Lesbian Nation
An autobiographical polemic, subtitled *The Feminist Solution*, written in a stunning, punning, stream-of-consciousness flow by Jill JOHNSTON, published in 1973. This is one of the earliest and best-known presentations of the case for LESBIAN-FEMINISM and SEPARATISM. It takes the position – based on Johnston's own experience rather than research or theory – that women's oppression is directly attributable to the institution of HETEROSEXUALITY. Heterosexual intercourse is an invasion of the woman, and men are the enemy. Women who sleep with men are traitors, and a feminist revolution will be possible only when all women withdraw from men to create a lesbian nation.

lesbianism

The term used for female homosexuality, it is derived from Lesbos, the island where SAPPHO, known as a lover of women, once lived. Homosexual behaviour has rarely been as severely condemned and punished in women as it has been in men; perhaps because, in a patriarchal culture, women's SEXUALITY is not considered to exist except in relation to men, and only PHALLOCENTRIC sex 'counts'. Only in the last one hundred years has homosexual activity been considered something which only a certain type of person – the homosexual – does, a category of abnormality constructed in opposition to the category of the normal heterosexual. Sheila Jeffreys (1986) has argued that the creation of lesbianism as a category was in reaction to the development of a feminist critique of male sexuality. As Lillian Faderman has demonstrated in *Surpassing the Love of Men* (1981), love between women was accepted and sometimes even encouraged for centuries. Only after women began to gain economic independence and to choose to satisfy their needs for companionship with other women rather than through marriage did women's love for each other threaten the social order. 'Love between women was metamorphosed into a freakishness, and it was claimed that only those who had such an abnormality would want to change their subordinate

status in any way. Hence, the sexologists' theories frightened, or attempted to frighten, women away from feminism and from loving other women by demonstrating that both were abnormal and were generally linked together.' (Faderman)

The threat of being considered lesbian and abnormal has been used against feminists since the turn of the century. As the RADICALESBIANS wrote in 1970: 'Lesbian is the word, the label, the condition that holds women in line. When a woman hears this word tossed her way, she knows. . .that she has crossed the terrible boundary of her sex role . . .Lesbian is a label invented by the Man to throw at any woman who dares to be his equal, who dares to challenge his prerogatives . . .who dares to assert the primacy of her own needs.'

Lesbianism as an issue caused one of the most serious internal disputes within the modern feminist movement. In 1971, the question of what recognition should be given to the specific oppression suffered by homosexual women was raised at the National Organization for Women's national conference. Betty FRIEDAN feared that what she called the 'LAVENDER MENACE' would sully NOW's public image, but the issue was raised, and solidarity among the membership ensured that a resolution approving 'a woman's right to define and express her own sexuality and to choose her own life-style' was passed. 'An end to discrimination against lesbians' became the sixth of the SEVEN DEMANDS of the 1975 National Women's Liberation Conference in Edinburgh.

But 'lesbian' is still used, often successfully, as a derogatory label to frighten and divide women, and despite a continued determination among most feminists to defend lesbianism as the woman's right to choose, no accepted feminist counter-strategy against lesbian-baiting has emerged.

Charlotte BUNCH has argued that the political importance of lesbianism for the women's movement is that it illustrated the way in which heterosexuality supported male domination. Love for other women, however it is expressed, is also vital to a movement to improve women's status. Yet lesbianism continues to be a divisive issue for feminists, who cannot agree on its meaning or its importance. Some consider it a matter of sexual preference, something private which need not affect the struggle to create a non-sexist, non-oppressive society. Others play down the erotic aspects and emphasize lesbianism as a political choice, the only life-style possible for the committed feminist.

Anna COOTE and Beatrix CAMPBELL (1982) have suggested that 'What remains to be done is to explore the experience that lesbians and heterosexuals *share* and to build on this common ground a political understanding of sexuality.'
(*See also* HETEROSEXUALITY; POLITICAL LESBIAN; GAY LIBERATION FRONT; LESBIAN-FEMINISM)

lesbian-feminism

The branch of RADICAL FEMINISM for which LESBIANISM is not simply a sexual preference or an issue of civil rights, but a whole way of life uniquely combining the personal with the political. In the 1970s, Rita Mae BROWN, Charlotte BUNCH, Ti-Grace ATKINSON, Jill JOHNSTON, and groups such as the FURIES and RADICALESBIANS developed the concept of political lesbianism. This is sometimes taken to the simplistic extreme of assuming that all lesbians are 'natural' feminists because of their rejection of men, but as Anne KOEDT (1971) has pointed out, this 'is a confusion of a personal with a political solution. Sex-roles and male supremacy will not go away simply by women becoming lesbians.' Because it rejects SEX-ROLES, radical feminism necessarily incorporates lesbianism, and the lesbian perspective has been crucial to the development of a woman-centred analysis. According to Charlotte Bunch (1975), 'Lesbian-feminist politics is a political critique of the institution and ideology of heterosexuality as a cornerstone of male supremacy. It is an extension of the analysis of SEXUAL POLITICS to an analysis of SEXUALITY itself as an institution. It is a commitment to women as a political group, which is the basis of a political/economic strategy leading to power for women, not just an "alternative community".'

Although Bunch presents lesbian-feminism as a political perspective and 'a fight that heterosexual women can engage in', some lesbian-feminists feel that heterosexual women are disqualified not only from lesbianism but also from feminism if they maintain emotional and/or sexual relationships with men. Groups such as the Leeds Revolutionary Feminists protest against not only the institution of HETEROSEXUALITY, but also its practice, seeing in any sexual relationship between a woman and a man the paradigm of women's oppression. This view sees lesbian-feminism as the only feminism. Women can be lesbian-feminists without having sexual relationships with other women: as POLITICAL LESBIANS they may choose CELIBACY as long as they withdraw their energies from men to devote their lives and feelings to women only. Some lesbian-feminists argue that all women are lesbians but are kept from realizing this through the imposition of COMPULSORY HETEROSEXUALITY. In this view, perhaps best articulated by Adrienne RICH in *Compulsory Heterosexuality and Lesbian Existence* (1980), lesbianism is redefined not only as sexual preference or even as a life style, but as a whole range of WOMAN-IDENTIFIED experience which Rich calls the LESBIAN CONTINUUM.

(*See also* LOVE YOUR ENEMY?; GAY/STRAIGHT SPLIT; SEPARATISM)

Lessing, Doris, 1919–
Rhodesian-born English novelist. Although she does not identify herself with feminism and has moved on to other concerns in her writing, her novel THE GOLDEN NOTEBOOK (1962) was a fictional forerunner of and a valuable contribution to the modern women's movement.

Letters on the Equality of the Sexes and the Condition of Women
Series of letters written by Sarah GRIMKÉ, first published at the beginning July 1837 in the *New England Spectator* and gathered together as a book in 1838. Lucretia Mott considered it 'the best work after Mary Wollstonecraft's *A Vindication of the Rights of Woman*'. In it, the author challenged her critics on their own grounds, that of religion and scriptural authority, basing her argument that God had created men and women equal on her own careful reading of the Bible. The core of her argument was that although men and women might play different roles in society, they had the same moral obligations as human beings: 'Rights and duties depend *not* on *sex* but on our *relations* in life; as women we have *no* particular duties, but as mothers, wives and daughters we have.'

liberal feminism

The best-known type of feminism, it was also the first to develop, growing out of liberalism which originated in the eighteenth century. Liberalism is founded on a belief in the importance and independence of the individual, and the belief that individuals have certain innate rights which must be protected both by and from the government, and that freedom (specifically, freedom to define and seek one's own form of happiness) is the greatest good. Although the first liberal philosophers were men, writing for and about men and often assuming that women were irrational creatures and in their irrationality less than human, it was inevitable that educated women would be inspired by this new philosophy and recognize its relevance to their own lives. Mary WOLLSTONECRAFT was the first great philosopher of liberal feminism, arguing in A VINDICATION OF THE RIGHTS OF WOMAN (1792) that equality of rights and opportunities should be extended to women in all areas of life. The classic work of liberal feminism is still THE SUBJECTION OF WOMEN (1869) by John Stuart MILL.

In the present, liberal feminism is also known as MAINSTREAM FEMINISM and, particularly in America, is often perceived as the only feminism. Its basic concern is with EQUAL RIGHTS, with extending to women the liberal values of liberty, equality and justice through legal and social reforms. Women are discriminated against, argue liberal feminists, because they are always judged first as women and only second as human beings, whereas men are judged individually, on their own merits, rather than according to sexual stereotypes. They are concerned with ending this discrimination through legal changes and through educating people. Sex should be considered only when relevant as, for example, in the provision of maternity benefits.

Typical strategies of liberal feminism are legal and legislative actions such as lobbying, class-action and individual legal suits; working within the political system and building coalitions to have women's issues incorporated into all areas; trying to influence public opinion through education and the media, eliminating sex-role stereotypes and presenting more varied and positive images of women. Liberal feminists also respond to women's immediate needs at the local level by setting up shelters for BATTERED WOMEN, RAPE CRISIS CENTRES, or CHILDCARE facilities, and emphasize the importance of self-improvement and individual achievement.

Objections to liberal feminism from other feminists are that it is basically reformist in nature; that it ignores the realities of class and racial oppression as well as the deeply entrenched nature of

PATRIARCHY; and that it accepts male values rather than challenging them from a woman-centred perspective. Zillah EISENSTEIN has argued that there is a basic contradiction between liberalism and feminism because feminism contains a sex-class analysis of women's oppression which is not compatible with the individualist values of liberalism. She believes that all feminism is liberal at root, but that its potential is radical.

(*See also* BOURGEOIS FEMINISM; MARXIST-FEMINISM; SOCIALIST FEMINISM; RADICAL FEMINISM)

liberated woman, the

A popular myth. The assumption behind the use of this term is that there are individual solutions to a universal problem, and that women can liberate themselves in their personal lives. In fact, no matter how 'liberated' a woman may be from men and the cultural expectations imposed upon women, no one is free from the effects of PATRIARCHY, and until all women are liberated, no one is. When used by men and in the media the term most often refers to a woman who has achieved success on male terms, or who is perceived to be attractive and sexually available.

(*See also* WOMEN'S LIBERATION MOVEMENT)

liberation

From the Latin *liber*, meaning free, this term was first used in the context of releasing a nation or group of people from the rule of a tyrannical government, and then came to be used in the sense of black or women's liberation to refer to the constraints imposed by laws, social expectations, psychological and religious taboos, and sex-roles.

Lilith

1) In Hebrew mythology, the first woman, created just as Adam was, of the dust of the earth, as his equal. When Adam tried to make her lie beneath him she refused to be treated as his inferior, and left him. Thus, the first feminist. Naturally, a patriarchal religion could not approve of a free and independent female, so she was subsequently referred to as a demon of the night.

2) The first Jewish feminist magazine, it was founded in New York in 1976. Published quarterly, it was named after the legendary precursor of Eve. Contents include fiction, poetry, articles, essays and reviews intended to help JEWISH FEMINISTS to rediscover and rework Jewish practice.

Lily, The

Monthly newspaper established by Amelia BLOOMER in 1849. It began as a temperance paper, but within a year had become strongly feminist, publishing articles by Elizabeth Cady STANTON under the pseudonym 'Sunflower'. In 1852 the masthead was changed from 'Devoted to Temperance and Literature' to 'A monthly journal devoted to the Emancipation of Women from Intemperance, Injustice, Prejudice, and Bigotry'. In 1856, with a national circulation of over 6,000 proving that it reached more homes than any other feminist journal, Amelia Bloomer moved to Iowa, far from printing facilities, and was forced to sell it.

literary criticism

Feminist literary criticism was part of the women's liberation movement from the beginning, as can be seen in Kate MILLETT'S classic text SEXUAL POLITICS (1970) in which she used literary criticism to make a larger cultural critique and to develop her theory of sexual politics.

Feminist criticism originated as an investigation into and exposé of the sexual stereotyping of women, but quickly branched out. There is no one precise definition for what constitutes feminist criticism; unlike some other schools, it is not governed by a rigidly defined theory, but usually expresses a reaction against such theories. Its attitude is one of openness. It asks new questions of old texts, and has been defined by Adrienne RICH as an act of 'RE-VISION'. Some of its aims are:

1. to search for an underlying, consistent female tradition
2. to uncover and interpret the symbolism specific to women's writing so that it does not seem as incomprehensible or unimportant as it might when judged by male standards and symbols
3. to rediscover 'lost' works of the past
4. to reassess male writers from a feminist standpoint
5. to learn to resist the sexism in a text – while admitting it may be important or valuable in other ways
6. to become aware of the politics of style and language

Books in this field include THINKING ABOUT WOMEN by Mary ELLMANN (1968), *Literary Women* by Ellen MOERS (1976), A LITERATURE OF THEIR OWN by Elaine SHOWALTER (1977), *The Madwoman in the Attic* by Sandra M. Gilbert and Susan Gubar (1979) and *How to Suppress Women's Writing* by Joanna RUSS (1983).

Literature of Their Own, A

Subtitled *British Women Novelists from Brontë to Lessing*, this book by Elaine SHOWALTER, published in 1977, remains one of the most influential works of feminist LITERARY CRITICISM. Like *The Female Imagination* by Patricia Meyer Spacks (1975) and *Literary Women* by Ellen MOERS (1976), it is concerned with establishing the reality of a specifically female literary tradition, and attempts to prove its existence and power by tracing common concerns, themes and images through works by both established and lesser-known British novelists of the nineteenth and twentieth centuries.

literature

See L'ÉCRITURE FÉMININE; LITERARY CRITICISM; NOVELS AND NOVELISTS; POETS AND POETRY; SCIENCE FICTION; THEATRE

Lockwood, Belva Ann Bennett McNall, 1830–1917

American lawyer, teacher and politician. After years of implementing her advanced ideas as a teacher, she opened one of the first private, co-educational schools in Washington, D.C. She completed a degree in law at the National University Law School in May 1873 and qualified to practise law in the District of Columbia. However, when one of her cases came before the federal Court of Claims that winter, she was refused, as a woman, the right to plead. The Supreme Court similarly denied her, and she took her argument to Congress, finally winning the right to practise law in the highest courts in the land when a bill to this effect was passed in 1879. In March 1879, she became the first woman to practise before the Supreme Court. A year later, she sponsored the first Southern black, Samuel R. Lowery, admitted to practise before the Supreme Court.

Her feminism had been encouraged by a meeting with Susan B. ANTHONY in 1860, and in 1867 she helped to found the Universal Franchise Association, the first suffrage group in Washington, D.C. She was active in the cause of women's suffrage throughout the 1870s, and helped pass bills to improve the rights of married and working women.

In 1884 a small group of women calling themselves the 'National Equal Rights Party' nominated Belva Lockwood for President. She ran on a platform of equal rights for all; uniform marriage and divorce laws; curtailment of the traffic in liquor; and universal peace. She attracted a great deal of attention, and received 4,149 votes in six States and believed she had been defrauded of more. She ran again in 1888, but with less impressive results.

Her presidential campaigns were disapproved of by Susan B. Anthony and other suffrage leaders, and she became estranged from the women's suffrage movement, instead turning her attention to the cause of world peace. She became involved with the INTERNATIONAL COUNCIL OF WOMEN, and served on the executive committee of the Universal Peace Union and on the nominating committee for the Nobel Peace Prize.

Longest Revolution, The

Essay by Juliet MITCHELL, published in *New Left Review* in 1966. Written before there was an active women's movement in Britain, and highly influential in its subsequent development, this article was a successful attempt to revive the 'woman question' within Marxist circles. Mitchell has said that she wrote it out of her involvement with the New Left, and her dissatisfaction with previous attempts to explain women's position on purely economic grounds. She did not agree with such earlier socialist theorists as ENGELS and BEBEL that women would be liberated by being integrated into the public workforce, because she recognized that women were oppressed by structures other than capitalism. She identified the various structures which SOCIALIST-FEMINISTS must tackle in order to change women's position as: production, reproduction, sexuality and the socialization of children. This argument was later expanded into her book *Woman's Estate* (1971).

Lorde, Audre, 1934–
American poet. A black lesbian feminist, she is at the forefront of the development of non-racist feminist theory intended to embrace the diversity of women of all races and classes. She has written on such subjects as racism, love, hatred, anger and the connections between sexism and racism, but difference and its importance is one of her major themes. As she wrote in 1979: 'Advocating the mere tolerance of difference between women is the grossest reformism. It

is a total denial of the creative function of difference in our lives. For difference must be not merely tolerated, but seen as a fund of necessary polarities between which our creativity can spark like a dialectic.' Despite her importance as a theoretical writer, she is best known – both popularly and critically acclaimed – as a poet, the author of such books as *The First Cities* (1968), *Cables to Rage* (1970), *From a Land Where Other People Live* (1973), *New York Head Shop and Museum* (1975), *Coal* (1976), *Between Ourselves* (1976), *The Black Unicorn* (1978), *Chosen Poems* (1982) and *Zami: A New Spelling of My Name* (1982). A collection of her speeches and essays, including the well-known 'Uses of the Erotic: The Erotic as Power', was published as *Sister Outsider* in 1984.

Love Your Enemy?
Pamphlet published in 1981 by ONLYWOMEN Press. Subtitled *The debate between heterosexual feminism and political lesbianism*, it contained a conference paper titled *Political Lesbianism: The Case Against Heterosexuality* written by the Leeds Revolutionary Feminists in 1979 (first published in WIRES 81) along with some of the letters received in response from the heterosexual, bisexual and lesbian women who disagreed with the paper's conclusion that because heterosexuality was the most basic foundation and support of male supremacy,

heterosexual women were collaborators with the enemy and could only contribute to a feminist revolution by becoming POLITICAL LESBIANS. Like Adrienne RICH's *Compulsory Heterosexuality and Lesbian Existence* (1980), this is one of the key documents contributing to a feminist analysis of HETEROSEXUALITY.

(*See also* REVOLUTIONARY FEMINISM)

Lucy Stone League

Founded in New York in 1921 by Jane Grant, Harold Ross and Ruth Hale, this organization was the first to help women cope with legal and bureaucratic problems they might face in keeping their birth names after marriage.

(*See also* STONE, LUCY; NAMES)

Lucy Stoners

Term used in nineteenth-century America for women who followed the example of Lucy STONE by keeping their own names after marriage.

Lutz, Bertha, 1899–1976

Brazilian zoologist. Founder, in 1922, of the Brazil Federation for the Advancement of Women, she was the Brazilian delegate to the Inter-American Commission of Women. She organized and led the Brazilian campaign for women's suffrage, granted in 1931. In 1936 she established a government department to deal specifically with problems faced by women, and she was also successful in forming a United Nations Commission on the Status of Women.

Lyndall

Heroine, partially autobiographical, of Olive SCHREINER'S THE STORY OF AN AFRICAN FARM. She has been called by Elaine Showalter 'the first wholly serious feminist in the English novel, and she remains one of the few who is not patronized by her author.' Before they met, Schreiner's husband-to-be had been so inspired by the book as to declare that he would marry when he met Lyndall.

Lysistrata

Fictional character, from play of the same name by Aristophanes, who brings about an end to war by convincing women on both sides to refuse sexual favours to their men until they stop fighting. This idea, sometimes referred to as a 'sex strike', has often been proposed as a way women have power over men, but this has never been proven by actual trial. In September 1977, a group of women in Italy presented a 'Lysistrata Petition' threatening to spread among women the idea of a strike against childbirth and, if necessary, a strike against all sexual relations with men, unless their demands (which included an end to all wars, military service and arms production, as well as the use of nuclear energy for any purpose) were met. Similar threats have met with a similar lack of response from men as a group.

Lytton, Constance (Lady),
  1869–1923

English. A militant suffragette, a member of the WOMEN'S SOCIAL AND POLITICAL UNION, and frequently imprisoned for her activities. As an upper-class woman she received preferential treatment, and was released whenever she went on hunger strike. Therefore, in 1911, she disguised herself and was arrested as 'Jane Wharton', a seamstress, and was forcibly fed with such violence that she suffered a stroke which partially paralysed her. Even after this she continued to work for the movement, writing articles and organizing suffrage petitions.

M

Macaulay, Catherine, 1731–91
English historian. Famous as the author of a controversial, eight-volume *History of England*, highly influential in political and intellectual circles of the 1770s in England, France and America, she is not often remembered as an important feminist contemporary of Mary WOLLSTONECRAFT. In her *Letters on Education* (1790) Macaulay may have been the first to present the very modern argument that the apparent differences between men and woman are the result not of biology, but of social and educational factors. She argued for the importance of boys and girls receiving an identical education, but although she believed in co-education, she was critical of the male-biased system. In A VINDICATION OF THE RIGHTS OF WOMAN (1792), Wollstonecraft expanded upon many of Macaulay's points and described her as the 'woman of the greatest abilities that this country has ever produced'.

McCormick, Katharine Dexter, 1875–1967
American philanthropist. She spent much of her inherited wealth on the causes closest to her heart: women's suffrage, women's EDUCATION, and BIRTH CONTROL. She became involved in the women's rights movement in 1909, when she spoke at the first open-air demonstration in Massachusetts, and subsequently served as treasurer and vice president of the NATIONAL AMERICAN WOMAN SUFFRAGE ASSOCIATION, as well as subsidizing publication of the *Woman's Journal*. Her Swiss château provided a meeting place for the INTERNATIONAL WOMAN SUFFRAGE ALLIANCE, and she helped Margaret SANGER by smuggling diaphragms into the United States. In the 1920s she began her life-long sponsorship of contraceptive research, believing that a foolproof, physiological birth control method was the key to women's freedom. She had received a B.S. in biology from the Massachusetts Institute of Technology (MIT) in 1904, and through her interest in contraception she developed expertise in judging biomedical projects. She recognized the potential, in 1953, of the experiments Gregory Pincus was doing with progesterone as an ovulation suppressant, and gave him the funds he needed to develop the first contraceptive pill, marketed in 1960 as Enovid.

McGill, Helen, 1871–1947
Canadian journalist and lawyer. Encouraged by her mother, a pion-

eering suffragist, she became the only woman to graduate from the University of Trinity College, Toronto, in 1888, and became a professional journalist. As editor of a daily newspaper in St Paul, Minnesota, she campaigned for penal reform and equal rights for women. In 1902 she moved to Vancouver and began to practise law. She was active in the International Association of Women Lawyers, a member of the International Council of Women, and a founder of the Vancouver Women's Building.

McIntyre, Vonda, 1948–
American SCIENCE FICTION writer. She writes most often about future societies in which neither women nor men are trapped by SEX-ROLES, and strong, capable women have adventures. She has said that her work arises from her personal egalitarian philosophy. Her books include *The Exile Waiting* (1975), *Dreamsnake* (1978), *Fireflood and Other Stories* (1979) and *Superluminal* (1984), and she was co-editor, with Susan Janice Anderson, of *Aurora: Beyond Equality* (1976), an anthology of non-sexist science fiction.

McKinney, Louise, 1868–1933
Canadian politician. Elected in 1917 to the Alberta legislature as a candidate for the Non-partisan League (which advocated public ownership of grain stores and flour mills), she was the first woman member of any legislative body in the British Empire. She did not run again after her defeat in 1921. Active in the struggle for women's legal rights, she supported Emily MURPHY in her campaign to have women admitted to the Canadian Senate.

Macmillan, Chrystal, 1871–1937
Scottish. Active all her life in feminist and pacifist causes, in 1908 she became the first woman to address the House of Lords when she appealed (unsuccessfully) for her right as a graduate to vote for the parliamentary candidate for the Scottish Universities seat. She was a member for many years of the NATIONAL UNION OF WOMEN'S SUFFRAGE SOCIETIES, and Secretary of the INTERNATIONAL WOMAN SUFFRAGE ALLIANCE, 1913–23. She was one of the organizers of the International Women's Congress at The Hague in 1915, which led to the foundation of the Women's International League for Peace and Freedom. In 1923 she founded the Open Door Council, and in 1929 became president of the Open Door International for the Economic Emancipation of the Woman Worker. She was also involved in the struggle for women's right to retain their nationality regardless of marriage, and in 1935 stood (unsuccessfully) as the Liberal candidate for Edinburgh.

Mcphail, Agnes, 1890–1954
Canadian politician. Active in the women's suffrage movement and

various radical groups, she became Canada's first woman member of parliament in 1921, and held her seat until 1940. At first she voted Progressive, but in 1924 broke away as part of the 'Ginger Group' which formed the Co-operative Commonwealth Foundation in 1932. A member of the Ontario legislature from 1943–51.

M-A-D

Term coined by Honor Moore, the initials stand for 'Male Approval Desire' and indicate that women who are driven by the desire for male approval of whatever they do are driven M-A-D, or mad.

magazines

See CONDITIONS; ENGLISH WOMAN'S JOURNAL; FEMINIST REVIEW; FEMINIST STUDIES; FREEWOMAN; HERESIES; HOT WIRE; JOURNAL OF FEMALE LIBERATION; LILY, THE; LILITH; MONTHLY EXTRACT, THE; MS.; NEW DIRECTIONS FOR WOMEN; SHREW; SINISTER WISDOM; SIGNS; SPARE RIB; SHIFRA; TIME AND TIDE; TROUBLE AND STRIFE; UNA, THE; VOICE OF THE WOMEN'S LIBERATION MOVEMENT; WOMAN'S DREADNOUGHT; WOMEN'S SUFFRAGE JOURNAL

mainstream feminism

Term used, mainly in America, to refer to the most widely accepted and professed form of LIBERAL FEMINISM. It is reformist rather than revolutionary in nature, characterized by a concern for EQUAL RIGHTS, and faith in the power of legislation. MS. Magazine is often considered the voice of mainstream feminism.

Maitland, Sarah, 1950–

British writer. Involved in the women's liberation movement since 1970, she became a part of the Christian feminist movement in 1978. She is the author of a study of feminism and Christianity entitled *A Map of the New Country* (1983), and co-edited, with Jo Garcia, a collection of women's thoughts and expressions of spirituality called *Walking on the Water* (1983). Her first novel, *Daughter of Jerusalem* (1979), won the Somerset Maugham Award.

Malakhovskaya, Natalia, 1947–

Russian. She became involved in the underground Russian feminist movement in the late 1970s and formed the illegal Christian women's organization Club Maria. With Tatyana MAMONOVA and others she wrote and edited the first feminist *samizdat* journal in the Soviet Union, for which she was forced into exile in 1980.

male chauvinism

Belief held by men that theirs is the superior sex. This term for self-centred, wrong-headed thinking gained popularity in the late 1960s, at a time when the word chauvinism (meaning an excessive, jingoistic patriotism) was much in use to describe America's military involvement in Vietnam. Similar terms, which never gained quite such wide acceptance outside the movement, include PHALLO-CENTRIC, masculist, and ANDRO-CENTRIC.

(*See also* MCP)

MCP (Male Chauvinist Pig)
Common pejorative term used by members of the women's liberation movement to describe male opponents, from the late 1960s. Although still used today, it has a faintly old-fashioned ring, and is more often used by men to describe themselves – often proudly – than by feminists.

(*See also* MALE CHAUVINISM)

male feminists
Rare. According to some, a contradiction in terms. Whether or not they exist depends on the definition of feminism. Politically, feminism affects both sexes, but because the changes it envisions are more obviously beneficial to women and require men to give up privileges, men who call themselves feminists are regarded with suspicion by both sides. Men are most at ease with the idea of feminism as human rights, with extending to women equal opportunities without radically changing the established structure of society, and a man, John Stuart MILL, is the most famous philosopher of LIBERAL FEMINISM.

(*See also* MEN'S LIBERATION MOVEMENT)

Mamonova, Tatyana, 1943–
Russian poet and artist. Experiences of sexism among the nonconformist artists' movement in Leningrad made her a feminist, and in 1979 she was a member of the group who wrote and edited the first feminist *samizdat* journal in the Soviet Union. Forced into exile in 1980, she became involved in the international women's movement.

-man
See PERSON

man
Term for adult, male human being which is still occasionally used in the obsolete sense to mean humanity, or a human being of either sex. That it *is* obsolete in this usage has been made clear through numerous studies on LANGUAGE use and comprehension as well as by the difficulty the people (usually men) who speak generically about 'man's progress' or 'man, the tool-using animal' have with what should be in this case the equally acceptable concept of 'man's pregnancy'. In Old English the word *man* did mean a human being of either sex, while the gender-specific terms for adult males and females were, respectively, *waepman* and *wifman*. While *wifman* evolved into the modern word *woman*, *waepman* was lost, replaced by *man*, and its use as a synonym for 'person' became more and more ambiguous. It could only continue to be used in the pseudo-

generic sense because it was men who used it in this way, speaking or writing for other men and thus seeing no discrepancy in assuming that the human beings they wrote of would always be male. Women, understandably, have never felt as comfortable with the notion that 'man' sometimes means 'women and men'. The use of *man* in the obsolete generic sense, whether intentionally or not, tends to make women's contribution to civilization effectively invisible.
(*See also* PRONOUNS)

Manchester Women's Suffrage Committee

The first organization devoted to winning the vote for women in Great Britain, it was a small group founded by Lydia BECKER in January 1867.

Manley, Mary, 1663–1724

English writer. The first English-woman to write a bestseller – *Secret Memoirs and Manners of Several Persons of Quality of Both Sexes From the New Atlantis, an Island in the Mediterranean* (1709) – she was also the first to be arrested for her writing when that same work, a political satire, was declared libellous. She collaborated with Jonathan Swift and succeeded him as the editor of the *Examiner*, a Tory publication, in 1711. In her writings she often attacked the DOUBLE STANDARD and defended women, presenting female characters who were strong, passionate and coura-geous. Her last work was *The Power of Love* (1720), about the corruption of female innocence by male lust.

Man's World, Woman's Place

Book by Elizabeth JANEWAY, sub-titled *A Study in Social Mythology*, published in 1971. Drawing on history, sociology, psychology and anthropology to trace the development of the concept of separate spheres, in this book Janeway revealed how the 'bargain' by which women held power in the home and men in the world resulted in women's oppression. The book was widely praised by reviewers and critics as a thoughtful, scholarly, elegantly written and comprehensive survey of women's situation.

Manus, Rosa, 1880–1942

Dutch. She began her lifelong struggle for women's rights in 1904, when she became involved in the women's suffrage movement in Amsterdam. Once the vote had been won in the Netherlands she extended her range, touring South America and Europe to campaign for women's rights, and becoming vice-president of the International Federation for Women's Suffrage in 1926. She was also a pacifist, and organized peace conferences in Dresden and Berlin. She organized an International Women's Congress in Istanbul in 1935. She was arrested after the German invasion of the Netherlands, and died in Auschwitz.

'March of the Women'

The official battle song of the WOMEN'S SOCIAL AND POLITICAL UNION, written in 1911 by Ethel SMYTH, with words by Cicely HAMILTON.

marriage

Of central importance in all human societies, the institution of marriage has always been of great interest to feminists. Providing the basic model for the sexual division of labour, it can be seen as a microcosm of patriarchal society, and details of her marital status are still considered by many to be the most important fact about an individual woman.

To the earliest feminists, marriage reform was a priority. The doctrine of COVERTURE, a basic principle of English common law which also applied in America and many European countries, meant that for a woman, marriage was civil death. The few rights she had possessed as a single woman were forfeited upon marriage, when her legal existence became incorporated into that of her husband. She lost all right to act for herself and her husband gained total control over her property, person and life.

From the 1820s women actively campaigned for more equitable marriage and divorce laws. Not all of them were feminists. Some, like Caroline NORTON, did not object to the division of power between men and women, but only sought protection from the misuse of this power by particularly brutal men. The first Married Women's Property Acts were passed in the United States in 1839, and in Britain in 1857, and with this very basic recognition of women as individuals the way towards legal equality with men began to open.

Despite the many changes in the legal and social perceptions of marriage since the 1820s, reforms continue to be needed and worked for in the 1980s. The idea that a woman gives up her individual identity and becomes the property of a man when she marries is a tenacious one, still expressed in many areas of law and custom today. Although marriage is often said to be an equal partnership, the woman is still expected to submerge her personality in that of her husband by taking his name and accommodating her life to his needs. A majority of women work at paying jobs outside the home but still work the 'DOUBLE SHIFT' by doing unpaid housework as well. In the 1960s the idea of 'marriage contracts' emerged in the women's liberation movement, and some women have found that spelling out the rights, needs and expectations of each partner before marriage is a useful way of reforming marriage on a personal level. But social, not merely personal, expectations of marriage must change if it is ever to become an equal partnership. The fact that marital rape is only rarely recognized as a crime (since the late 1970s, under pressure from feminist groups, some American states changed their laws on rape to allow husbands to be prosecuted, but in Britain husbands may still rape their wives) is probably the most glaring example of how married women are still denied recognition as individuals. Although women who marry are not specifically told this, the legal assumption is that in agreeing to marry a man a woman not only consents to sexual relations with him, she gives up the right to withdraw that consent for as long as the marriage lasts.

Mary WOLLSTONECRAFT was the first to label marriage 'LEGAL PROSTITUTION', and from her time to the present there has been a strong feminist tendency which sees reform as worse than useless, and calls for the abolition of marriage. Before the availability of effective BIRTH CONTROL measures, marriage was often seen as providing the necessary security for women and their children, and as a means of controlling potentially dangerous male SEXUALITY. Now, when more women have the material means to support themselves and to decide when, whether and under what circumstances they will bear and raise children, they also have the freedom to look more critically at marriage.

Marxist theory sees monogamous marriage as a capitalist structure based on the domestic slavery of the wife, Friedrich ENGELS declaring that within the family the husband was the bourgeois and the wife the proletarian. Once the capitalist state is destroyed, and women are a full part of the public work force, in this view there will be no economic inequality, and therefore no other inequality within marriage.

Radical feminists recognize other forms of inequality and oppression within marriage besides the economic. They have defined marriage under PATRIARCHY as SEXUAL SLAVERY, with the linked institutions of marriage and family identified as the structures which reproduce and perpetuate women's subordination. In 1969 the American group called THE FEMINISTS declared: 'We can't destroy the inequalities between men and women until we destroy marriage. We must free ourselves. And marriage is the place to begin.' Among the many feminists who called upon women to free themselves, Germaine GREER wrote in 1970: 'If independence is a necessary concomitant of freedom, women must not marry.'

Yet however oppressive and unsatisfactory the present reality of marriage, as an ideal it has a powerful hold on the imagination and emotions. Writers of non-sexist UTOPIAS have suggested various forms future egalitarian marriages might take, based on the raising of children, shared interests, love or liking – based on almost everything except the economic necessity and social coercion which has marked marriages in the past. And in their own lives many women are experimenting with different forms of partnership, temporary or life-long, monogamous or not, homosexual, heterosexual or group, in attempts to find non-oppressive ways of living together.

Marsden, Dora, 1882–1960
English philosopher. A militant suffragette, she was first an active member of the WOMEN'S SOCIAL AND POLITICAL UNION (WSPU) then of the WOMEN'S FREEDOM LEAGUE. Unwilling to take orders or submerge her own ideas, she went her own way in 1911, founding the FREEWOMAN, which she edited (with the help of Mary GAWTHORPE) until 1914. At that time she withdrew from public life to think and write. She was a visionary feminist, more interested in metaphysics than in politics, and her chief concern in life was linguistic philosophy and the nature of thought. She constructed a new philosophical system which she attempted to reveal to the world through her books: *The Definition of the Godhead* (1928), *Mysteries of Christianity* (1930) and *The Philosophy of Time* (1955). Her friend and publisher Harriet Shaw Weaver, who was at the same time sponsoring James Joyce, believed that both writers were geniuses who would open new horizons in their respect-

ive fields of literature and philosophy, but although Joyce made the expected impact, Marsden's books were scarcely noticed.

Martin, Anne Henrietta,
1875–1951
American. She founded and headed the history department at the University of Nevada in 1897. During a visit to England (1909–11) she joined the WOMEN'S SOCIAL AND POLITICAL UNION and the Fabian Society, was arrested for demonstrating for women's rights, and began to write on social issues under the name Anne O'Hara. She returned to Nevada at the end of 1911 and led the Nevada Equal Franchise Society in a campaign which triumphed with the ratification of a state suffrage amendment in November 1914. After 1914, she became involved with the NATIONAL AMERICAN WOMAN SUFFRAGE ASSOCIATION and the CONGRESSIONAL UNION FOR WOMAN SUFFRAGE. In 1917 she became vice chairman and legislative chairman of the National Woman's Party, and proved to be one of the Party's most effective speakers. In 1918 she resigned and returned to Nevada to begin her campaign for Senator, becoming the first woman to run for the United States Senate. She chose to run as an independent, wanting to give women an alternative to male-dominated party politics, and although she polled only 20 per cent of the vote, she attracted

much support from other women.

In 1921 she moved to California and wrote many articles and essays for British and American magazines, calling upon women to express 'sex solidarity' by supporting other women and challenging the male control of politics and culture. She also became active in the WOMEN'S INTERNATIONAL LEAGUE FOR PEACE AND FREEDOM, and served on the national board from 1926–36.

Martineau, Harriet, 1802–76
English writer and political economist. Her first article was published when she was nineteen, but it was not until the family business collapsed in 1829 that she was able to stop apologizing for her 'unwomanly' interests and devote herself to her writing career as she became the chief financial support of the Martineau family. Her series *Illustrations of Political Economy* (1832–4) made her a literary celebrity and she was offered the editorship of a new economics journal – a position she refused because of her brother's disapproval. In 1849 she became Secretary of Bedford College for Women in London. Her interest in reform was concentrated chiefly on the abolition of slavery, economic change, and the 'Woman Question'. A lifelong feminist, she campaigned for better education for women, and believed that women must be given the opportunity for economic independence. Her 1859 article 'Female Industry' inspired the formation of the SOCIETY FOR PROMOTING THE EMPLOYMENT OF WOMEN. Among her books are the novel *Deerbrook* (1839), *Life in the Sickroom* (1844) and her *Autobiography*, published posthumously in 1877.

Marxist-feminism
Although Marxism is theoretically committed to women's liberation, there has been a long and continuing dispute between feminism and Marxism. This is usually presented as an argument about whether class or sexual oppression should take priority, since traditionally Marxism considers the class struggle to be basic, whereas feminism (particularly radical feminism) believes male domination of women is fundamental. According to ENGELS – whose ORIGIN OF THE FAMILY, PRIVATE PROPERTY AND THE STATE is the foundation upon which all Marxist analysis of the WOMAN QUESTION is built – monogamy is the primary institution for the oppression of women, and monogamy is MARRIAGE based on the idea of private ownership, hence inextricably linked to CAPITALISM and a class society. Capitalism must be destroyed not only to free the workers, but to emancipate women both as workers and in their particular relation to REPRODUCTION. Marxists do not see this as a matter of a class revolution having to pre-

cede one to free women, but see inevitable connections between capitalism and PATRIARCHY as the common enemy of women and the working class. They reject both RADICAL and LIBERAL FEMINISM as BOURGEOIS FEMINISM, a form of FALSE CONSCIOUSNESS which only serves the interests of the ruling class by obscuring class differences and thus delaying the revolution. They argue that women should not unite as women, but should recognize the long-term interests they have in common with working-class men and achieve liberation through a shared struggle. SOCIAL-IST FEMINISM is dependent upon Marxist analysis, and committed to Marxist goals, yet feminists recognize that traditional Marxism fails to acknowledge the full extent of women's oppression. While explaining how capitalism benefits from patriarchy, Marxism does not explain how patriarchy also works independently of capitalism, nor why women as a group are oppressed by men as a group even in pre-capitalist societies.

In 1973, a number of American women were driven by the contradictions they felt between their feminism and their continuing commitment to Marxism to form Marxist-feminist Group I (M-F I) in the hope of forming a synthesis, a genuinely new method for understanding and working to overcome all forms of oppression. Subsequently, at least four more M-F groups were formed. One of the members, Rosalind Petchesky, defined M-F as being neither an organization nor a movement, but 'the structural expression of a political and personal tendency: the urge of a considerable number of women, long active in both the women's movement and the independent left, to integrate the two major aspects of their own political thought and practice'. (1979)

BEYOND THE FRAGMENTS was another attempt to develop a new, productive form of feminist social-ism or socialist feminism which would draw upon the insights of both Marxism and feminism. Some feminists feel that the struggle to resolve the contradictions in what has been called 'the unhappy marriage of Marxism and feminism' is worthwhile and necessary; others, that Marxism is another male-dominated, therefore limited, ideology which oppresses feminism as much as any chauvinistic husband, so that divorce is preferable.

(*See also* BEBEL, AUGUST)

materialism

Historical materialism is a fundamental tenet of Marxism: the belief that human consciousness is determined by social conditions rather than being the pre-existing determining factor itself. Regardless of any connection with or rejection of Marxism, feminism holds by definition a materialist conception of human nature. As Christine DELPHY has argued in 'For a Materialist Feminism' (1975) (English translation, 1981), the very existence of feminism as a social movement is based on the idea of changing the situation of women and the idea that a situation can be changed implies belief in the social (rather than 'natural' or inevitable) origins of that situation. Feminist materialism attempts to identify the material interests which are satisfied by the systematic oppression of women, and to point out the benefits men derive from it, as a necessary first step towards a feminist revolution. THE DIALECTIC OF SEX (1970) by Shulamith Firestone was one of the first attempts to develop a materialist view of history based on sex.

maternal instinct

Probably imaginary. An excuse used to justify and perpetuate SEXISM. The idea that women have an 'instinct' for CHILDCARE hides the reality of psychological and cultural conditioning, as well as all the social pressures upon women to bear and raise children. Recent research on other mammals has shown that the potential for maternal behaviour exists in both sexes and will manifest itself in adults of either sex in response to prolonged exposure to the new-born. Biologists Evelyn Shaw and Joan Darling (1985) have suggested that women rather than men mother not because of any-

thing physiologically or psychologically innate, but simply because women are there when a baby is born.

(*See also* MOTHERHOOD; BIOLOGICAL DIFFERENCES)

matriarchy

Literally, the rule of the mothers; a society governed by women. It has sometimes been depicted as the mirror-image of PATRIARCHY, a system under which women dominate men, but this is not how the term is most often used by feminists. Marxists mean by it an egalitarian, pre-class society where women and men share equally in production and power. Some object to the implication of a hierarchical structure in the word and prefer to use such terms as MATRISTIC or MATRIFOCAL to name a woman-centred alternative to patriarchy. Those feminists who do define matriarchy as a system in which women rather than men have the power conceive of female power as something very different from the manipulative, domineering and aggressive power of males. The rule of women is seen as being in harmony with nature, non-coercive, non-violent, valuing wholeness and the sense of connection between people.

J. J. BACHOFEN was the first (1861) to propose the theory that matriarchy had preceded patriarchy: that MOTHER RIGHT had existed before the rule of the father.

Others who have written in some depth on the case for prehistoric matriarchy include Matilda Joslyn GAGE, Helen DINER, Elizabeth Gould DAVIS, Evelyn Reed, Merlin Stone and Elizabeth Fisher. Although most anthropologists reject the idea of a universal, prehistoric matriarchy which was overthrown by the rule of men, there is certainly much evidence that women's position was very different in prehistoric societies, and GODDESS-worshipping societies may have been matriarchal in some sense. There are no matriarchal cultures in the world today (matrilineal societies, sometimes misleadingly referred to as MATRIARCHAL, figure kinship through the mother's line, but power is still held by males) and the case that they ever existed rests on fragmentary, tantalizing evidence from myth and archeology.

Whether matriarchies ever existed in fact may be less important than the concept that they might. As a symbol, matriarchy helps women believe in their own power and to struggle against male domination, which is no longer seen as inevitable. The idea of a matriarchy as a golden age for women has inspired many poets, philosophers, artists and dreamers, and it provides an ideal to strive for in the future, whether or not it can be found in the past. As Monique WITTIG wrote in her novel *Les Guérillères*: 'You say there are no

words to describe this time, you say it does not exist. But remember. Make an effort to remember. Or, failing that, invent.'

(*See also* UTOPIA; SPIRITUALITY; HISTORY)

matrifocal

Literally, 'mother-focused'. Anthropological term coined in 1956 by Raymond T. Smith, it is used to refer to societies in which the role of the mother is highly valued, giving her economic and political power within the kin group, and in which the relationship between the sexes is relatively egalitarian.

matrilineal

Term used for a society which traces kinship and inheritance through the mother's line. Although some anthropologists have suggested matriliny may be a remnant of a prehistoric MATRIARCHY, most agree that even in matrilineal cultures men rather than women have the power. Uncles, rather than fathers, have authority according to this system. Women may be more highly valued in such a society (as opposed to the more common patrilineal societies) – if so, it may be referred to as a MATRIFOCAL culture.

matristic

Term sometimes used as an adjective in preference to 'matriarchal' to describe woman-centred, women-supportive societies on the grounds that the structure of the word 'matriarchal' implies a hierarchy which would not actually exist in such a society.

matrophobia
Term coined by poet Lynn Sukenick, meaning the fear of becoming one's own mother, which has been the theme of much women's literature. Adrienne RICH suggested that 'the mother stands for the victim in ourselves, the unfree woman, the martyr' and that 'the loss of the daughter to the mother, the mother to the daughter, is the essential female tragedy.' As a cure for matrophobia, Mary Daly has proposed the recognition of DAUGHTER-RIGHT.

Mattapoisett
Future non-sexist utopia described by Marge PIERCY in her novel WOMAN ON THE EDGE OF TIME (1976).

Mead, Margaret, 1901–77
American anthropologist. Enormously influential and admired, her greatest contribution was in making the insights of ANTHROPOLOGY accessible to ordinary people through her many books, lectures and films. She was one of the first to study child-rearing practices and connect them with the overall pattern of the society. Two of her books, *Sex and Temperament in Three Primitive Societies* (1935) and *Male and Female* (1949), offered cross-cultural perspectives to reveal

that woman's role was far more socially than biologically determined. It was this work which later feminists were able to build on in formulating the distinction between sex and GENDER and denying the primacy of innate, biological distinctions.

Memoirs of an Ex-Prom Queen
One of the first novels to emerge from the American women's liberation movement, it was written by Alix Kates SHULMAN and published in 1972. Not unlike the later *Fear of Flying*, it is the emotional and sexual odyssey of one young woman in the contemporary world, but a powerful feminist consciousness informs the writing throughout, revealing how the FEMININE MYSTIQUE constantly defines and limits Sasha Davis, the 'ex-Prom Queen' of the title, as she struggles against and yet is trapped by her own beautiful image.

Men Against Sexism
The first Men Against Sexism group started in Brighton in 1971, made up chiefly of men who were involved with women in the women's liberation movement. During the 1970s MAS groups were formed in other parts of Britain, and a newsletter occasionally published to keep the groups in touch with each other. These groups have alternated in purpose between trying to help women (practically, by providing child-

care, and on a longer-term basis by attempting to change men's attitudes) and existing to put men in touch with each other and to learn more about their own health, sexuality and emotions.

(*See also* MEN'S LIBERATION MOVEMENT; EFFEMINISM)

men's liberation movement

This began in 1969 with the establishment of the first male consciousness-raising group in New York City, and then followed the growth of the women's liberation movement in Britain and America on a much smaller scale, attracting chiefly young, white, middle-class, leftist men who were feeling isolated by their exclusion from the sisterhood their female colleagues and partners had discovered.

From the very beginning there has been a division in the men's movement between those who feel their main aim is to provide support for the women's liberation and gay liberation movements, and those men drawn together in their own interests. The first group is less likely to use the term 'men's liberation' because it sounds as if it is in opposition to women's liberation. They prefer to call themselves MEN AGAINST SEXISM, or EFFEMINISTS, or anti-sexist or pro-feminist men. They are aware of the difference between institutional and personal sexism, and realize that even if a man refuses to oppress the women he knows, he is still part of a privileged group, and benefits from (even if he is emotionally crippled by) the institution of sexism. They are consciously aware of the dangers of men's involvement in feminism: that they might, even unintentionally, co-opt the women's movement by channelling energies into male-determined directions; and that their consciousness-raising groups, instead of making them more aware of their own sexist attitudes, might simply be another form of male bonding, to women's detriment.

The other group, proponents of men's liberation, hold the view that men and women are somehow equally oppressed by sexism. They see sexism as an institution which prescribes crippling, harmful, stereotyped sex-roles, and rather than exploring how men benefit from the perpetuation of sexism they look at how men are harmed by it. These men are, therefore, less concerned with aiding the women's movement than with learning to get in touch with their own emotions and break out of the traditional male role. This attitude led, by the 1980s, to the development of a definite hostility towards feminism in some men's groups.

Men's Political Union for Women's Enfranchisement (MPU)

Militant British organization founded by Victor Duval in 1910 as the male auxiliary of the WOMEN'S

SOCIAL AND POLITICAL UNION. By 1913, the WSPU had officially excluded men from their fight, and the connection with MPU was severed. Many of the men involved chose to join the United Suffragists.

menstruation

Throughout history, all over the world, menstruation has been considered either a sign of female weakness (making women unfit for certain jobs and responsibilities) or as a powerful, dangerous phenomenon to be surrounded by taboos. Although Elizabeth Gould DAVIS theorized that menstrual taboos originated during a prehistoric MATRIARCHY as a means of protecting women and enhancing their power, these taboos have always been used by men as an excuse to exclude women from certain aspects of life. Even where there are no explicit rules and regulations regarding menstruating women, the force of superstition and custom is enough to make this natural bodily function seem shameful. Modern feminists have tried to overcome this shame by sharing experiences and trying to develop different attitudes towards menstruation through increased understanding. Rather than denying this aspect of their lives as women, more writers and artists have felt free to use it. Judy CHICAGO's 'Menstrual Bathroom' in Womanhouse (1971–72) is one example in art, and such books as

The Wise Wound by Penelope Shuttle and Peter Redgrove (1978) and *Menstruation and Menopause* (UK: *Female Cycles*) by Paula Weidegger (1976) have explored the positive as well as negative aspects of 'the curse'. Judy GRAHN and Emily Culpepper are among those who have suggested that it is actually a blessing we should glorify and learn from, while others would agree with Germaine GREER that 'Menstruation does not turn us into raving maniacs or complete invalids; it is just that we would rather do without it.' (1970). One of the most revolutionary ideas to emerge from the women's health movement in America during the early 1970s was that of menstrual extraction. In 1971, feminists developed a simple extraction device (consisting of a tube attached to a collection bottle, and a syringe used as a pump) to remove the entire menstrual flow on the day that it began, and promoted its use as part of a self-help, self-examination routine. There are drawbacks – risks of infection, and unknown possible long-term effects – yet the concept itself, and the willingness of women to help themselves, emphasize how women are reclaiming their bodies.

Meredith, George, 1828–1909
British writer. Author of *Diana of the Crossways* (1885), a novel based on the life of Caroline NORTON. He had an affinity with intellectual

women who established relationships with men on their own terms, and supported women's suffrage.

Méricourt, Théroigne de,
1762–1817

French. Women's organizer and leader in the French Revolution. Dressed as an AMAZON, she was one of the first in the storming of the Bastille, and led the Women's March to Versailles. She travelled around Paris in a riding habit giving speeches to women about their rights and duty to fight alongside men, and she organized women's clubs which antagonized male Jacobins. In 1793 she fell from popularity and was attacked and beaten by a gang of Parisian women. Either a blow or the shock affected her mind, and she spent the last twenty years of her life in an asylum.

metaethics

Term from meta (beyond or of a higher logical order) + ethics (study of moral principles) used in Mary DALY's GYN/ECOLOGY: *The Metaethics of Radical Feminism* (1978). She defined radical feminist metaethics as not merely the study of ethics, but as a whole new discipline, 'of a deeper intuitive type' than patriarchal ethics, and capable of uncovering the hidden structure of patriarchal thinking.

metaphysical feminism

Term used by Robin MORGAN in *Going Too Far* (1977) for her idea of 'an all-encompassing feminist vision which goes literally beyond the physical (yet never leaves it behind)'. She did not use the word 'metaphysical' in the traditional philosophical sense, but derived it from the name Samuel Johnson gave to a group of seventeenth-century English poets (including Donne, Herbert, Crashaw and Marvell) with whom she felt modern feminists had a particular affinity in their 'demand for synthesis, the refusal to be narrowed into desiring less than everything'.

M-F 1–5
See MARXIST-FEMINISM

middle-class feminism
See BOURGEOIS FEMINISM; IMPERIAL FEMINISM; MAINSTREAM FEMINISM

Mikhailov, M.L., 1829–65
Russian. He wrote a series of articles on 'the woman question' between 1859–65 which made it an established subject in Russian intellectual circles. His writings had a great influence on the consciousness of women, and although he didn't raise the question of political rights, he promoted the idea of equal education, equal marriage, and economic independence for women.

militant suffragists

Term used for nineteenth- and early twentieth-century campaigners for women's rights who believed in DIRECT ACTION to force through legal changes. In order to draw attention to their demands they waged a war which included public demonstrations, civil disobedience, trespassing, disrupting political speeches, and damaging and destroying both public and private property. The main force behind the militant campaign in Britain was the WOMEN'S SOCIAL AND POLITICAL UNION. Alice PAUL learned militant tactics in England and brought them to America when she founded the CONGRESSIONAL UNION FOR WOMAN SUFFRAGE. Militant tactics were less common in other countries, although there were usually some who would try them when the polite, socially acceptable methods were seen to fail. Militant suffragists were also known, especially in Britain, as SUFFRAGETTES.

Mill, Harriet
See TAYLOR, HARRIET

Mill, John Stuart, 1806–73
English philosopher, economist and politician. Probably the best known, most influential man in the history of feminism, he presented the classic liberal argument for women's rights in THE SUBJECTION OF WOMEN (1869). It was through his intellectual and emotional partnership with Harriet TAYLOR, whom he met in 1830, that his belief in the principle of equal rights for women developed from an abstract ideal into a powerful commitment.

He not only wrote on the subject, but acted on it. Standing for Parliament, he announced his conviction that women were entitled to equal representation, and was elected as a Liberal M.P. for Westminster. During his term (1865–8) he presented the KENSINGTON SOCIETY's suffrage petition to the House of Commons in 1866, and in 1867 he introduced a motion – the first of its kind in Britain – to enfranchise women on the grounds that taxpayers must not be deprived of representation. The motion was defeated by 196 votes to 73.

Miller, Elizabeth Smith,
1822–1911
American. Best remembered as the designer of what became known as BLOOMERS. Finding trailing skirts a nuisance when she gardened, she made herself what she called the 'short dress', which came to four inches below the knee and was worn over voluminous, ankle-length trousers. Early in 1851 she wore this costume while visiting her father's cousin, Elizabeth Cady STANTON. Impressed by its comfort and practicality, Elizabeth Cady Stanton and Amelia BLOOMER made themselves similar outfits, and Amelia Bloomer advocated it in THE LILY, as a result of which the dress became known by her name. Elizabeth Smith Miller wore bloomers for another seven years, longer than any of her followers, before giving up her personal battle

for DRESS REFORM. She continued to be involved in the women's rights movement, through her friendship with Susan B. ANTHONY and as a financial supporter of both National and New York woman suffrage associations, and was honorary president of the Geneva Political Equality Club until her death.

Millett, Kate, 1934–
American writer and artist. One of the earliest and most influential theorists of the Women's Liberation Movement, she came to political activism through her involvement in the civil rights movement of the 1960s, and was a founding committee member of the NATIONAL ORGANIZATION FOR WOMEN (NOW). Her first book, SEXUAL POLITICS (1970) became a cornerstone of the new movement. A radical feminist, she demanded not only the legal and economic changes to which NOW was committed, but also called on women and men to examine and change their personal and sexual attitudes. During the crisis over LESBIANISM (the GAY/STRAIGHT SPLIT) within the American Women's Liberation Movement in 1970, she spoke openly about her bisexuality. She was attacked by the media for this (*Time* claimed this disclosure had discredited her as a spokeswoman for feminism and cast doubt on her theories) but as gay and straight women united in her support the ultimate result was to strengthen

the movement. She continued throughout the 1970s to be active in feminist politics, her scope becoming international. In 1979 her activities on behalf of women's rights in Iran caused her to be expelled from that country. She has also continued her work as a sculptor, with shows in New York and Los Angeles. Her other works include a film about women, *Three Lives* (1971), an autobiography, *Flying* (1974), and other books including *The Prostitution Papers* (1976), *Sita* (1977), and *The Basement: Meditation on a Human Sacrifice* (1979).

Mink, Paule, 1839–1900
French. While still a teenager, she joined Republican and feminist societies in Paris, and in 1868 she founded a women's mutual aid society and began giving public lectures on women's work. She continued to work for women's interests in various socialist groups in France, and by 1893 was working for women's suffrage. In 1893 she became a member of the Comité Révolutionnaire Central, and stood as one of the five women candidates for the National Assembly. She led the socialist women's movement in France from 1896 until her death.

Mitchell, Juliet, 1940–
British psychoanalyst. Her essay 'THE LONGEST REVOLUTION', published in *New Left Review* in 1966, was important as the first attempt in decades to combine

socialism and feminism, to use Marxist theory to try to understand the reasons behind women's oppression. This essay, as well as her later pamphlet, 'Women's Liberation and the New Politics' (1969), had a profound effect on the development of modern feminism. A later book, *Psychoanalysis and Feminism* (1974) continued her concern with the ideologies underlying women's position, this time taking FREUD's theories about the unconscious and the construction of FEMININITY and demonstrating their importance as tools for analysing – and challenging – patriarchal society. Her other writings include *Woman's Estate* (1971) and *Women: The Longest Revolution* (1984), a collection of essays on politics, feminism, literature and PSYCHOANALYSIS.

Moers, Ellen, 1928–79

American critic and scholar. Best known as the author of *Literary Women* (1976), in which she established the existence of a specifically female literary tradition by her examination of great woman writers through the ages, and thus contributed substantially to the development of feminist LITERARY CRITICISM.

monogamy

See MARRIAGE

Monster

Collection of poems by Robin MORGAN, published in America in 1972. The first book of militant, explicitly feminist poems ever to be published by a major, commercial publishing house.

Montagu, Lady Mary Wortley, 1689–1762

English writer. Author of a series of published letters based on her experiences in Turkey from 1716–18, as well as a poet and playwright, she is also remembered for her introduction of smallpox vaccinations to England. As the publisher of a periodical called *The Nonsense of Common Sense*, she was one of the earliest female political journalists in England, as well as an influential salon hostess. While her feminism is evident in her letters and her journalism, there is some question as to whether she went further, to develop a systematic, feminist critique of society. Although she never claimed it, most scholars believe that she used the pseudonym 'SOPHIA', and that, as the author of WOMAN NOT INFERIOR TO MAN (1739), she should be mentioned, with Mary ASTELL, as one of the earliest of English feminists, a pioneering foremother of Mary WOLLSTONECRAFT and others.

Monthly Extract, The

Subtitled *An Irregular Periodical*, this was the first newsletter of the women's HEALTH MOVEMENT. Founded in August 1972 by Millie Alleyn and Lolly and Jeanne Hirsch, it was based in Connecticut and published throughout the 1970s, containing reports, letters, ideas, newspaper clippings and health information. It was crucial as a means of creating a network of communication for women interested in health and medical issues in America and abroad, and helped to strengthen and spread the growth of the feminist health movement.

Morgan, Lewis Henry, 1818–81
American anthropologist. Author of *Ancient Society* (1877), a book based on his field studies of native American cultures which greatly influenced Karl Marx and provided the ethnological base for Friedrich ENGELS' THE ORIGIN OF THE FAMILY, PRIVATE PROPERTY AND THE STATE. In his book, Morgan developed a theory of the evolution of the human family from primordial promiscuity, through group marriage and matrilineal families, to the late development of patriarchal monogamy. Although he himself drew no political implications from his theory, and although his assumptions are now out-dated, he was an important influence on feminist and matriarchal theorists who followed. By opposing the widely accepted idea of his contemporaries – that the monogamous, patriarchal family had always been the basic unit of human society – he opened the way for the recognition that women's oppression was not natural, but culturally imposed.
(*See also* MATRIARCHY)

Morgan, Robin, 1941–
American writer. As an activist, theorist, poet and reporter she has been one of the most visible participants in the women's liberation movement since its beginning. She edited *Sisterhood is Powerful* (1970), the first anthology of writings from the modern women's movement to reach a wide audience. She is the author of two non-fiction books, *Going Too Far: The Personal Chronicle of a Feminist* (1978) and *The Anatomy of Freedom* (1982), which combine autobiography, polemic, speculation and reportage in developing feminist theory. Her feminism is also expressed in her poetry, which has been collected in several volumes, including MONSTER (1972) and *Lady of the Beasts* (1976). In addition to being a leading figure in the American movement, she is also active in international feminism, and edited *Sisterhood is Global* (1984), an anthology about women's issues and status all over the world.

Mother Right
From the German term *Mutterrecht*, as used by the matriarchal theorist J. J. BACHOFEN, it refers to the matrilineal social structure (i.e. one in which kinship and line of descent are reckoned only through the mother), which is not necessarily one in which women have any particular rights or powers. Jane ALPERT adopted the term as the title for her 1973 essay in which she

declared her belief that the capacity to bear and nurture children was the source of women's greatest power, and called for a feminist revolution to overthrow the rule of men and re-establish a MATRIARCHY.

motherhood

For many young women in the late 1960s and early 1970s, the women's liberation movement meant liberation from motherhood. They were rejecting the role traditionally offered to women and demanding the autonomy of REPRODUCTIVE FREEDOM, which included the right to cheap, safe abortions and effective birth control which would make motherhood a genuine choice rather than an inevitable destiny. Shulamith FIRESTONE, in THE DIALECTIC OF SEX (1970), located the cause of women's oppression in biological motherhood, and saw the possibility of a feminist revolution offered by new reproductive technologies to free women from the necessity of 'barbaric' pregnancy and birth.

A deeper, more thoughtful analysis of motherhood, which recognized that it was more complicated than mere biology, began to develop in the mid-1970s, most influentially in OF WOMAN BORN by Adrienne RICH.

Rich identified two aspects of motherhood: motherhood as experience, and motherhood as institution. It was the institution of motherhood, created by PATRIARCHY, which oppressed women. Under patriarchy, motherhood is forced labour. Men control it all, deciding when children will be born and how they are to be raised, even though women do the actual work. The institution of motherhood is the fundamental process in reproducing male dominance and keeping women oppressed. According to Rich, it is an invisible edifice constructed of such elements as RAPE, the economic dependence of MARRIAGE, the concept of illegitimacy, laws concerning abortion, unsafe birth control methods, the rights (and token responsibilities) of fathers over children, unequal pay for women and inadequate public CHILDCARE, the unrecognized emotional work women do in the family, and feelings of love and guilt.

To destroy the institution of motherhood is not to abolish motherhood itself, but rather to release it from male control. Within the actual experience of motherhood, Rich and many other feminists have located a source of strength for women, and many positive values which provide not only great joy, satisfaction and creativity for individual women, but also the basis for a new female culture.

(*See also* CHODOROW; FAMILY)

Mott, Lucretia, 1793–1880
American. One of the most prominent women in the ABOLITION MOVEMENT, she was also a founder

of the first women's movement.
The experience which led her, with
Elizabeth Cady STANTON and
others, to call the first convention
for women's rights in 1848, in
SENECA FALLS, New York, took
place in London at the 1840 Anti-
Slavery Convention when Mott,
Stanton, and all the other female
delegates were refused seats. She
presided over the third national
women's rights convention in 1852,
in Syracuse, addressing more than
2,000 members. Described by
historian Mary BEARD as 'a genuine
radical with balance', Mott was
widely loved, and combined ideal-
ism with practicality. She was disturbed by the division in the
movement which resulted in two
separate groups (NATIONAL WOMAN
SUFFRAGE ASSOCIATION and AMERI-
CAN WOMAN SUFFRAGE ASSOCI-
ATION), and refused to take sides
herself, trying unsuccessfully to the
end of her life to reunite the two
factions by stressing the goals they
had in common.

Mozzoni, Anna Maria,
1837–1920

Italian. A founder and leading
member of the women's movement
in Italy, she was inspired by her
vision of 'the renaissance of
women' (*risorgimento delle donne*),
and argued that women were
humanity's only hope against the
destructiveness of men. She
founded La Lega promotrice degli
interessi femminili (League pro-

moting women's interests) in Milan
and drew up an 18-point plan for
reforming the legal status of
women, including education,
employment, political and family
rights. She campaigned for
women's suffrage and social purity,
and also wrote on many issues concerning women.

Ms.

American magazine launched in
1972 as a way of spreading word of
the WOMEN'S LIBERATION MOVEMENT
to non-political women. By the end
of 1973 it had a monthly circulation
of 350,000, with a 70 per cent
renewal rate, and it has continued to
be a success. The best known, most
widely read and readily available of
all feminist periodicals, it is often
accepted as the voice of
mainstream, liberal American feminism. It contains news, opinion,
the arts, fiction, poetry, non-sexist
children's stories, reviews, letters,
and articles on famous women and
almost any subject considered of
interest to women. In its attempt to
be all things to all women its feminism is sometimes stretched rather
thin, and although it reaches many
women (and some men) who
would be frightened off by anything more obviously radical, it has
received at least as much criticism as
praise, particularly from within the
women's movement.
(*See also* STEINEM, GLORIA)

Ms.

Title used before a woman's name,

the equivalent of Mr used before a man's name, instead of Miss or Mrs. Although usually defined as 'courtesy titles', Miss and Mrs could more accurately be called 'availability titles' since, unlike Mr or Ms, they immediately define the person as married or single and contribute to the culture of sexism which defines a woman primarily by her relationship with a man. Ms. was first suggested in secretarial handbooks of the 1940s, as a solution to the awkwardness of addressing someone whose marital status was unknown but it did not begin to catch on until, with the second wave of feminism in America in the late 1960s, more and more women demanded to be treated as individuals, regardless of whether they were divorced, married, widowed, single, using their husband's name or their father's, a lover's or their own. The 1972 American Heritage School Dictionary was the first dictionary to include an entry for Ms. Also in 1972, the first issue of MS. Magazine appeared, and with its success came somewhat more widespread acceptance of the title.

Mud March, The

First outdoor procession held by the NATIONAL UNION OF WOMEN'S SUFFRAGE SOCIETIES on 7 February 1907, so called because of the pouring rain through which at least 3,000 women marched from Hyde Park Corner to the Exeter Hall in London.

Muller, Mary, 1820–1902

New Zealander. Although she had to work in secret, due to her husband's disapproval, she was an influential and pioneering feminist who did much to ensure the eventual achievement of women's suffrage in New Zealand. Under the name 'Femina' she wrote many passionate newspaper articles calling for women's emancipation, and in 1869 published *An Appeal to the Men of New Zealand*. Active not only in her own country, she was also in correspondence with many British feminists, including John Stuart MILL.

Murphy, Emily, 1886–1933

Canadian lawyer and writer. Working as a social reformer in Alberta from 1904, she became particularly involved in the suffrage movement and in working to further the legal rights of women. She helped establish the Women's Court (where women's evidence could be heard in cases of rape, sexual assault and divorce) in Edmonton in 1916, and became the first woman magistrate in the British Empire. Yet during her first case the defence lawyer challenged her right to be there, claiming that, as a woman, she was not legally a person. Her position was upheld by the Supreme Court of Alberta in 1916, and she began a campaign to admit women to the Senate. In 1928 the Supreme Court ruled that women were no more legally 'persons' than were children, idiots or criminals, but an appeal to the British Privy Council resulted in the 1929 ruling that women *were* 'persons' and therefore eligible for seats in the Senate.

Murray, Judith Sargent,
1751–1820

American writer. First American-born woman dramatist to have plays professionally performed. Her essays for the *Massachusetts Magazine* dealt with the need for better educational opportunities for women and similar topics, the best known being 'On the Equality of the Sexes', published in 1790, and were first published under the pen-name Constantia.

Murray, Margaret, 1863–1963

British scholar. Active in the women's movement from 1886, she is best remembered today for her highly controversial view of folklore and WITCHES as expressed in *The Witch-Cult in Western Europe* (1921) and *The God of the Witches* (1931).

music and musicians

Women's absence from musical history is even more striking than their absence from the history of art. Feminist musicology is still in its early stages, but a regular pattern of discrimination can be recognized which curtailed women's opportunities at every turn. In the past, women might be allowed to learn to play a musical instrument and they might even compose, but having their works published, circulated or performed was another question. Women in music have usually appeared in secondary, supportive roles: as the wives, daughters and sisters of composers, or as teachers and performers rather than innovators creating their own work. Even such determined exceptions as Ethel SMYTH were forgotten after their deaths until feminist scholars rediscovered them.

The future may be more promising, in part due to changing opportunities for women, and in part due to the development of the phenomenon known as women's music.

Women's music has its roots in popular music, chiefly folk and rock, and it developed in the early 1970s, after the women's liberation movement had raised feminist consciousness and created a large audience of women who were dissatisfied with the sexist lyrics and male-dominated attitudes of most popular music. Precursors of women's music came from such political-musical groups as the Northern Women's Liberation Rock Band in England and the New Haven Women's Liberation Rock Band in the United States, who performed at women-only events, changing the lyrics of well-known rock songs to make feminist points. A new step was taken with the release of LAVENDER JANE LOVES WOMEN in 1973, the first women-produced record, and followed soon after by the founding of OLIVIA RECORDS and, in 1974, the First National Women's Music Festival in Urbana-Champaign, Illinois.

The concept of women's music caught on quickly, and the audience for it grew rapidly after that. Women's music is usually defined in opposition to traditional, male-dominated music, as being WOMAN-CENTRED, WOMAN-IDENTIFIED, and offering affirmative, realistic and various images of women.

Another difference in women's music can be seen in its presentation. Everyone involved in the concerts or in record production is considered to be equally important. The performer is not an isolated 'star' and everyone has a responsibility to do her job to the best of her ability. Ruth Scovill, who wrote her master's thesis on feminist music, has defined the concert environment as being different in three areas: accessibility, vulnerability, and responsibility. These all refer to the performer, who makes herself accessible by meeting her audience after the performance; who admits to her own weaknesses, and takes responsibility for presenting the music and the message of her songs as honestly as she can. Some performers play only to women while others enjoy mixed audiences. Most feel that there is a discernible difference in the experience of singing only to women as opposed to a group with even a few men in it.

Differences in lyrics and in presentation are clear enough, but whether women's music has a distinctly different form is arguable. Few composers have ventured beyond traditional forms, and women today as much as in the past have been taught and influenced by men and male-defined forms. Kay GARDNER is a composer, conductor and musician who believes she has found and identified a musical form which may be described as innate to women. She calls this a 'circular form', in which the climax, or moment of most tension, is found in the middle, with the structure following the climax being the same as that leading up to it, only reversed. She relates this circular form to such recognized musical forms as the round and the rondo, and compares it to women's natural cycles, and to women's experience of orgasm, pointing out that the traditional musical form with the climax at the end could equally well be related to male sexual experience.

Some of the best-known names in women's music include Cris WILLIAMSON, Meg CHRISTIAN, Alex Dobkin and Holly NEAR. The women's music network includes record companies, distributors, clubs, regular festivals and magazines.

(See also HOT WIRE; PAID MY DUES;

NOT JUST A STAGE; WOMEN'S REVO-
LUTIONS PER MINUTE; WILD; WOMAN-
CULTURE.)

Muslim feminists

At issue for feminists in Muslim
societies is a set of laws and customs
oppressive to women but not, as in
Judaeo-Christian societies, an
ideology of female inferiority.
Islam does not presume that
women are naturally inferior to
men; rather, that women are potentially equal. The existing inequality
between men and women under
Islam is the result of specific social
institutions: segregation and legal
subordination in the family structure. Pre-Islamic sexuality is described in Arab literature as rampant
and promiscuous, whose essence is
women's self-determination and
freedom to choose or discard sexual
partners without regard for paternal
legitimacy. Thus, all sexual institutions (polygamy, repudiation, sexual segregation) are strategies for
containing potential female power.
Muslim marriage is based on male
dominance because women are
considered a potentially destructive
element who must be confined and
kept under male authority. In
*Beyond the Veil: Male–Female
Dynamics in Muslim Society* (1975),
Fatima Mernissi argues that this
very belief in women's power
makes the idea of women's liberation far more threatening than it is
in the West, but also means that
Muslim women are likely to set
higher, broader goals than just
equality with men. Muslim women
will achieve liberation not only for
themselves, but will bring about the
revision and reorganization of the
whole social structure if they are
successful: 'American women will
get the right of abortion but it will
be a long time before they can prevent the female body from being
exploited as a marketable product.
Muslim women, on the contrary,
engage in a silent but explosive
dialogue with a fragile ruling class
whose major task is to secure
economic growth and plan a
future without exploitation and
deprivation.'

The feminist movement emerged
as the result of Arab–Muslim
nationalism. Two men, in particular, Qasim Amin (1863–1908)
and Salama Musa (1887–1958), considered that the liberation of
women was necessary for Arab–
Muslim societies to be liberated
from Western domination. They
argued that in order to rival the
West in terms of power and produc-
tivity, women must be freed to
become fully involved in production, and they advocated full sexual
equality in all spheres of social, legal
and political life. But their attempts
to back up their argument by claiming that women's exclusion from
social affairs was due not to Islam
but to secular customs failed in the
face of the more popular Traditionalists.

The controversy continues today

between Traditionalists who claim that Islam prohibits any change in sex roles, and Modernists who claim that Islam allows for the liberation of women and the desegregation of society.

Mussey, Ellen Spencer,
1850–1936

American lawyer. She taught law to women students and when they were refused admission to Columbia, started her own Washington College of Law. An active suffragist, she served as chairwoman of the National Council of Women, and drafted legislation pertaining to property rights, the status of women, and citizenship rights.

'Myth of the Vaginal Orgasm, The'

One of the most revolutionary and influential articles from the WOMEN'S LIBERATION MOVEMENT, it was written by Anne KOEDT for distribution at the first American national women's liberation conference in Chicago, November 1968. She later expanded it and it was published in *Notes from the Second Year* (1970). This article represents the first awareness within the women's movement that women were oppressed not only politically, economically and socially, but also by assumptions about the nature of SEXUALITY. Using scientific findings, Koedt refuted the Freudian idea that a woman incapable of having an ORGASM from coitus was sexually immature or frigid. All orgasms originate in the clitoris, which has no function except sexual pleasure, and not in the vagina, which is related to the reproductive function. Although the facts were well known about the sensitivity of the clitoris and the insensitivity of the vagina, Koedt suggested that men continued to perpetuate the myth of vaginal orgasm because they preferred vaginal penetration to any other form of sexuality; because they maintained power by refusing to consider women as independent human beings with desires of their own; and because they were afraid of being considered sexually expendable if the clitoris were substituted for the vagina as the centre of pleasure for women. She called upon women to redefine their sexuality, to discard the male-defined concepts of 'normal' sex and replace them with the idea of mutual sexual enjoyment. Many women who read the article did attempt to do this, and many found it a liberating experience as they were able to experience pleasure for the first time without shame, whether with another woman, a man, or by themselves. Yet other readers found the concept of a clitorally-based sexuality too threatening to accept because it implied that HETEROSEXUALITY was only an option, not an imperative.

(*See also* ORGASM; VAGINAL ORGASM)

N

names

Names in our society are the property of men. Fathers give their names to their children as a means of acknowledging and legitimating them. Although both girls and boys bear the father's name, traditionally boys are expected to bring honour to that name as men, whereas women are expected to exchange their father's name for a husband's. People may choose to change their names to symbolize that they are changing their lives, but when a new name is imposed this indicates a lack of power. Names are closely tied to identity, and that women are named according to their relationship to a man reveals the expectation that women need not be recognized as individuals. Because of this tradition, women have often preferred to be known by their first name – the one part of their name which is indisputably and individually their own. The custom of referring to a married woman by her husband's full name, with the addition of the title 'Mrs' is the most blatant example of how women become invisible in a male-dominated society. Names have long been a feminist issue. In 1847 Elizabeth Cady STANTON wrote to a friend, 'I have very serious objections, dear Rebecca, to being called Henry.

There is a great deal in a name . . . The custom of calling women Mrs John This and Mrs Tom That, and colored men Sambo and Zip Coon, is founded on the principle that white men are lords of all. I cannot acknowledge this principle as just, therefore, I cannot bear the name of another.' Some feminists went further: as early as 1832, Jeanne DEROIN refused to change her last name upon marriage, and Lucy STONE made her name among American feminists by retaining it when she married in 1855. The LUCY STONE LEAGUE was founded in 1921 to encourage more women to follow her example. Recognizing that by refusing to take their husband's name they are still allowing themselves to be identified by the father's, some modern feminists have chosen to name themselves after their mothers or a female ancestor, or to create new, personally meaningful names. Laura Shaw Murra, for example, renamed herself Laura X, choosing X to stand for the anonymity of women's history.

(*See also* NAMING; LANGUAGE)

naming

Term for what is usually seen as one of the central tasks of radical feminism: to liberate women through

LANGUAGE, by changing our perception of reality. Because all existing descriptions of the way things are have been distorted by male bias, and because patriarchal language has concealed how women are oppressed, women's experiences cannot be fully understood until they have been named. This may involve the actual construction of new words (like SEXISM), but a situation may also be named by being described and acknowledged as real. Among those who have made naming of central concern in their work are Mary DALY, Dale SPENDER, Cheris Kramarae and Adrienne RICH.

National American Woman Suffrage Association
(NAWSA)

Organization formed in 1890 by the merger between the two branches of the American suffrage movement, the once-radical NATIONAL WOMAN SUFFRAGE ASSOCIATION (its leaders old and nearing retirement) and the more conservative, now almost respectable, AMERICAN WOMAN SUFFRAGE ASSOCIATION. Elizabeth Cady STANTON was elected its first president, followed by Susan B. ANTHONY (1892), Carrie Chapman CATT (1900) and Anna Howard SHAW (1904).

Although the merger was seen as positive, in that it healed old rifts and presented a united working front for the same end, some of the older feminists (like Matilda Joslyn GAGE) withdrew, while others who stayed (like Susan B. Anthony) regretted the lack of the old passionate intensity which had led to the original split. It was soon obvious after the merger that the movement had entered a stagnant period, and little was accomplished.

Arriving home from England, where she had learned from the militant suffragettes, Alice PAUL promised to revive the fight for a federal woman suffrage amendment in 1913. A conflict arose, however, which resulted in another split: this time, the radical wing of the movement was represented by Paul's CONGRESSIONAL UNION. In contrast, NAWSA seemed paralysed and virtually powerless.

The turning point came at the end of 1915, when Carrie Chapman Catt agreed to become the NAWSA president. With an efficient, hand-picked staff, and a definite, though secret plan of action (called the 'Winning Plan'), Catt turned NAWSA into a genuine political force.

Unlike the CONGRESSIONAL UNION which held President Wilson and the Democrats to blame for the lack of a women's suffrage amendment, NAWSA tried to win him over. Their tactics succeeded to the extent that he appeared, with his wife, at the NAWSA convention in 1916 and, although he did not then commit himself, he later proved willing to help.

Victory came, finally, in 1920,

and NAWSA became the LEAGUE OF WOMEN VOTERS.

National Black Feminist Organization (NBFO)

Based in Washington, D.C., this American organization was founded on 15 August 1973 to address the specific needs of and provide a voice for black women who suffer the dual oppressions of racism and sexism.

National Organization for Women (NOW)

The largest, most visible, and most broadly-based feminist organization in the United States, its goals are to bring women into full participation in American society, to address and advocate women's issues at a national level, and to work for their realization on a local level. It was founded in 1966 by Betty FRIEDAN, Aileen HERNANDEZ, Pauli Murray, and two dozen other influential, highly placed women determined to enforce recognition of women's civil rights. As the only activist organization concerned with women's rights it attracted a membership with diverse aims, and at the second national conference in November 1967, conflicts among the 1,200 members were obvious. Some believed NOW should concentrate on improving women's employment and educational opportunities through legal changes, while others, indifferent to a 'respectable' image, wanted to

fight SEXISM and change society far more radically. Disagreements on such emotive issues as abortion legislation and sexual preference often threatened to tear the group apart, yet it has survived and continued to grow. A system of state-level committees was set up, and the national office (founded in 1969) coordinates local activities with national priorities. NOW is sometimes praised as a democratic membership organization with a largely decentralized power structure, and sometimes criticized as being too hierarchical and bureaucratic. In 1977, NOW made ratification of the EQUAL RIGHTS AMENDMENT its top priority, and until defeat in 1982 it was effectively a one-issue organization with other issues and conflicts downplayed or suppressed. In the 1980s, NOW's increasing emphasis on electoral politics has led to a loss of more radical members, but it has also forced public recognition of women's issues, and made MAINSTREAM FEMINISM a political presence in America. Membership, which is open to all women and men who believe in equal rights for women, is in excess of 250,000.

National Plan of Action

Programme adopted at the NATIONAL WOMEN'S CONFERENCE in November 1977, in Houston, Texas, and presented to the President and Congress of the United States of America. It contained twenty-six 'planks' covering a whole gamut of issues affecting women's lives. Demands included the elimination of violence against women, support for women's businesses, equal credit, federally funded, nonsexist CHILDCARE, a policy of full employment, protection of homemakers, reproductive freedom, an end to the sexist representation of women in the media, welfare reform, and an end to discrimination on grounds of sex or sexual preference. Recommendations as to how these demands might be met ranged from the specific – passage of new laws and ratification of the EQUAL RIGHTS AMENDMENT – to more general hopes for the restructuring of society to end poverty, SEXISM and violence. The plan, along with a report on the conference, was published as *The Spirit of Houston* (1978).

National Union of Women's Suffrage Societies (NUWSS)

The largest of the organizations working for women's suffrage in Britain, it developed in 1897 out of a number of smaller local groups, its stated aim 'to obtain the Parliamentary Franchise for women on the same terms as it is or may be granted to men.' It was democratically run with an elected president Millicent Garrett FAWCETT, and a national executive committee, and published THE COMMON CAUSE. In 1912, after the Labour Party had officially declared itself for women's suffrage, the Union overturned its traditional non-party status to support Labour candidates, probably more for tactical reasons (to pressure the Liberals) than from genuine socialist commitment, although the membership of the NUWSS embraced all parties and classes at truce for their common cause. World War I led to a serious split and mass resignations in 1914, when Fawcett declared it 'treason to talk of peace', counter to the conviction many members felt that the War was man-made and in opposition to true suffragist and democratic principles. In 1918, with the passage of the Representation of the People Act, membership declined still further, despite the statements from the Union that the struggle was not over: 'The enfranchisement of women is not a matter of the vote alone . . . until we have a world in which there are no sex barriers . . . the purpose of the Suffragists will not be fulfilled.' In 1919 its name was changed to the National Union of Societies for Equal Citizenship.

National Woman Suffrage Association

Organization founded in 1869 by Elizabeth Cady STANTON, Susan B. ANTHONY and their followers out of disillusionment with the male-dominated AMERICAN EQUAL RIGHTS ASSOCIATION. It admitted only women as members, but was willing to work with anyone, regardless of their other views, so long as they wholeheartedly supported women's suffrage. It represented the more radically feminist part of the American women's movement, both in philosophy and in tactics, and although the vote was seen as important, it was not an end in itself. In 1870, an article in the association's newspaper, THE REVOLUTION, stated, 'The ballot is not even half the loaf; it is only a crust – a crumb. The ballot touches only those interests, either of women or men, which take their root in political questions. But woman's chief discontent is not with her political, but with her social, and particularly her marital bondage.' More conservative women, who found themselves unable to join an association which spoke out for marriage reform, questioned organized religion and favoured unions for working women, were represented by the AMERICAN WOMAN SUFFRAGE ASSOCIATION. For many years the split in the movement seemed impossible to bridge, but in 1890 the two organizations merged to become the NATIONAL AMERICAN WOMAN SUFFRAGE ASSOCIATION.

National Woman's Party

Oldest existing women's rights organization in the United States, it is a one-issue party, its goal the ratification of the EQUAL RIGHTS AMENDMENT. Founded in 1916 by Alice PAUL as a militant, activist group dedicated to getting the vote for women. Instead of disbanding after the vote was won in 1920, it reorganized to work for full legal equality for women. In 1923 members drafted an equal rights amendment, introduced it to Congress, and continued over the years to lobby for its passage. It ensured that the Equal Rights Amendment remained a live issue during the years when there was no active women's movement in the United States.

National Women's Conference

Also known as the Houston Women's Conference, or simply 'Houston', this was held 18–21 November 1977, in Houston, Texas, the end result of a government-sponsored commission formed to study and report on the status of women in the United States. Both commission and conference were in response to the United Nations' INTERNATIONAL WOMEN'S YEAR. Over 1,800 were in attendance, selected on a state level and representing many different minority, racial, ethnic, religious, class and political groups. Unusually, white, middle-class women were actually under-represented, and in order to meet the racial balance requirements, white 'at-large' delegates had to be added to some state delegations. Although most of the delegates were feminists, some specifically anti-feminist organizations were also represented. The purpose of the conference was to discuss, debate, amend and vote on a NATIONAL PLAN OF ACTION for improving women's situation and status in all areas of American society. Bella ABZUG was the presiding officer. The conference was widely perceived to have been a success in placing feminist issues on the national political agenda and in demonstrating the strength women could have in working together politically.

National Women's Liberation Conferences

The first national women's liberation conference in Britain was held at RUSKIN COLLEGE, Oxford, in February 1970. At that time the WOMEN'S NATIONAL COORDINATING COMMITTEE was established, a short-lived attempt to link the autonomous groups around the country into one unified movement. This lasted only a year. But although the women's liberation movement was from the start too diverse to follow a single party line, national conferences bringing the many different groups together continued to be held: at Skegness in 1971, at Manchester in 1972, at Edinburgh in 1974, at Manchester in 1975, and at Birmingham in 1978. Internal divisions, particularly the bitter conflict between heterosexual and lesbian feminists on the political importance given to HETEROSEXUALITY, became so over-

whelming that no one was prepared, after 1978, to attempt to bring together the fragmented movement as a unified whole.

National Women's Political Caucus (NWPC)

American multi-partisan membership organization dedicated to increasing women's participation in politics at all levels, ending legal inequalities suffered by women, and supporting non-sexist, non-racist candidates. Over 300 women met in Washington, D.C. in July 1971, founding the NWPC 'to awaken, organize, and assert the vast political power represented by women'. Members of the first National Policy Council, included Bella ABZUG, Shana Alexander, Liz Carpenter, Shirley CHISHOLM, Betty FRIEDAN and Gloria STEINEM. By 1973 the NWPC had active local caucuses in every state. It continues to be an active and visible part of the political GENDER GAP – during Reagan's first year as President, NWPC membership increased by 8,000. Among its achievements: raising the percentages of women delegates to the Democratic and Republican national conventions, from the 1968 level of 13 and 17 per cent, to 39 and 30 per cent respectively in 1972; in 1979, in conjunction with the NATIONAL ORGANIZATION FOR WOMEN (NOW), it organized feminists into the Coalition for Women's Rights.

Near, Holly, 1949–
American singer and songwriter well known in the field of women's music. Her singing career was linked with political consciousness from the start, when she joined the 'Free the Army' tour as part of the protest against American involvement in Vietnam. This stirred her interest in other political movements, inluding feminism, gay liberation, nuclear disarmament, and international peace. Requests for her music from people who had seen her on tour led her to form Redwood Records and record her first album in 1973 (*Hang in There*). Her albums include *You Can Know All I Am* (1976), *Imagine My Surprise* (1979), *Fire in the Rain* (1981), *Speed of Light* (1982) and *Lifeline* (with Ronnie Gilbert, 1983).
(*See also* MUSIC AND MUSICIANS)

neo-feminism
Term occasionally used (chiefly by historians) to distinguish the current or SECOND WAVE OF FEMINISM (circa 1970) from all earlier women's movements.

Nevinson, Henry, 1856–1941
British journalist. With Henry Noel Brailsford, he resigned from *The Daily News* in protest at the paper's support of a government which refused women the vote. A militant suffragist, he was chairman of the Men's Political Union.

New Directions for Women
Started in 1972 as a mimeographed newsletter for feminists in New Jersey, by 1985 its national circulation of 55,000 made it the most widely-read feminist journal in America after MS. Magazine. With the aim of fighting SEXISM, racism, ageism and homophobia, it reports on legislation, health, CHILDCARE, EDUCATION, employment, books, feminist theory and the arts. It is published bi-monthly in tabloid format.

New Feminist Theatre (also called the New Feminist Repertory and Experimental Ensemble, or New FREE)
Generally recognized as the first feminist THEATRE group, it was founded in New York City by Anselma dell'Olio in 1969. According to dell'Olio, the intention of the group (which was composed of both women and men) was to 'contribute to the liberation of women from centuries of political, social, economic, and above all, cultural oppression . . . not just "to give women a chance" in the arts . . . but primarily to give a dramatic voice to the new feminist movement'.

New Feminists
Whenever feminism is believed to have disappeared as a meaningful philosophy or social movement, its rediscovery is heralded with the label 'new'. Members of the

Women's Liberation Movement, which is sometimes referred to as the SECOND WAVE OF FEMINISM, were referred to as the new feminists until, by the mid-1970s, they were no longer perceived by the media as news. In an article (*The Guardian*, 21 January 1986) protesting against the use of the term 'POST-FEMINISM', Lucy Hooberman suggested it would be more realistic to call post-1970s feminists the New Feminists.

New Left

The breeding ground of the WOMEN'S LIBERATION MOVEMENT, this is a political tendency which began in Britain in the mid-1950s, developing out of a disenchantment with the old left from which it stemmed. In the early 1960s a somewhat different version appeared in America, born of the CIVIL RIGHTS MOVEMENT and opposition to American involvement in Vietnam. The driving force behind the many different strands of the New Left was an idealistic quest to overthrow 'the system' and eliminate the sources of established power by DIRECT ACTION, including violence. Many women became radicalized by the conflict between their shared political belief in equality and the treatment they actually received from their male comrades. Realizing that privilege was invested in sex as much as in race, they began to organize around their own oppression, for the liberation

of women. The New Left occupies much the same position in regard to contemporary feminism as the ABOLITION MOVEMENT did to the FIRST WAVE OF FEMINISM.

New York Radical Feminists

A short-lived group founded in late 1969 by Minda Bikman, Diane Crowthers, Shulamith FIRESTONE, Anne KOEDT and Cellestine Ware, it was an important, though unsuccessful, attempt to create a mass-based radical women's movement in America. Its manifesto, 'THE POLITICS OF THE EGO' articulated the RADICAL FEMINIST position. Rejecting hierarchies, the movement was composed of brigades of between five and fifteen women. Whenever a new brigade formed, it was required to spend three months of CONSCIOUSNESS-RAISING, followed by three months of reading and discussing feminist literature, at which point the women were considered full and equal members. By 1971 membership was over 400, with new brigades forming at the rate of several per week, yet under charges of elitism the founding brigade had disbanded, and there was no coherent structure to unite the many small groups into a unified force.

Nichols, Clarinda I., 1810–85

American newspaper editor. She published a series on women's civil rights in her Vermont newspaper and was active in lobbying for a married woman's property act and in the first American women's movement.

Nin, Anaïs, 1903–77

French-born American writer. Her novels and short stories are impressionistic, dream-like renderings of female experience, but her diaries, which began to be published in 1966, brought her to fame. Her close examination of her own inner life, and her reflections on female–male relationships, made her a heroine to many feminists in the 1970s, although her respect for psychoanalysis and a traditional, mystical vision of what is masculine and what feminine have caused other feminists to find her writings deeply suspect and even anti-feminist. She herself believed she made a psychological, but not political, contribution to the women's liberation movement.

Nineteenth Amendment

United States Constitutional guarantee of women's suffrage, sometimes called the ANTHONY AMENDMENT in honour of Susan B. ANTHONY, although it was actually written (modelled after the Fifteenth Amendment) by Elizabeth Cady STANTON. It was first voted on – and defeated – by Congress in 1886. After that it was proposed and defeated every year until 1896, then not again until 1913. It was finally ratified in 1920, the successful end to a struggle which had started for

American women in 1848 at SENECA FALLS. The amendment declares: 'The right of citizens of the United States to vote shall not be denied or abridged by the United States or by any State on account of sex.'

No More Fun and Games

See JOURNAL OF FEMALE LIBERATION, A

nonaligned feminism

Term used by Charlotte BUNCH to describe 'a direction for feminism that is both radical and independent and that integrates the political, cultural, economic and spiritual dimensions of women's lives.' In 'A Manifesto for Nonaligned Feminism', published in QUEST in 1976, she declared:

'Our assertion of nonaligned feminism involves keeping the feminist struggle and perspective at the fore as we evaluate all questions, coalitions and issues. It also recognizes the need to expand what is called "feminist" so that the term responds to the realities of all women, across class, race, sexuality, and national boundaries in order to avoid merely reflecting the interests and needs of only one group.

'It requires a willingness to explore every possible source for analysis – not only the works of women but also of men like Fanon, Freud, Galbraith, Mao, Marx, and Proust – regardless of how others have used their insights and without compulsion to declare ourselves *a priori* for or against any of their theories. It implies an openness to explore coalitions with other forces for change, to evaluate and reassess them constantly, according to how they affect women and our long-range goals. As we engage with others, declare positions on a wide range of issues, and make ourselves available instead of self-segregated, it is also crucial that we keep our own communities, projects and organizations intact. We must not lose our independent feminist base; it is the source of our political power. It is the inspiration and touchstone for theory and strategy. And it is the source of our personal and communal sustenance.'

Norton, Caroline, 1808–77
English writer and campaigner for women's rights. Her activities to improve women's legal position in Britain concentrated on the rights of mothers to their children, and of wives to keep their own property, and stemmed from her own suffering at the hands of a cruel and vindictive husband. When she left him to escape his brutality, she found herself deprived of all financial support and of her own property. She was not allowed to see or communicate with her children. She had no legal recourse against her husband, but she applied for custody and wrote pamphlets arguing the rights of mothers which influenced the passage of the Infant Custody Bill in 1839 and resulted in her being reunited with her children. She wrote to support herself and them, but in 1853 her estranged husband deprived her of her living by suing successfully for her copyrights. This prompted her to write more pamphlets which helped bring about the passage of the 1857 Marriage and Divorce Act, and the first Married Women's Property Bill. Although her contributions to the improvement of women's legal situation in England have made her a feminist heroine, she would not have seen herself in such a role. Although concerned with obvious inequities in the law, especially as they affected her, she never questioned or seriously challenged male-dominated society or women's place in it. She is also remembered as the model for George MEREDITH's heroine *Diana of the Crossways* (1885).

Not Just a Stage
Chicago-based group formed in 1984 by Toni Armstrong, Michele Gautreaux, Ann Morris and Yvonne Zipter with the aim of being a catalyst to develop and maintain a network of creators of women's culture. They publish the magazine HOT WIRE and organize events for the creation, enjoyment, sharing and celebration of woman-identified music, writing and performing arts.
(*See also* WOMANCULTURE)

novels and novelists

In her influential book *Literary Women* (1976) Ellen MOERS pointed out that the rise of the novel cannot be separated from the rise of women to professional literary status. From the beginning, women have written novels without facing quite the intensity of male disapproval and discouragement they have met in other areas of literature, such as poetry and the essay. Yet the novel is not considered a female art form. Although critics such as Elaine Showalter and Patricia Meyer Spacks, as well as Moers, have argued for the existence of a specifically female literary tradition, the dominant tradition in the novel, whether written by men or women, is ANDROCENTRIC.

Some feminists have assumed that any WOMAN-CENTRED novel is particularly valuable, an attitude both fostered and expressed by the VIRAGO Modern Classics series and other publishing ventures dedicated to reclaiming our feminist literary heritage. But although there is a tradition of women writing against the dominant mode, there is an equally long tradition of 'women's stories' which reinforce such patriarchal ideals as male dominance and female submission.

The feminist novel is not merely woman-centred – it is a direct challenge to androcentric and patriarchal thought. Patricia Stubbs, in *Women and Fiction* (1979), declared that 'A genuinely feminist novel must surely credit women with more forms of experience than their personal or sexual entanglements.'

But this is an ideal – or perhaps a description of the POST-FEMINIST novel. Although the limitations of women's traditional concerns are recognized, and a common theme is a woman's struggle to reject stereotyped images and define herself, most contemporary feminist novels still explore this theme chiefly through a woman's emotional, sexual and personal relationships.

Feminist ideas have been explored in novels ever since they began to be articulated. Among the most famous novels to explore the development of a feminist consciousness through a woman's dissatisfaction with the limited role she is allowed to play are THE AWAKENING by Kate CHOPIN (1899) and THE STORY OF AN AFRICAN FARM by Olive SCHREINER (1883). Other novels which tackled 'the Woman Question' and depicted early feminists include THE BOSTONIANS by Henry James, *The Odd Women* by George Gissing, ANN VERONICA by H. G. Wells, THE CONVERT by Elizabeth ROBINS, and THE JUDGE by Rebecca WEST.

Since the Women's Liberation Movement made feminist questions once more part of the general culture, novels have been written by, about, and for feminists in increasing numbers, and have been published successfully not only by women's presses but by commercial publishers. In 'Are Women's Novels Feminist Novels?' (1980) Rosalind Coward adapted Fay Weldon's comment on THE WOMEN'S ROOM by Marilyn FRENCH (1977) to call this new genre 'novels that change lives'. Attempting to define what made a feminist novel, Coward suggested that most of these books shared such elements as the quasi-autobiographical female voice, the use of CONSCIOUS-NESS-RAISING as a fictional device, and – sometimes – an expressed allegiance to the Women's Liberation Movement.

For the most part, as Coward recognized, the identification of a novel as feminist is an arguable and individual decision. A reader may decide a novel is feminist because she feels a sense of kinship with the main character and recognizes her problems as her own, or because of what she knows about the author's own beliefs and life, as much as because of any political assessment of the book as a whole. Equally, a lack of sympathy with the main character – or the author – may cause her to decide that the book is not, despite appearances, really feminist. A book such as FEAR OF FLYING by Erica JONG (1973) might be welcomed as a liberating experience one month, and denounced as reactionary the next, simply on the basis of public reaction and the suspicion that anything

so popular could not be politically correct. One branch of feminist literary criticism has demonstrated how to read 'against' or 'beyond' the text, so that a valuable feminist interpretation may be given to a book such as *Clarissa* (1747–8) which author Samuel Richardson surely never intended.

A list of contemporary 'life-changing' novels of particular interest might include THE GOLDEN NOTEBOOK by Doris LESSING, *The Odd Woman* by Gail Godwin, *Small Changes* and *Braided Lives* by Marge PIERCY, *Kinflicks* by Lisa Alther, MEMOIRS OF AN EX-PROM QUEEN and BURNING QUESTIONS by Alix Kates SHULMAN, *Surfacing* and *The Edible Woman* by Margaret ATWOOD, *Rubyfruit Jungle* by Rita Mae BROWN and *A Piece of the Night* by Michèle ROBERTS.

Some critics, Joanna RUSS and Patricia Stubbs among them, have suggested that the future of the feminist novel, and a genuinely liberating alternative to patriarchal literature, must be found in some form other than that of traditional realism. Some writers have found SCIENCE FICTION the ideal form for exploring ideas which can hardly be expressed, certainly not experienced, in the modern world. Depictions of FEMALE FUTURES and feminist UTOPIAS can be found in such novels as HERLAND by Charlotte Perkins GILMAN, WOMAN ON THE EDGE OF TIME by Marge PIERCY, THE WANDERGROUND by

Sally Miller GEARHEART, and LES GUÉRILLÈRES by Monique WITTIG.

Another aspect of literary experimentation can be found in the idea of L'ÉCRITURE FÉMININE, the term for a specifically female type of writing, based in women's bodily experience, which is presumed to have the potential to be truly liberating, to bring down the old phallocentric universe and re-create the world. Hélène CIXOUS is the chief proponent of this, but the idea of *l'écriture féminine* can be seen to be related to the earlier question of whether there are fundamental differences in the way men and women write – what these sex-linked differences are, and their meaning. Writers such as Dorothy RICHARDSON, Anaïs NIN and Virginia WOOLF have been proposed as essentially feminine writers, yet attempts to codify or prove sexual differences between writers often end in contradiction and absurdity, as what Cynthia Ozick has called the 'ovarian theory' of literature. Since feminists have delighted in pouring ridicule on testicular theories and PHALLIC CRITICISM, why should the female version be exempt?

(*See also* LITERARY CRITICISM; POETS AND POETRY; PUBLISHING; LANGUAGE; GATEKEEPERS)

NOW

See NATIONAL ORGANIZATION FOR WOMEN

O

Oakley, Ann, 1944–
English sociologist and writer. Her
feminism first became apparent in
her decision to study women's
attitudes towards HOUSEWORK as
her Ph.D. topic in 1969, and soon
thereafter she became involved in
the women's liberation movement.
Her books, which explore gender
roles, MOTHERHOOD, and other
aspects of women's experiences,
include *Sex, Gender and Society*
(1972), *The Sociology of Housework*
(1974), *From Here to Maternity* (first
published as *Becoming a Mother*)
(1979), *Subject Women* (1981) and
her autobiography, *Taking it Like a
Woman* (1984).

objectification
One of the means – some would say
the primary means – by which
women's oppression is perpetuated. The term describes the process
of viewing women not as
individual, complex persons, but as
sexual objects which exist only in
relation to male desire. This is done
by identifying women solely with
their bodies, either whole, or fragmented and fetishized as parts, and
is considered by radical feminists to
be a form of VIOLENCE against
women. It can be recognized in the
existence of PORNOGRAPHY, PROSTI-
TUTION, sexual harassment, and the
representation of women in mass
media and art. Although it was
originally men who identified
women as sex objects, female
narcissism and sexual alienation can
be recognized as the fate of a
woman who has so internalized
dominant male values as to become
a sex object to herself, according to
Sandra Bartky (1982).
(*See also* OTHER, THE)

Obstacle Race, The
History of women painters by
Germaine GREER, published in 1979.
She addresses what she calls 'the
false question' of 'Why are there no
great women artists?' by offering a
comprehensive survey of female
painters in Western art, examining
them in context, taking into consideration such things as social
attitudes towards women, legal
restrictions, the perceived character
of the artist, the cost and availability
of materials, sources of patronage,
training, etc. Wide-ranging and
well-documented, the book is
invaluable as a starting point for the
feminist art historian or critic.
Greer's conclusion is that '. . . it is
to our advantage to become the
women artists' audience, not in a
foolishly partisan way so that
everything a woman does is good in
our eyes, but to offer the kind of

229

constructive criticism and financial, intellectual and emotional support that men have given their artists in the past. The first prerequisite is knowledge, not only of women's work, but of the men's work to which it relates, and not in vague generalizations but precise examples.'

Of Woman Born

Book by Adrienne RICH, subtitled *Motherhood as Experience and Institution*. Published in 1976, it was the first in-depth examination of MOTHERHOOD – psychological, historical, theoretical and personal – to be written from a feminist consciousness. In it, she examines the experience of motherhood as it is shaped by the demands and expectations of PATRIARCHY, moving from the personal to the history of childbirth, obstetrics, the family, birth control, female experience and male ideas about that experience. It explores the reasons that the creation and nurturing of life has been turned into an institution oppressive both to women and children.

off our backs

The earliest (founded three months after the demise of VOICE OF THE WOMEN'S LIBERATION MOVEMENT) and longest-lasting national women's liberation newspaper in America. Founded in 1970, it continues to be published eleven times a year by the off our backs collective

covering national and international news, feature articles and reports on various aspects of the women's movement, and on work, health, education, penal and lesbian issues.

Older Women's Liberation
(OWL)

This began forming in 1970, part of the larger Women's Liberation Movement in America. Like the larger movement, it is an informal, leaderless network of groups organized on a local level. Some groups mobilize around a specific issue (such as legislation concerning retirement age or health care) while others may be more concerned with consciousness-raising in regard to public and personal attitudes towards the elderly. Although many of the problems faced by older women are shared with older men, there is a particularly close link between SEXISM and AGEISM. Not only are women the majority of the population over the age of sixty-five, but because such a high premium is placed on youth and attractiveness in a woman, age comes sooner and may be far more devastating to her than to a man in a patriarchal society.

(*See also* GRAY PANTHERS)

Olivia Records

American record company founded in 1973 by Ginny Berson and Meg CHRISTIAN, it is probably the best known and most successful example of a feminist business collective.

It is a woman-only company which, although it does have dealings with men, has advocated SEPARATISM as a longterm, transitional strategy. It was founded with the aim of making a range of musical opportunities open to women, incuding the chance for lesbians to record their own music without male pressure to change it. Olivia has produced albums by Meg Christian, Cris WILLIAMSON, June Millington, Linda Tillery and Teresa Trull, among others.
(*See also* MUSIC AND MUSICIANS)

Olsen, Tillie, 1913–

American writer. Although her output is small, almost everything she has written has achieved the status of a modern classic – the short stories 'Tell Me A Riddle' and 'I Stand Here Ironing', for example, which concern the ordinary lives of working people. Her non-fiction book SILENCES (1978), a sustained meditation on the relation of circumstances – including class, colour and sex – to the creation of literature, is one of the basic texts and resources of feminist literary theory.

Onlywomen Press

Radical lesbian feminist PUBLISHING collective established in London in 1974 with the intention of printing and publishing feminist books, pamphlets and posters, with all production carried out entirely by women. Among the books they have published are *One Foot On the Mountain* (1979), an anthology of British feminist poetry; *Women Against Violence Against Women* (1985), a collection of papers presented at national women's liberation conferences in 1980, 1981 and 1982; and *Brainchild* (1981), a novel by Eve Croft.

oppression

The imposition by one group of unjust constraints upon the freedom of another. This concept, particularly prominent in Marxist thought, implies a view of society which includes at least two groups with conflicting interests, and suggests that the oppressed group has the right to fight against the oppressor. One of the central ideas of modern feminist thought is that women share a common oppression greater than any differences of race or class. Some aspects of the oppression of women by men are the exclusion from public life and power; rape and physical abuse; social expectations that women will bear the main burden of CHILDCARE and housekeeping; and the sexual OBJECTIFICATION which alienates women from their own bodies. As a class, women have less money, power and physical freedom than men.

The idea that women are oppressed as a group, not merely discriminated against as individuals, defines feminism as a radical political struggle and encourages the recognition of SISTERHOOD. As Bell HOOKS has pointed out, however, in the United States the emphasis on the common oppression of all women enabled more privileged women to shape feminism to their own ends while ignoring the fact that not all women are oppressed in the same way or to the same degree, and that the end of the feminist struggle cannot simply be the extension of male, white, middle-class privilege to white, middle-class women.

orgasm
Freudian theory, widely accepted in Western society, postulates two different types of orgasm for women: the immature clitoral orgasm, and the far superior VAGINAL ORGASM. Freud's thought, ossified into common knowledge by the 1950s, was that to become fully mature, the woman must transfer sexual primacy from the clitoris to the vagina. No matter how orgasmic she might be under other circumstances, the woman who could not reach orgasm solely through penetration would be classified as neurotic, immature, and frigid. Women were therefore encouraged to remain passive and submerge their actual desires. In 1966, scientific research reached the public through William Masters and Virginia Johnson's tremendously influential book, *Human Sexual Response*, and declared the clitoral/vaginal dichotomy a false one.

However it was produced and however it was experienced, there was only one kind of orgasm, and anatomically the woman's orgasm originated in the clitoris.

The first feminist writer to draw political conclusions from this discovery was Anne KOEDT, whose article 'THE MYTH OF THE VAGINAL ORGASM' appeared in 1968. In it, she showed how men have benefited from the denial of the clitoris and the distortion of female SEXUALITY. As long as women believed they could be fulfilled only as the passive recipients of male desire, men could continue to define women only in relation to themselves, not as independent individuals. Male power relies, at least in part, on the continued sexual dependency of women, argued Koedt.

The revolutionary potential of this discovery threatens the whole heterosexual institution. With the clitoris substituted for the vagina as the centre of sexual pleasure, men fear they will become sexually expendable. Anatomy alone can no longer be used to explain why women should continue to choose men as sexual partners – 'normal' sexuality must be reconsidered and redefined, with the female experience finally taken into consideration.

Origin of the Family, Private Property and the State, The
Written by Friedrich ENGELS and published in 1884, this was the first

major attempt ever made to uncover the material causes of women's subordination, and remains the classic Marxist statement on women. Engels located the source of women's oppression in monogamous MARRIAGE, which he described as based on the domestic slavery of the wife, and which he theorized had originated in the male desire to ensure knowledge of paternity in order to pass on ownership of private property. In his theory, he described monogamous marriage as the equivalent of capitalism, and sex as the equivalent of class, writing: 'The first class opposition that occurs in history coincides with the development of antagonism between man and woman in monogamous marriage, and the first class oppression coincides with that of the female sex by the male.' And as sexism and class struggle were connected in origin, Engels felt the death of one would bring about the end of the other: male domination would no longer exist once women were a regular part of the paid work-force and economics ceased to have a role in sexual relations.

There are problems with Engels' equation of sex with class: as Sheila ROWBOTHAM has pointed out, throughout history individuals have managed to move from one class to another, yet women cannot become men (transsexuals notwithstanding). Contemporary Marxists usually criticize – or excuse – some

of the flaws in *The Origin of the Family, Private Property and the State* on the grounds that it was based on the now-outdated anthropological theories of Lewis Henry MORGAN. Yet regardless of all its limitations, this book has been enormously influential, and remains the starting point for most Marxist and socialist feminist theorists – so much so that even those who reject it feel obliged to explain why.

Other, the

A major concept, derived from Hegel and Sartre, in the philosophy of Simone de BEAUVOIR, which she uses in THE SECOND SEX to explain the oppression of women. Women are the Other in all cultures, not only to men – who should logically be the Other in regard to women – but to women themselves, who have accepted their OBJECTIFICATION and play the role of Other as defined by men. This came about, according to de Beauvoir, from the basic dualism of human consciousness which perceives from the very beginning a difference between Self and Other. This is not intrinsically sexual, since to the individual the world may be divided into 'us' (family, tribe, comrades) and 'them' without reference to sex, and the distinction between human and animal, civilization and nature, or person and god are equally primordial. In a world, however, in which man has kept the power for himself and made the rules, the sexual division has come to be seen as the most basic, and women have not been allowed to be fully human. Women need not be defined as inferior – the effect is the same if feminine virtues are mystified and worshipped, which is why de Beauvoir is so critical of ESSENTIALISM, and urges women to refuse otherness and strive for full equality.

Otto-Peters, Luise, 1819–95

German. Well known as a social novelist under the pseudonym Otto Stern, she is generally considered the founder of the German women's movement. During the unsuccessful revolution of 1848 she demanded full equal rights for women, including the vote. But later, as President of the Allgemeiner Deutscher Frauenverein (General German Women's Association), she was far more moderate, rejecting such advanced notions as women's suffrage, and campaigning only for modest reforms in education and marriage laws.

Our Bodies Ourselves

Subtitled *A Health Book By and For Women* and first published in America in 1971, this is the classic text of the women's health movement, and one of the most widely-read, influential books to come out of the women's liberation movement.

It was the result of a discussion group on 'Women and Their Bodies' at a Boston women's conference in 1969. The women from the conference – later known as the BOSTON WOMEN'S HEALTH BOOK COLLECTIVE – continued to research, discuss and develop a feminist perspective on such interrelated topics as women's sexuality, pregnancy, childbirth, birth control, abortion, health, standard and alternative health care etc., and eventually published their findings for the use of other women.

Although full of useful information on health care and sexual questions, the book has had an even more important impact in encouraging women to consider how we are defined and valued by society, and how we can regain control of our bodies and our lives.

Over the years the book has become a bestseller and has been reprinted frequently, with foreign editions in eleven languages. In 1978, Angela Phillips and Jill Rakusen adapted the book for British readers. In 1985 *The New Our Bodies Ourselves* was published, nearly twice as long as the original and reflecting new problems, interests and changes in the 1980s while maintaining the original philosophy and style.

Outsiders' Society

An imaginary organization invented by Virginia WOOLF, it was in fact no organization at all, but rather a feminist alternative to traditional male societies. Writing about it in *Three Guineas* (1938) Woolf compared the potential effectiveness of the Outsiders' Society to the actual effectiveness of existing organizations in achieving such goals as peace, freedom and equality, suggesting, '. . . we can best help you to prevent war not by repeating your words and following your methods, but by finding new words and creating new methods.'

Outwrite
Britain's first national newspaper for women, launched on 8 March 1982. Produced collectively and published monthly, it campaigns against women's oppression, racism, imperialism and lesbian oppression, and prints news and features on women's struggles and achievements internationally.

OWL
See OLDER WOMEN'S LIBERATION

P

pacifism

This term first came into use at the beginning of the twentieth century to describe movements advocating the reduction of armaments and an end to war, and to describe the refusal of individuals to undertake military service on grounds of conscientious objection to war. Women have always made up a large proportion of pacifist groups, and much of the vigour of the pacifist movement preceding World War I came from active feminists. Although some argued that women were 'natural' pacifists with a biologically based reverence for life, and although some suffragists extended this into a reason for giving women political power, others rejected such ESSENTIALISM but combined their belief in the necessity of equal rights for women with a growing sense of the urgency of establishing world peace. Jane ADDAMS made a theoretical connection between feminism and pacifism: she believed that men, being physically stronger than women, could continue to use their strength to oppress women until warfare and all other forms of violence were eradicated. Pacifism must succeed, for women could never achieve true equality in a society which sanctioned violence. With Crystal EASTMAN and Lillian

Wald in 1915 she founded the WOMEN'S INTERNATIONAL LEAGUE FOR PEACE AND FREEDOM, hoping it would be a base to rid the world of both war and sexism. The war split the women's movement between nationalists and pacifists, and after the 1920s pacifists and feminists went their separate ways, both belonging to dwindling, unpopular movements. Not until the rebirth of the PEACE MOVEMENT in the 1960s did feminist-pacifists re-emerge.

Paid My Dues

American quarterly journal about women and music published from 1973–80. It was the first, and for a time the only, feminist music journal, and provided an on-going history of the development of women's music as well as an important communication link for women interested in women's culture.
(*See also* MUSIC AND MUSICIANS)

Palm, Etta Aelders (Baroness d'Aelders), 1743–93?

Dutch. Born in Holland, she travelled to Paris in 1774 to report on local conditions to her government, and was drawn into the revolutionary struggle by her interest in women's rights. In 1791 she petitioned the legislative assembly, giving a well-received speech in favour of equal rights for women in education, employment, politics and law, and she tried to organize a national system of women's clubs. Accused of being a spy, no more is known of her after 1792.

Pankhurst, Adela (Adela Walsh), 1885–1961

English-born Australian. Daughter of Emmeline Pankhurst, sister of Christabel and Sylvia, she was a forceful speaker and organizer for the WOMEN'S SOCIAL AND POLITICAL UNION until her commitment to socialism (she led WSPU members in support of a textile workers' strike in Yorkshire) led to conflict with her mother. Determined to continue working for the women's movement, she emigrated to Australia in 1914 to join Vida GOLD-STEIN's Women's Peace Army in 1914, and was quickly recognized as a leader of the socialist-feminist movement in that country. In 1917 she resigned from the women-only WPA to become an organizer for the Victoria Socialist Party, and married militant socialist Tom Walsh. During the 1920s she was considered the most influential woman in Australia, and throughout her life, although her causes changed, she was an active, charismatic speaker and campaigner for unions, peace and national unity.

Pankhurst, Christabel, 1880–1958

English. Daughter of Emmeline

PANKHURST and probably the best-known figure from the British women's suffrage movement, she was the courageous, charismatic organizer of the WOMEN'S SOCIAL AND POLITICAL UNION, and was practically worshipped by her followers. Despite being prohibited, as a woman, from practising as a lawyer, she studied law and received a joint first LLB in 1906. Arrested many times for her militant activities, in 1912 she was forced by the threat of a conspiracy charge to flee to France where she continued to rule in exile under the *nom de guerre* Amy Richards, and to direct the militant campaign through her paper, *The Suffragette*.

Her series of articles on venereal disease and women's sexual oppression became a book, *The Great Scourge and How to End It*, in 1913. She argued that the 'scourge' of disease was the direct result of men seeing women only in sexual terms and forcing them into the categories of wife or prostitute. The winning of the vote was the necessary first step which would enable women to break free from sexual slavery: political equality would bring with it the possibility of legal and economic independence.

In 1914, with the outbreak of war, her patriotic fervour turned her towards war work as she decided that the vote was of less importance than national victory. After the war, and the vote, had been won, she stood as a candidate for Parliament but was defeated.

By 1920, her politics were overwhelmed by Christianity. She spent the rest of her life in America, preaching the second coming of Christ.

Pankhurst, Emmeline

(Mrs Pankhurst), 1858–1928
English. She attended her first suffrage meeting with her mother at the age of fourteen, and from then on her whole life was devoted to the women's movement. In 1879, she married Dr Richard Pankhurst, who was also committed to legal equality for women, and together they worked on the Manchester Women's Suffrage Committee, the Married Women's Property Committee, and founded the WOMEN'S FRANCHISE LEAGUE in their London home in 1889.

In 1903, now a widow but with the aid of her daughters, she founded the WOMEN'S SOCIAL AND POLITICAL UNION, which she was to lead throughout that organization's existence. From 1908, as the militant campaign began to escalate, she was arrested and imprisoned more than a dozen times for conspiracy, incitement to violence, and assorted acts of protest. Her many hunger, sleep and thirst strikes badly damaged her health, yet she continued to appear in public to inspire her followers, even when she was too weak to walk and in danger of immediate re-arrest.

When World War I broke out in 1914 her energies were diverted from suffrage to recruitment, for she felt victory against Germany was a more immediate priority than the vote. After the war, she toured Canada lecturing on social purity and child welfare. Returning to England in 1926, she joined the Conservative Party and was a prospective Parliamentary candidate for the Whitechapel district of London.

Pankhurst, Richard Marsden

('Dr Pankhurst'), 1838–98
English social reformer and politician. Husband of Emmeline Pankhurst, father of Christabel, Adela and Sylvia. Devoted to the cause of women's rights all his life, he helped to found the Women's Suffrage Society in Manchester in 1865; drafted the Married Women's Property Bill; and, with Emmeline, founded the WOMEN'S FRANCHISE LEAGUE.

Pankhurst, Sylvia, (Estelle)

1882–1960
English writer and artist. Daughter of Emmeline PANKHURST and sister of Christabel, she became effectively the official artist of the WOMEN'S SOCIAL AND POLITICAL UNION, designing the Women's Exhibition, the WSPU membership card, posters, badges, banners, the HOLLOWAY BROOCH, and even a suffragette tea-service. For her political activities she was imprisoned

thirteen times and often forcibly fed while on hunger strike.

In 1911, she went to America to speak about the women's suffrage movement in both countries, and received an enthusiastic welcome, becoming only the second woman ever invited to address a joint session of the Senate and House of Representatives (the first woman had been Susan B. Anthony forty years earlier). On her return to Britain, she decided to give up art and commit herself totally to the women's movement.

Believing that the WSPU was too middle-class and needed a broader base, Sylvia founded a branch in the East End of London in 1912. By 1914, however, Emmeline and Christabel Pankhurst declared they wanted only hand-picked women for their movement, and disavowed Sylvia's working-class women. Her followers then became the East London Federation of Suffragettes and she began a weekly paper, the WOMAN'S DREADNOUGHT, as a forum for the voice of the working woman.

She had written articles on women's affairs for the *Westminster Review* signed 'Ignota', and her first book, *The Suffragette: The History of the Women's Militant Suffrage Movement 1905–1910*, was published in 1911. It was not until 1924, however, that she became a full-time writer.

Her most important book is probably *The Suffragette Movement*, an autobiographical history published in 1931, but she interested herself in many other causes besides that of women's rights, and wrote books on such subjects as India, maternity conditions in Britain, the prospect of creating an international language, Romanian authors, and the plight of Ethiopia.

Pappenheim, Bertha, 1859–1936 German social worker. In 1904 she founded the Judischer Frauenbund (League of Jewish Women), the heart of the German Jewish feminist movement. This organization was chiefly concerned with the white slave trade – forced PROSTITUTION on an international scale, particularly as it affected Jewish women – and with establishing women's equality with men in the Jewish community and religious life. In 1907 she founded the first home for unmarried Jewish mothers and disturbed girls. Throughout her life she emphasized the importance of career training for women as she worked to improve the status and self-image of Jewish women. The author of plays, prayers, essays and factual reports, Pappenheim is best known as the German translator of Mary Wollstonecraft's VINDICATION OF THE RIGHTS OF WOMEN. She is also remembered, through the writings of Breuer and FREUD, as 'Anna O.', the first woman to be psychoanalysed, and it was she who first defined this form of psychological treatment as 'the talking cure'.

Park, Maud Wood, 1871–1955
American. She was active in women's suffrage campaigns and civic reform from her student days. In 1900 she became chairman of the Massachusetts Woman Suffrage Association, and in 1901, executive secretary of the Boston Equal Suffrage Association for Good Government (BESAGG), an organization which became a forum for the more progressive young feminists in Massachusetts. With her friend Inez Haynes IRWIN she organized the first chapter of the College Equal Suffrage League in 1901, and later spent several years travelling around the country organizing college women. In 1916 she was persuaded by Carrie Chapman CATT to join the Congressional Committee of the NATIONAL AMERICAN WOMAN SUFFRAGE ASSOCIATION (NAWSA), and headed the 'front door lobby' which worked, successfully, to push a women's suffrage amendment through Congress. Later she said that if Catt had been the architect of the NINETEENTH AMENDMENT, she had been the builder. She became the first president of the LEAGUE OF WOMEN VOTERS when it was formed in 1919, and when the Women's Joint Congressional Committee was formed in 1920 to coordinate the activities of ten different women's organizations, including the League of Women Voters, and to lobby for social feminist goals such as legislation protecting women and children, she served as its head. Illness caused her to resign her office in 1924, but she always remained involved in the women's movement, and when she took up playwriting later, the life of Lucy STONE provided the subject of her most successful play. In 1943, working with Edna Stantial, an old friend from BESAGG, she collected written materials related to the women's movement in Massachusetts which became the nucleus of the Woman's Rights Collection of the Schlesinger Library at Radcliffe College.

Parkes, Bessie Rayner (Mrs Louis Belloc), 1828–1925
English. Member of the LANGHAM PLACE GROUP and a close friend of Barbara BODICHON, with whom she often travelled and worked. A founding member of the SOCIETY FOR PROMOTING THE EMPLOYMENT OF WOMEN, and an advocate of higher education for women. In 1858, inspired by a suggestion from the author Anna JAMESON, she bought a minor periodical which was for sale and turned it into the ENGLISH WOMAN'S JOURNAL, the first magazine of its kind, which became a major forum for the women's movement.

Parkhurst, Charley (Charlotte), 1812–79
American stagecoach driver. Honoured with a plaque in the Soquel, California fire station; as

the first woman to vote in an American presidential election (1868), she spent most of her life as a man, her real sex only being discovered after her death.

Parren, Kalliroe, 1861–1940
Greek. In 1888 she founded and edited *The Women's Newspaper*, produced exclusively by and for women. With it she did much to inform Greek women and direct attention to women's rights. In 1894 she founded the Union for the Emancipation of Women, and in 1911 she founded the Lyceum of Greek Women, to support women in education, childcare and job orientation. Her campaigns influenced government policy on laws affecting children and working women, and she ran classes to increase literacy among women. She also wrote a feminist play, a study of women in history, and a history of Greek women from 1650–1860.

Parturier, Françoise, 1919–
French journalist and essayist. A regular contributor to *Figaro* from 1956, she collaborated on three books with Josette Raoul-Duval using the name 'Nicole' before going on to write books under her own name from 1959. In 1970 she was accepted as one of four candidates for election to the Académie française: although she was not elected, her candidacy was precedent-setting, being the first time a

woman had been considered for membership since the founding of the Académie in the seventeenth century. She is one of the most accessible and popular feminist writers in France. Her books include *Lettre ouverte aux hommes* (1968), *L'Amour?, Le Plaisir?* (1968) and *Lettre ouverte aux femmes* (1974).

paternity
The knowledge of biological fatherhood is necessary to the construction of PATRIARCHY, which relies on the idea of inheritance through the male line. The male role in reproduction is not intuitively obvious: Australian aborigines remained unaware until quite recently of the connection between coitus and pregnancy. Not surprisingly, many theorists have made the connection between the discovery of paternity and the development of patriarchy. Elizabeth Fisher suggested in *Woman's Creation* (1979) that it was the domestication of animals, and the development of practices for their breeding, which led to male control of female reproductive capacity: enforced chastity, enforced pregnancy, and other forms of sexual repression designed to ensure that men can confidently claim ownership of the children their wives give birth to. As Germaine GREER pointed out in *The Female Eunuch* (1970): 'It is known that a father is necessary, but not known how to identify him, except

negatively.' She went on to advise women to refuse men the guarantees of paternity they've relied on for so long. By not marrying, having children by their own choice and insisting that all men are fathers to all children, Greer suggests that women have the power to make the patriarchal family impossible.

Paterson, Emma, 1848–86
English. Founder of the Women's Provident and Protective League (which became the Women's Trade Union League in 1891), in 1874 she began organizing women in bookbinding, dressmaking, millinery, upholstery and other trades. In 1875, she was the first woman to attend the Trades Union Congress. A suffragist, she opposed protective legislation, fearing it would create fewer employment opportunities for women. In 1876, she began editing the monthly *Women's Union Journal*, taught herself printing, and founded the Women's Printing Society.

patriarchy
The universal political structure which privileges men at the expense of women; the social system which feminism is determined to destroy. The term is frequently used by contemporary feminists, who are not always in agreement as to what they mean by it. It is used sometimes as a synonym for male domination; sometimes to refer to a specific, historical, social structure. Literally it means 'rule of the father', and was originally used by anthropologists to describe the social structure in which one old man (the patriarch) has absolute power over everyone else in the family. Feminists then began to point out that *all* societies, whatever their economic, political or religious differences, are patriarchies. All known societies are ruled by men, who control and profit from women's reproductive capabilities. Under some systems women have more privileges, even token power, than in others, but everywhere men are dominant, and the basic principles, defined by Kate MILLETT in *Sexual Politics* (1970), remain the same: 'male shall dominate female; elder male shall dominate younger'.

The concept of patriarchy has been an important one to feminists, providing a way of working towards a theory of male domination and female subordination, and of recognizing that, despite the different forms it takes, all women suffer a similar oppression which cannot be ended merely by changing the economic system.

The origin of patriarchy is unknown, and because it is universal it can seem monolithic, unassailable, even inevitable. It has often been assumed (not usually by feminists) that patriarchy is rooted in biology, in the fact that men are physically bigger and stronger than women, who are additionally weakened by child-bearing. Yet civilization (and other forms of oppression, like racism or slavery) is not founded on brute strength; the role of GENDER is not identical to biological sex; and alternatives to patriarchy may at least be imagined. Many have suggested that a prehistoric MATRIARCHY existed, and even those historians and anthropologists who find no evidence for a matriarchy suggest there must have been prepatriarchal social forms, and that patriarchy developed for some historical reason. Kate Millett has suggested that it may have been the discovery of PATERNITY which led to the establishment of male control over women. Juliet MITCHELL, in *Psychoanalysis and Feminism* (1974) argued that the patriarchal kinship systems evolved out of the universal existence of the incest taboo and the Oedipus complex.

If patriarchy *is* the inevitable outcome of biology, then it cannot be ended until not only SEX-ROLES, but sexual differences themselves are abolished. Shulamith FIRESTONE, in *The Dialectic of Sex* (1970), called for a biological revolution, seeing in the new reproductive technologies women's chance to rid themselves of the barbaric burden of pregnancy, and foreseeing the non-patriarchal future as an androgynous one.

Not all feminists find the term 'patriarchy' useful; some alternatives which have been used for the same basic concept include 'SEX-

GENDER SYSTEM' (Gayle Rubin); 'the planetary Men's Association' (Mary DALY); 'phallocracy' or simply 'SEXISM'.

Patriarchy Study Group
British organization founded in 1978 as a support system for feminists involved in research and trying to formulate a theory of PATRIARCHY.

Paul, Alice, 1885–1977
American. While studying in England in 1907, she became a member of the WOMEN'S SOCIAL AND POLITICAL UNION, and was militant enough to be arrested six times. On her return to the U.S. in 1910, she joined the NATIONAL AMERICAN WOMAN SUFFRAGE ASSOCIATION but soon grew impatient with the lack of energy in the American movement. In April 1913, with her friend Lucy BURNS, she founded the CONGRESSIONAL UNION FOR WOMAN SUFFRAGE to work for the passage of a federal amendment for women's suffrage, using tactics learned from the English suffragettes. In 1917, she was jailed for picketing the White House. After the vote was won in America she reorganized the NATIONAL WOMAN'S PARTY TO WORK for total legal equality for women. She drafted the first EQUAL RIGHTS AMENDMENT and submitted it to Congress in 1923. At the same time she had become involved in the international women's movement, and divided her time between

Europe and the United States until
the outbreak of World War II. She
succeeded in getting the Equal
Nationality Treaty accepted by the
League of Nations, and the Equal
Nationality Act passed in the U.S.
in 1934. She founded the WORLD
WOMAN'S PARTY in Geneva in 1938,
and was elected its president. From
1941, she devoted the rest of her life
to lobbying and organizing for the
Equal Rights Amendment.

peace movement
Ever since Fredrika BREMER founded
the first women's peace organization in Europe in 1854, women
have been organizing separately
from men to work for peace. Yet,
with a few notable exceptions like
Jane ADDAMS, most of the women
who combined PACIFISM with a
belief in equal rights lacked a
feminist analysis to connect the
two struggles. Most accepted
the prevailing notion that women
were naturally more peaceful than
men, and felt that this proof of
moral superiority was the best
reason why women should have the
vote.

The idea that women are
'naturally' peaceful is still around
today, and many women in the
contemporary peace movement are
content to play their traditional
role, sacrificing themselves for the
good of others. Some feminists feel
that the revolutionary potential of
the women's liberation movement
has been threatened by the tradi-

tional nature of the women's peace
movement, which they believe
represents a loss of genuinely
feminist principles and actions and
has become the acceptable face of
women-only actions. Yet although
many women in the peace movement may be indifferent or even
antagonistic towards feminist
goals, the traditional notion of
woman as peace-maker has a strong
hold on many feminists. In particular, radical feminists have often
accepted the idea that men have a
biological predisposition towards
VIOLENCE, and that women's
biology gives them a special close-
ness to all life. If this is so, then
peace is inarguably a woman's
issue, and the only hope for human
survival lies in what Sally GEARHART
has called a FEMALE FUTURE.

The women's peace movement
became larger, more visible, and
more diverse than ever in the 1980s,
and more groups began to organize
out of the felt need to focus feminist
consciousness on the issue. Instead
of making a choice between peace
and women's issues, feminist pacifists are attempting to recognize the
movements for peace and women's
liberation as aspects of the same
vision of a better world. If, as the
Nottingham Women Oppose the
Nuclear Threat (WONT) have
said, the primary source of violence
is the construction of GENDER, then
as long as society remains deeply
SEXIST, no peace movement will
achieve any meaningful success. In

Piecing it Together: Feminism and Nonviolence (1983) the Feminism and Nonviolence Study Group claim that violence is so basic to the structure of PATRIARCHY that it cannot be used for women's liberation. Nuclear weapons and war are both sub-categories of militarism, which both reflects and reproduces patriarchy, and as feminism is committed to ending the patriarchy, it must by definition oppose militarism. Peace is a woman's issue, therefore, not because that is part of women's traditional role, and not for a biological reason, but because war, violence and women's oppression all grow from the same roots, and one cannot be wiped out while the others remain.

(*See also* GREENHAM)

Peck, Annie, 1850–1935

American mountaineer. World famous as a mountain-climber, she considered her achievements to be to the glory of all women. In 1911, she climbed Mt Coropuna in Peru, to plant a 'Votes for Women' sign at the summit. In 1927, the Lima Geographical Society named the north peak of Huascarán after her.

Pelletier, Madeleine, 1874–1939

French doctor and writer. She became part of the women's suffrage movement in the 1890s and, influenced by the WOMEN'S SOCIAL AND POLITICAL UNION, adopted flamboyant and militant tactics, one of the few French feminists to do so.

She often wore male clothing from the waist up, including a tie and bowler hat, to symbolize her demand for equality. She edited a feminist journal, *La Suffragiste*, and wrote several books about feminism and sexual freedom. In 1905 she became Secretary of La Solidarité des Femmes, the radical wing of the French women's movement. She worked for women's suffrage and equal rights from within the socialist movement until 1913, when she joined the anarchists, finding their policies more egalitarian. Trained as a physician, in 1906 she became the first woman in France allowed to qualify to work in mental hospitals. Towards the end of her life she campaigned for women's rights to birth control and legal abortions, and practised abortions herself until her arrest in 1939.

-person

Suffix, at first sight the obvious non-sexist replacement for the pseudo-generic -man, as in chairman. But in practice, while chairwoman often becomes chairperson, a male chairperson is still called chairman, with the result that -person is coming to seem a euphemism for -woman, and -man remains the norm.

'Personal is Political, The'

This phrase encapsulates one of the most radical and important concepts of the WOMEN'S LIBERATION MOVEMENT. It was developed in the

United States in the late 1960s, and first appeared in print in 1970 in *Notes from the Second Year* as the title of an article by Carol Hanisch which justified the importance of CONSCIOUSNESS-RAISING groups and refuted the false dichotomy between 'personal' and 'political'. Although the idea has been interpreted in various ways – including the prescriptive that a feminist must lead a politically correct life – basically it expresses the insight that there is a politics to sex. Family life is defined by power relationships just as much as the state, and one is a reflection of the other. The act of defining women's shared problems as 'personal', and therefore not suitable for public discussion or change, is simply another means by which men have kept women from realizing the extent of their oppression. Under PATRIARCHY, women have been identified with the private and men with the public sphere, and the two have been kept separate. Masculine power is reinforced most strongly precisely through the most 'personal' institutions of marriage, childcare, violence, love and sexual relationships, and only when the personal is treated as seriously and critically as the public can the roots of sexism be found.

(*See also* SEXUAL POLITICS)

Pethick-Lawrence, Emmeline,
1867–1954

English. After Emmeline and Christabel PANKHURST, she was undoubtedly the most tireless worker and influential leader of the militant suffrage movement. In 1906 she became Treasurer of the WOMEN'S SOCIAL AND POLITICAL UNION. With her husband Frederick, she edited the paper VOTES FOR WOMEN from 1907. She was frequently arrested and imprisoned for her militant activities. In 1912, the Pethick-Lawrences were abruptly dismissed from the WSPU; they subsequently joined the United Suffragists. In 1918 she became President of the Women's Freedom League. A pacifist, she was as active in the international peace movement as she was in the struggle for women's rights. She travelled to the United States as representative of the Women's International League for Peace in 1912, and in 1915 she attended the women's peace congress at The Hague.

Pethick-Lawrence, Frederick,
1871–1961

English politician. Born Frederick Lawrence, he added his wife's name to his own on his marriage to Emmeline Pethick in 1901. He was drawn into the women's suffrage movement as a fully participating member of the WOMEN'S SOCIAL AND POLITICAL UNION when Emmeline was arrested during a demonstration at the House of Commons. When she was arrested, he took over her job as treasurer of the WSPU, and their London home was soon headquarters for Christabel PANKHURST. The only man with an official position in the militant suffrage movement, he was arrested for his part in demonstrations, and even forcibly fed. He founded, financed and co-edited the paper VOTES FOR WOMEN, and wrote a book called *Women's Fight for the Vote* (1910). After their dismissal from the WSPU, the Pethick-Lawrences joined the United Suffragists. He became a Labour Member of Parliament in 1923, and his maiden speech to the House of Commons, written with Emmeline's aid, was about pensions for widows. Although he continued to have strong feminist sympathies, in later years they took second place to his interest in foreign affairs and economics.

phallic criticism
Term used by Mary ELLMANN for the practice of regarding the sex of the author as of primary importance in assessing the value of a work of literature. Examples, given in THINKING ABOUT WOMEN, include Norman Mailer's belief that male genitalia are more necessary to the writer than pen and ink. Cynthia Ozick has called this the 'testicular theory' of literature. Its complement, which she called the 'ovarian theory', claims that a woman writer, being a woman, will write in a style recognizably feminine, in what Virginia WOOLF claimed to

find in Dorothy RICHARDSON's works: a woman's sentences.

phallocentric
Term, like ANDROCENTRIC, which points out the masculine bias of our culture. Literally meaning 'phallus-centred', the term gained currency among modern feminists (largely displacing the earlier term androcentric) through PSYCHOANALYSIS. In psychoanalytic thought the phallus is not considered to be the same as the penis, but is rather the symbol of the difference between the sexes and the signifier of the status which has been socially conferred upon biological maleness. Phallocentrism, therefore, is the belief that maleness is the centre and the norm against which everything must be judged.

phallocracy
Social, political, ideological system which perpetuates the domination of men and the subordination of women. Another term for PATRIARCHY, it literally means 'rule of the phallus', thus emphasizing that, far from being natural or rational, patriarchy is based on penis worship.

phallogocentrism
Term developed by Jacques Derrida to suggest that logocentrism (the primacy of the word, or LANGUAGE) and PHALLOCENTRISM are the same thing; that language is the realm of the fathers and the phallus is the

'privileged signifier'. The development of a specifically female way of writing, or L'ÉCRITURE FÉMININE, is the feminist challenge to phallogocentrism.

Piercy, Marge, 1936–

American poet and novelist. A political activist, she came to the women's liberation movement via the civil rights movement, and anti-war activities. Her poetry and novels reflect her politics and are concerned with the realities of women's lives today. Among her novels are WOMAN ON THE EDGE OF TIME (1976), in which she created a non-sexist UTOPIA, and *Vida* (1979) about the experiences of a political radical and fugitive in the America of the 1960s and 1970s. Her many collections of poetry include *To Be of Use* (1973), *The Moon is Always Female* (1980), and *Circles on the Water: Selected Poems* (1982). A collection of her essays, reviews and interviews, many of them concerned with women's writing, women's lives, and connections between feminist politics and culture, was published in 1982 as *Parti-Colored Blocks for a Quilt*.

Pilgrimage

Long novel by Dorothy RICHARDSON, published in thirteen volumes over the course of fifty-two years. It reveals, in stream-of-consciousness fashion, the experiences of the autobiographical Miriam Henderson as she comes to maturity between the 1890s and 1915. Most of the characters are based on people Richardson knew, including H. G. Wells who appears as 'Hypo Wilson', but the chief interest of the book is less in the people and events than in the viewpoint character's changing perceptions of reality. Writing contemporaneously with Proust and Joyce (a French critic later described the work as '*proustienne avant Proust*'), yet from a thoroughly female consciousness, Richardson found few readers sympathetic to her new and apparently difficult technique. The idea expressed in the book, that women perceive and live more deeply and truly than men, alienated some male critics, but Virginia Woolf, May Sinclair and others hailed the early volumes as evidence of a welcome development in the art of the novel. A rediscovery, and re-evaluation, of *Pilgrimage* began in the mid-1970s, and no one in search of a female aesthetic can afford to ignore it.

Pizan, Christine de, 1365–?1430

Italian-born French writer. After the death of her husband in 1389, she supported herself, her three children, and other family members by writing, an almost unimaginable career for a woman of her time. She is considered by some to be the first feminist writer; according to historian Joan Kelly, de Pizan 'defined what was to become the modern feminist sensibility'. During her lifetime she produced some fifteen volumes of work, including history, biography, philosophy and poetry, in which she established herself as a defender of her sex and carried out a campaign against literary misogyny. This she did by recording the deeds and lives of strong and praiseworthy women from HISTORY; by criticizing the male DOUBLE STANDARD and violence against women; and by arguing strongly for women's right to an EDUCATION, claiming that women had a sharper understanding than men and needed only the opportunity to exercise it. Her arguments sparked off the debate which became known as the QUERELLE DES FEMMES, and for centuries she was inevitably quoted in any discussion of women's nature. Today her best-known works are *The Book of the City of Ladies* (1404) and its sequel, *The Treasure of the City of Ladies* (1405), also known as *The Book of the Three Virtues*. Her last known work was a song in honour of JOAN OF ARC (1429).

Pizzey, Erin, 1939–

British social reformer and writer. She founded Chiswick Women's Aid in 1971 and was responsible for forcing public awareness of the plight of BATTERED WOMEN, and making it a public issue. She has often clashed with other feminists, and has said that she was 'drummed out of the women's movement' for her unpopular belief that women in violent situations may be in control of the VIOLENCE and addicted to it, not simply victims. She has written books on battered women, violence-addiction and incest, as well as novels.

Plamnikova, Franciska, 1875–1942

Czech teacher and politician. Remembered as the founder of Czech feminism, she founded the Women's Club of Prague in 1901, and the Committee for Women's Suffrage in 1905, both strongly nationalistic feminist organizations. She became the first Chairwoman of the Czech Council of Women in 1923, and was also the Vice-Chairwoman of the International Council of Women.

plays and playwrights
See THEATRE

poets and poetry

There have been women poets as long as there has been poetry, and even in times without a formal woman's movement some poems have been about feminist concerns or written from a recognizably feminist sensibility. Poetry that was too explicitly feminist tended to be ignored, lost, or misinterpreted by the male GATEKEEPERS of our culture who decide what is and is not acceptable from a woman. One of the achievements of the women's liberation movement has been the rediscovery of the strength and variety of women's poetry, and the reclaiming of male-defined 'minor' poets as important. Elizabeth Barrett BROWNING, for example, usually remembered for her love poems to her husband, was also the author of AURORA LEIGH, a verse novel which inspired Susan B. ANTHONY and many other 'first wave' feminists.

Like the polemic, poetry is a traditional form for political protest and as such has been made use of by feminists in all ages. Sylvia PANKHURST and other militant suffragettes wrote poems about their cause while in prison.

In the late 1960s, as part of the women's movement in Britain and America, there was a positive explosion of poetry. Many of the leading theorists of the new movement were poets – Robin MORGAN, Susan GRIFFIN and Adrienne RICH, among others – and since language was recognized as one of the tools by which perceptions were formed and women oppressed, the role of poetry in reclaiming language for women was obviously vital. The understanding that 'THE PERSONAL IS POLITICAL' also led naturally to poetry. Creating poems out of their own feelings and experiences, women could come to a new understanding and also share this understanding with other women. Poetry was sometimes seen as a form of CONSCIOUSNESS-RAISING, something any woman could do, sitting at the kitchen table, fitting it in among other tasks, and because of its

length it could easily be copied and shared with others.

Networks developed, bringing women together in writing workshops, printing collectives and public readings, as well as through the pages of magazines and self-published books. Investigating the feminist cultural renaissance in 1974, Susan Rennie and Kirsten Grimstad collected more than 130 self-published volumes of women's poetry from all parts of America.

Commercial publication of explicitly feminist poetry began in America in 1972 with MONSTER by Robin Morgan, followed by a number of influential, steadily selling anthologies of work by women poets. In Britain, although poetry played an equally important role in the women's movement from at least 1969, it remained underground, hardly noticeable in mass-market publishing until the 1980s. In 1981, Anna Carteret, Sue Jones-Davies and Fanny Viner calling themselves The Raving Beauties launched a performance of poems by women called 'In the Pink'. This was a success at the 1982 Edinburgh Festival and became first a television show and then an anthology published by The Women's Press.

Yet although the women's movement created a much greater interest in women's poetry, not all poems written by women are feminist poems. Poet Jan Clausen has described the 'core revelation' being sought and expressed in early feminist poetry as simply 'I am a woman'. This is a liberating notion in patriarchal culture, but is it enough? Towards the end of the 1970s the question of what defined a poem as feminist began to be asked, and distinctions made between poems about female experience, and those written from a feminist awareness.

As Jan Clausen suggested in her essay 'A Movement of Poets: Thoughts on Poetry and Feminism', feminists usually have certain expectations of their poetry: the feminist poem should be both useful and accessible. It is political (in the largest sense of the word), usually written from personal experience and without distancing techniques, and written explicitly for an audience of women. Janet Montefiore has said that the task of feminist poetry is the work of re-definition: to combat sexist language and create feminist meanings; and Adrienne Rich has frequently written, in poems as well as prose, of the need for women to develop a new language, and a whole new poetry.

Because feminist poetry emerged from a rejection of patriarchal culture, refusing its definitions of what was allowed to be considered poetry, some feminists mistrust the idea of any critical standards applied to poetry just as they dislike the divisiveness of choosing to recognize one individual poet and not another. Some poets, although

feminist in intent, feel that to be called a 'feminist poet' is too narrow a label. Bearing that in mind, here is a short list of some of the better-known contemporary feminist poets writing in English: ALTA, Alison FELL, Judy GRAHN, Susan GRIFFIN, Marlyn Hacker, June JORDAN, Judith Kazantzis, Audre LORDE, Lyn Lifshin, Robin MORGAN, Pat Parker, Marge PIERCY, Adrienne RICH and Alice WALKER.

political lesbian

1) Woman who has become a lesbian as a conscious, political decision through the impact on her life of feminist theory.

2) A woman-identified woman who, although she may never have a sexual relationship with another woman, has committed her life totally to women.

3) Lesbian who has been politicized, who understands her oppression in both gay liberation and feminist terms.

Political Lesbianism
See LESBIAN–FEMINISM; LOVE YOUR ENEMY?

Political Lesbianism: The Case Against Heterosexuality
See LOVE YOUR ENEMY?

politicos
Term used by American feminists in the late 1960s and early 1970s for women who called themselves feminists but did not accept the idea

of feminism as a political struggle in its own right; they saw women's issues as part of a larger struggle for social change. These women would not call themselves politicos, but would say they were feminist-socialists or Marxists.

'Politics of the Ego'

Manifesto composed by Anne KOEDT and Shulamith FIRESTONE and presented by them on 5 December 1969, to a group of about forty women who subsequently became known as the NEW YORK RADICAL FEMINISTS. It was the first major paper to outline the basic beliefs and goals of RADICAL FEMINISM, declaring that the purpose of MALE CHAUVINISM is 'primarily to obtain psychological ego satisfaction' and that female oppression is not the fault of capitalism or any other economic system, because 'the political oppression of women has its own class dynamic; and that dynamic must be understood in terms previously called "non-political" – namely the politics of the ego.' Certain institutions – MOTHERHOOD, MARRIAGE, love and sexual intercourse – constructed and maintained the position of women in regard to men. The goal of radical feminism was defined as the destruction of the sex class system through women helping each other to learn to resist, 'by constructing alternate selves that are healthy, independent and self-assertive' and by transferring 'the

ultimate power of judgment about the value of our lives from men to ourselves.'

politics

Although in common usage the terms politics and political usually refer to government, public affairs, civil administration and legislative action, politics is interpreted in a broader sense in feminist theory to refer to POWER relationships of all kinds.
(*See also* SEXUAL POLITICS)

Pollitzer, Anita Lily, 1894–1975

American. A meeting with Alice PAUL in 1916 caused her to join the NATIONAL WOMAN'S PARTY (NWP), and from then on it was at the centre of her life. She travelled around the country speaking, lobbying and organizing on behalf of women's suffrage, and won over many state legislators with her charm. After the vote had been won she devoted her energies to campaigning for the EQUAL RIGHTS AMENDMENT. She also worked for the INTERNATIONAL WOMAN SUFFRAGE ALLIANCE, and for women's equality within the United Nations, and in 1933 she became vice chairman of the WORLD WOMAN'S PARTY. In 1945 she was elected to the chair of the National Woman's Party, a position she held until 1949.

Popp, Adelheid, 1869–1939

Austrian. Leader of the Austrian Socialist women's movement from

1892. In 1893 she led the first women's strike, in a clothing factory near Vienna, and founded a group called Libertas to give women experience in political debate. She consistently fought male trade unionists' resistance to women's interests, and in 1896 failed by only one vote to get the Austrian Trade Union Congress to back an official women's organization. She continued, until the Nazi takeover, to work for equal rights for women, including the right to equal pay, divorce reform, and the provision of childcare.

pornography

This emerged as an important issue in the latter half of the 1970s and has been dividing feminists ever since. Even if most feminists feel some sort of gut-level reaction against pornography, not all agree whether, or how, that feeling should be translated into political action. Even a widely-accepted definition of pornography has yet to be formulated, although there have been many attempts.

Legislation to regulate or outlaw pornography is an uneasy area particularly for liberal feminists and socialist feminists, not only because censorship conflicts with the liberal ideals of freedom of speech and personal privacy, but also because of the awareness that censorship has always been used against women: anti-pornography laws could be used to ban publication and sale of anything from lesbian erotic fiction, to self-help health texts and birth control information, to radical feminist theories of human sexuality. Feminists with a strong anti-pornography stance have often found themselves, willingly or not, sharing a platform with right-wing moralists who oppose pornography not because it degrades women, but because they consider any depictions of sexual activity to threaten the patriarchal family.

Despite disagreement about what should be done, most feminists share a view which differs from that held by the non-feminist liberal or conservative. Rather than considering SEXUALITY as a given, a biological urge which must be controlled (conservative) or allowed harmless expression (liberal) for the good of society, feminists see sexual behaviour as being culturally determined. Pornography, therefore, while it expresses cultural attitudes towards sex and women, also may create or reinforce that attitude in those who are exposed to it, and thus influence subsequent behaviour. The extent to which an individual believes exposure to pornography influences behaviour (the results of studies are far from conclusive) will obviously affect her feelings about the dangers of pornography. If it is merely a symptom of our sexist society, reflecting the same attitudes found in advertising and all forms of popular culture, then outlawing one particular expression won't solve the deeper problem; if pornography is in itself an act of VIOLENCE against women which causes or increases women's oppression, then concern for freedom of speech is beside the point.

The modern debate on pornography grew out of concern with RAPE and other obvious instances of male VIOLENCE against women. Robin MORGAN coined the phrase 'Theory and Practice: Pornography and Rape' in 1974, and Susan BROWNMILLER made the same link, calling pornography 'anti-female propaganda' in her important book about rape, AGAINST OUR WILL (1975). Among the first active anti-pornography groups were WOMEN AGAINST VIOLENCE AGAINST WOMEN (from 1976) and the London Revolutionary Feminist Group (1977).

Some women oppose official censorship but believe in taking direct action. Angry Women in England, and the Preying Mantis Women's Brigade in California have vandalized and burned down pornographic bookshops. Other individuals and groups have expressed their objections by picketing, public demonstrations, and spray-painting over offensive advertising, as well as organizing on a local level to stop the sale of pornographic books, films and videotapes.

In 1985 Andrea DWORKIN and Catharine MacKinnon drafted a model antipornography law which departed from the usual tradition of relying on public standards to decide what was offensive, and instead confronted pornography as a violation of women's civil rights.

The first section contains a statement of policy which describes pornography as sex discrimination: 'Pornography is a systematic practice of exploitation and subordination based on sex that differentially harms women. The harm of pornography includes dehumanization, sexual exploitation, forced sex, forced prostitution, physical injury, and social and sexual terrorism and inferiority presented as entertainment. The bigotry and contempt it promotes, with the acts of aggression it fosters, diminish opportunities for equality of rights in employment, education, property, public accommodations and public services; create public and private harassment, persecution and denigration; promote injury and degradation such as rape, battery, child sexual abuse, and prostitution and inhibit just enforcement of laws against these acts; contribute significantly to restricting women in particular from full exercise of citizenship and participation in public life, including in neighbourhoods; damage relations between the sexes; and undermine women's equal exercise of rights to speech and action guaranteed to all citizens under the Constitution and laws of the United States.'

The second section defines pornography as 'the graphic sexually explicit subordination of women through pictures and/or words that also includes one or more of the following: (i) women are presented dehumanized as sexual objects, things, or commodities; or (ii) women are presented as sexual objects who enjoy pain or humiliation; or (iii) women are presented as sexual objects who experience sexual pleasure in being raped; or (iv) women are presented as sexual objects tied up or cut up or mutilated or bruised or physically hurt; or (v) women are presented in postures or positions of sexual submission, servility or display; or (vi) women's body parts – including but not limited to vaginas, breasts, or buttocks – are exhibited such that women are reduced to those parts; or (vii) women are presented as whores by nature; or (viii) women are presented as being penetrated by objects or animals; or (ix) women are presented in scenarios of degradation, injury, torture, shown as filthy or inferior, bleeding, bruised, or hurt in a context that makes these conditions sexual.'

The law then defines as unlawful:

1. coercion into pornography;
2. trafficking in pornography;
3. forcing pornography on a person; and
4. assault or physical attack due to pornography.

The Feminist Anti-Censorship Task Force (FACT) responded by filing a legal brief opposing an Indiana ordinance based on this model law. Among other objec-

tions to the law, they argued that rather than being feminist, it was actually sexist, since it is partly based on the idea that women are weak, and less than legally adult, since proof that a woman consented to take part in the creation of sexually explicit material would be no defence against a charge of coercion. They also objected that the definition was vague enough to be used against women's own free sexual expression – not everyone would agree on what constituted a posture of 'sexual submission'.

The fact that feminists are publicly opposing each other on this issue – and that, for some feminists, pornography has become the most important single issue – has been recognized as a danger threatening the women's movement in the 1980s, and a search for common ground and recognition of common goals continues along with the debate. As Joanna RUSS has said about the two sides taken by feminists on pornography: 'we're both right – and both wrong'. Russ has suggested that underlying the disagreement is the fact that 'women's experience of SEXUALITY under sexism is inescapably double'.
(*See also* TAKE BACK THE NIGHT)

positive discrimination
To deliberately choose the members of a certain group (for example, women) not merely on a basis of equal opportunity, but in pre-

ference to members of a previously privileged group (white men). Those who disapprove see this as no better than the original practice of discrimination which excluded women from certain jobs or privileges. Those who favour the practice of positive discrimination (also called reverse discrimination) see it as a temporary stage, necessary to balance the original injustice, leading to a time when all unfair discrimination will be ended.

positive language

The use of the feminine for every indefinite or generic reference in speaking or writing. (For example: 'God in *her* infinite wisdom . . .'; 'Each student should finish *her* work . . .') Like POSITIVE DISCRIMINATION in employment, positive language is considered by some a way of righting the balance which usually works against women. It is also a way of pointing up the bias which results in HE/MAN LANGUAGE. (*See also* PRONOUNS)

post-feminist

A term which has been used in the past (particularly in reference to the decades following the achievement of women's suffrage until the birth of the WOMEN'S LIBERATION MOVEMENT in the late 1960s) and which has acquired a disturbing new life in the mid-1980s. Contemporary use of the term may be hostile, revealing the wish that feminism was a mere passing fashion, or it may

express the well-meaning but misguided belief that feminism belongs to history because the feminists have 'won', freeing today's postfeminist women from the necessity of being feminists. In *Making for the Open*, a collection of poetry by contemporary women published in 1985, editor Carol Rumens defended the term 'post-feminist' by saying that it expressed a psychological rather than political condition. She wrote: 'It implies a freedom which a few outstanding women in any age have achieved, and which many more, with increasing confidence, are claiming today.' Yet no matter how the term is redefined or justified, its use is anti-feminist, for it works against the continuing feminist struggle by seeking to limit feminism, to define it and place it in history. Although all feminists hope and work for a post-feminist future, to believe that we have achieved it when we so clearly have not is to be defeated without even realizing it, and to risk losing the gains feminism has achieved.

Post Partum Document

Six-part artwork (1973–9) by Mary KELLY which investigates the developing mother/child relationship from the mother's point of view, choosing key moments of individuation, starting with the baby being weaned from the breast (Part I) and continuing to the point where the child has learned to write

(Part VI). Each section consists of two parts: a 'fetish' (infant clothes, her son's first drawings etc.) and an accompanying text which analyses what is happening through dense psychoanalytic language, Lacanian diagrams, charts etc. The work has been greatly criticized, but also recognized as one of the few major feminist artworks.

(*See also* HAYWARD ANNUAL II)

Potonie-Pierre, Eugénie,
1844–98

French co-founder, with Léonie Rouzade and Marguerite Tinayre, of the Union des Femmes in 1880. In 1889 she founded La Ligue Socialiste des Femmes, and in 1891 co-founded, with Maria Martin, La Groupe de la Solidarité des Femmes. In 1892 she united eight separate feminist groups in Paris as the Federation Française des Sociétés Feministes. She led the French deputation to the feminist congress in Brussels in 1897.

power

The ability to do or act. The most visible forms of power are those legitimated by authority, and throughout history men as individuals and in groups have wielded power while it has been denied to women. Although the 'separate spheres' argument would have it that there is a balance between the sexes, so that while men have power in the public realm, women have power within the home and family, there is no such neat division in reality. Men's power in the public realm has consequences in the private: laws concerning MARRIAGE, RAPE, BIRTH CONTROL, ABORTION and employment, as well as male control of education and religion, ensure that women are denied not merely public power but the power to control their own lives and bodies. Men have power not only over each other, but over women. One of the major goals of feminism has always been to ensure redistribution of social power and reclaim some of it for women: the long fight for women's suffrage is the most famous example of how public power was fought for and achieved by women. Yet another task of feminism has been to rethink and redefine power, not merely to enable women to share in the powers held by men, but to question the validity of those powers, and to recognize that women already have certain powers. These powers may be psychological and spiritual as well as material, and they exist whether or not they are authorized, legitimized or generally acknowledged by men. Many works of feminist theory have necessarily dealt with the issue of power since the development of the concept of SEXUAL POLITICS and the recognition that the PERSONAL IS POLITICAL. Two recent, full-length works on power are *Powers of the Weak* by Elizabeth JANEWAY (1980) and *Beyond Power* by Marilyn FRENCH (1985).

Power of Women Collective
See WAGES FOR HOUSEWORK

President's Commission on the Status of Women

The first official body to examine the status of women in the United States. On 14 December 1961, at the suggestion of Esther Peterson, President John F. Kennedy established the commission to examine and suggest ways of combating the 'prejudices and outmoded customs' which prevented women from enjoying full human rights.

Chairing the Commission were Eleanor Roosevelt, Esther Peterson and Richard A. Lester.

The Commission's report, *American Women*, was released in 1963. Although filled with hard facts showing that most women worked for a living, for lower wages and status than men, and that many laws openly discriminated against women, the tone of the report, and recommendations for improvements, were moderate in the extreme.

One result of the Commission was the formation of fifty state commissions to do similar research on the state level. These commissions were composed primarily of women, and by bringing together politically active, informed women to uncover evidence of women's

unequal status in the expectation that something positive would be done about it, groundwork was laid for SECOND WAVE FEMINISM, the modern women's movement.

Principles of Feminist Journalism
See JOURNALISM

problem that has no name

Term used by Betty FRIEDAN in THE FEMININE MYSTIQUE to describe the growing dissatisfaction felt by American women in the 1950s and 1960s. As she defined it, the problem was that women were not allowed to be grown-up individuals, genuine human beings, but were expected to follow a false, infantile pattern of femininity and live through their husbands and children. She recognized that this was a genuine social problem, and not just the matter of individual maladjustment it was said to be. Subsequently, feminists have named the problem SEXISM.

pro-choice

Term describing those who support a woman's right to choose whether or not to bear a child. A more accurate descriptive than 'pro-abortion'.

Proctor, Adelaide Ann, 1825–64

English poet who also wrote under the name Mary Berwick. Well-loved by the Victorians for her verse, she was a member of the LANGHAM PLACE GROUP and devoted her short life (she died of tuberculosis) to the women's movement. With Barbara BODICHON and Jessie BOUCHERETT she founded the SOCIETY FOR PROMOTING THE EMPLOYMENT OF WOMEN.

pronouns

The English language has no singular form of a common-gender pronoun, and the need for one can be seen in the persistent use of 'they' as a singular, despite the fact that this is widely taught and believed to be incorrect. Grammatical rules (formulated by men in the eighteenth century) prescribe that the male gender is more comprehensive than the female, and, therefore, that 'he' and 'his' should be used when the sex of the subject is uncertain. This implies that the generic being is male, and that the female is a deviant or exceptional form. While men may be happy referring to unknown individuals as 'he', women have always felt less comfortable with this, knowing that despite the laws of grammar, 'he' does not always mean or include 'she'. Feminists writing about this (and about the use of MAN as a generic term for human beings) have sometimes referred to it as the HE/MAN problem.

A number of ways of avoiding this problem have been suggested: to use *they* as a singular (more commonly acceptable in spoken than in written LANGUAGE); to restructure sentences to avoid the necessity of a singular 'universal' pronoun; to use 'she and he' or 'she and/or he' every time; to use 'she' as the universal; or to invent a new set of pronouns.

Varda One discussed alternatives in her 'Manglish' column in *Everywoman* in 1971. Her own invention was ve (he or she), vis (his or hers), ver (him or her) and verself. Mary Arovan came up with co, cos, co and coself, while Dana Densmore preferred she, heris and herm.

Kate Miller and Casey Swift, writing in the first issue of MS. (1972), suggested that a common-gender pronoun could most easily be derived from they: tey for he or she, ter or ters, and tem.

In her 1973 novel *The Cook and the Carpenter*, June ARNOLD went one step further by abolishing the distinction between he and she and using only one pronoun – na – for everyone as a way of questioning the importance of gender and in the future society depicted in Marge Piercy's WOMAN ON THE EDGE OF TIME (1976) per (from person) has replaced he and she, his and hers.

prostitution

Feminists past and present have seen in prostitution the paradigm of the male–female relationship under PATRIARCHY, in which women are forced to sell themselves in exchange for economic survival. This analysis recognizes MARRIAGE as another form of prostitution, and both as SEXUAL SLAVERY. Although a woman may choose to marry, or choose to become a prostitute, these apparently free choices may be forced upon her because she has so few other options.

The traditional, patriarchal attitude considers prostitution a necessary evil, something which must be discouraged but cannot be abolished because of human nature. Prostitutes are seen as wickedly exploiting the natural male sexual urge; therefore, when police enforce laws against prostitution, it is usually the women they arrest, while letting the customers go free. Feminists have broken down this traditional view by pointing out how social, economic and psychological factors, as well as outright coercion and entrapment in many cases, have forced women into perpetuating a system which is entirely for male benefit.

Yet to presume that the prostitute is always a victim in need of rescue is not entirely satisfactory. Although there was a strong feminist strand in the SOCIAL PURITY MOVEMENT of the nineteenth century, many of the middle-class followers of Josephine BUTLER were reluctant to admit that working-class women had the right to determine and control their own SEXUALITY.

Prostitutes began organizing and speaking for themselves publicly in the 1970s, working for the decriminalization of prostitution through such groups as the English Collective of Prostitutes and COYOTE.

From the mid-nineteenth century, when the CONTAGIOUS DISEASES ACTS were successfully fought, to the present, when the women's liberation movement has backed prostitutes protesting against unjust laws and unsafe working conditions, most feminists would agree that, whatever their personal feelings about prostitution, it must be removed from patriarchal control.

Although it is usually presumed that women's liberation would do away with prostitution, this is far from certain. From the liberal feminist viewpoint, there is no reason why an individual should not sell her sexual services as readily as she might any other skills or abilities. Why should there be any special stigma attached to a woman who makes her living as a sexual partner rather than as a secretary, a teacher, or a surgeon? Yet the feminist must always question how genuinely free the choice of prostitution can be so long as women are seen (and socialized into seeing themselves) first and foremost as sexual objects, and as long as their opportunities for other types of employment remain limited.

proto-feminism

The beginning of feminism as a social movement is usually set no earlier than mid-seventeenth-century England. At that time, women played a powerful role in the formation of many new radical religious sects, and the Protestant concept of the equality of souls was resulting in their growing demands to be treated with the same equality on earth as they would be in heaven. The first moment in English history in which women took independent political action on the national level, as women on behalf of women, was in January 1642 when at least 400 women petitioned Parliament for their rights as workers, as worshippers, and within marriage. As a coherent philosophy, equal rights feminism was established in the eighteenth century, part of the radical movement which also led to the French and American Revolutions.

Yet even before feminism existed as a movement or a recognized theory, it can be argued that feminists existed. As long as women have been oppressed there have been individuals who have resisted that oppression, some on a personal level and others quite consciously on behalf of their sex. Such women are sometimes referred to as proto-feminists, to recognize their status as foremothers of later women's movements. A short list of proto-feminists might include SAPPHO, Jane ANGER, JOAN of Arc, Christine de PIZAN, THEODORA, and Aphra BEHN.

pro-woman line

Political stance first defined and promoted by the REDSTOCKINGS in 1969, it countered traditional, psychological explanations of women's position by declaring that women are not responsible in any way for their own oppression. As expressed in the Redstocking Manifesto (7 July 1969): 'We also reject the idea that women consent to or are to blame for their own oppression. Women's submission is not the result of brainwashing, stupidity, or mental illness but of continual, daily pressure from men. We do not need to change ourselves, but to change men.'

Although an original, positive theory which contributed greatly to feminist thought, the pro-woman line can also be criticized for leading to the glorification of the victim, and a stalemate as far as action is concerned since it declares that there is no point in women trying to change their lives.

The other aspect of the pro-woman line, which continues to be an important consideration for many feminists, was expressed in the Manifesto as: 'In fighting for our liberation we will always take the side of women against their oppressors. We will not ask what is "revolutionary" or "reformist", only what is good for women.'

psychoanalysis

The theory and THERAPY developed by Sigmund FREUD and his followers. Although it has been used as a weapon against many women, denying their political insights as it

261

forces them into an ill-fitting but socially acceptable SEX-ROLE, psychoanalysis is not the ideology later popularizers made it out to be, but rather a method of investigation. As such, it is a tool now used by many feminist theorists, including Juliet MITCHELL, Gayle Rubin and Nancy CHODOROW, to try to understand how GENDER is constructed. In France, a movement originally called *Psychanalyse et Politique*, combines the use of Marxist theory (to explain the current historical and economic situation) with psychoanalysis (especially as interpreted by Jacques Lacan) to explain the ideology of PATRIARCHY and the meaning of sexual differences within society.

'Psychology Constructs the Female'

Paper by Dr Naomi WEISSTEIN presented to a meeting of the American Studies Association at the University of California, 26 October 1968, and widely circulated within the women's liberation movement. (It was published under the title '*Kinder, Küche, Kirche* As Scientific Law: Psychology Constructs the Female' in *Sisterhood is Powerful* (1970).) The argument of the paper is that PSYCHOLOGY knows nothing about the true nature or desires of woman – or, for that matter, man – in part because it consists largely of myths rather than properly tested theories, but also because 'personality theory has looked for inner traits when it should have been looking at social context'. Drawing on the results of experiments which demonstrated that experimental results with both people and animals were affected by the expectations of the experimenters, the presence and attitudes of other people, and other changes in the social context, Weisstein concluded that personality is far more affected by changes in the environment than is usually admitted, and that statements about women's nature reveal more about what men want from women than anything essentially true.

psychology

Like biology, a branch of science used to justify the oppression of women by explaining SEX-ROLES as being inherent in human nature. In 1968, Dr Naomi WEISSTEIN presented her brief but devastating critique, 'PSYCHOLOGY CONSTRUCTS THE FEMALE', exposing psychology's inability to explain 'what women are really like'. In WOMEN AND MADNESS (1972) Phyllis CHESLER demonstrated how the business of psychology and psychiatry had been used to oppress women. Feminists do not accept psychological justification for SEXISM any more readily than biological ones, but as a science, psychology can be useful in trying to understand how PATRIARCHY came about, and how it can be demolished. Among those who have been reinterpreting psychology from a woman-centred viewpoint are Carol GILLIGAN, Nancy CHODOROW and Jean Baker Miller.

publishing

Feminist publishing emerged with the Women's Liberation Movement, in response to the feeling that certain books were needed, and no one else would publish them if feminists did not do so themselves. The first books produced by the new women's presses were collections of poetry, and of articles from the women's movement, all considered 'unpublishable' by contemporary standards, yet which found their audience through the women's bookshops which began to open at about the same time.

As feminist publishers became more established and numerous (despite increasing financial pressures on small presses throughout the 1970s and 1980s, the 1985 *Index/ Directory of Feminist Media* listed more than seventy-five women-owned presses) they also became more diverse in their approach and politics. Some are commercially successful, reaching an ever-growing audience with a wide range of books, while others may publish only one or two books a year, deliberately aimed at a special interest group, and consider themselves lucky if they don't lose too much money. The very existence of feminist publishers has had an effect on the entire publishing industry, because it has proved the existence of a feminist 'market', and thus widened the range of books considered commercially viable. Once the publishers of books no one else would risk, now feminist publishers often find themselves in competition with larger, more established, male-dominated companies for the same authors, titles and readership. Yet this boom in women's books could be just a passing fashion. Although many women work in publishing, and despite the efforts of such groups as the London-based Women in Publishing to improve women's status, the real power and money remain in the hands of the few at the top – who are almost entirely men. Without the commitment to women's interests found only in organizations dedicated to feminism rather than profits, there can be no certainty that feminist writing will continue to be published when the fashion changes.

Feminist publishing differs from patriarchal publishing not only in its product, but also in its structure, attitude and reason for being. Most feminist publishers replaced the standard hierarchies with collectives or cooperatives in which all the women share in tasks and decision-making. Some feminist presses have made more or less uneasy alliances with the capitalist and patriarchal institutions they are in philosophical and political opposition to: for example, England's

THE WOMEN'S PRESS, although it has editorial autonomy, is financially backed by the Namara Publishing Group. But others have always seen the goal of feminist publishing as more than the books they cause to exist. As Polly Joan and Andrea Chesman wrote in their *Guide to Women's Publishing* (1978): '. . . feminist publishing is also feminist politics. It is not an alternative to male publishing. It is a political act as creative and diverse as the Women's Movement itself.'

SHEBA and ONLYWOMEN PRESS, both London-based collectives, each decided from the beginning that it was as important to change to a more feminist way of working as it was to produce feminist books. Daughters, Inc. and Diana Press, two American publishers now defunct but very active and influential during the 1970s, were among those representing the political position for SEPARATISM in women's publishing. They saw this as less a matter of lesbianism than of economics, maintaining that only when women are willing and able to support all-women's businesses will they be able to build the structures necessary for genuine economic independence which will make women's liberation a reality.

Other existing English-language feminist presses include VIRAGO in England, Stramullion in Scotland, Alice James Books, Cleis Press, Crone's Own Press, Down There Press, Firebrand Books, Frog in the Well, Kitchen Table: Women of Color Press, The Naiad Press, New Victoria Publishers, Shameless Hussy Press, Seal Press, Spinsters Ink and Womyn's Braille Press, Inc., in the United States.

Q

querelle des femmes

The medieval version of the WOMAN QUESTION. The term is French and means, literally, 'quarrel of women' or the women's argument. Sparked by the writings of Christine de PIZAN, it took place in European literary circles between 1400–1789, and historian Joan Kelly has argued that it marks the beginning of feminist theorizing as such. Within the *querelle*, or debate, male writers demonstrated their misogyny by attacking women, and justified their ideas by quoting earlier and equally misogynistic writers as authorities on the nature of women. Instead of merely attacking men as the men attacked women, the PROTO-FEMINISTS who set out to defend their sex attempted to transcend the accepted, ANDRO-CENTRIC values of their day, to achieve a more universal viewpoint, and argued that women and men were created as much by culture as by nature.

Quest

American quarterly journal committed to exploring and advancing feminist theory and developing strategies for the future. It was founded in 1974 in Washington, D.C. by Dolores Bargowski, Rita Mae BROWN, Charlotte BUNCH, Jane Dolkart, Beverly Fisher-Manick, Alexa Freeman, Nancy Hartsock, Karen Kollias, Mary-Ellen Mautner, Emily Medvec, Gerry Traina and Juanita Weaver, who remained the core staff for the next five years, after which a new editorial group emerged. The journal was envisioned as a tool for the already committed feminist, rather than as a mass-market magazine. Each issue is built around a general theme: Women and Spirituality; Leadership; Work; Theories of Revolution etc.

Question of Silence, A

Film made in the Netherlands by Marleen Gorris in 1981 to which audience and reviewer response is clearly divided by gender: women usually like it; men are offended and/or misunderstand it. It tells the story of three women who kill a male boutique owner. There is no obvious motive, they refuse to explain themselves, and four women who witnessed the killing also keep silent. A woman psychiatrist assigned to the case comes to believe these women are not mad or even unusual. The climax of the film comes in court, when the male prosecutor declares that he could see no difference in the case if the victim had been a woman and the murderers three men. At this, one of the accused begins to laugh. She is joined by the other two accused, and then the women witnesses, and then the psychiatrist, and female laughter swells and fills the court and will not be silenced.

R

radical feminism

The branch of feminism which grew out of and is most closely identified with the WOMEN'S LIBERATION MOVEMENT. The term was first used to identify women from the political NEW LEFT who had become feminists, and then came to indicate their belief that women's oppression was the root of all systems of oppression. (Radical = 'of the roots'.)

The other major types of feminism – LIBERAL FEMINISM and SOCIALIST FEMINISM – are identified with previously existing political/philosophical systems. Radical feminism, born in the late 1960s, is something completely new. Not only is it the first political approach to take women's common experience as its chief concern, it questions the very things other systems have taken for granted, and redefines the area called political.

Radical feminism begins with the insight that GENDER distinctions – usually unrecognized, or unquestioned because they are assumed to be 'natural' – structure every aspect of our lives. Instead of examining public, traditionally political institutions for the answer to why women are universally oppressed, radical feminists have declared the 'PERSONAL IS POLITICAL' and examined the way human REPRODUCTION is controlled and socialized through such institutions as MARRIAGE, COMPULSORY HETEROSEXUALITY, and MOTHERHOOD. Reforms in the public sphere – surface equality – will not touch the deeper oppression: radical feminists seek to create an entirely new social system.

They work for this new system in small groups, without LEADERS, part of a diverse, grass-roots movement which has no single agreed philosophy or overall plan, and which is divided even in how it would define the goals and meaning of radical feminism.

All radical feminists believe in the necessity of an autonomous, women-only, women's movement. Men – not merely 'the PATRIARCHY' or male-dominated institutions – are identified as the enemy, because all men benefit from women's oppression. Therefore, all radical feminists agree with the need for some degree of SEPARATISM. Some see it as a necessary but temporary stage, whereas others envision it as the first step towards a women-only society. Radical feminists are concerned with creating feminist alternatives in all areas of life, from communal, separatist societies, to women-run businesses such as restaurants, bookshops and record companies, to new forms of religion, healthcare, and the development of WOMANCULTURE. All these various pursuits are a form of living the revolution, for they not only help women to cope and provide for needs not met by patriarchal society; they are also designed to bring about social change by building the new feminist society.

The concept of the WOMAN-CENTRED analysis was developed by radical feminists as a part of the continual need to question all male-defined structures and values. In looking for alternatives to the PATRIARCHY, radical feminists have reclaimed many of the aspects labelled feminine and devalued by male-dominated society. Yet the positive celebration of womanhood can lead to an acceptance of the very forms of dualistic and hierarchical thinking which earlier radical feminists identified as being one of the reasons for the SEX/GENDER SYSTEM and women's oppression. Many radical feminists tend towards a kind of ESSENTIALISM, accepting the patriarchal concept of deep and significant differences between male and female, merely turning that idea around by claiming that there is something better in FEMININITY, a source of positive strength in women which is denied to men. Alice Echols (1984) has argued that early radical feminists sought the elimination of GENDER as

a meaningful category, whereas most of those who would identify themselves as radical feminists today treat gender differences as if they represented deep and unchangeable truths. Because of this break with original radical feminist theory she prefers the term CULTURAL FEMINISM for the newer, now more dominant, strain. Other off-shoots of radical feminism are LESBIAN-FEMINISM and REVOLUTIONARY FEMINISM.

Radical Women

The first women's liberation group in New York City, and one of the first in the United States (although it predated the use of the term 'women's liberation'), it was founded by Pam Allen and Shulamith FIRESTONE in October 1967. It consisted of a core of up to twenty women who helped organize many more in public actions including 'THE BURIAL OF TRADITIONAL WOMANHOOD' at an anti-war demonstration in Washington, D.C., in January 1968, and the Miss America Contest protest in Atlantic City, New Jersey, 7 September 1968. In June 1968 they published a mimeographed journal called *Notes from the First Year*. Most of the Radical Women had some previous involvement with new left political organizations, the civil rights movement and/or the peace movement, and from the beginning there was an unresolved division among the members between the POLITICOS and the avowed feminists. This resulted in a final split late in 1968, and the emergence of three separate new organizations: WITCH, RED-STOCKINGS, and THE FEMINISTS.

Radicalesbians
First avowedly feminist, lesbian organization in the United States, it began in 1970 as a group of women calling themselves the LAVENDER MENACE in protest against the heterosexism of the women's liberation movement. Although in existence only a few years, it led the way for other lesbian-feminist groups, and was highly influential in forcing LESBIANISM to be recognized as a political issue. (*See also* WOMAN-IDENTIFIED WOMAN)

Ramabai, Pandita, 1858–1920?
Indian. A pioneering Indian feminist, she was an active campaigner for changes in the status of women, and was particularly successful in helping women enter the fields of medicine and education. She travelled to the United States and England to lecture on the condition of women in India, and wrote books on the same subject. In 1882 she founded the Sharada Sadan, a home for widows.

Rankin, Jeanette, 1880–1973
American politician. First woman elected to Congress; in 1971, she was called 'the world's outstanding

living feminist' and honoured as the first member of the Susan B. Anthony Hall of Fame. She became actively involved in the women's suffrage movement in 1910 in Washington State, and went on to lead the campaign to victory in her home state of Montana (1912–14). She then ran as the Republican candidate and, in 1917, became the first woman to enter the House of Representatives, where she supported protective legislation for women and children, and peace – her vote against entering World War I lost her her seat. After the war she became involved with the WOMEN'S INTERNATIONAL LEAGUE FOR PEACE AND FREEDOM. Re-elected to Congress in 1940, she was again the only dissenting voice against America's entry to World War II. Her political career ended in 1942, but she continued to be involved in the international peace movement and, in 1968, feminism and PACIFISM united as she led the Jeanette Rankin Brigade in an anti-war demonstration in Washington, D.C.

rape
An act of political terrorism, used systematically by all men to intimidate and oppress all women. Feminist analysis in the early 1970s transformed the concept of rape from that of a sexual act and a crime involving property rights (as it has been traditionally perceived under patriarchy) to that of the major tactic used by men to keep women in

subjection, and a metaphor for all male–female relations in a sexist society. The ideology of rape, as defined by Susan BROWNMILLER in her major work on the subject AGAINST OUR WILL (1975), was the prehistoric discovery by men that rape was possible. Because they *could* rape women, men did; and because women could not retaliate in kind, male genitalia became a weapon, and the symbol of male superiority.

Andrea DWORKIN and Susan GRIFFIN have also written about rape following a similar chain of reasoning, and many feminists have accepted the concept of rape as the archetype of marriage and the material basis for women's oppression by men. Others, however, including Elizabeth WILSON (1983) have objected to the acceptance of rape as a universal, biological mandate rather than as something cultural which can be changed as the structure of society is changed. Wilson suggests that a high level of political consciousness and/or the integration of women into full participation in social and political life (as among the revolutionary Chinese, the Hopi and the Arapesh) may practically eliminate rape except as a rare and loathed crime of violence.

In our society, although rape was recognized as a crime long before feminist redefinitions began, it is also treated as a joke, and as something which certain women want or 'ask for' despite their denials. As a crime, rape is an act of sexual intercourse which a man forces on a woman against her will. Rape is therefore usually considered a 'normal' male sexual response, and the question of whether or not it is a crime hinges on whether or not the woman gave her consent. Whether she agreed or refused is not determined by what the woman herself says, but what others, mostly men, decide on the basis of her race, class, marital status, age, clothing and other such non-related evidence. If a woman has at one time given her consent to sexual intercourse with a man who later rapes her – particularly if she is married to that man – it is usually presumed that she can never again *not* consent: she has given up the right to her own body and is the sexual property of her husband or lover. Under PATRIARCHY, rape is still widely seen as a crime against property, something one man does to another with the body of a woman as the medium.

In 'Theory and Practice: Pornography and Rape' (1974), Robin MORGAN suggested that a radical feminist definition of rape would recognize that rape exists 'any time sexual intercourse occurs when it has not been initiated by the woman, out of her own genuine affection and desire'. The final qualifier was important, she said, because when a woman permits sexual intercourse against her own desires because she doesn't want to lose a man, or hurt his feelings, or risk his anger, she is responding to pressure and fear just as surely as if he held a knife against her throat.

The destruction of the old myths and definitions of rape and the creation of new understandings of all aspects of SEXUALITY is one of the major tasks of feminism, but it is only the first step. Another achievement of the modern women's movement has been to increase public awareness of the reality and prevalence of rape. As a result, more women have felt able to overcome feelings of guilt or shame, to report rapes, and to feel less isolated and helpless. There have been investigations of ways of preventing rape, and campaigns to change the man-made laws which have in the past functioned to protect men – whether as rapist or as the women's 'owner' – and to force the legal system to become more responsive to women's needs. The establishment of RAPE CRISIS CENTRES has also been particularly important.

rape crisis centres

The aim of rape crisis centres is to provide a woman-centred framework of support to help rape victims with advice, counselling and supportive companionship through encounters with the uncaring, often abusive, legal and medical systems. Depending on funds, a rape crisis centre may offer a twenty-four-hour hot line, counselling sessions, practical information about the legal process, VD and pregnancy testing, lists of non-sexist doctors, or self-defence classes.

The first one, the Rape Crisis Center, was established in Washington, D.C. in 1972. It offered counselling and advice, and volunteers accompanied rape victims to the hospital and to the police, with the result that women began to receive better treatment. It published a booklet, 'How to Start a Rape Crisis Center', and now acts as a clearing-house for other rape crisis centres. During the 1970s, some 600 rape crisis centres were established throughout the United States, but cuts in government spending forced nearly a quarter of them to close by the end of 1981.

In Britain, the first Rape Crisis Centre opened in North London in March 1976, in a house donated by the Department of the Environment, but with no government funding. Most of the women who work there are unpaid volunteers working as a collective to provide sympathy and practical advice in a woman-centred atmosphere. Others opened in other cities, and today there are about twenty-five rape crisis centres throughout Britain.

(*See also* WOMEN AGAINST RAPE; RIGHTS OF RAPE VICTIMS)

Rat

Leftist New York newspaper of the late 1960s which mixed radical politics with pornography. On 26 January 1970, the women on the staff seized control and, with the help of members of the women's liberation movement, ran the paper as a collective for a year. This was seen as a breakthrough, both symbolic and actual, for women on the Left, and other newspapers followed their lead. Despite being produced by women, including some feminists, the 'women's *Rat*' remained a male-oriented paper; the more committed feminists lost interest and, after many changes of staff, the paper ceased publication in 1971.

Reclaim the Night

British name for night-time marches or demonstrations by feminists protesting about violence against women, sometimes directed at sex-shops, pornographic films etc., and often held in response to a particular act of violence, and taking place in the locality where a woman alone at night was attacked. The first Reclaim the Night demonstration was held on 12 November 1977 simultaneously in Leeds, Manchester, Newcastle, York and London. These protests developed into the more sustained campaign of WOMAN AGAINST VIOLENCE AGAINST WOMEN.

(*See also* TAKE BACK THE NIGHT)

Red Rag

British Marxist-feminist journal, chiefly theoretical, published between 1972 and 1980.

Redstockings

Radical feminist organization founded in 1969 in New York by Ellen Willis and Shulamith FIRESTONE, who coined the name to represent a synthesis between the intellectual BLUESTOCKINGS and the red of revolution. It was the first group to articulate and advocate the function, purpose, process and use of CONSCIOUSNESS-RAISING. Although it dissolved as a formal group after 1970, some members continued to carry on the Redstocking line of political analysis and to use the name. In 1981 Redstockings reorganized with the proposal of becoming 'the equivalent of a multi-issue, radical think tank' for the WOMEN'S LIBERATION MOVEMENT.

(*See also* PRO-WOMAN LINE)

religion

Recognizing in religion one of the most powerful institutions for perpetuating sexism and patriarchal authority, feminists have responded in different ways. Some reject all forms of religion, believing that it is an oppressive and negative force, a trap which hinders women in the struggle for material change in their lives. Others believe that there is a spiritual as well as a material aspect to life, and seek alternatives to male-defined religions in GODDESS worship and other forms of woman-centred THEALOGY. Still others, while recognizing the patriarchal bias of

Christianity, Judaism and Islam, believe that there are spiritual truths in these religions which cannot be denied, and feel that it is therefore necessary to work for reform from within, rather than breaking away. Some religious feminists work for equality, while others believe that female superiority should be recognized in spiritual matters; some reject what they consider oppressive traditions, while others believe there is strength to be found in reclaiming and redefining women's traditional roles.

(*See also* CHRISTIAN FEMINISTS; JEWISH FEMINISTS; MUSLIM FEMINISTS; SPIRITUAL FEMINISM; WITCHES; WOMAN'S BIBLE, THE; WOMANSPIRIT)

Reproduction of Mothering
See CHODOROW, NANCY

reproduction
In Marxist theory there are two major types of human activity, production and reproduction. Reproduction is an aspect of production because it replaces the means of production (whether machine-parts, seed-corn, or the babies who will become new workers) and maintains the ideological superstructure through social relationships, education, entertainment and culture. The division between production and reproduction is seen as gender-linked because, although men obviously contribute to the procreation and socialization of children as well as to the broader areas of reproduction, women are seen as primarily responsible for reproduction (not only childbearing but CHILDCARE, HOUSEWORK, and emotional nurturance of both children and men) and men are engaged primarily in production. Many feminists have accepted this distinction (although they may find the terminology of 'reproduction' to be inappropriate or misleading) in their attempt to formulate a theory of women's oppression based on this primary gender-linked division of labour. Alison Jaggar (1983), however, has suggested that the distinction between 'production' and 'reproduction', whatever terms are used, is artificial, a relic of the masculine, dualistic thinking in which 'personal' is divided from 'political', 'public' from 'private', and which feminists have criticized in many other contexts. A feminist understanding of reproduction is crucial, but, Jaggar argues, it must be reconceptualized, not seen in isolation from other forms of socially meaningful human activity, but fully a part of what men have designated WORK.

(*See also* MARXIST-FEMINISM; SOCIALIST FEMINISM)

reproductive freedom
Defined by feminists in the 1970s as a basic human right, it includes the right to ABORTION and BIRTH CONTROL, but implies much more. To be realized, reproductive freedom must include not only woman's

273

right to choose childbirth or abortion, sterilization or birth control, but also her right to make those choices freely, without pressure from individual men, doctors, governmental or religious authorities. It is a key issue for women, since without it the other freedoms we appear to have, such as the right to education, jobs and equal pay, may prove illusory. Provisions of CHILD-CARE, medical treatment, and society's attitude towards children are also involved.

Of particular concern in the 1980s is the rapid growth of new reproductive technologies, including developments in embryo transfer, *in vitro* techniques, cloning, ectogenesis (artificial wombs), sex predetermination, and related practices such as surrogate motherhood and artificial insemination. Although writers such as Shulamith FIRESTONE and Marge PIERCY have envisioned a brave new world in which women have been released from biological slavery through technology, and both sexes share equally in the creation and care of children, there is no sign in our own world that these new developments will be used for feminist aims. Far from being used on behalf of women, such techniques as cloning, artificial wombs and using amniocentesis to determine the sex of a foetus could result in a world in which women were a true minority, kept only for the pleasure of men. The FEMINIST INTERNATIONAL NET-WORK OF RESISTANCE TO REPRODUCTIVE AND GENETIC ENGINEERING (FINRRAGE) was formed in 1985 to monitor the development of and protest against the misuse of new reproductive technologies. They called upon all women 'to resist the take-over of our bodies for male use, for profit-making, population control, medical experimentation, and misogynous science'.

reverse discrimination
See POSITIVE DISCRIMINATION

revisionist feminism
Term used by Zillah EISENSTEIN for what she sees as the major internal threat to feminism in the 1980s, a rejection of the basic feminist demand for sexual EQUALITY in favour of stressing the importance of sexual differences. Although this is not the same as anti-feminism, Eisenstein sees danger in the similarities between the new revisionist feminism and the larger neo-conservative political climate, in the similar sexual and moral views shared by some feminists (for example, among those who have adopted PORNOGRAPHY as their single-issue fight) and members of the Moral Majority in America. Both, she says, are frightened by the radical potential inherent in the idea of sexual equality. She identifies Betty FRIEDAN – at least since publication of *The Second Stage* (1981) – as 'a major spokesperson for revisionist liberal feminism'.

(*See also* CULTURAL FEMINISM; ESSEN-
TIALISM; FEMININISM)

re-vision

Term used by Adrienne RICH to
define the new feminist approach to
literature, culture, art and history:
'the act of looking back, of seeing
with fresh eyes, of entering an old
text from a new critical direction –
is for women more than a chapter in
cultural history: it is an act of
survival'. (From *On Lies, Secrets and
Silence* [1979])

Revolution, The

Women's rights newspaper
founded by Susan B. ANTHONY and
Elizabeth Cady STANTON with
funding from wealthy eccentric
George Train. Published weekly
from 8 January 1868–May 1870, it
contributed more to the cause than
its brief lifespan and modest circulation would suggest. It gave the
women's movement a forum and a
guiding force as it took on a variety
of causes, particularly on behalf of
the exploited woman worker and
the social outcast. But its willingness to consider controversial issues
(prostitution, divorce, religion, the
double standard) meant it would
never have the success of its more
conservative competitor, *Woman's
Journal*, and the potential audience
was too small to support them
both. Its motto: 'Men, their rights
and nothing more; women, their
rights and nothing less!'

revolutionary feminism

Militant tendency which developed
in Britain in 1977, it is a form of
LESBIAN-FEMINISM and an outgrowth of RADICAL FEMINISM, also
called revolutionary/radical feminism. Discussions at the National
Women's Liberation Conference in
Edinburgh in 1977, and a paper by
Sheila Jeffreys, 'The Need for Revolutionary Feminism' (1977) caused
a number of radical feminist groups
to reconstitute themselves along
revolutionary lines, and was
divisive of the Women's Liberation
Movement as a whole. Revolutionary feminism is a declaration of war
between women and men. It
involves the determination to turn
radical feminist theory into a revolutionary strategy for confronting
men as the enemy and ending their
domination. Heterosexual women
are identified as collaborators (if not
actually the enemy themselves) and
urged to join the revolution by
becoming POLITICAL LESBIANS.
HETEROSEXUALITY is considered to
be the foundation of women's
oppression, and SEPARATISM the
only acceptable political stance.
(*See also* LOVE YOUR ENEMY?)

Rhondda, Lady (Margaret Haig), 1883–1958

Welsh. A militant suffragette in her
teens, she devoted her life to
improving the legal and political
status of women. She campaigned
for women to be full members of
both Houses of Parliament, and

although she did not realize this aim in her lifetime, she did receive royal permission to attend the House of Lords herself. In 1920, she founded the feminist political weekly TIME AND TIDE which she published and financed for over thirty years, also contributing to it as writer and editor (from 1926). She also founded the SIX POINT GROUP to press for legal reforms needed by women.

Rich, Adrienne, 1929–
American poet. In the early 1970s her POETRY reflected her growing commitment to feminism, and from 1974, when she rejected the National Book Award as an individual but accepted it with Alice WALKER on behalf of all women, she has been a much-loved and honoured member of the lesbian/feminist movement. Her collections of poems include *The Will to Change* (1971), *Diving Into the Wreck* (1973), *The Dream of a Common Language* (1978) and *A Wild Patience Has Taken Me This Far* (1981). Her contributions as a theorist, in prose, have also been important. Some of her attempts to define a female consciousness were collected as *On Lies, Secrets and Silence* (1979) and include essays on honour, on 'the common world of women', on education, motherhood, neglected women writers, and racism. She wrote about MOTHERHOOD both as personal experience and as an institution in OF WOMAN BORN

(1976). A frequent contributor to feminist journals, she is a co-editor of SINISTER WISDOM.

Richardson, Dorothy, 1873–1957
English writer, author of the thirteen-volume, autobiographical, stream-of-consciousness novel, PIL-GRIMAGE. Virginia WOOLF said that Richardson had invented 'a sentence which we might call the psychological sentence of the feminine gender. . . . It is a woman's sentence, but only in the sense that it is used to describe a woman's mind by a writer who is neither proud nor afraid of anything that she may discover in the psychology of her sex.' Richardson would probably not have called herself a feminist, since she was uninterested in the struggle for political and economic equality. As her viewpoint character, Miriam, says in *Deadlock* (volume 4 of *Pilgrimage*), 'Those women's rights people are the worst of all. Because they think women have been "subject" in the past. Women never have been subject. Never can be.' Nevertheless, Richardson has been claimed as an important feminist writer, with good reason. Her entire body of work asserts that male and female consciousness are fundamentally different, and attempts to transmute a woman's experience of the world into a unique work of art.

Richer, Léon, 1824–1911
French journalist. With Maria

DERAISMES, the leader of the feminist movement in France during the 1870s and 1880s, co-founder of Société pour l'Amélioration du Sort de la Femme (Society for the Improvement of Women's Lot). Founder and editor of the magazine *Le Droit des Femmes* (1869–91). He was always politically cautious and anti-revolutionary, believing in the gradual reform of French society through the establishment of better education and economic independence for women, and the legalisation of divorce, but he did not support female suffrage. In 1878 he held what was meant to be an international feminist congress in Paris, but most of those who attended were male and French. In 1882 Richer reacted against Deraismes' growing radicalism (as he perceived it) by founding a more conservative group, Ligue Française pour le Droit des Femmes (French League for Women's Rights). This organization never became the mass movement he hoped for, but remained small, reformist, and male-dominated. Richer retired from feminist politics in 1891.

Riddles of the Sphinx

Film by Laura Mulvey and Peter Wollen, released in 1976. An experimental film about a woman's experience of motherhood and the alienation women feel in patriarchal society, it was made as a conscious attempt to create an alternative, feminine form of cinema, to express ideas the dominant male culture represses.
(*See also* FILM)

Rights of Rape Victims

The demands of the Rape Crisis Center, Washington, D.C., are that any victim of sexual assault should have the right:

'to be treated with dignity and respect during questioning

'to be educated about procedures and the law in a rape case and her role as witness for the state

'to free medical and psychological treatment by sensitive, trained personnel

'to choose what preventative medical measures will be taken

'to the best possible collection of evidence for court

'to have support resources like rape crisis groups, to be accompanied by sympathetic friends etc.

'to legal representation that supports the victim, since the victim cannot have legal counsel of her choice as the defendant can (because it is the *state*, not the woman, who is prosecuting the rapist)

'to a preliminary hearing in each case when an arrest is made

'to personal privacy (prior sexual experience should not be admissible as evidence)

'to be considered a credible witness equal to one in any other crime

'to consent to sexual relations with the spouse without violence and without coercion 'to be protected from any violent sexual assault regardless of the weapon used, and regardless of which part of the body is violated

'to submit to rape from fear alone without this being seen as consent, or to ward off the attack without being liable to prosecution herself.' (*See also* RAPE CRISIS CENTRES)

Rights of Women (ROW)

London-based organization founded in 1975 as a legal resource and pressure group for women's rights. Their aims are to create a legal profession which is accessible to women and responsive to their interests, and to become a resource centre on a national basis for information affecting women's rights and a referral list of lawyers responsive to women's interests. Their activities include advising individual women on their legal rights and how to realize them; helping women's campaigns draft model legislation; and producing news sheets and guides to aspects of the law.

Roberts, Michèle, 1949–

British novelist and poet. Involved in the women's liberation movement since 1970, she has worked in a variety of women's groups, including writing collectives and *Spare Rib* (1975–77). As a writer, she has been particularly concerned to explore images of the female self. Her novels include *A Piece of the*

Night (1978), *The Visitation* (1983) and *The Wild Girl* (1984).

Robins, Elizabeth, 1863–1952

American-born actress, novelist, playwright and campaigner for women's rights. She abandoned the study of medicine at Vassar to become an actress, first on tour in America, and then in London, where she was instrumental in getting Ibsen's plays produced and achieved the reputation of 'England's first great intellectual actress' (Mrs Patrick Campbell).

It was the struggle to produce Ibsen's plays in London which made her a feminist, she said later, and once committed to the cause she put all her talents to work for women's suffrage. She helped organize the Actresses' Franchise League, joined Emmeline and Christabel PANKHURST on the board of the WOMEN'S SOCIAL AND POLITICAL UNION, and forged a connection between that group and the Women's Trade Union League of America, which was headed by her sister-in-law, Margaret Dreier ROBINS. With Cicily HAMILTON and Bessie Hatton she founded the Women Writers' Suffrage League in 1908.

Her play VOTES FOR WOMEN! and its sister novel THE CONVERT were both commercial successes. She shared the profits with the WSPU and then bought Backsettown Farm in Henfield, Sussex, as a haven for herself, her sister suffragettes, and the women medical students she supported. In her career as a writer Robins published a dozen novels, a book about Ibsen, her memoirs, and a collection of letters from Henry James. Many of her feminist essays were published as *Way Stations* (1913), and *Ancilla's Share: An Indictment of Sex*, which Jane Marcus has called her 'most important feminist work', was published anonymously in 1924, by which time her once large and responsive audience appeared to have vanished.

Robins, Margaret Dreier,
1868–1945

American. Sister of Mary Elisabeth DREIER and, like her, devoted throughout her life to the interests of working women. In 1904 she joined the new Women's Trade Union League (WTUL) which sought to organize women into trade unions and to secure legislation bettering their working conditions, hours and wages. After her marriage to the religious and political reformer Raymond Robins (brother of Elizabeth ROBINS) in 1905, she began working with Jane ADDAMS in Chicago. In 1907 she became president of both the Chicago and the national WTUL, and helped organize effective garment workers' strikes in New York, Philadelphia and Chicago between 1909 and 1911. She was also active in the women's suffrage movement and, in the 1920s, with pacifist organizations.

robotitude
Term coined by Mary DALY (1978) to describe the 'robot state' of life reduced to mechanical actions. Although not gender-specific, this existence is forced most particularly upon women in our culture. For illustration, see *The Stepford Wives* by Ira Levin.

role reversal
1) Literary and/or psychological technique used to raise consciousness about SEXISM, it depicts passive, subordinate, traditionally 'feminine' men contrasted to women demonstrating what are usually considered masculine traits (authority, strength, rampant sexuality etc.) in order to make the point that sex roles are imposed rather than natural. This technique, however, is also used against feminists, to misrepresent feminism as an unnatural desire for female domination.

2) A heterosexual partnership in which the woman goes out to work while the man tends the house and raises the children.
(*See also* GENDER)

Room of One's Own, A
Classic essay on women and fiction by Virginia WOOLF, first published in 1928. The often-quoted title comes from Woolf's statement that, in order to write fiction, a

woman should have an independent income and a room of her own. She considered, however, that the main obstacles faced by the woman who would write were the 'Angel in the House' (the Victorian ideal of the self-sacrificing woman) and the difficulty of writing honestly about her physical, sexual self. Although considered the first major work of feminist LITERARY CRITICISM, it presents the idea that the true artist is somehow androgynous, somehow above the confines of gender, and some modern feminists object to Woolf's description of feminine anger as a limitation or weakness.

Rose, Ernestine, 1810–92

Polish-American. Born in Poland, the daughter of a rabbi, at the age of sixteen she successfully sued in a Polish court to overturn the marriage contract her father had arranged for her, and to regain property inherited from her mother. By 1829, she had moved to England, where she became a disciple of Robert Owen. In 1836, she moved to the United States with her husband, William Rose, another Owenite. With her husband's financial and emotional support, she was able to devote all her energies to reform, and became active in the anti-slavery, temperance, free thought and women's rights movements. In advance of the organized women's movement, she gave free public lectures on the subject of women's rights in many American towns and cities, and her presence was strongly felt at all the early national conventions. She presented the first petition for married women's property rights to the New York legislature in 1836, and continued to petition until a law was finally passed in 1848.

Rossi, Alice

Contemporary American sociologist. She made a substantial contribution to the contemporary women's movement as a scholar, editor and writer, providing an historical background for feminism in such books as *Essays on Sex Equality by John Stuart Mill and Harriet Taylor Mill* (1970) and *The Feminist Papers: From Adams to de Beauvoir* (1973). She has defined herself as an 'integrationist', believing that SEPARATISM – even to the extent of separate WOMEN'S STUDIES courses – is wrong and feminists should encourage men to understand women. Although she has always been active in the movement for political and economic equality for women, she is at odds with most contemporary feminists in combining an equal rights stance with the belief that sex roles are in part physiologically based and genetically determined.

Rowbotham, Sheila, 1943–

British. Active in the socialist movement since the early 1960s and active in the women's liberation movement since it began in the late 1960s, she has written many widely read books combining socialism, feminism and history. They include *Women, Resistance and Revolution* (1972), *Hidden from History* (1973), *Women's Consciousness, Man's World* (1973), *A New World for Women* (1977) and *Dreams and Dilemmas* (1983). With Hilary Wainwright and Lynne Segal she contributed to *Beyond the Fragments* (1979), and has continued to be involved, in the 1980s, in exploring the practical and theoretical connections between socialism and feminism.

Rubyfruit Jungle
See BROWN, RITA MAE

Rukeyser, Muriel, 1913–80
American poet. A political activist all her life, she became involved in the women's liberation movement via her involvement in the anti-war and civil rights movements. Her poetry, uniting political awareness with sensuous imagery, speaks to the experiences of many modern women.

Ruskin College, Oxford
Site of the first national modern feminist gathering in February 1970, and usually seen as the formal beginning of the WOMEN'S LIBERATION MOVEMENT in Britain. About 600 women attended to discuss the aims and methods best suited to modern feminism. Their first formal act was to set up a WOMEN'S NATIONAL COORDINATING COMMITTEE, a loosely-structured body whose function was to circulate information among the many small groups which made up the women's movement, and to organize future national conferences. A consensus emerged that feminists should continue to ignore the usual forms of politics and hierarchies, and to operate in small groups, without leaders, outside the system.

Russ, Joanna, 1937–
American writer and academic. Her first story was published in 1959, but it was not until the publication of her first novel, *Picnic on Paradise* (1968) that she made a strong impression on the SCIENCE FICTION scene. This first novel was notable for many reasons, not least of which was the strong, positive character of the female protagonist, Alyx. 'When it Changed', about an Amazonian UTOPIA called WHILE-AWAY, won the Nebula Award for best short story of 1972. In THE FEMALE MAN (1975), a classic of feminist science fiction, she went on to chronicle life on Whileaway – as well as life in our own and other cultures as they might be seen by an outsider. Other books of interest include *We Who Are About To . . .* (1977) and *The Two of Them* (1978), both works of science fiction which angrily and brilliantly, demolish sexist assumptions; *Kittatinny* (1978), a tale of magic and adven-

ture for young feminists; and a 'coming out' novel, *On Strike Against God* (1980). In addition to her fiction, Russ has written many perceptive critical essays and *How to Suppress Women's Writing* (1983), an examination of the treatment given by the literary establishment to women who dare to write.

Russell, Dora, 1894–
English. A dedicated feminist and radical socialist from her earliest years, she campaigned for the availability of birth control and maternity leave throughout the 1920s, founding the Workers' Birth Control Group in 1924. In 1927, with her first husband, Bertrand Russell, she founded the liberal, experimental Beacon Hill School, which she ran until 1939. From the 1950s, she was active in the Campaign for Nuclear Disarmament and, in 1958, led the Women's Caravan of Peace across Europe to protest against the Cold War. Among the books she has written are an assessment of sexual politics called *Hypatia: or Women and Knowledge* (1924); an attack on sexual repression, *The Right to be Happy* (1927); and her theory of education, *In Defence of Children* (1932).

Rye, Maria Susan, 1829–1903
English. A member of the LANGHAM PLACE GROUP, she worked for the SOCIETY FOR PROMOTING THE EMPLOYMENT OF WOMEN and went on to found, with Janet Lewin, the Female Middle Class Emigration Society in 1862. As her associates in both societies became more involved in the struggle for women's suffrage, she turned her attention to the problems of destitute children, helping to found the Church of England Waifs and Strays Society in 1891, which occupied her until her retirement.

S

Sand, George (pseudonym of Amandine Aurore Lucie Dupin, Baronne Dudevant), 1804–76
French. A prolific and very influential writer in her time, she is remembered today chiefly for her life style as a passionate, free-spirited woman who had many affairs, wore trousers, and smoked cigars in public. She scorned conventional marriage and glorified both sensual and spiritual love in her novels. Like her contemporary, Flora TRISTAN, she inspired both outrage and worship, and was sometimes thought to be the female messiah predicted by Saint-Simon and other utopian socialists. Among her many novels, those of particular interest for their female characters include *Indiana* (1832), *Valentine* (1832) and *Lélia* (1833). Her autobiography was published in 1854.

Sander, Helke, 1937–
German filmmaker. She began making films in 1966, and became involved in the women's liberation movement in the late 1960s. She helped found the German Council for Women's Liberation and organized the First International Women's Film Workshop in 1973. She founded the first feminist film journal in Europe in 1974, *Frauen und Film*. Her first feature film was *The All Round Reduced Personality/ Redupers* (1977).

Sanger, Margaret, 1883–1966
American. A pioneer of sexual freedom, her declaration that 'No woman can call herself free who does not own and control her body' was the driving force behind her lifelong crusade to supply more and more women with BIRTH CONTROL information and methods. While working as a nurse on New York's Lower East Side, her experience of the poverty, illness and death that resulted from unwanted pregnancies made her more radical. Believing that sexual satisfaction was of as much importance to women as to men, she did not consider celibacy or 'self control' a reasonable answer. In 1914, she was prosecuted for writing an 'obscene' pamphlet, *Family Limitation*, and began publishing a journal called *Women Rebel* (later, *Birth Control Review*) until forced to flee to England to escape prosecution. In 1921, she founded the American Birth Control League and in 1927, she organized the first World Population Conference in Geneva. She constantly lectured, campaigned, wrote and lobbied for legislative changes to make birth control

SAPPHO

information widely available, and gradually laws and public attitudes changed. She became the first president of the Planned Parenthood Federation in 1953.

Sappho, born *c.* 613BC
Greek poet. Little is known of her life, except that she taught music and poetry to a school of girls on the island of Lesbos, and that her students were both audience and subjects of her loving, erotic poems. Her poems were collected in nine books, and her fame was such that she was named one of the nine terrestrial muses.

Sarachild, Kathie (Amatniek)
American. A founder of the WOMEN'S LIBERATION MOVEMENT. She was among the group of radical women who planned the 'BURIAL OF TRADITIONAL WOMANHOOD' action to bring some feminist consciousness to an anti-war demonstration in Washington, D.C. in January 1968, and it was in a leaflet written for this demonstration that she first publicized the slogan SISTERHOOD IS POWERFUL. Most important was her work in developing the concept and technique of CONSCIOUSNESS-RAISING. She did this with a group of radical women in New York, in touch with other feminists in Florida, and wrote 'A Program for Feminist "Consciousness Raising"' for distribution at the First National Women's Liberation Conference, held near Chicago over

Thanksgiving weekend in 1968. She was also a member of REDSTOCKINGS.

Schapiro, Miriam, 1923–
American artist and teacher. Met Judy CHICAGO in 1970 and began to collaborate with her, founding the Feminist Art Program at the California Institute of the Arts, co-sponsoring the WOMANHOUSE project (1971–2), writing a monograph on vaginal iconography, and visiting other women artists. The result of these experiences was to change her art, as she became more concerned 'to acknowledge and to underscore the realities of women's lives', and found the personal was political. She also collaborated with her students on two books in which she hoped to balance the standard art histories by offering more information on the works and lives of women artists: *Anonymous was a Woman* and *Art: a Woman's Sensibility*.

Schmidt, Auguste, 1833–1902
German educator. Among her pupils were many who became leading feminists, including Clara ZETKIN. In 1888 she became head of the General German Women's Association (Allgemeiner Deutscher Frauenverein), and in 1894 the first president of the Federation of German Women's Associations (Bund Deutscher Frauenverein). Unlike her more radical, socialist pupils, she was always conservative

in her feminism. She wished to improve women's status and employment opportunities, but believed in the moral superiority of women and in the importance of marriage, charity work, and self-sacrifice.

Schreiber, Adele, ?–1957
Austrian politician. A founder-member of the INTERNATIONAL WOMAN SUFFRAGE ALLIANCE; in 1910 she founded the German Association for the Rights of Mothers and Children and did much to help unmarried mothers. Vice-President of the International Alliance of Women, she also wrote several books.

Schreiner, Olive, 1855–1920
South African writer. Her first book, THE STORY OF AN AFRICAN FARM, caused a scandal when published in 1883, yet the recognition that it was a work of original genius gained her entry to London literary and intellectual circles where she met Eleanor Marx, Havelock Ellis, Edward Carpenter and Karl Pearson, among others. Plagued by ill health, she found writing difficult except when possessed by the trance-like state in which she wrote her allegories, published as *Dreams* (1891) and *Dream Life and Real Life* (1893). Back in South Africa, in 1894, she married farmer and politician Samuel Cronwright, and together they campaigned for suffrage, racial

justice and the Boer cause. Later, in England, she was active in both the suffrage and the peace movements. She was hugely influential in her day, both personally and for her ideas about relationships between the sexes. The suffragettes read her allegories aloud to each other in Holloway prison; WOMAN AND LABOUR (1911) was hailed as the 'Bible of the Woman Movement'; her political opinions and support were sought by men and women in South Africa and Britain. She also inspired women writers who came after her, including Virginia WOOLF, Dorothy RICHARDSON and Doris LESSING. Her first novel, *Ondine*, and the ambitious work she had been writing and rewriting for most of her life, *From Man to Man*, were both published by her husband after her death.

Schwarzer, Alice, 1942–
German writer. Founding editor and publisher of *Emma*, the major West German feminist magazine, she has been active in the women's movement both in West Germany and France since 1970.

Schwimmer, Rosika, 1877–1948
Hungarian. Founder of the Union for Women's Rights in 1904, she led the Hungarian women's suffrage movement using militant tactics inspired by the British WOMEN'S SOCIAL AND POLITICAL UNION. She was also a pacifist, and became one of the founders of the WOMEN'S

INTERNATIONAL LEAGUE FOR PEACE AND FREEDOM in 1915.

science fiction

Despite its male-dominated history, science fiction offers a unique potential for the feminist writer and reader. As Joanna RUSS has pointed out, women writers are handicapped because there are so few possibilities for stories in which women can be the protagonists. This is not the case in science fiction. Because it is not concerned with the working out of specifically male or female roles, but rather with human adaptability to change, and because it is theoretically not culture-bound, the hero of any science fiction story may as easily be female as male – or even a non-human hermaphrodite. Unlike realistic, contemporary novels which are limited in range, science fiction can offer the image of strong, active women and provide examples of a wide variety of life styles and options which we can then work for in our own world.

More women began writing science fiction in the 1960s and 1970s, refusing to be bound by the traditional male-oriented concerns. Some male writers also began to write more freely about strong female characters and alternatives to contemporary gender-roles.

Works of particular interest include THE LEFT HAND OF DARKNESS (1969) and The Dispossessed (1974) by Ursula K. LE GUIN; THE FEMALE MAN (1975) and The Two of Them (1978) by Joanna RUSS; Walk to the End of the World (1974) and Motherlines (1978) by Suzy McKee CHARNAS; WOMAN ON THE EDGE OF TIME (1976) by Marge PIERCY; The Wanderground (1978) by Sally Miller GEARHEART; and short stories and novels by James TIPTREE, Jr (pseudonym of Alice Sheldon), Kate Wilhelm, Vonda McIntyre, Marion Zimmer Bradley, C. J. Cherryh, Suzette Haden ELGIN, Josephine Saxton, Zoë FAIRBAIRNS, Tanith Lee, Elizabeth Lynn, Pamela Sargent, Angela CARTER, Chelsea Quinn Yarbro, Mary Gentle, and many others.

(See also UTOPIA)

Scott, Rose, 1847–1925

Australian. Founder of the Womanhood Suffrage Society in Sydney in 1891, she worked for years with Vida GOLDSTEIN and shared her conviction that women must fight for their own interests and not be distracted by party politics. She campaigned not only for suffrage, but also for protective legislation and social purity, and she was active in the peace movement. She founded and presided over the League for Political Education in 1910.

Scum Manifesto

Written by Valerie SOLANAS in 1967, published by the Olympia Press in Paris in 1968 and 1970. In 1977 Solanas reprinted it herself with a short introduction in which she accused Maurice Girodias of Olympia Press of changing her title from 'Scum Manifesto' to 'S.C.U.M. (Society for Cutting Up Men) Manifesto'. It was reprinted in London in 1983 by the Matriarchy Study Group as an important part of our feminist heritage.

It is a strange, nihilistic document, full of an energizing female rage. Men are defined as biological accidents, incomplete females who desperately seek out women to claim female characteristics for their own. As a solution to the problem of men, Solanas encourages women to become *scum* (which she describes as 'dominant, secure, self-confident, nasty, violent, selfish, independent, proud, thrill-seeking, free-wheeling arrogant females who consider themselves fit to rule the universe') and wipe out those men who won't kill themselves. Once they have inherited the universe, she predicts that the remaining female *scum* will eventually stop reproducing themselves.

Sebestyen, Amanda, 1946–
British. A radical feminist, active in the WOMEN'S LIBERATION MOVEMENT in Britain since 1969. She was a member of the SPARE RIB collective from 1977–80, has helped organize conferences and written for such publications as SHREW and *Catcall*, and co-edited *No Turning Back* (1981), an anthology of writings

from the British women's movement in the late 1970s.

Second Sex, The
Classic feminist text by Simone de BEAUVOIR, originally published in French in 1949 (*Le deuxième sexe*) and translated into English in 1952. Published nearly twenty years in advance of the modern women's movement, it is sometimes claimed to mark the beginning of the feminist renaissance, but, as Alice ROSSI has argued, it is more accurate to view it as a product of the transitional period between the old and new feminism. Neither a polemic nor a call to action (as many books influenced by it were), it is a scholarly, apolitical book written before de Beauvoir had come to identify herself as a feminist. It is a long and brilliant exploration of woman as 'the OTHER'. Drawing on history, art, psychoanalysis, biology, myth, literature and existential philosophy, de Beauvoir shows how men have consistently denied the right of humanity to women, creating an artificial construct which they define in opposition to themselves and call 'Woman'. Reprinted many times since its original publication, it is a groundbreaking work in which many later feminist theorists have found inspiration.

second wave feminism
Term used for the contemporary women's movement, which began

in the 1960s, to differentiate it from FIRST WAVE FEMINISM, which is considered to have subsided by about 1920. Another name for the WOMEN'S LIBERATION MOVEMENT (WLM).

Second Wave, The

Political journal founded in 1971, published twice a year (formerly quarterly) from Cambridge, Massachusetts. The editors have defined it as 'a tool with which we hammer at existing social and economic structures to open up new directions for a woman's revolution'. It features articles, analysis, poetry, fiction, art and reviews, all related to feminism.

Seneca Falls

New York town considered the birthplace of American feminism because it was the site of the first women's rights convention, 19–20 July 1848.

When Lucretia MOTT and Elizabeth Cady STANTON met in London in 1840 an important friendship was born. Their shared experience of being denied seats at the World Anti-Slavery Convention because of their sex convinced them that women were as much in need of emancipation as were slaves. In July 1848 they met again in New York State, and, at a tea-party with Martha C. Wright (Lucretia Mott's sister) and Mary Ann McClintock, a discussion of women's rights led to the writing of an advertisement, published the next day in the *Seneca County Courier*, calling upon all interested parties to attend a convention to discuss the social, civil, and religious condition and rights of women.

At least 300 people, some of them travelling by foot or wagon from as far as fifty miles away, arrived at the Wesleyan Chapel in Seneca Falls on 19 July, and because forty of them were men, the idea of a women-only meeting was dropped, and Lucretia's husband, James Mott, was named to the chair, with Mary Ann McClintock as secretary. Speeches and articles were read, and then Elizabeth Cady Stanton presented her 'DECLARATION OF SENTIMENTS', a description of women's grievances closely modelled on the Declaration of Independence and followed by twelve resolutions. After discussion, eleven resolutions were passed unanimously; the twelfth, 'that it is the sacred duty of the women of this country to secure to themselves their sacred right to the elective franchise' was more controversial but eventually passed by a small majority.

Now that the subject of women's rights had been publicly raised a need was felt for more discussion and action. A second convention was held in Rochester, New York, two weeks later, and others soon followed in Ohio, Massachusetts, Indiana, Pennsylvania and other parts of New York State: the

American women's movement had begun.

Although the actual Wesleyan Chapel where the first convention was held has been demolished, the National Women's Rights Historical Park was officially opened on 17 July 1982, in Seneca Falls to commemorate it.

separatism

The belief and practice of a community of women separate from men, sometimes as a temporary or partial measure, sometimes as an ideal or absolute goal. The idea of separatism has been around for a long time: it is segregation from a positive point of view. Instead of having it forced upon them by the dominant group (ghettoization), some women choose separatism as a means of escape from male domination.

In the past as well as the present, women have found emotional, spiritual and/or economic independence by setting up women-only alternative communities like the BEGUINES or the WOMAN'S COMMONWEALTH, or in their private lives by choosing to live with families of women friends. The results of separatism on a grand scale have been explored by writers who have imagined women-only UTOPIAS as well as less pleasant SCIENCE FICTION scenarios.

Separatism was part of the women's liberation movement from the beginning, as a means of defining and maintaining a specifically feminist stance, divorced from other political concerns. Although some Marxist and liberal feminists have always objected to the idea of a women-only movement, declaring that the system, rather than men, is the enemy and that men, too, are oppressed by sexism, in practice most feminists (like other oppressed groups) recognize the need for some separatism. They promote the creation of WOMANSPACE, to allow women to define their own struggle without male interference.

The most radical extreme of separatism can be seen in the refusal of some LESBIAN FEMINISTS to ally with women who maintain any emotional connections with men, including male infants.

At this extreme, separatism seems to be a dead end. It is a retreat rather than a political response. Instead of encouraging struggle against the system, it offers an escape into an alternative woman's culture. This is positive and valuable as it sustains women in the present and provides energy and ideas for the future; but when it is seen as the only proper feminist response to the world, it seems to imply that women are wasting their energies trying to fight male supremacy, because it is biologically ordained and cannot be changed. If this is true, then separatism may be the only freedom available to women, but it is not likely that many women will want, or be able, to take it.

Because middle-class, able-bodied white women are more likely than others to find a separatist life style possible, and because the assumption behind separatism ignores the fact that, despite their common problems as women, some groups may have interests in common with groups of men which they can neither ignore nor fight for alone (e.g. racism, rights of the handicapped, etc.), the concept of separatism has been criticized as élitist and racist.

Separatism is probably most valuable as an emotional ideal, which reminds women of the reality of sisterhood, and as an occasional, energizing retreat, rather than as a practical life style.

Seton, Grace Gallatin, 1872–1959 American writer and explorer. Active in the suffrage campaign from the age of seventeen, she worked for women's rights throughout her life. She belonged to many feminist organizations and was particularly concerned with gaining recognition for women writers. She served as president of the Connecticut Woman's Suffrage Association (1910–20), president of the National League of American Pen Women (1926–8 and 1930–2), and as chairman of letters of the National Council of Women (1933–8). During the 1930s she established the Biblioteca Femina, a collection of 2,000 volumes and 100 pamphlets by women from thirty-seven countries, which was later donated to the Northwestern University Library. Her experience of travelling and camping out in the American West during the late 1890s led her to found the Camp Fire Girls in 1912. She travelled widely throughout the 1920s and 1930s, visiting Japan, China, Indochina, Egypt, India and South America, and wrote books about her travels which include not only her own experiences but discussions of each country's history, customs, politics, with attention to the status of women. Of particular interest is *Poison Arrows* (1938) in which she writes about the Moi tribes of Vietnam as an example of a matriarchal culture. Her other books include *A Woman Tenderfoot* (1900), *Chinese Lanterns* (1924), *Magic Waters* (1933) and a collection of poetry, *The Singing Traveler* (1947).

Seven Demands, The
If the women's liberation movement in Britain has one single, unifying creed, it is probably this. They began as the FOUR DEMANDS announced in 1970, grew to six in 1975, and at the national conference in Birmingham in 1978, an introductory assertion and final, two-part, demand were added to create this declaration:

'The women's liberation movement asserts a woman's right to define her own sexuality and demands:

1. Equal pay for equal work;
2. Equal education and job opportunities;
3. Free contraception and abortion on demand;
4. Free 24-hour community controlled child care;
5. Legal and financial independence for women;
6. An end to discrimination against lesbians;
7. Freedom for all women from intimidation by the threat or use of male violence. An end to the laws, assumptions and institutions that perpetuate male dominance and men's aggression towards women.'

sex
See GENDER; SEXUALITY

Sex Discrimination Act

Enacted in the British Parliament on 29 December 1975, it outlaws discrimination on grounds of sex in such public areas as employment, education, training, housing and the provision to the public of goods and services, and includes the concept of indirect discrimination as well as direct.

The first Bill against sexual discrimination was introduced by Joyce Butler, Labour M.P. for Wood Green, in 1967. Similar bills were proposed in subsequent years, and by 1972 the need for such legislation had become the focus of a large campaign uniting the women's liberation movement with such older feminist organizations as the FAWCETT SOCIETY and the SIX POINT GROUP, and with some trade unions.

Yet despite the enthusiasm with which eventual passage of the Sex Discrimination Act was greeted, it has proved to be full of loopholes and difficult to enforce. Vaguely defined differences are permitted as reasons why only one sex might be genuinely qualified for a particular job, and employers have argued successfully that some cases of indirect discrimination are 'justifiable'. Individual action must be taken in a case of alleged discrimination, and it can be difficult for a woman to know and to prove that she has been the victim of unlawful discrimination. While enshrining the principle of equality between the sexes under law, the Sex Discrimination Act, like much other legislation, has had little material effect on the lives of women.

sex/gender system

Gayle Rubin was the first, in 1975, to use this term in preference to the more vaguely-defined PATRIARCHY. Her definition: 'the set of arrangements by which a society transforms biological sexuality into products of human activity, and in which these transformed sexual needs are satisfied'.

This is the means by which biological differences are linked to

291

socially constructed characteristics and then used to define the roles of men and women, and to justify the established relationship between the sexes.

For example, to be physically equipped to bear and nurse children does not necessarily mean that women are also endowed from birth with certain psychological characteristics shared with all other women but not with men. The sort of characteristics our society believes to be feminine include passivity, emotionalism, empathy, etc. in contrast to such presumably masculine characteristics as aggression, objectivity, and rational thought. Linking SEX with GENDER presumes that temperament is determined before birth, in connection with biological sexual characteristics. If women are as naturally incapable of looking after themselves or thinking logically as men are incapable of giving birth, the existence of SEX ROLES may be considered fixed, with male dominance inevitable. But one of the basic concepts of feminism is that gender is not innate, but a social construct which may be detached, at least conceptually, from sex.
(*See also* SOCIAL MYTHOLOGY)

sexism
Term, constructed by analogy with racism, first used around 1968 in America within the WOMEN'S LIBERATION MOVEMENT, now in widespread, popular use.

It may be defined as the system and practice of discriminating against a person on the grounds of sex. Specifically, it refers to unfair prejudice against women, the stereotyping of women (SEX-ROLES), the defining of women in regard to their sexual availability and attractiveness to men (OBJECTI-FICATION), and all the conscious or unconscious assumptions which cause women to be treated as not fully human, while men are identified as the norm.

Although men also claim to be the victims of sexism, either in personal relationships or in regard to AFFIRMATIVE ACTION programmes, this is more accurately known as 'inverse sexism' or 'reverse sexism', and is actually a response to the institutionalized sexism which oppresses all women.

Like racism, sexism presumes an essential superiority grounded in specific physical manifestations. No justification for sexist attitudes is necessary when men are considered to be naturally better than women: male domination is seen as natural, and therefore right.

In the past, sexism had no name. It was simply the way things were, had always been, and always would be. A term like male dominance described the situation without implying criticism. Feminism, by naming sexism, has made the system visible and therefore open to change.

Different theories for the origin

of sexism have been proposed, most of them based on the BIOLOGICAL DIFFERENCES which have tied women to the process of reproduction as men are not. Some radical feminists, like many sexist males, have considered male dominance a biological mandate, so that the only possibility for freedom for women lies in SEPARATISM. Others, like Shulamith FIRESTONE and Marge PIERCY, have suggested that only when the link between sex and reproduction has been broken by new reproductive technologies making old-fashioned pregnancy unnecessary, will women and men be freed from the tyranny of sex-roles.

Juliet MITCHELL, Nancy CHODOROW and Dorothy Dinnerstein are the best known of those who have linked the perpetuation of sexism to psychology rather than biology. Dinnerstein has theorized that because the primary caretaker for nearly all infants is a woman, that children of both sexes resolve their infantile feelings of ambivalence towards the mother by rejecting female authority and investing power in men. In order to break this pattern, human psychology must be changed by a new form of child-rearing in which both sexes take an equal part.

In *Woman's Creation* (1979) Elizabeth Fisher theorized that sexism, or 'the domestication of women' followed the domestication of animals: that with animal-keeping (which may have been the earliest form of private property) and selective breeding, came the male desire to 'own' children, and that by analogy with their treatment of animals, men began to control women's reproductive capacity by enforcing chastity and sexual repression.

Those who see sexism as culturally imposed call for reforms in law, education and personal relationships to bring about the gradual elimination of the rigid sex-roles which both result from and perpetuate sexism. Marxist and socialist feminists generally believe that sexism can be overcome only as part of the abolition of the class system and capitalism.

Yet however they may differ on theories of how it came about and how it can be abolished, all feminists are agreed that sexism is the evil which feminism exists to fight. (*See also* PATRIARCHY)

sex-object
See OBJECTIFICATION

sex-roles
The concept of sex-roles (which might more appropriately be called gender-roles) was developed by sociologists as a way of describing the appropriate social functions filled by men and women. Behind the term was the assumption that there were certain traits and qualities which were naturally masculine or feminine, and which explained why

women were best suited to the 'role' of wife and mother and supportive companion, whereas men were suited to a much wider range of roles as an individual in the world. Feminist theorists adopted this terminology but transformed the meaning of it. Instead of considering the sex-role as something naturally dictated by biology, feminist analysis saw it as an assignment from society which linked certain psychological characteristics (such as aggression or passivity) with anatomical sex. Sex-roles (or the SEX/GENDER SYSTEM) were seen as something which psychologically damaged women, and the destruction of sex-roles was seen as a prerequisite for women's liberation. THE FEMINISTS (founded in 1968) called themselves 'A Political Organization to Annihilate Sex Roles'. By the mid-1970s, however, there was a general shift away from describing women's oppression in terms of sex-roles. Women trying to change themselves and society discovered that even when they were recognized, it was no easy matter to change or abandon these sex-roles: they were more deeply entrenched than the term 'role' implied. GENDER was recognized as something more complex than just the system of stereotypes which oppresses women, and questions were raised about why and how the sex-role system was developed and maintained.

sexual discrimination

Practice of making an unfair distinction in the treatment of individuals on the basis of their sex. The term is always used in the sense that one sex is privileged or restricted in comparison with the other: providing separate toilet facilities for men and women is not an example of sexual discrimination, but refusing to hire a woman as a toilet cleaner on the grounds that toilets have always been cleaned by men, is direct sexual discrimination. There are very few jobs – acting and wet nursing are among them – for which the sex of the applicant could be seen as relevant. Sexual discrimination is based not on the abilities or needs of individuals, but on stereotyped sex roles, tradition, and on benefits to men of keeping women economically oppressed. Although men, too, may be discriminated against and refused jobs which are considered more suitable for women, in general sexual discrimination works to the disadvantage of women.

Besides direct sexual discrimination, the concept of indirect discrimination has also been recognized in law. Because it is more complex, indirect discrimination is more difficult to prove. It involves applying a particular requirement or condition which places one sex at a relative disadvantage. For example, setting an age limitation on promotion to certain job-levels privileges those men (and women) who follow the traditional masculine career-pattern over the many women who take time off work in their twenties or thirties to have and rear children.

sexual harassment
Term for unreciprocated, unsolicited, unwanted male behaviour which has as its aim the reduction of a woman to a sex object. This may take the form of flattery or verbal abuse, casual comments or demands for sexual favours, embraces, 'accidental' bodily contact, or even the threat of rape. Like rape, sexual harassment is about power, not desire; it is a means of asserting male dominance. Before the modern women's movement there was no name for it; it was considered natural masculine behaviour, and if there was blame it was attached to the woman who complained. Now it is recognized not as a personal problem but as an issue faced by all women, an aspect of sexual politics. Although it may take place anywhere, most attention has been focused on sexual harassment in the workplace, with attempts to have it legally recognized as a form of sexual discrimination.

Sexual Politics
A modern classic, one of the basic texts of the women's liberation movement, written by Kate MIL-LETT and published in 1970. Beginning with the proposition that the relationship between the sexes

should be looked at as a power relationship – as, indeed, the most fundamental and pervasive model for all political relationships – Millett drew on the concepts of sociology, psychology, economic history, philosophy and literature in order to formulate a theory of PATRIARCHY, and to define patriarchy as a political institution. And yet, although it can be referred to as political, in the sense that it concerns a power relationship, Millett recognized that 'So deeply embedded is patriarchy that the character structure it creates in both sexes is perhaps even more a habit of mind and a way of life than a political system.'

Much of the book, which Millett described as a hybrid of literary criticism and cultural criticism, consists of the detailed analysis and deconstruction of the way four modern male writers – D. H. Lawrence, Henry Miller, Norman Mailer and Jean Genet – wrote about sex. Millett revealed that the urge to dominate was the major force in their vision of SEXUALITY. Power, not love or sexual passion, was always the real issue at stake in every erotic encounter, and the inclusion of a homosexual writer simply reveals that the sexual role is not tied to biology, but rather to class or caste.

sexual politics
The concept of sexual politics is at the very heart of modern feminist

theory. Like the slogan 'THE PER-SONAL IS POLITICAL' it represents a different way of thinking about male-defined reality, and connects two areas (private=sexual + public=political) which had previously been presumed to be dichotomous. In 1968, Kate MILLETT wrote 'Sexual Politics: A Manifesto for Revolution', in which she declared, 'When one group rules another, the relationship between the two is political'.

She was not, as she explained at greater length in her 1970 book SEXUAL POLITICS, using the term POLITICS in its customary narrow sense, because she believed it was imperative to define a theory of politics which went beyond the idea of traditional, formal politics. Chiefly, the relationship between the sexes had to be looked at in a new way in order to be understood. Disguised by ideology, psychology and ideas about love and human nature, the relationship between the sexes was not usually recognized as one involving power. Yet relationships between classes and races had been recognized as political in the broader sense that sociologist Max Weber called *herrschaft*, a relationship of dominance and subordinance. As Millett wrote: 'Groups who rule by birthright are fast disappearing, yet there remains one ancient and universal scheme for the domination of one birth group by another – the scheme that prevails in the area of sex.' And

sexual domination, as she argued throughout her brilliant and influential book, remains 'perhaps the most pervasive ideology of our culture and provides its most fundamental concept of power'.

sexual sexual politics

SEXUAL POLITICS concerns the power relationship between the sexes; sexual sexual politics is concerned with the same thing, but narrows the focus to concentrate on how male dominance is expressed and maintained through COMPULSORY HETEROSEXUALITY.

sexual slavery

Although the term is usually used to refer to forced PROSTITUTION and the international traffic in women who are kidnapped, drugged, and physically and mentally abused for men's sexual pleasure, many feminist writers as early as Hedwig DOHM and Olive SCHREINER have recognized that sexual slavery can take far more subtle forms – that it is an inevitable part of life for many women under PATRIARCHY. Denied economic independence, denied the education and work which would allow the development of other skills and abilities, women through the ages have had nothing to sell but their bodies. Schreiner argued, in WOMAN AND LABOUR, that women are forced to become sexual parasites, and that the difference between selling oneself to one man in MARRIAGE or to many as a prostitute was not great. More recently, in *Female Sexual Slavery* (1979), Kathleen Barry, writing about the difficulty of defining prostitution as something women choose, rather than are forced into, defined sexual slavery as 'present in *all* situations where women or girls cannot change the immediate conditions of their existence; where regardless of how they got into those conditions they cannot get out; and where they are subject to sexual violence and exploitation.'

sexual violence
See RAPE; PORNOGRAPHY; WOMEN AGAINST VIOLENCE AGAINST WOMEN; VIOLENCE

sexuality
There is a confusion in our very language between sex, meaning male or female, and sex, meaning sexual activity; and because women's oppression as a sex is often expressed *through* sex, sexuality has, inevitably, been one of the most vital topics for feminist examination. There is an obvious need for a feminist analysis of sexuality, yet the subject has polarized the contemporary feminist movement.

Joanna RUSS has nicknamed the two sides the 'Perverts' and the 'Puritans'. The perverts are sex radicals who believe that women suffer from sexual repression, and wish to see a sexual revolution to liberate both women and men.

They question whether any consensual sexual acts should be forbidden, and think that a hierarchy of sexual acts in which some are privileged, some tolerated, and others banned is as oppressive as any other system of rank. The puritans believe that sexual freedom – at least as it has been demonstrated in our culture – is only an extension of male privilege and dangerous to women. They believe that normal female sexuality is gentle and loving, in contrast to violent, oppressive male desires. The first view tends to concentrate on the pleasures of sex; the second to see its dangers. For women under PATRIARCHY, sexuality always presents the potential for pleasure and danger – sometimes even within the same experience – and it is unrealistic to look at sex only from one side.

In the past, sex was usually perceived as a natural force existing prior to and restrained by the structures of society. This attitude still underlies most of our unconscious assumptions, whether we believe that force to be basically life-enhancing, or destructive. But just as feminists have recognized that GENDER is created by society, not nature, so feminist theories about sexuality begin with the radical premise that sex is a social construction. Yet how and where is it constructed? Can it be consciously reconstructed at either the social or the personal level? Should it be?

Can some sexual practices be considered 'better' or more 'normal' than others? What is the connection between practices of sexual dominance and submission, and male dominance in the world; between desire and the relationship between the sexes? Is women's sexuality profoundly – or inevitably – different from that of men? How deeply is HETEROSEXUALITY implicated in women's oppression?

Some feminists are asking these questions and attempting to find answers by exploring their own and others' fantasies, desires and experiences. Others feel threatened that the questions are even being asked, having established for themselves an idea of what a politically correct feminist sexual practice should be. A misunderstanding of the slogan 'THE PERSONAL IS POLITICAL' has caused it to be seen as prescriptive, so that many women feel guilty because their sexual urges cannot be changed by an act of will to match their political understanding.

'Sexual acts are burdened with an excess of significance', according to Gayle Rubin (1984). 'Although people can be intolerant, silly, or pushy about what constitutes proper diet, differences in menu rarely provoke the kinds of rage, anxiety and sheer terror that routinely accompany differences in erotic taste.'

An example of this was seen in the feminist backlash against a feminist conference at Barnard College, New York, in 1982. The Ninth Annual Scholar and Feminist Conference addressed 'women's sexual pleasure, choice, and autonomy, acknowledging that sexuality is simultaneously a domain of restriction, repression and danger, as well as a domain of exploration, pleasure and agency. This dual focus is important, we think, for to speak only of pleasure and gratification ignores the patriarchal structure in which women act, yet to talk only of sexual violence and oppression ignores women's experience with sexual agency and choice and unwittingly increases the sexual terror and despair in which women live.' (Carole S. Vance, 1984) A coalition organized by Women Against Pornography and other groups held a ZAP ACTION and circulated leaflets denouncing the conference for inviting 'anti-feminist' speakers, and attacking individual participants as morally unacceptable.

For many feminists, as this demonstrates, sexuality has become the defining issue. Male heterosexuality is seen as the cornerstone of women's oppression, expressed most vividly in PORNOGRAPHY and acts of VIOLENCE against women, and it is fought not only on the institutional level, but also in the bedroom, where the private expression of sexual desire is heavily weighted with significance. Yet this redefining of feminist sexuality seems an act less of liberation than of drawing new boundaries, creating a charmed circle for the politically correct. Desire is not so easily controlled. Despite disagreements about what is and is not acceptable sexual behaviour, an important achievement of modern feminism has been to claim women's right and power to define their own sexuality, instead of having it defined, as for so long, by men.

(*See also* LESBIANISM; ORGASM)

Shafiq, Dori'a, 1910–75
Egyptian. She founded Bint-E-Nil (Daughters of the Nile) and in 1951 led a procession of 1,500 women into the Egyptian parliament to demand the vote (which was not granted until 1956).

Shange, Ntozake, 1948–
American poet and novelist. She began experimenting with poetic drama as both a writer and a performer in 1975, achieving public acclaim with the Broadway production in 1976 of her first 'choreopoem', *For colored girls who have considered suicide/when the rainbow is enuf.* Her books inlude *Nappy Edges* (1978) and *Sassafrass, Cypress & Indigo* (1982). Her name, which she chose herself, is Zulu for 'she who comes with her own things'/'she who walks like a lion'.

Sh'arawi, Huda, 1882–1947
Egyptian. She led the first women's organization in Egypt, founded in

1920, and in 1923 represented Egypt at the International Conference of Women in Rome. In 1924 she founded the Women's Union and its journal, *Egyptian Woman*. In 1944 she helped establish the All Arab Federation of Women, and continued to attend both national and international women's conferences until 1946.

Shaw, Anna Howard, 1847–1919
American orator, preacher and doctor. Despite the opposition of her family and society, she worked her way through college and Boston University to become both a Doctor of Divinity (ordained in 1880 by the Protestant Methodist Church) and a Doctor of Medicine (1885). She came in contact with the women's suffrage movement as a lecturer for the WOMEN'S CHRISTIAN TEMPERANCE UNION (WCTU) and served as president of the NATIONAL AMERICAN WOMAN SUFFRAGE ASSOCIATION (NAWSA) from 1904–15. She was a brilliant and influential speaker who won many admiring followers to the cause, but her lack of administrative ability meant she was not the strong leader NAWSA needed at that time. Recognizing this, she willingly stepped down for Carrie Chapman CATT.

Sheba
London-based feminist PUBLISHING collective founded in 1980. They follow no particular 'line' of feminism and state their criteria: 'We

won't publish any books that are anti-lesbian or have any kind of racist content. We give priority to black women's writing and that of working class women.' They published seven new titles in 1985, and hoped to increase the number the following year. Their publications include children's books, poetry, non-fiction and novels.

Sheehy-Skeffington, Hannah, 1877–1946

Irish. A founder-member of the Irish Association of Women Graduates in 1901, in 1908 she co-founded the Irish Women's Franchise League with Constance Markiewicz. She was imprisoned for two months and dismissed from her teaching job in 1912 because of her militant activities. She took part in many marches and demonstrations both in London and in Dublin on behalf of women's suffrage, and in 1913 became head of the Irish Franchise League. In 1916 her husband witnessed the shooting of an unarmed boy by British soldiers and was himself arrested and shot without trial. After this, her life was dominated by Irish nationalism almost to the exclusion of feminism. She travelled to the United States to raise funds for the IRA, and became involved in local politics in Dublin.

Sheldon, Alice, 1915–

American psychiatrist and writer. She is best known for her SCIENCE FICTION novels and short stories published under the pseudonym James TIPTREE Jr, but has also published some of her more 'overtly feminist' stories under the name Racoona Sheldon.

Sheppard, Kate, 1848–1934

Scottish-born New Zealand feminist. An interest in DRESS REFORM and temperance drew her into the women's suffrage movement, and between 1885 and the granting of the vote in 1894 she actively wrote, spoke and organized petitions. In 1896 she became the first President of the National Council of Women. She was made honorary vice-president of the INTERNATIONAL COUNCIL OF WOMEN in 1909, and was the author of *Women's Suffrage in New Zealand* (1907).

Sherfey, Mary Jane, 1933–

American psychiatrist. While researching the reasons for the development of MENSTRUATION in humans, Sherfey was inspired by the work of William Masters and Virginia Johnson showing that women had the physical capacity for unlimited ORGASMS. This led her to write 'A Theory on Female Sexuality' (1966), later expanded into *The Nature and Evolution of Female Sexuality* (1972). Her theory of female SEXUALITY included a theory of the development of PATRIARCHY: she suggested that women's sexuality, allowed its natural expression, was so powerful and uncontrollable as to make what we consider normal family life an impossibility. Men, therefore, had dominated women, suppressing the true nature of female sexuality and forbidding its expression.

Shifra

Jewish feminist journal launched in Britain in December 1983, it aims to provide Jewish women with a forum to discuss and understand their experiences. It is named after a Jewish woman active in the Warsaw resistance until murdered by the Nazis in 1943. Because her surname is unknown, the editors felt Shifra symbolized the cause of Jewish feminists by speaking and acting in her own name, not the name of her father or husband.

(*See also* JEWISH FEMINISTS)

Showalter, Elaine, 1941–

American. Professor of English at Princeton University, she is influential in the field of feminist LITERARY CRITICISM, where she has been concerned with defining a specifically female literary aesthetic. She is best known as the author of A LITERATURE OF THEIR OWN (1977), and has edited several books, including *Women's Liberation and Literature* (1971) and *The New Feminist Criticism* (1985).

Shrew

First widely-circulated newsletter of the women's movement in Britain, it began in July 1969. With the object of giving as many women as possible a voice, editorship was passed with each issue to a different group within the London Women's Liberation Workshop. It attained a circulation of about 5,000 and was published several times a year until 1974; after isolated appearances in 1976 and 1977, it ceased publication.

Shulman, Alix Kates, 1932–

American writer. Her first book, written after her children entered nursery school, was a mathematical fantasy for children without a single female character. After finishing it, in 1968, she became involved in the Women's Liberation Movement, and her life was changed. She devoted more of her energies to writing, and 'from then on, I focused my attention on the lives, works, and history of women, and I became a fighter in our movement' (from 'Living Our Life', 1984). She was an early member of REDSTOCKINGS, and founded Feminists for Children's Media, the first group to begin developing a feminist critique of children's literature. Her books include *To the Barricades: The Anarchist Life of Emma Goldman* (1971); *Red Emma Speaks* (1972), a collection of speeches and essays by Emma GOLDMAN; and three novels, MEMOIRS OF AN EX-PROM QUEEN (1972), BURNING QUESTIONS (1978), and *On the Stroll* (1981).

Signs

American quarterly subtitled *Journal of Women in Culture and*

Society, founded in 1975. An inter-disciplinary journal, it attempts to represent the most original and rigorous new thinking about women in social science, humanities and natural science, all from an international perspective.

Silences

Non-fiction book by Tillie OLSEN, first published in America in 1978. It consists of interlinking essays which explore the social circumstances which inhibit and silence creative writers. One section in particular, 'One Out of Twelve: Writers Who Are Women in Our Century', first given as a talk in 1971, is important as a basic text of feminist literary theory.

Sinclair, May, 1863–1946

English novelist. In 1908 she became involved with the Women's Freedom League and fund-raising, marching for women's suffrage, writing articles for *Votes for Women*, and other feminist activities, including writing a pamphlet, *Feminism*, for the Women Writers Suffrage League. Besides poetry, short stories, criticism and philosophical works, she wrote twenty-four novels. Of particular interest are *The Tree of Heaven* (1917), a fictional treatment of the women's movement, based on her own experiences between 1908–12; *Mary Olivier: A Life* (1919), the fictional biography of a poet, with particular emphasis on the mother-daughter

relationship, told using the stream-of-consciousness technique which Sinclair so admired in the work of Dorothy RICHARDSON; and *Life and Death of Harriett Frean* (1922), often considered her best novel.

Sinister Wisdom

American quarterly journal founded in 1976 to publish theory, fiction, poetry, drama, art and reviews to appeal 'to the lesbian imagination in all women'. The title was taken from a line in THE FEMALE MAN by Joanna RUSS, chosen to represent a turning to the creative 'left' in revolution against the rational, patriarchal 'right'.

sisterhood

The bonding together of women in love, solidarity and a recognition of shared oppression, the first step towards liberation. Although the concept is similar to fraternity, it is not simply the feminine counterpart of brotherhood – Mary DALY has argued that it is in fact totally different. Because women, in a patriarchal society, are conditioned to mistrust, compete with and betray each other for men, female friendship can be a form of rebellion. Many women have always instinctively recognized the importance of bonds between women. Feminism gave this a name, and made sisterhood a major political goal.
(*See also* LESBIAN CONTINUUM; WOMAN-CENTREDNESS; WOMAN-IDENTIFIED WOMAN)

Sisterhood is Powerful

1) Slogan coined by Kathie SARACHILD which first appeared in a leaflet distributed at the 'BURIAL OF TRADITIONAL WOMANHOOD' demonstration in January 1968, in Washington, D.C., it expresses the sense of power women can find in solidarity with each other, and was very popular during the early years of WOMEN'S LIBERATION MOVEMENT.

2) One of the first, most influential anthologies of writings from the Women's Liberation Movement, edited by Robin MORGAN and published in America in 1970. It contains essays, polemics, personal testimony and poetry. Contributors include Kate MILLETT, Marge PIERCY, Valerie SOLANAS, Leah FRITZ, Roxanne DUNBAR, Mary Jane SHERFEY, and Naomi WEISSTEIN.

Six Point Group, The

British organization founded in 1921 by Lady RHONDDA as a discussion and political pressure group for women's interests; the name came from the 'six points' upon which Parliament was urged to act to improve the status of women. These were:

1. Satisfactory legislation on child assault.
2. Satisfactory legislation for the widowed mother.
3. Satisfactory legislation for the unmarried mother and her child.
4. Equal guardianship.
5. Equality of pay for men and women teachers.
6. Equality of pay and opportunity for men and women in the Civil Service.

If one point was settled, another of equal importance could be put in its place. In 1981, the group was disbanded by its last president, Hazel Hunkins HALLINAN – not because all objectives had been achieved but, sadly, because not enough younger women were interested in sustaining it.

slave name

Term used for a married name, or any name not chosen by the woman herself which implies male ownership. The first American feminists, emerging from the abolition movement, saw similarities between the slave forced to bear his master's name, and the woman who had her identity absorbed in marriage. During the second wave of feminism, under the influence of black power and black pride movements, it was recognized that all women have 'slave names', being identified either as their father's daughter or their husband's wife. Some women have chosen to express their liberation in the same way as many emancipated slaves did – by choosing a new name with personal significance for themselves.

(*See also* NAMES; LUCY STONERS)

Smeal, Eleanor (Ellie), 1939–

American. Known as the first housewife to become president of the NATIONAL ORGANIZATION FOR WOMEN (in 1977), she is also the author of a study of the political GENDER GAP, *Why and How Women Will Elect the Next President* (1984).

Smedley, Agnes, 1890–1950
American writer. From a poor, working-class background herself, she tried through her writing to provide a voice for those who are usually unheard, and her life was dedicated to helping the oppressed, wherever she found them. She became involved with Margaret SANGER's birth control movement and also the Indian nationalist movement in New York in 1917. Imprisoned for her activities, she moved to Germany in 1920, where she was soon at the centre of the overseas Indian freedom movement. Her close relationship with the leader of this male-dominated movement in Berlin resulted in a nervous breakdown, from which she recovered through writing a fictionalized autobiography, *Daughter of Earth* (1928). Her political and personal lives were always inseparable, but she never again became emotionally dependent upon a man. In 1929, she went to China as a journalist, and her intense sympathy for the oppressed, particularly the women, of China soon involved her in their struggle. Her books about China include *China's Red Army Marches* (1934), *China Fights Back: An American Woman with the Eighth Route Army* (1938)

and *Battle Hymn of China* (1943). She became one of the targets for the Anti-Red hysteria in America in the late 1940s and early 1950s, and her books went out of favour. She was almost forgotten until THE FEMINIST PRESS chose *Daughter of Earth* as one of their first reprints, in 1973.

Smith, Barbara, 1946–
American. A black lesbian-feminist writer and activist, she has contributed substantially to the development of BLACK FEMINISM in theory and in practice. She helped found the COMBAHEE RIVER COLLECTIVE and Kitchen Table: Women of Color Press. She co-edited *Conditions Five: The Black Women's Issue* (1979) and edited *Home Girls: A Black Feminist Anthology* (1983).

Smith, James Elishana, 1801–57
English Presbyterian minister. Wrote *Doctrine of the Woman* expressing his belief that women and men were equal yet different, two halves which made up one whole. He believed that women would be emancipated from their present dependent role with the coming of a female messiah who would transform and save the world.

Smyth, Ethel, 1858–1944
English composer. She was well established, famous for her orchestral works, chamber music and operas, when, in 1910, her life

changed dramatically as the result of hearing Emmeline PANKHURST speak on the subject of women's rights. She became converted to the cause, and took part in the most militant suffrage campaigns, as a result of which she was arrested and imprisoned for two months. In 1911 she composed 'MARCH OF THE WOMEN', which became the official song of the WOMEN'S SOCIAL AND POLITICAL UNION. The libretto of her 1916 opera, *The Boatswain's Mate*, reflects her involvement in the women's movement, and she wrote about her experiences and convictions in various autobiographical books, including *Female Pipings in Eden* (1933). She fought the male-dominated musical establishment for recognition not only of her own work, but for that of other women. During World War I she succeeded in finding jobs in major orchestras for many women musicians. After the war, seeing these women dismissed and replaced by men, she began what was virtually a one-woman campaign in support of women musicians, and fought male prejudice until the end of her life. Her friend Virginia WOOLF said of her: 'She is of the race of the pioneers: she is among the ice-breakers, the window smashers, the indomitable and irresistible armoured tanks who climbed the rough ground; went first; drew the enemy's fire and left a pathway for those who came after her.'

social constructionism
The idea that the status of women, and the apparently natural differences between male and female, are not directly attributable to biology, but rather to the way that biology is interpreted within a given society; that SEX-ROLES are constructed and women and men made rather than born. The opposite of this point of view is called BIOLOGICAL DETERMINISM or ESSENTIALISM.

social feminist
1) Term devised by William O'Neill in writing about the first wave of feminism in America to denote women active in broad social reforms which they considered more urgent than attaining legal rights for themselves; used in contrast to the suffragists or 'hardcore' feminists.

2) As defined and used by Naomi Black: 'Social feminists believe that women have produced a set of values and practical skills that are excluded, along with women, from the larger society that is organized and run by men. . . . An authoritative public role for women is therefore necessary in order to improve the defective social system.'

social mythology
Term used by Elizabeth JANEWAY to explain women's subordination to men, similar to such terms as SEX/GENDER SYSTEM and PATRIARCHY. According to Janeway, male domination in most areas of life

came about and has persisted through male propaganda (internalized by women) about women's nature, and partly through an unspoken bargain by which women have agreed to let men rule the world in exchange for a measure of power in the private sphere.
(*See also* SEX-ROLES)

social purity movement

A series of campaigns designed to protect women and children from the most damaging effects of male sexual behaviour, which flourished between 1880–1914 as part of the larger women's movement. It included campaigns against state regulation of PROSTITUTION, projects to provide women with alternatives to prostitution, and attempts to encourage men to change their own attitudes and behaviour. Although not everyone involved in this movement was feminist, it was in part inspired by the feminist recognition that male sexuality was not an uncontrollable natural force, and in fact was used as a means of controlling women. Josephine BUTLER was one of those who made the connection between the economic and sexual oppression of women, as was Christabel PANKHURST with her slogan 'Votes for Women; Chastity for Men!'

socialist feminism

Combining the insights of RADICAL FEMINISM with Marxist analysis, socialist feminism is committed to the abolition of both class and GENDER. It aims to overthrow the current social order (sometimes described as capitalist patriarchy), to end all forms of exploitation, and create a society in which maleness and femaleness are socially irrelevant.

Like radical feminists, socialist feminists believe the PERSONAL IS POLITICAL. Rejecting the concept of a division between private and public spheres of existence, they broaden the Marxist conception of the material base of society to include all aspects of what is sometimes called REPRODUCTION. Recognizing that the structuring of SEXUALITY, MARRIAGE and the FAMILY are basic to women's oppression, socialist feminists believe in the importance of challenging the norm and practising alternatives in their own lives (through communal living, egalitarian marriages, all-women households, etc.) yet also realize that individual solutions are limited by society. Lifestyle changes in themselves will not bring about an end to sexism, but they can be a way of preparing for a post-revolutionary, non-sexist society.

Socialist feminists also accept the need for a certain degree of SEPARATISM, and for an autonomous, women-only women's liberation movement. Men, not merely 'the system', are seen as the enemy, because as PATRIARCHY operates in men's interests they are less likely to want or to be able to resist it. Yet socialist feminism, while recognizing that all women are oppressed on the basis of their sex, also admits the existence of other types of oppression. Differences of nationality, race, age, ability, religion and class all cut across gender lines, ensuring that women in different groups, while sharing a universal oppression with all other women, will also share equally important interests with men of their same race, class, ability, etc. Rather than arguing that oppression on the basis of sex or class is the fundamental oppression, socialist feminists argue that every issue is a women's issue, as well as having class and race implications, so that it is neither possible nor desirable to separate 'the WOMAN QUESTION' from other political questions. While believing that women must organize around their own oppression, they also see a necessity for coalitions with other socialist and revolutionary groups.

(See also LIBERAL FEMINISM; MARXIST-FEMINISM; BEYOND THE FRAGMENTS; ROWBOTHAM, SHEILA)

Society for Cutting Up Men (S.C.U.M.)
See SCUM MANIFESTO

Society for Promoting the Employment of Women
English organization founded in 1860 by Jessie BOUCHERETT, Barbara BODICHON and Adelaide PROCTOR for the purpose of opening more careers to women and encouraging education and training for such diverse jobs as farming, nursing, engraving, photography, bookkeeping and hairdressing. Printing, formerly a male preserve, became another possibility when the Society founded the VICTORIA PRESS.

Sojourner
National women's paper established in 1975 and published monthly from Boston. Named after Sojourner TRUTH.

Solanas, Valerie, ? 1940–
American artist and writer, part of the New York avant-garde in the 1960s. Offered a contract by Maurice Girodias of The Olympia Press to write her autobiography, she instead produced a document called SCUM MANIFESTO which was published as the S.C.U.M. (Society for Cutting Up Men) Manifesto in 1968. In 1968 she was briefly notorious for shooting and wounding the artist, Andy Warhol, after which she was put under psychiatric observation.

Somerville, Edith, 1858–1949
Irish novelist. Most of her books were written in partnership with her cousin and lifelong friend, Violet Martin (Martin Ross), and even those written after her partner's death were published as by 'E. Œ. Somerville and Martin Ross'. The book they considered their best was

307

The Real Charlotte (1894). Always a feminist, she was president of the Munster Women's Franchise League.

Somerville, Mary Fairfax, 1780–1872

Scottish mathematician and science writer. A staunch feminist, she broke new ground for women not only by her example, but also by writing books which made the sciences more comprehensible to her countrywomen. Hers was the first signature on the first petition for women's suffrage presented to Parliament.

Song Qingling (Soong Ching Ling; Madame Sun Yat-sen), 1893–1981

Chinese leader. Western-educated, she felt that Western-style feminism was out of place in China, arguing that it was incongruous for women to fight against male oppression if at the same time they oppressed other members of their own sex. She urged women to fight with men for China's freedom as well as struggling for their own emancipation. After the establishment of the People's Republic of China (1949), she continued to be a prominent figure in the Chinese women's movement and, in 1957, was made honorary President of the Women's Federation.

Sophia, a Person of Quality

Name used by the author of WOMAN NOT INFERIOR TO MAN, a contro-versial pamphlet published in London in 1739. Her true identity was never revealed, but scholars believe she was probably Lady Mary Wortley MONTAGU.

Spare Rib

British magazine started in 1972 by Rosie Boycott and Marsha Rowe as a popular journal for women of all ages and backgrounds; the title was a joke, a pun on the biblical origin of woman. Early issues had articles by men and ran feminist analysis side-by-side with columns on beauty, cooking and celebrities. It became a collective with its eighteenth issue, and the format changed to offer more information and less artwork, the content becoming both more political and more practical. It became one of the main contacts of the British women's movement and provided a starting place for many of the most prominent feminist writers of today. In the 1980s, with a circulation well over 25,000, the magazine committed itself to greater reader participation and began to address such major issues as racism and the oppression of women internationally; it actively recruited more black, third world and disabled women as members of the collective.

Speaking Bitterness

Sometimes translated as Speaking Pain, this practice was used by the revolutionary Chinese as a form of CONSCIOUSNESS-RAISING: individuals were encouraged to speak about their oppression within a group, and then to work to overcome it. Some believe that this was the model used for the development of consciousness-raising groups in America; Jo FREEMAN, among others, has said that the technique of consciousness-raising, while very similar to the practice of Speaking Bitterness, was not directly influenced by it.

Spence, Catherine, 1825–1910
Australian writer. Her novels, at first published anonymously, made her the first successful woman novelist in Australia. They include *Tender and True: A Colonial Tale* (1856), *Mr Hogarth's Will* (1865), *The Author's Daughter* (1868) and *A Week in the Future* (1889). She also wrote textbooks, journalism, and critical essays for Australian and British publications, often stirring controversy with her feminist viewpoint. She became involved with reform work, chiefly on behalf of orphaned children, in the 1870s. In 1891 she became vice-president of the Women's Suffrage League of South Australia, and after the vote had been won she continued to be active in both the Australian and the international women's movements, touring both the United States and Britain as a lecturer. She was active in many campaigns, including proportional representation, tax reform, educational improve-

ments, women's rights, and the peace movement.

Spence, Thomas, 1750–1814
English. A working-class radical, he envisioned a socialist UTOPIA called Spensonia in which all men and women achieved citizenship and full equality at the age of twenty-one.

Spencer, Anna, 1851–1931
American minister and social reformer. Author of *Woman's Share in Social Culture* (1912) which emphasized the importance of woman's contribution to public life, the arts and industry from the earliest times.

Spender, Dale, 1943–
Australian. A prolific writer, she has emerged as one of the key feminist theorists of the 1980s, concerned with recovering, preserving and popularizing women's HISTORY. Her main thesis is that men have traditionally retained power by controlling LANGUAGE, EDUCATION, and all areas of knowledge, so that the control of knowledge is one of the most crucial areas of feminist struggle. She has taught both in Australia and in England, and is the editor of *Women's Studies International Forum*. Her books include *Man Made Language* (1980), *Men's Studies Modified: The Impact of Feminism on the Academic Disciplines* (1981), *Invisible Women* (1982), *Women of Ideas and What Men Have*

Done To Them (1982), *Feminist Theorists: Three Centuries of Key Women Thinkers* (1983), *There's Always Been a Women's Movement This Century* (1983), *Time and Tide Wait for No Man* (1984), and *For the Record: The Making and Meaning of Feminist Knowledge* (1985).

spinster
Term which originally meant a woman who spins, and came by the seventeenth century to mean an unmarried woman. It has now been reclaimed and enriched by Mary DALY (1978) to mean a self-identified woman 'who defines her Self, by choice, neither in relation to children nor to men' and who, in an elaboration on the potential meanings of the verb to spin, 'participates in the whirling movement of creation'.

spiritual feminism
Feminist spirituality, sometimes called WOMANSPIRIT, emerged spontaneously on a grass-roots level during the 1970s. Dissatisfied with or alienated by patriarchal religions yet still feeling the need for a spiritual dimension to their lives, more and more sought alternatives. Some found it in the rebirth of GODDESS worship, others became WITCHES, while many more used art or some form of divination or personally devised ritual to develop previously suppressed aspects of themselves. The first women's spirituality conference was held in Boston in 1976, attended by over 1,500 women, and by now, as well as being one aspect of modern feminism, spirituality can be recognized as a movement of its own.

While some feminists welcome the development of spiritual feminism, others consider it a threat to women's liberation, calling it escapist, a waste of women's energy, and even, by diverting attention from the practical, material struggle, ultimately suicidal. As the OFF OUR BACKS collective declared in 1977: 'Religions, even women-identified ones, have misled the oppressed rather than encouraging them to struggle against their situation'. This attitude, by opposing the spiritual to the political, accepts the dualistic view of the world which spiritual feminists claim is one of the major traps of PATRIARCHY. Feminist spirituality, according to its adherents, seeks to integrate the political and the personal by recognizing that there is a spiritual dimension to every aspect of life. Feminist spirituality does not seek to replace male gods and churches with female ones, but to develop a new feminist vision.

An argument for spiritual feminism which has been made by author Charlene Spretnak (1982) is that people have a deep-seated, psychological need for religious symbols and rituals in their lives, and that this is not under rational control. It is not enough to reject the patriarchal religious systems which oppress women – they must be replaced by something else which will satisfy the deep, psychic need. Without a feminist spirituality, women will continue to revert, in times of need, to the familiar structures of patriarchal religion. Since these structures underlie, and validate, male-dominated society, any purely political movement against patriarchy will leave the roots untouched and thus fail. But if women develop their own, feminist spirituality, they will be able to believe in the legitimacy of female power and will be able to provide a genuine, revolutionary alternative.

(*See also* DALY, MARY; RELIGION)

Stanton, Elizabeth Cady,
1815–1902

American. Founder, philosopher and leader of the first women's movement in America. Her interest in women's rights began as a child in her father's law office, where she saw at first hand how women were denied their rights and property by unjust laws. Marriage to a fellow abolitionist, Henry Stanton, led to a honeymoon at the London Anti-Slavery Convention in 1840. There she met Lucretia MOTT, and their shared experience of being denied seats because of their sex made them plan the first women's rights convention, which they finally organized in 1848, in SENECA FALLS,

New York.

In 1851, when she met Susan B. ANTHONY, a fifty-year friendship and productive political collaboration were born. Together, with Anthony the chief strategist and public speaker and Stanton the philosopher and writer, they shaped the women's movement.

She was the founder and first President of the NATIONAL WOMAN SUFFRAGE ASSOCIATION in 1869, and travelled widely, lecturing on women's rights, childcare, education and family life. From 1881–6 she wrote and compiled the HISTORY OF WOMAN SUFFRAGE with Susan B. Anthony and Matilda Joslyn GAGE.

Her outspoken views on divorce and religion had always made her a radical and, in the late 1880s, she was at odds with the now respectable suffrage movement as she devoted most of her energy to goals more far-reaching than just winning the vote. Her chief target was organized religion, which she saw as being responsible for the origins and justification of women's oppression. With a group of other women scholars, she wrote a feminist analysis and critique of the bible, published in two parts as THE WOMAN'S BIBLE (1895, 1898).

Her last appearance at a national convention was in January 1892, at the National American Woman Suffrage Association convention in Washington, D.C., where she delivered what many considered her greatest speech, 'The Solitude of Self'. This expressed her personal credo; that a woman was first and foremost an individual and not to be denied any of the rights of choice and development which men expected to have as individuals, and not to be judged solely in regard to her duties as a mother or wife any more than a man was as a father or husband.

Her daughter, Harriot Stanton BLATCH, also played an important role in the women's rights movement.

Stasova, Nadezhda, 1822–95

Russian. With Mariya TRUBNIKOVA and Anna FILOSOFOVA she formed the 'Triumvirate' generally credited with being the beginning of Russian feminism. Their work was primarily philanthropic and did not challenge the political system, being concerned with improving the lot of women through establishing cooperatives to provide good, cheap lodgings and more work for unmarried women. In 1868 she became involved with Evgenia KONRADI's campaign for higher education, and throughout her life she had a particular interest in helping women students.

Stein, Gertrude, 1874–1946

American writer. She is remembered as much today for her openly lesbian life style as for her often deliberately obscure experimental writings. Nearly all her writing, whether prose, verse or drama, was about women, much of it about her life with Alice Toklas. She wrote some of the first overtly feminist operas and dramas, including *Mother of Us All* (1946) about Susan B. ANTHONY.

Steinem, Gloria, 1934–

American journalist. She emerged as one of the leading lights of the women's liberation movement in the late 1960s, and is still one of the most widely recognized, and respected, liberal feminists in America. Co-founder of the WOMEN'S ACTION ALLIANCE in 1970 and of the National Women's Political Caucus in 1971, she is best known as one of the founding editors of MS. Magazine, and for her articles on such subjects as politics, the EQUAL RIGHTS AMENDMENT, women and work, networking, and her interviews with people as different as Patricia Nixon and Linda Lovelace. One of her first major stories was 'I Was a Playboy Bunny' (1963), and in addition to serious campaigning pieces and personal essays she has also explored social and sexual injustice in lighter pieces such as 'If Men Could Menstruate' (1978). In 1983 a collection of her best-known articles was published as *Outrageous Acts and Everyday Rebellions*.

stereotypes

See SEX-ROLES

Stevens, May, 1924–

American artist. Her work combines a highly personal response to her family and working-class background with an overtly political message, a good example of the modern feminist insight that 'the personal is political'. A portrait of her father evolved into the anti-imperialist, anti-patriarchal 'Big Daddy' series in the late 1960s. 'Mysteries and Politics', a 1978 painting, was inspired by reading *Of Woman Born* by Adrienne RICH. A founding editor of the feminist arts journal HERESIES, she also writes poems, many of them about her mother 'whose aborted life is for me the clearest argument for the liberation of women' (1977).

Stöcker, Helene, 1869–1943

German. One of the founders of the Deutscher Verband für Frauenstimmrecht (German Union for Women's Suffrage), she became involved in the fight for better education, women's suffrage, and the social purity campaign against PROSTITUTION from the late 1890s. Unlike most other feminists in the social purity movement, she argued not that men should develop self-restraint to match that of women, but instead that women should be allowed to express their own SEXUALITY more freely. She also believed that, married or not, women needed useful work and public recognition just as much as men did. But it was her call for

legalized ABORTION which led to the major split between Stöcker and her followers, and the majority of German feminists. In 1904 she established the Bund für Mutterschutz und Sexualreform (League for the Protection of Motherhood and Sexual Reform), which became notorious for its belief in free love. It collapsed, amid much scandal, by 1914, but after World War I (during which Stöcker's PACIFISM drove her even further from the conservative women's movement) she revived it.

Stone, Lucy, 1818–93

American. The first abolitionist to lecture solely on women's rights, she was active and influential in both the Anti-Slavery Society and the new women's rights movement, travelling around the country to lecture on either or both subjects in the 1840s and 1850s. Although she had said she would never marry, objecting to the laws which made a married woman her husband's possession, in 1855 she finally accepted Henry BLACKWELL's promise to renounce all his unfair male privileges, and agreed to marry him on a basis of absolute equality.

The most obvious symbol of their equal partnership, and what she is best remembered for, was the fact that Lucy Stone did not change her name on her marriage. That a woman should keep her own identity, and name, was her firmest conviction, and she never wavered. In 1879, women in Massachusetts were permitted to vote in school elections, and although she had fought hard for this right, she chose not to vote rather than register under her husband's name as the law required.

In 1866, she became a member of the American Equal Rights Association and the AMERICAN WOMAN'S SUFFRAGE ASSOCIATION. With her husband she financed and edited the *Woman's Journal*, and organized the Massachusetts' Woman's Suffrage Association. After her death, both her husband and their daughter, Alice Stone BLACKWELL, continued to work for the women's suffrage movement.

Stopes, Marie, 1880–1958
English. After an unsatisfactory marriage (annulled in 1916 on the grounds of non-consummation) she began her lifelong campaign for BIRTH CONTROL and sex education, both of which she recognized as necessary for women's sexual fulfilment. Her books, including *Married Love* (1918), *Wise Parenthood* (1918), *Radiant Motherhood* (1920) and *Enduring Passion* (1928), were all bestsellers and she had a grateful public, despite being denounced by the British medical establishment for the 'monstrous crime' of spreading information about contraception.

Story of an African Farm, The
Novel by Olive SCHREINER, first published in 1883 under the pseudonym 'Ralph Iron'; a powerfully felt, partially autobiographical, symbolic tale concerning the dreams and thwarted ambitions of three white children growing up on an isolated South African farm: Waldo, who searches for meaning and finds his only pleasure in nature; Em, the stoic, subdued female who accepts her oppression; and LYNDALL, beautiful and brilliant, who seeks fulfilment in both love and work, refuses to shackle herself in the bonds of marriage, and dies after bearing an illegitimate child. Along with Ibsen's *A Doll's House*, it was a major artistic force for awakening women to feminist ideas. An immediate success when first printed, it continues to speak to women today. Despite its flaws (Lyndall shines like a beacon throughout the book, yet we are shown no relation between her moving monologues on the bitterness of women's lot and the reality of her life) it is a unique and timeless classic.

Stowe, Emily (Jennings),
    1831–1903
Canadian. The first woman authorized to practise medicine in Canada, she was also a leading SUFFRAGIST and organized the Dominion Woman Suffrage Association in 1893.

Strachey, Ray (Costelloe),
  1887–1940
English. Best known today as the author of THE CAUSE (1928), that classic history of the women's movement in Britain, she also wrote biographies of Frances WILLARD and Millicent Garrett FAWCETT. Coming from a family with a strong, feminist tradition, it is not surprising that she not only wrote about but also worked for women's interests throughout her life. She served as Parliamentary Secretary for the NATIONAL UNION OF WOMEN'S SUFFRAGE SOCIETIES, and, was an editor of the *Woman's Leader*. After World War I, she was particularly active in regard to women's employment, serving on many committees including one for the legal profession, the civil service, and the Society of Women Welders, and as Secretary of the Women's Employment Federation. She was one of the first sixteen women to stand for Parliament, as an Independent, when it became legal in 1918 (she stood again in 1922 and 1923), and when Nancy Astor was elected in 1919, she offered to work, unpaid, as her secretary.

Stritt, Marie, 1856–1928
German. In 1891 she became involved in the movement for better education for women, and by 1895 was leading the group called Reform. In 1899 she became president of the Federation of German Women's Associations (Bund

Deutscher Frauenvereine), and under her leadership that previously conservative group began to endorse more radical policies. But her increasing involvement with Helene STÖCKER's Bund für Mutterschutz und Sexualreform (League for the Protection of Motherhood and Sexual Reform) and campaigns for a 'new morality' which would include the legalization of abortion and free love, led to her being ousted from leadership of the Federation, to be replaced by the conservative Gertrud Baumer.

Subjection of Women, The
Classic of liberal feminism, first published in 1869, written by John Stuart MILL with the assistance of his stepdaughter, Helen Taylor, expressing ideas developed after years of discussion with Harriet TAYLOR. It is an eloquent, controlled argument for equal rights and opportunities for women, presenting the case that not only is the legal subordination of one sex to the other wrong in itself, like any other form of slavery, but that the oppression of women is a hindrance to the advancement and happiness of the human race as a whole. Without denying the existence of sexual differences, Mill declared that it was impossible to know what these differences might be, since what is regarded as 'woman's nature' is a totally artificial creation imposed by her subordinate relationship to man. Arguing that if

women were naturally incapable of performing certain tasks, laws to prevent them from doing so would be unnecessary, Mill believed that once all legal disabilities were removed, individual women and men would be able to follow their inclinations and discover the roles that best suited them.

Appearing in translation in France, Germany, Austria, Sweden and Denmark in the same year as it was published in Britain, America, Australia and New Zealand, the book made a tremendous impact on educated women all over the world and provided the major sustained argument for the women's suffrage movement. It is still readable today, for although LIBERAL FEMINISM has changed and the limits of Mill's masculine orientation are more obvious, his essay remains a clear statement of the pure liberal stance on women's rights.

suffrage movement
See WOMEN'S SUFFRAGE MOVEMENT

suffragette
Term used in Britain for a woman member of a militant suffrage society (chiefly the WOMEN'S SOCIAL AND POLITICAL UNION) before 1918. It was first used in the *Daily Mail*, 10 January 1906, and was widespread by March of that year, as a means of differentiating the militant campaigners from other SUFFRA-GISTS. The members of the WSPU themselves embraced the name,

using it as the title of their newspaper. In America the term was seldom used, except derogatorily.

Suffragette Fellowship
British organization founded in 1931 to perpetuate the memory of the pioneers of women's emancipation, particularly those connected with the militant suffrage campaign from 1905–14. Dedicated to the aim of improving women's political, civic, economic, educational and social status on the basis of equality between the sexes, it publishes a yearly newsletter and cooperates with other organizations sharing its aim.

suffragist (from *suffrage*, the right to vote)
Term for one who advocates the extension of the right to vote, usually to women, and, by implication, an advocate of women's rights. When used by contrast with SUFFRA-GETTE, it meant one who advocated the vote be obtained by legal means only.

Swanwick, Helena M.,
    1864–1939
British journalist. An ardent suffragist, she worked with the constitutionalists rather than the militants. The level of her involvement can be seen in the fact that in 1908, in addition to her organizing activities in Manchester and London, she spoke at more than 150 public

gatherings in England and Scotland, often to hostile crowds. She was the founding editor of THE COMMON CAUSE, a position she held from 1909–12. With the advent of World War I, her activities for peace became foremost, and she presided over the British branch of the Women's International League for Peace and Freedom. Her books include *The Future of the Women's Movement'* (1913), *Women in the Socialist State* (1921), *Builders of Peace* (1924) and her autobiography, *I Have Been Young* (1935).

Sweet Freedom

History of the Women's Liberation Movement in Britain, written by Anna COOTE and Beatrix CAMPBELL, and published in 1982.

T

Takamure, Itsue, 1894–1964
Japanese writer and historian. An established poet and writer, at the age of thirty-seven she withdrew from the public world to devote the rest of her life to the study of women's history. She uncovered proof that matrilineal (possibly matriarchal) society had preceded PATRIARCHY, and wrote the first substantial, consistent history of Japanese women, published in 1966 in four volumes.

Takayama, Shigeri, 1899–1977
Japanese journalist. Active in the movement for women's rights in Imperial Japan, she was one of the founders of the League for Defence of Women's Rights, which campaigned for women's involvement in government. In the 1950s she headed Chifuren, a women's civil rights organization. A member of the Upper House of the Japanese parliament, 1965–71.

'Take Back the Night'
American slogan originating in the late 1970s as a rallying cry for women to unite against PORNOGRA-PHY and other forms of male violence against women. It was used as the theme for a night-time protest march in San Francisco, organized by Women Against Violence in Pornography and Media in November 1978, in which over 5,000 women took part, and subsequently as the title for other, similar demonstrations in other cities.

Take Back the Night
An important work, subtitled *Women on Pornography*, which presents through a collection of essays, articles, interviews and reports, an in-depth, coherent feminist philosophy of PORNOGRAPHY as it relates to sexism, male violence and female oppression. Contributors include Alice WALKER, Adrienne RICH, Gloria STEINEM, Susan BROWNMILLER, Robin MORGAN, Kathleen Barry, Ann Jones, Andrea DWORKIN and Audre LORDE. It was edited by Laura Lederer and first published in America in 1980.

Taylor, Harriet (Harriet Mill), 1808–58
English. Her career as a feminist theorist is so closely bound up with that of John Stuart MILL as to be obscured by his, although he always declared that his masterpiece, THE SUBJECTION OF WOMEN, although written after her death, had developed out of his discussions with her and from her own profound understanding of women's situation.

She met Mill in 1830 and a close intellectual and emotional partnership began, although she was already a wife and mother and continued to live with her husband. She married Mill in 1851, two years after her husband's death.

The only published work positively identified as hers is 'Enfranchisement of Women', an article published anonymously in *The Westminster Review* in 1851. Mill, however, always acknowledged the extent of her contribution to the work which was published under his name alone, and claimed that most of his writings after 1840, particularly *On Liberty*, were 'joint productions'.

Terrell, Mary Church, 1863–1954
American social reformer, community leader and suffragist. During the 1890s she became a public speaker, chiefly on issues concerned with women's rights. She was also involved in campaigns against lynching and discriminatory laws, and the celebration of black history and achievements. She addressed the 1898 convention of the NATIONAL AMERICAN WOMAN SUFFRAGE ASSOCIATION on 'The Progress of Coloured Women', and spoke on the same subject, in German and French, as a representative at the INTERNATIONAL COUNCIL OF WOMEN in Germany in 1904. In 1896, she became President of the National Association of Colored Women

and, after serving three terms, was voted honorary president for life. She was a charter member of the National Association for the Advancement of Colored People, picketed the White House with the NATIONAL WOMAN'S PARTY for suffrage, and addressed the second congress of the Women's International League for Peace and Freedom in Zurich, 1919. Her autobiography, *A Colored Woman in a White World*, was published in 1940. She remained politically active until the end of her life: at the age of eighty-five she broke the colour bar in the American Association of University Women, and at eighty-nine was leading picket lines in a campaign to desegregate restaurants in Washington, D.C.

Terry, Megan, 1932–
American playwright. She has been called 'the mother of American feminist drama', with her play *Calm Down Mother* (1965) considered the first truly feminist American drama. Her plays for the most part do not analyse society in political terms, but seek to reveal the lives of women and to find strength and the possibility for change within everyday life. She has said herself that feminist drama is 'anything that gives women confidence, shows themselves to themselves, helps them to begin to analyse whether it's a positive or negative image'. *Viet Rock* (1966), an anti-war as well as anti-sexist play, was

the work which brought her public attention. In 1972 she joined with other women playwrights to form the Women's Theatre Council. In 1974 she left New York for Omaha to become the resident playwright of the Omaha Magic Theatre, which had as one of its major aims the crashing of barriers against women in THEATRE. Her plays include *Approaching Simone* (1970) about the life of Simone Weil; *Babes in the Bighouse* (1974), a musical fantasy set in a women's prison which had both male and female actors playing women; and *American King's English for Queens* (1978) which explores sexism in language.

thealogy

From Greek *thea* (goddess) + logy (study of). Suggested by Naomi Goldenberg as a more appropriate term than theology (derived from *theos*, the Greek term for a masculine god) for the study of feminist spirituality, GODDESS-centred religions, or WITCHCRAFT.

theatre

Since its known beginnings, the theatre has been male-centred and male-dominated. Even when allowed to take an active role, women have been presented as characters chiefly in relation to men in plays written from a masculine viewpoint. An alternative to this did not emerge until the early 1970s when the radical theatre trends of the 1960s met the women's libera-

tion movement. In addition to the playwrights who found the existence of the women's liberation movement gave them the courage and incentive to write from their own experience, new theatre groups were formed. Between 1969–84 more than 100 feminist theatre groups came into existence in the United States, the first one being the NEW FEMINIST THEATRE in New York. In Britain feminist theatre groups, some women-only and some mixed, grew out of the tradition of political theatre. The longest lasting of the women-only groups is the WOMEN'S THEATRE GROUP.

Feminists in the theatre, like feminists in all the media, are fighting a battle on two fronts. One is to raise women's participation to a full 50 per cent of the work force; the other is to develop a specifically feminist theatre, to change not only theatrical conventions but society itself by bringing a feminist consciousness to bear on both the content and the form of drama.

Feminist theatre is not simply the female side of traditional, male-dominated theatre – but there is no widely held agreement about what precisely it is or should be. Some feminist playwrights, including Megan TERRY and Myrna Lamb, are against any too-explicit formulation of feminist theatre, believing this would create implicit restrictions which could be harmful to the development of a genuinely new art form. Yet some attempts at definition have been offered.

Michelene WANDOR has said that because of the usual male-dominated imbalance, 'almost any play that takes a woman's point of view has a feminist element in it. So any play which has its focus in women's experience or the concerns of sexual politics is feminist'.

Similarly, Megan Terry suggests that any play which is useful in revealing women to themselves is feminist.

Helen Keyssar has proposed that feminist theatre contains the power of transforming *all* theatre, and sees the essence of feminist drama as lying in the idea of transformation – as opposed to traditional drama, which she considers to centre on the moment when the fixed, unchanging truth about the self is discovered.

Janet Brown has provided a definition based on the critical theory of Kenneth Burke: 'a feminist drama is one in which the agent is a woman, her purpose autonomy, and her scene a society in which women are powerless'.

On the other hand, playwright Martha Boesing has suggested that 'True feminist theatre perhaps cannot be created in this society. The theatre of this new society, a matriarchy which embraces both men and women, will be a collective theatre which performs ritualistic and participatory events that would indeed change people's lives.'

Ritual is an element which often occurs in feminist theatre, as do collective organization, collective playwriting, focus on women's experience, and a pro-woman stance even when negative images of women are being presented. Feminist theatre may be defined as didactic because it supports a cause, but that didacticism may be overt, or it may be so subtle as to be unnoticeable.

Although feminist theatre groups first nurtured feminist drama and made it possible, they are no longer the only source of it. There is now a recognizable audience for plays by and about women, although plays which present the simplest, least threatening aspects of feminism are the ones most likely to become widely successful.

Some of the most popular and best-known contemporary plays which can be considered feminist include: *Birth and After Birth* by Tina Howe, *Mourning Pictures* by Honor MOORE, *But What Have You Done for Me Lately?* and *The Mod Donna* by Myrna Lamb, *Trafford Tanzi* by Claire Luckham, *Rites* by Maureen Duffy, *Calm Down Mother* and *Comings and Goings* by Megan TERRY, *For colored girls who have considered suicide when the rainbow is enuf* by Ntozake SHANGE, *Cloud Nine*, *Top Girls* and *Fen* by Caryl CHURCHILL, *Uncommon Women and Others* by Wendy Wasserstein, *Steaming* by Nell Dunn, *Skirmishes* by Catherine Hayes, *'night, Mother* by Marsha Norman and *Crimes of the Heart* by Beth Henley.

Theodora, 497–548

Byzantine Empress. Ruled, with her husband the Emperor Justinian, from 527. Her brilliance, skill and authority were widely recognized, and she was unique among rulers of her era in her attention to women's rights. She altered divorce laws, gave daughters the right to inherit and wives the right to their own property. In 535 she passed an edict which forced brothel keepers out of the cities and made the procurement of prostitutes a crime. She also personally purchased the freedom of many young women who had been sold into prostitution.

Theodoropoulou, Avra, 1880–1963

Greek musician. She had a life-long commitment to the idea that women and men should be equal. In 1911 she founded a School for Working Women, and in 1920 she founded the League for Women's Rights, serving as its president for thirty-seven years.

therapy

During the SECOND WAVE OF FEMINISM, psychotherapy came to be seen as one of the oppressive tools of PATRIARCHY: a way of forcing women to fit into the conventional feminine role and reinforce social attitudes as the only ones possible.

Then, based on the insights of consciousness-raising groups, in the early 1970s an alternative, feminist therapy began to be developed. Rather than seeking personal solutions for personal problems, feminist therapists encourage clients to recognize that many of their problems are common to all women and are not the result of any personal disability. Once they feel stronger within themselves, women may decide to take action to work for political and social changes. The relationship between therapist and client is based on the idea of equals meeting to work through problems together, and much feminist therapy is group-based, often in leaderless, self-help groups adapting various techniques to their specific needs. The goal of feminist therapy is not adjustment, but change. It is not considered an end in itself, or a substitute for political action, but as a tool to help reach beneath conditioning and to understand ourselves better.

Thinking About Women

Book by Mary ELLMANN, first published in America in 1968. An early, major contribution to the development of a feminist theory of LITERARY CRITICISM. With wit and elegance the book reveals and demolishes the structure of PHALLIC CRITICISM, shows up the absurdity and self-contradiction in sexual analogies and female stereotypes, and raises questions about tone, style and authority which have since been explored by other writers.

Thomas, M. Carey, 1857–1935
American educator. At a time when women were not allowed to pursue advanced studies in America, she went to Leipzig to study philology. Denied a degree for her work there, she was granted a doctorate with distinction in Zurich in 1882, becoming one of the first American women with a Ph.D. At the age of twenty-six, she became Dean of the newly-opened Bryn Mawr College for Women. Although she distrusted male educators, and particularly masculine attitudes towards women, she based Bryn Mawr's new, academically demanding curriculum on that of the best men's colleges, realizing that, in a male-dominated world, women educated to any other standard would be at a disadvantage. She was made President of Bryn Mawr in 1894 and remained so until her death. She instituted the first university school of social work in 1915, ran summer school programmes for working women, helped more women enter professions, and was active in both the women's suffrage and peace movements.

Thompson, Dorothy, 1893–1961
American journalist. She became involved in the women's suffrage movement while a student at Syracuse University and, after graduat-ing in 1914, worked as a publicist for the New York State Woman Suffrage Association. She was also active in the upstate area as a lecturer. After the vote was won she went to Europe where she became a foreign correspondent, with a particular interest in politics, for American newspapers. From the 1930s to the 1950s, she was widely read and frequently controversial on many topics as a syndicated columnist.

Thompson, William, 1775–1833
Irish. A forerunner of Karl Marx, he was, with Robert Owen, one of the leaders of the Cooperative Movement in Britain. His major contribution to feminism was the book APPEAL OF ONE-HALF THE HUMAN RACE, WOMEN, AGAINST THE PRETENSIONS OF THE OTHER HALF, MEN, TO RETAIN THEM IN POLITICAL AND THENCE IN CIVIL AND DOMESTIC SLAVERY (1825) which he wrote in association with Anna WHEELER.

300 Group, The
British organization founded in 1980 with the intention of encouraging women of all races and democratic political beliefs to stand for Parliament, the European Parliament, and local councils, and to provide them with training and advice from experienced women and men in politics.

Three Marias, the
Maria Isabel Barreno, Maria Fátima Velho da Costa, and Maria Teresa

Horta, Portuguese authors of *New Portuguese Letters*, first published in 1972. The book grew out of their decision to meet and talk – and write about – their shared problems as women and writers. Using the seventeenth-century classic *Letters of a Portuguese Nun* as a starting point, they wrote many variations on the themes of love, sexuality, spirituality, motherhood, and relationships of all kinds between women and women and men. As soon as it was published their book was banned, and the 'Three Marias' arrested on charges of outraging public decency. Their cause was taken up by the women's liberation movement worldwide, and their trial finally ended in April 1974 with all charges dropped and the book declared a work of literary merit.

three-sex theory
Term used by Betty FRIEDAN for the barely conscious rationalization which allows many women to share prejudices against women without feeling personally affected: the idea there are men, there are women, and 'there's me'.

Through the Flower
Subtitled *My Struggle as a Woman Artist*, this autobiography of Judy CHICAGO was first published in America in 1975 and immediately recognized as a classic of feminist literature. Besides being an inspiring story of the development of a feminist artist, the book presents a coherent theory of the importance of female imagery in art, and suggests the potential women artists have, through self-awareness, for transforming our whole culture.

Time and Tide
English magazine founded in 1920 as a political feminist weekly written by and for women. Most of those involved with it had been active in the women's suffrage movement. The original board of directors was composed of Mrs Chalmers Watson, Viscountess RHONDDA, Helen Archdale, Helen Gwynne-Vaughan, Mrs H. B. Irving, Christine Maguire and Elizabeth ROBINS. Among the many who wrote for it were Rebecca WEST, Vera BRITTAIN, Winifred HOLTBY, Cicely HAMILTON, Crystal EASTMAN, Rose Macaulay and Virginia WOOLF. The staunchly feminist stance faded in subsequent decades, and the magazine became more of an arts and literary review, finally vanishing in 1963. A very different magazine, with no feminist affiliations, was launched under the same title in 1984.

Tiptree, James, Jr (pseudonym of Alice SHELDON), 1915–
American psychiatrist who has used a pseudonym for her science fiction stories since 1967. Despite the strongly feminist stance of some of the Tiptree stories (in particular 'The Women Men Don't See' and 'Houston, Houston, Do You

Read?' the author was usually presumed to be male – one writer went so far as to claim there was something 'ineluctibly masculine' in the Tiptree writing style – until Alice Sheldon revealed her identity in 1977. Some of her stories were also published under the name Racoona Sheldon. Her short stories have been collected as *Ten Thousand Light Years From Home* (1973), *Warm Worlds and Otherwise* (1975), *Star Songs of an old Primate* (1978) and *Out of the Everywhere and Other Extraordinary Visions* (1981).

tokenism

Practice of minimum effort by the dominant group (men) in response to pressure to share their power and privileges, meant to give the impression, without substantially changing the status quo, that the formerly excluded group (women) have now been allowed into their territory on equal terms. As a symbolic gesture, this can do more harm to women than straightforward exclusion. The presence of a few women in a male preserve – whether a university, a coal mine, or a board of directors – implies that institution offers equal rights and opportunities, and allows it to get away with perpetuating SEXISM in working and hiring practices. The token woman becomes a weapon to be used by the male establishment, the implication being that the system is open to women, and need not be changed; anyone who com-

plains is revealing her own inferiority. The token woman herself, holding out the illusory prospect of hope for other women, and at the same time filling the only available niche, is isolated both from other women and the men around her; she faces the dangerous choice between being the 'token feminist', and risking her job, or becoming 'one of the boys' and helping perpetuate the system.

transsexualism

Term first used in 1953 and widely accepted by the mid-1960s to refer to the psychological syndrome characterized by an individual's denial of his (or her) biological sex and attempts to change his (or her) body in accordance with the felt gender identity. This is not considered to be a psychosis, but a problem which can be dealt with by surgery and hormone treatments. Transsexualism has also been called 'gender dysphoria'. Most transsexuals (who are born male rather than female by a ratio of about four to one) would describe their problem in terms similar to 'a female mind trapped in a male body'.

Because it detaches GENDER from biology (any man might 'really' be a woman, despite lack of any obvious signs) yet reinforces the importance of sexual stereotypes (certain physical attributes, abilities, behaviours and attitudes are assumed to be so indisputably male or female that they cannot be harboured in a body of the 'wrong' sex), the concept of transsexualism is a contradiction which raises and disturbs many of the questions feminists have been asking about differences between the sexes and what they mean. It is a subject which makes most feminists uneasy.

Gloria STEINEM probably expressed the liberal feminist viewpoint best, writing in MS Magazine in 1977: 'Feminists are right to feel uncomfortable about the need for and the uses of transsexualism. Even while we protect the right of an informed individual to make that decision, and to be identified as he or she wishes, we have to make clear that this is not the goal we have in mind. . . . Better to turn anger outward toward changing the world than inward toward transforming and mutilating bodies.'

Janice Raymond, in the first definitive feminist analysis of the subject, *The Transsexual Empire* (1979), said that transsexualism is not the human problem it is usually presented as being, but a male problem only, female-to-male transsexuals being tokens which disguise the true nature of transsexualism. She believes that PATRIARCHY, by creating SEX-ROLES, is the first cause of transsexualism, which is an ideology serving to reinforce the image of women created by men.

Controversy has been raised in feminist communities by transsexuals (male-to-female) identifying

themselves as lesbian-feminists. Janice Raymond and Mary DALY are among those who have argued that transsexually constructed lesbian-feminists should not be accepted as women because they are really still men who have found this way of invading women's space and appropriating women's energy. A man may wish all his life to be a woman, act like a woman, have his body surgically altered and even believe he is a woman, but, argued Raymond, this does not give him the personal history of living as a woman under patriarchy and he can never share the same experiences as those born female. Other feminists have objected to this argument as elitist, and point out that women, particularly lesbians, have always suffered from not being allowed to define themselves, from having boundaries drawn and definitions of womanhood imposed on them by others.

trashing

A type of politically motivated malicious gossip which Jo FREEMAN has defined as 'a particularly vicious form of character assassination'. It is used as punishment within the women's movement for feminists who are perceived as being overly concerned with individual achievement, and often has the result of causing women who have been picked out by the media as feminist leaders to cut all ties with the movement, disenchanted with the reality of sisterhood although their ideals remain unchanged.

Tristan, Flora, 1803–44
French socialist. Inspired by FOURIER and Robert Owen, Flora Tristan spent much of her brief, adventurous life analysing social conditions in England and France, writing about them, and personally spreading her ideas of reform among the working classes. Although Marx later dismissed her writings as bourgeois and utopian, many responded to the vision of *L'Union ouvrière* (1843) and her call for an international cooperative movement of workers for a peaceful revolution. Like Mary Wollstonecraft before her, Tristan believed that men and women possessed the same potential for development, and should be given equal opportunities. She emphasized the importance of education for working-class women in particular. Being very much of her time, however, she believed that women could redeem and elevate men through their superior moral power, and expressed this idea in her only novel, *Méphis* (1838).

Trivia
American magazine founded in 1982 and published three times a year. The title is from 'Trivium' (crossroads), one of the names given to the Triple Goddess, and acknowledges that women's ideas and achievements have customarily been trivialized in patriarchal history as it seeks to redress the balance by publishing feminist essays, theory, reviews, scholarship and translations.

Trouble and Strife
British radical feminist magazine founded in 1983 and published three times yearly by a collective. The title, cockney slang for 'wife', was chosen 'because it acknowledges the reality of conflict in relations between women and men'.

Trubnikova, Mariya, 1835–97
Russian. She hosted a salon in St Petersburg from 1855 and met and corresponded with feminists in other countries including Josephine BUTLER, Jenny D'HERICOURT and Marie GOEGG. Their examples inspired her to form the 'Triumvirate' of early Russian feminism with her friends Nadezhda STASOVA and Anna FILOSOFOVA, to try to improve the lot of women in Russia. Their work was primarily philanthropic rather than political, and although successful, affected a relatively small number of women. In 1859 they set up a Society for Cheap Lodging to help unmarried women, and in 1863 they established a Women's Publishing Cooperative to provide educated women with interesting work. She also joined Evgenia KONRADI in petitioning for the creation of a women's university. Illness and financial problems caused her to

withdraw from the Russian women's movement after 1881.

Truth, Sojourner, 1777–1883
American. Born a slave, she escaped and won her freedom in 1827. After some time in New York City, she became an inspired travelling preacher, speaking at revival meetings throughout the Eastern states. She became involved in the ABOLITION MOVEMENT, and subsequently in the women's suffrage movement where she was notable not only as one of the few black women active in a predominantly white, middle-class campaign, but also for the power of her speeches. The one most often quoted was given in 1851 at the women's rights convention in Akron, Ohio. As the other women were being shouted down by male hecklers, Sojourner Truth took the floor and said in response to the jibes about women's weakness: 'The man over there says women need to be helped into carriages and lifted over ditches, and to have the best place everywhere. Nobody ever helps me into carriages or over puddles, or gives me the best place – and AIN'T I A WOMAN? Look at my arm! I have ploughed and planted and gathered into barns, and no man could head me – and ain't I a woman? I could work as much and eat as much as a man – when I could get it – and bear the lash as well! And ain't I a woman? I have born thirteen children, and seen most of 'em sold into slavery, and when I cried out with my mother's grief, none but Jesus heard me – and ain't I a woman?'

U

Una, The
One of the first periodicals in America to be devoted to women's issues, it was published monthly from 1853–6 by Paulina Wright DAVIS, and provided a forum for discussing such topics as equal rights, equal pay, marriage and dress reform, as well as circulating reports of the women's conventions.

unisex
Term coined by Kate MILLETT in 'Sexual Politics: A Manifesto for Revolution', written in the winter of 1968 in connection with the organization of the first women's group at Columbia University (New York). It refers to an androgynous ideal which would be brought about by a sexual revolution. She defined unisex as: 'the end of separatist character-structure, temperament and behaviour, so that each individual may develop an entire – rather than a partial, limited and conformist – personality.'

The word caught on quickly with the media as a tag for fashions, clothes and hair-styles shared by both sexes. As it gained this connotation of superficiality, it ceased to be used by feminists to describe a world without SEX-ROLES. (*See also* ANDROGYNY)

universalism
The development of feminism required a recognition of femaleness as a universal which all women shared, the acceptance of the idea that GENDER was an important category in the structure of all human societies, so that whatever their differences, women shared a common oppression simply because they were women. This becomes a false universalism, however, when feminists assume that what women share as women is so fundamental that it makes all class, economic, cultural and racial differences in experience unimportant.

utopia
The word utopia was coined by Sir Thomas More in 1516, derived from the Greek 'no-place' (*ou+topos*), and it has come to be used as the generic term for an ideal, imaginary society.

Women's utopias are very different from men's. Most men, whatever else they want to change, seem happy to perpetuate SEXISM and ignore the needs of women in their dreams. Not surprisingly, although there are no men-only utopias, many women have imagined ideal worlds without men.

Feminist utopias offer alternatives to and criticisms of contemporary values and conditions, usually pinning the blame for social ills squarely on men or male institutions. In some utopias, like Marge PIERCY'S MATTAPOISETT, men and women live together in egalitarian harmony, having given up GENDER roles and privileges; but despite attempts by both male and female SCIENCE FICTION writers to imagine non-sexist futures, more feminist utopias are inhabited by women only, men left out either because they are too dangerous, or because imagining the truly non-sexist male is too difficult a task.

Most modern feminist utopias have certain elements in common. They are usually depicted as small, communal, even tribal societies in a rural setting. Government is minimal, if it exists at all; the use of force and hierarchical structures have vanished. Technology is usually distrusted, and there is a strong concern for ECOLOGY and the natural world. All the women have the freedom to choose their own place in the world and control their own reproductive functions.

Some of the better-known feminist utopian novels include HERLAND by Charlotte Perkins GILMAN (1915), *The Kin of Ata are Waiting for You* by Dorothy Bryant (1971), *The Dispossessed* by Ursula K. LE GUIN (1974), THE FEMALE MAN by Joanna RUSS (1975), *The Shattered Chain* by Marion Zimmer Bradley (1976), WOMAN ON THE EDGE OF TIME by Marge PIERCY (1976), *Motherlines* by Suzy McKee CHARNAS (1978), THE WANDERGROUND by Sally Miller GEARHEART (1979) and *The Demeter Flower* by Rochelle Singer (1980).

V

vaginal orgasm

Myth used to oppress women. Inspired by Sigmund Freud's *Three Essays on the Theory of Sexuality* (1905) and perpetrated by the common male refusal to consider women as independently sexual beings, it presumes that vaginal penetration by a penis is necessary for female ORGASM.

(*See also* 'MYTH OF THE VAGINAL ORGASM')

Vaginal Politics

Book by Ellen FRANKFORT published in 1972. It grew out of a column she wrote for *The Village Voice* in which, from 1968, she reported on the women's HEALTH MOVEMENT. The book was important for exposing the way in which women were kept ignorant and powerless by the American medical establishment, and it was influential in spreading the feminist health movement by alerting women to the possibilities of radical, political change through self-help clinics and consumer pressure groups. Among other subjects, the book discusses the economics of ABORTION, the drug industry, the sex-power syndrome of traditional psychiatry, feminist THERAPY, and the doctor–patient relationship as it really is,

and as feminist consciousness might transform it.

Van Grippenberg, Baroness Alexandra, 1859–1913

Finnish. A leading member of the Finnish Women's Association (Finsk Kvinnoførening), she campaigned not only for women's suffrage, but for equal rights in all areas, including EDUCATION, politics, employment and MARRIAGE. She was also active in the campaign to end state-regulated prostitution. In 1889 she became Vice President of the INTERNATIONAL COUNCIL OF WOMEN. After 1906, when women in Finland won the vote, she actively encouraged women's participation in politics. In 1909 she was elected to the Finnish Diet where she argued against protective legislation on the grounds that women and men should be treated equally. She founded the Finnish National Council of Women in 1912.

Van Hoosen, Bertha, 1863–1952

American surgeon. Founder and first president of the American Medical Women's Association, which was formed in Chicago in 1915 to fight against discrimination against women in medicine. As an inspiring teacher to female medical students, and through her devotion to women's health issues, she did much to advance the position of women in medicine. She helped develop better methods of prenatal care, lectured on sex education from a feminist point of view, pioneered the use of scopolomine-morphine anaesthesia in childbirth (known as twilight sleep, its use was controversial, but championed by a number of American feminists who demanded the right to painless childbirth in 1914) and established the first human breast-milk bank in Chicago in 1930.

Varda, Agnes, 1928–
French film director. Her feminism is expressed through films which focus on women's lives and strong, individual female characters. Among her best-known films are *Cléo de 5 à 7* (1961), *Le bonheur* (1965), *L'une chante, l'autre pas* (*One Sings, the Other Doesn't*, 1977) and *Vagabonde* (1985).

Venturi, Emilie Ashurst,
? 1820–93
English. After the death of her husband in 1866, she became deeply involved in the women's movement. She was one of the leading campaigners against the CONTAGIOUS DISEASES ACTS, and edited the newspaper of that campaign, *The Shield*, from 1871–86. She studied law (although prohibited by her sex from becoming a practising lawyer), and actively supported

higher education for women as well as women's suffrage and other legal campaigns.

Vernon, Mabel, 1883–1975
American. A concern for women's rights and friendship with Alice PAUL drew her into the women's suffrage movement, and from 1913 she worked as a full-time organizer for the CONGRESSIONAL UNION FOR WOMAN SUFFRAGE. She became the first militant SUFFRAGIST in America when she interrupted a speech by President Woodrow Wilson in Washington, D.C., on 4 July 1916, and later that same year was one of the first suffragists to be sent to prison, for picketing the White House. After the vote had been won she continued to work for women's rights, touring the country to lecture on feminism and supporting women candidates for Congress. In 1926 she became executive secretary for the NATIONAL WOMAN'S PARTY and campaigned for passage of the EQUAL RIGHTS AMENDMENT. From 1930, when she joined the WOMEN'S INTERNATIONAL LEAGUE FOR PEACE AND FREEDOM, she devoted the rest of her life to the cause of peace and disarmament.

Victoria Press
First feminist printing press in England, founded in 1860 by the SOCIETY FOR PROMOTING THE EMPLOYMENT OF WOMEN under the direction of Emily FAITHFULL in London.

Vindication of the Rights of Woman, A

Long polemical essay by Mary WOLLSTONECRAFT, first published in England in 1792. A new political philosophy, liberalism, emerged in the eighteenth century, to promote the idea of human rights, yet even the most radical of the male liberals tended to believe that these 'rights' applied to the male of the species only, and that women were 'naturally' weak and in need of protection. Mary Wollstonecraft was one member of this intellectual and political movement who extended the ideas of liberalism to her own sex. In the *Vindication* she argued that women's weakness was due to social conditioning and could be corrected by extending an equality of education to both girls and boys, to be followed by equal rights and opportunities in all spheres. The book was widely read and praised, but equally widely attacked, sometimes in parodies which extended her arguments about women to children or animals. Later, as facts of the author's unconventional life became widely known, her work was shunned, even by avowed feminists, until it was rediscovered in the twentieth century.

violence

The issue of male violence has always been of concern to feminists. Violence, or the threat of violence, is one of the most obvious means by which patriarchal power is expressed and maintained. Feminists have recognized that acts of violence against women include not only the beatings, rapes and murders which are considered personal, but also such institutionalized procedures as involuntary sterilization or forcing women with unwanted pregnancies to bear children. The potential threat of violence, whether from an individual man or an impersonal state, runs throughout our lives to keep women subordinate.

Many of the most important campaigns of the WOMEN'S LIBERATION MOVEMENT have been attempts to make women safe from various forms of male violence. These include direct actions against RAPE and PORNOGRAPHY by WOMEN AGAINST VIOLENCE AGAINST WOMEN and similar groups; the provision of refuges for BATTERED WOMEN; and training women in methods of self-defence. Yet although it is important to ensure that all types of violence against women are recognized as crimes and punished, and that women gain strength both collectively and individually by learning that there are alternatives to being victimized, none of these activities will eliminate violence. Although the use men make of violence is obvious, its origins are not. Feminists have different attitudes towards the meaning of violence and how it can best be controlled or eliminated. A thorough, widely-agreed feminist analysis of violence has yet to be developed.

Some see violence as the extreme form of power relationships, and believe that only when the hierarchy and authority allowing these power relationships are replaced by a free, egalitarian system will there be an end to violence. In this view, PATRIARCHY is both maintained by and creates violence. In a MATRIARCHY – or some other, non-hierarchical, feminist society – there would be no reason for and no reinforcement of violence, and violent acts would be deviant and rare.

Others believe that it is *because* men are violent that this patriarchal system which rewards violence exists. If the aggression which leads to violence is a human rather than masculine trait, displayed less often by women because of social conditioning or lack of opportunity, then presumably men could learn to be more like women. Men could be raised and trained in such a way as to develop the peaceful, nurturing qualities which our culture defines (and devalues) as feminine. But there have been many suggestions that aggression is biologically rather than culturally determined, and that males have a particular capacity for violence which females lack. This is usually located in the so-called male hormone, testosterone. If an abundance of testosterone leads inevitably to violence, then as long as men are men, women's only hope for a free and peaceful life lies in SEPARATISM, or the destruction of men.

THE SCUM MANIFESTO is probably the most famous call for the eradication of men; science fiction writers including Joanna RUSS and James TIPTREE Jr have speculated that women will have to literally fight and win the battle of the sexes if some useful plague doesn't wipe out ninety-nine of every one hundred men; and the idea that rapists should be castrated has a perennial appeal to even the most peace-loving women – yet the use of violence against men, even in self-defence, has seldom been considered as a serious solution by feminists. This may or may not prove that women in fact are inherently less violent than men, or at least prove the strength of our conditioning against appearing aggressive, but it does reveal something important about the nature of feminism. Unlike many other social movements and philosophies, feminism does not presume that its goal is more important than the means used to achieve it. Means and ends are indivisible. Violence is a weapon used by patriarchy, and it is not possible to create a non-violent society through violence, or a non-sexist one by using sexist tactics. Reflecting another meaning of the slogan 'THE PERSONAL IS POLITICAL', feminists attempt to create the conditions for liberation in their own lives even as they are struggling to make it a wider reality.

Virago

The first British feminist PUBLISH-ING imprint, it was established in London in 1975, published nine books in its first eighteen months, and soon found a large and loyal audience. The 'Modern Classics' list, launched in 1978 with the aim of demonstrating the existence of a female tradition in literature, is probably its biggest success. The name 'Virago' was chosen for its earlier meaning of a woman warrior.

Voice of the women's liberation movement

The first national newsletter of the women's liberation movement in America, it was published monthly from March 1968–June 1969. Written and edited by a group of Chicago feminists, it served as a much needed forum and communications link uniting radical women across the country and made 'women's liberation' a widely accepted term. The first issue consisted of three mimeographed pages, largely hand-distributed to 200 women; the last issue had grown to twenty-four offset pages with a print-run of 2,000.

Von Suttner, Bertha, 1843–1914

Austrian writer. Her controversial anti-war novel, *Die Waffen nieder* (1889; translated as *Lay Down Your Arms*) inspired Alfred Nobel to found his Peace Prize, and in 1905 she became the first woman to receive it. An active suffragist and feminist whose novels were often concerned with the position of women, she put most of her energy into the peace movement, and founded the International Peace League.

Von Trotta, Margarethe, 1942–

German film director. Her films explore relationships between women, mixing the psychological and personal with the political as the tensions of sisterhood are examined against the background of contemporary Germany. They include *The Second Awakening of Christa Klages* (1977), about a woman who organizes a bank robbery to finance a crèche, and her odd relationship with a young, female bank teller; and *The German Sisters* (1981), about two sisters, one a feminist journalist, the other a terrorist (based on Gudrun Ensslin of the Baader-Meinhof group).

'Votes for Women and Chastity for Men'

Slogan created by Christabel PANKHURST for the WOMEN'S SOCIAL AND POLITICAL UNION in 1913, reflecting her understanding that the subordination of women – the fact that men saw women as sexual objects divided into 'good' (wives) and 'bad' (prostitutes) – was the root cause of venereal disease.

Votes For Women!

A play, subtitled 'A Tract', by

Elizabeth ROBINS, first produced by the Vedrenne-Granville-Barker management at the Court Theatre in London in April 1907. A witty, comic melodrama based on the on-going movement for women's suffrage, it was popular with theatre-goers both in London and in New York, where in March 1909, it opened at Wallack's. It was the first play written by Robins, already known as an actress, novelist, essayist and campaigner for women's rights, and, knowing that she might be attacked by male critics for the subject matter, she asked and received help from Henry James, H. G. Wells, and William Archer in rewriting every scene. At the same time, she wrote a novel version of the play, titled THE CON-VERT, which was published in 1907.

Votes For Women
English women's suffrage journal, begun as the official organ of the WOMEN'S SOCIAL AND POLITICAL UNION in October 1907, with a circulation of 2,000. By 1910 it was a 24-page weekly with a circulation approaching 40,000. When, in late 1912, Frederick and Emmeline PETHICK-LAWRENCE were forced out of the WSPU, they retained the title for their paper, and the official organ of the WSPU became the SUFFRAGETTE. In July 1914 *Votes for Women* became the journal of a relatively new suffrage group, the United Suffragists.

W

Wages for Housework

Campaign founded by Selma JAMES in 1970 and run in Britain by the Power of Women Collective. Although it developed out of the women's liberation movement, it has become an international, single-issue movement which many feminists consider dangerous and divisive to feminist aims. Throughout the 1970s, the suggestion that 'wages for HOUSEWORK' be included as one of the demands of the British women's liberation movement continued to be raised and rejected. Opponents object that the idea of paying women for child-, house- and husband-care simply reinforces the very traditions and prejudices which keep women in the home. Supporters assert that until the value of women's work is recognized, no external reforms will be effective and many women will have no realistic hope of financial independence. The Power of Women Collective argues that if women refused to labour in the home, industry would collapse overnight. It is only because women keep the home going with their unpaid work (women who have paid jobs outside the home usually do the housework, too, which means they work a DOUBLE-SHIFT) that our economy can be sustained. A study by *Woman's World* Magazine in 1981 estimated the worth of the average house-wife's work to be £180 per week; an American study in 1977 estimated that the full-time homemaker should be paid between $20,000 to $40,000 for her year's work.

The slogan of the Wages for Housework campaign is 'Wages for housework – all women are workers'. Supporters of this campaign argue that wages for housework would not only give women the dignity which comes from having one's efforts recognized and valued, but would offer women a choice of occupations, the freedom to choose housework or to reject it for work outside the home.

Waisbrooker, Lois Nichols, 1826–1909

American. Dubbed 'the Abraham Lincoln of women', she was an anarchist, feminist and pacifist, known as an advocate of free love and arrested several times for lecturing on women's rights to control their own bodies. She edited a free love journal called *Lucifer, the Light Bearer* (1883–1907), and during the 1880s and 1890s published her own journal, *Foundation Principles*, in Kansas, Iowa and California. Her writings include *Suffrage for Woman:*

The Reasons Why (1868) and *Nothing Like It; Or, Steps to the Kingdom* (1875) and many works of didactic fiction. Today she is best remembered as the author of a feminist UTOPIA called *A Sex Revolution* (1894), in which women take control of the world for fifty years in order to bring about an end to war.

Walker, Alice, 1944–
American novelist and poet. Active in the Civil Rights movement in the 1960s, she is equally involved in the women's liberation movement and has spoken and written about the double burden of oppression – sexism and racism – carried by black women. She prefers to call herself a WOMANIST rather than a feminist, declaring 'Womanist is to feminist as purple is to lavender'. A consulting editor of MS. Magazine, she has also taught women's studies and black studies courses. A collection of her 'womanist prose' was published in 1983 as *In Search of Our Mothers' Gardens*. Her books include two collections of short stories, three collections of poems, and the novels *The Third Life of Grange Copeland* (1970), *Meridian* (1976) and the Pulitzer Prize winning *The Color Purple* (1983).

Walker, Mary Edwards, 1832–1919
American doctor and journalist. With a degree from Syracuse Medical College in 1855, she practised medicine in Ohio and New York until the outbreak of the Civil War, when she went to work as a volunteer in tent hospitals in Virginia. In 1863, she became the first woman to hold a commission as an official army surgeon. In 1865, her devotion and bravery during the war were recognized, and she became the first woman to receive the Congressional Medal of Honor. After the war, she became one of the first women journalists in America, working for a New York newspaper and writing two books. She preferred to wear trousers, and habitually did so, despite being harassed and occasionally arrested for 'masquerading in men's clothes'. As well as providing an example in her own life of what a woman could do, she also travelled widely to lecture on women's rights and, in 1897, founded a colony for women which she called Adamless Eden.

Wallace, Michele, 1952–
American. She became famous with the publication of her controversial polemic *Black Macho and the Myth of the Superwoman* (1979). Because many black women considered the women's liberation movement to be white, middle class and meaningless to their own lives, her public assertion of a feminist identity meant that to the public eye Michele Wallace was for some time seen as *the* black feminist. Her book took the stance that there was a deep distrust between black men and

black women which could be blamed partly on racism, but was also due to SEXUAL POLITICS. She called upon black women to develop their own feminist analysis as a necessary step towards both racial and sexual liberation.
(*See also* BLACK FEMINISM)

Wanderground, The

A series of linked tales by Sally Miller GEARHART, published as a book subtitled *Stories of the Hill Women* in 1978 and swiftly achieving the status of a modern feminist classic. Set in the near future, the world of the book is dramatically different from our own. The Hill Women have left the violent, male-dominated cities to live free with nature in the Wanderground. Through rediscovered psychic powers and with the help of the plant and animal life around them, they have created a loving UTOPIA for women. This work of visionary SCIENCE FICTION illustrates the concept of the FEMALE FUTURE which Gearhart believes all women should be working for.

Wandor, Michelene, 1940–

English playwright, poet and critic. She edited the first anthology of writings from the British women's liberation movement, *The Body Politic* (1972) and is a significant figure in the creation of modern feminist THEATRE. In addition to editing collections of plays by women, she has written one of the

few examinations of the development and importance of feminist theatre, *Understudies* (1981). Her own plays include *The Day After Yesterday* (1972), about the 1971 Miss World Contest; *To Die Among Friends* (1974) about the psychic realities of sexual politics; *Care and Control*, written for the Gay Sweatshop in 1977 on the subject of how society attempts to regulate MOTHERHOOD; *Floorshow*, a cabaret on women and work written with Caryl Churchill and Bryony Lavery in 1977; and *Correspondence* (1979) about a divorced woman's reassessment of her life. She also dramatized Elizabeth Barrett Browning's poem AURORA LEIGH (1979) and has written a number of other dramatizations and original plays for radio and television. Her poetry, short stories and essays have been widely anthologized.

Warrior, Betsy, 1940–

American. Her involvement with feminism began in 1968 as a contributor to the *Journal of Female Liberation*. She was particularly interested in popularizing the idea of self-defence for women, and in identifying the unpaid labour of HOUSEWORK as a central issue in women's economic oppression. In 1975 she worked with Chris Womendez to organize the first shelter for BATTERED WOMEN in New England. Since 1976 she has edited and published the annual *Battered Women's Directory* to disseminate information on where battered women can find help in the United States and other countries.

Weisstein, Naomi, 1939–
American experimental psychologist. In the early 1960s she became involved in the CIVIL RIGHTS MOVEMENT and NEW LEFT organizations, where she became known as a champion of women's rights. With her husband Jesse Lemisch she gave talks on equality in marriage; she organized women's caucuses, and in 1966 taught one of the earliest WOMEN'S STUDIES courses at the University of Chicago. She was a founder-member of one of the first Women's Liberation groups, in Chicago in 1967. She presented her paper, 'Kinder, Küche, Kirche As Scientific Law: PSYCHOLOGY CONSTRUCTS THE FEMALE', to a meeting of the American Studies Association at the University of California in 1968. Widely circulated in the women's movement, subsequently published in Sisterhood is Powerful (1970) and other anthologies, this paper is a classic demolition job on PSYCHOLOGY as men have used it to excuse and explain women's oppression. She was organizer and pianist for the Chicago Women's Liberation Rock Band from 1970–3. Her research is in the area of vision, perception and cognition, and her papers have been published widely in scientific journals. She is also known as an inspiring speaker and feminist comedian.

Wells-Barnett, Ida, 1862–1931
American journalist. Remembered chiefly as a crusader for the civil rights of black Americans, for her anti-lynching campaigns and tireless work as an organizer, and as a co-founder of the National Association for the Advancement of Colored People, she was also active in the woman suffrage movement from about 1900, and founded the Alpha Suffrage Club of Chicago, the first black woman suffrage organization.

West, Rebecca (Cicily Fairfield Andrews), 1892–1983
British writer. Independent, widely-travelled, multi-talented, with many interests and causes throughout her long life, she always remained a feminist, a fact which is obvious in her novels, her journalism, her criticism and philosophy. Her involvement with the women's movement began in her teens, when she worked for the WOMEN'S SOCIAL AND POLITICAL UNION; her first published piece was a letter to The Scotsman on the subject of women's suffrage, written when she was sixteen. At eighteen, she was writing regularly for THE FREE-WOMAN and, by 1912, was also writing political journalism and criticism for The Clarion. She left the WSPU in 1912, partly through distaste for Christabel PANKHURST's campaign for purity, and partly because she knew there was more to feminism than a single-minded

concentration on winning the vote. Her second novel, THE JUDGE (1922) is a serious treatment of the problems faced by unmarried mothers. She was made a Dame of the British Empire in 1959.

What is to be done?
Russian novel by Nikolai CHERNYSHEVSKY, first published in 1864. Closely based on the triangular relationship between three of his friends, it is a classic document of the need for sexual freedom and was considered a bible for advanced Russian women for more than fifty years, inspiring Alexandra KOLLONTAI, among others. During the course of the novel the heroine, Vera Pavlovna, gradually awakens to consciousness as a full human being, not only a woman, as she recognizes her needs for independence, love, and work.

Wheeler, Anna, 1785–?
Irish. Married at the age of fifteen, she managed to educate herself while coping with a drunken husband and bearing six children in twelve years. After leaving her husband she became widely known among French and British radical and intellectual circles for her speeches and writings on the condition of women. The Saint Simonians hailed her as 'the most gifted woman of the age' and as the 'Goddess of Reason'. She is best remembered now for her intellectual partnership with William THOMPSON, which resulted in his APPEAL OF ONE-HALF THE HUMAN RACE, WOMEN, AGAINST THE PRETENSIONS OF THE OTHER HALF, MEN, TO RETAIN THEM IN POLITICAL, AND THENCE IN CIVIL AND DOMESTIC SLAVERY (1825). Although this book bore only Thompson's name as author, he dedicated it to her, used her portrait as a frontispiece, and credited her with the major responsibility for the views and ideas he had expressed. Her great granddaughter was a well-known suffragette, Lady Constance LYTTON.

Whileaway
A women-only UTOPIA imagined by Joanna RUSS in her short story 'When it Changed' (1972) and her novel THE FEMALE MAN (1975).

White Goddess, The
Book by Robert GRAVES published in 1948 which became, in the 1970s, one of the key texts used by feminists in search of evidence for a prehistoric MATRIARCHY. The GODDESS of the title is the earliest known European deity, who presided over birth, love and death, and whom Graves also identifies as the muse of poetry. His proposition is that true poetry is written in the language of myth and has but a single theme, which is connected with the ancient cult-rituals surrounding the Goddess.

WILD (Women's Independent Label Distributors)
A network of nine American

woman-owned record distribution companies, formed in 1979 out of their shared feminist philosophy of mutual help and support. Committed to making women's music widely available, they are an important part of the WOMANCULTURE. (*See also* MUSIC AND MUSICIANS)

Wilkinson, Ellen, 1891–1947

English politician. She began working for the NATIONAL UNION OF WOMEN'S SUFFRAGE SOCIETIES in 1913, at the same time as she was making her name as a speaker for the Independent Labour Party. Like Sylvia PANKHURST, she was particularly influential in expanding the predominantly middle-class women's movement to include the concerns of working women. From 1915–25 she worked as a national women's organizer for the Amalgamated Union of Co-operative Employees. In 1924 she became the first woman Labour member of Parliament.

Willard, Frances, 1839–98

American. Involved with the WOMEN'S CHRISTIAN TEMPERANCE UNION from its foundation in 1874, becoming its National President in 1881 until her death. Her zeal for temperance was matched by her feminism and, under her leadership the WCTU poured more money and organizers into the women's suffrage campaign than did any of the official suffrage organizations. After her death, however, the character of the WCTU changed, and it ceased to be an ally of the suffrage movement.

Williams, Fanny Barrier, 1855–1944

American. She attracted national attention with her 1893 speech on 'The Intellectual Progress of Colored Women of the United States Since the Emancipation Proclamation' at the Chicago World's Fair World Congress of Representative Women. She was the first black and the first woman appointed to the Chicago Library Board.

Williamson, Cris

Contemporary American musician. She began composing and performing as a folk artist while still at school, and recorded three albums for Avanti Records in the mid-1960s. In 1972, she gave a performance at American University in Washington, D.C. and met Meg CHRISTIAN, who introduced her to the concept of women's music. The two women became friends, and it was a suggestion from Cris Williamson which led to the founding of OLIVIA RECORDS in 1973. Her album, *The Changer and the Changed*, was released by Olivia in 1975, and quickly established her as the bestselling artist in the women's music industry. Despite little advertising and almost no airplay, it became one of the most successful albums ever produced by an independent label, selling nearly 100,000 copies. Her other albums include *Live Dream* (1978), *Strange Paradise* (1980), *Lumiere* (1982), *Blue Rider* (1982), *Prairie Fire* (1985) and *Snow Angel* (1985).

(*See also* MUSIC AND MUSICIANS)

Wilson, Elizabeth, 1936–
English social worker, teacher and author. She became involved in the women's liberation movement in 1971, and was on the editorial board of RED RAG. In 1977 she became a member of the editorial collective of FEMINIST REVIEW. Her books include *Women and the Welfare State* (1977), *Only Halfway to Paradise: Women in Postwar Britain 1945–1968* (1980), and *What is to be done about violence against women?* (1983).

wimmin
See WOMON

Windeyer, Mary Bolton,
1836–1912
Australian. From charity work she became involved in the Women's Christian Temperance Union, and then in women's rights organizations. She supported the right to birth control, campaigned for higher education, and joined Louisa Lawson's Dawn Club. She became the first President of the Womanhood Suffrage League in 1891, and in 1895 was the founder and first President of the Women's Hospital in Sydney. In addition to campaigning in her own right, she influenced her husband to support women's interests: when he became Attorney General in 1878, he introduced the Married Women's Property Act.

WIRES
The British WOMEN'S LIBERATION MOVEMENT national information service, established in May 1975. The name is an acronym for Women's Information, Referral and Enquiry Service, and although it was initially based in Leeds, it moves to a different city every year or two. A voluntary, women-only network, it functions as an information service, keeping files on groups, contacts, campaigns, etc. throughout the women's movement, and it issues a newsletter (also called WIRES) to keep different areas, groups and individuals in touch with each other.

WITCH
Politically left-wing, loosely organized group which emerged from the NEW YORK RADICAL WOMEN. Out of CONSCIOUSNESS-RAISING discussions on the subject of female power and its historical context came the idea of women as witches. The first coven, dressed in witch costumes, made an appearance on Hallowe'en 1968, to hex the New York Stock Exchange. Other such ZAP ACTIONS were held subsequently as more covens sprang up in other cities.

The acronym stood originally for Women's International Terrorist

Conspiracy from Hell, but the meaning was no more fixed than the membership, and it was frequently changed, depending on the target of the current action. For example: Women Inspired to Commit Herstory; Women Incensed at Telephone Company Harassment; Women Interested in Toppling Consumption Holidays.

WITCH defined itself as 'all-women Everything. It's theatre, revolution, magic, terror, joy, garlic flowers, spells. It's an awareness that witches and gypsies were the original guerrillas and resistance fighters against oppression – particularly against the oppression of women – down through the ages.'

Because of its theatrical style of confrontation, WITCH received much publicity and was generally approved of by the male Left, but many women felt alienated. This became clear in February 1969 during the protest actions at the New York Bridal Fair and simultaneously at the Bridal Fair in San Francisco. The intention of WITCH was to ridicule the industry which profits from selling romantic myths to women, but the would-be brides at the fair, and many women outside, felt they were under attack from feminists. Realizing that they were harming their own cause, WITCH abandoned street theatre for a period of study and discussion.

Although WITCH did not last very long, it had a powerful impact on the women's movement, both by demonstrating that feminist actions could be spontaneous and fun, and by awakening many women to the positive image of the witch. As the New York covens proclaimed, 'You are a Witch by being female, untamed, angry, joyous, and immortal.'

witches

The image of the witch – powerful, wise, feared by men – has been reclaimed by modern women. In 1968 the WITCH Manifesto described witches as the first feminists, and many feminist writers since have imagined witches in the same way, as rebels, revolutionaries, and worshippers of the GODDESS. One of the most striking and horrible examples of male hatred of women can be seen in the savage persecution known as the BURNING TIMES, or witch-craze, throughout fifteenth, sixteenth and seventeenth-century Europe. During that time between two and nine million people accused of witchcraft, most of them women, were murdered. Some of the victims may have been practising witches, but most were killed for not conforming to the very limited role men wished women to fill: for being too intelligent, for refusing sexual advances or for making them, for being ugly, old, solitary, single or eccentric.

Today, some women looking for spiritual sustenance and an alternative to male-dominated religions have turned to witchcraft, also known as The Craft and Wicca. Most feminist witches have chosen to reject the standard, male–female polarities of the traditional Craft rituals, substituting their own, personally meaningful rituals within the context of an all-female coven. Some feminists claim that all women are witches by birth-right, and that it is not a religion men can join. The Susan B. Anthony Coven, started in California in 1971 by Z. Budapest, may have been the first explicitly feminist coven. Its manifesto states: 'We believe that without a secure grounding in women's spiritual strength there will be no victory for us. . . . We are equally committed to political, communal and personal solutions.'

As Margot Adler pointed out in her book on witches and other pagans in modern America, feminist covens differ from standard covens not only in their rituals, but also in not separating religious activities from their daily lives: political struggle and spiritual development are perceived as interdependent, so that most feminist covens devote much of their energies to the women's movement or community activities.

According to religious scholar Naomi Goldenberg, witches believe fantasies are as real as remembered facts, since both influence present actions. Rituals are psychological tools, used to change women's internal image of themselves. Once women recognize the divinity within themselves and are no longer convinced by the image of a male god, according to this theory, they will be less accepting of male dominance in everyday life, and political change will then accompany spiritual development.

Matilda Joslyn GAGE and Margaret MURRAY were the first to analyse witchcraft from a feminist point of view. Contemporary writers who have found the image of the witch a particularly powerful one include Mary DALY, Andrea DWORKIN, Erica JONG and Robin MORGAN.

Wittig, Monique, 1935–
French writer. Author of LES GUÉRILLÈRES (1969), an innovative, poetic epic of women warriors which has inspired many feminists; a radical lesbian feminist who was one of the early leaders of the women's liberation movement in France. In 1970 she founded Féministes Révolutionnaires, a radical separatist group dedicated to the total destruction of PATRIARCHY, and she was a founder-member of the International Lesbian Front in 1974, but since the mid-1970s she has remained outside organizational alliances, while still contributing to the international women's movement. In 1979 she presented a short but influential paper at The Second Sex Conference in New York City:

'One is Not Born a Woman'. In this paper she declared that, far from being 'natural', the very categories of 'man' and 'woman' are artificial creations of patriarchal society: 'what we believe to be a physical and direct perception is only a sophisticated and mythic construction, an "imaginary formation" which reinterprets physical features through the network of relationships in which they are perceived'. The object of women's liberation, therefore, must be 'to suppress men as a class, not through a genocidal, but a political struggle. Once the class "men" disappears, women as a class will disappear as well, for there are no slaves without masters.' Her other works include *L'Opoponax* (1964), *Le corps lesbien* (1973, published in English as *The Lesbian Body*, 1976), and, with Sande Zeig, *Lesbian Peoples: Material for a Dictionary* (1980).

WLM
See WOMEN'S LIBERATION MOVEMENT

Wollstonecraft, Mary, 1759–97
English feminist, radical and writer, self-educated and driven from an early age by anger at the way in which women were oppressed. She established, with her sister Eliza and friend Fanny Blood, a school for girls at Newington Green where, despite the school's failure, she was rewarded by becoming a part of a network of nonconformist and liberal thinkers.

She is known as one of the English Jacobins, that group of radical intellectuals which included Thomas Paine, Joseph Johnson, Henry Fuseli, Mary HAYS and William Godwin (whom Wollstonecraft married in 1797, their shared objections to marriage overcome by her pregnancy).

Her first published work was *Thoughts on the Education of Daughters* (1787), followed by the novel *Mary* (1788), but she is best remembered as the author of one of the earliest sustained arguments linking liberalism to feminism, A VINDICATION OF THE RIGHTS OF WOMAN (1792). This passionate plea for equal rights and opportunities created a great stir and was widely read, drawing both praise and attack. As frequently happens with women's work, it was not judged on its merits alone but viewed in connection with the author's behaviour and appearance.

Wollstonecraft led an unconventional and adventurous life which included involvement in the French Revolution, several love affairs, one illegitimate child and two suicide attempts, and she was attacked as much for her life as for her views, dubbed 'a philosophical wanton' and 'a hyena in petticoats'. She died giving birth to her second daughter (who would grow up to become known as the writer Mary Wollstonecraft Godwin Shelley), and her husband's *Memoirs of Mary Wollstonecraft* (1798), although written out of love and respect, cast a veil of scandal over her name for many years. Early nineteenth-century feminists felt, as Harriet Martineau wrote, that Wollstonecraft could not be considered 'a safe example, nor as a successful champion of Woman and her Rights'. But by 1889, Susan B. ANTHONY and Elizabeth Cady STANTON thought highly enough of the author of *A Vindication* to put her name first on the dedication page of the HISTORY OF WOMAN SUFFRAGE.

Wolstenholme-Elmy, Elizabeth, 1834–1918

English. Her life was devoted to the women's movement, beginning with the campaign in the 1850s for the Married Women's Property Bill and continuing through the most militant struggles of the WOMEN'S SOCIAL AND POLITICAL UNION. She took a radical stance on SEXUALITY and, under the pen-name Ellis Ethelmer, wrote books and articles about the abuses and ideals of sexual love. She did not wish to sacrifice her independence by marrying but, when she became pregnant, her sister suffragists persuaded her to marry Ben Elmy, rather than risk damaging the cause of women's legal rights with any scandal.

woman

An artificial social construct, always defined in opposition to man, as the OTHER. The term comes from Old English *wifman* (*wif*+*man*) meaning a female person. The complementary term meaning a male person (*weapman*) was lost, and 'man' came to mean both male human being and human being. Femaleness became the marked quality; maleness was implied as the norm. Without the category 'woman', feminism could not exist. Without the category 'woman', feminism would not be necessary, for SEXISM could not exist.

Some writers differentiate between women – a class of being identified by sex – and 'Woman', the mythical being invented by men. William O'Neill (1971) traced the origins of feminism to the recent, deliberate creation of Woman: 'The Victorians taught women to think of themselves as a special class. Having become conscious of their unique sexual identity, however – a consciousness heightened by the common experiences forced upon them by the cult of purity – they could no longer accept uncritically those role definitions drawn up for them by the alien male. Victorian society created The Woman, where before there had been only women.'

For the most part, feminists have sought to redefine woman from a woman-centred perspective. Only a few – Andrea DWORKIN and Monique WITTIG most prominently – have suggested she might not exist at all. In *Woman Hating* (1974) Andrea Dworkin wrote, 'The discovery is, of course, that "man" and "woman" are fictions, caricatures, cultural constructs. As models they are reductive, totalitarian, inappropriate to human becoming. As roles they are static, demeaning to the female, dead-ended for male and female both. ... *We are, clearly, a multisexed species which has its sexuality spread along a vast fluid continuum where the elements called male and female are not discrete.*'

(*See also* FEMININITY; GENDER)

Woman and Labour

Book by Olive SCHREINER first published in 1911 and hailed as the 'Bible of the Woman's Movement' by early twentieth-century feminists. In it, Schreiner argues that modern civilization has robbed women of most of their traditional work and, although society will not tolerate idleness in men, women are encouraged to become 'sex parasites'. While exalting MOTHERHOOD as the noblest work of all, she emphasizes that it fulfils only part of the need every human being feels for social activity and meaningful labour. The book ends with the belief that women would be able to teach men the desirability of equality, and the ancient equilibrium of true partnership would be restored.

Woman in the Nineteenth Century

Book by Margaret FULLER published in 1845. It first appeared, in shorter form, as an essay entitled 'The Great Lawsuit. Man versus Men. Woman versus Women.' in the July 1843 issue of *The Dial*, a Transcendental literary quarterly. After Sarah GRIMKÉ'S LETTERS ON THE EQUALITY OF THE SEXES AND THE CONDITION OF WOMEN, this was the first major work by an American to examine woman's place in society and offer an extended argument for equal rights. It was widely read and influential both in America and Britain, and provided the major intellectual foundation for the women's movement in the nineteenth century.

Woman Movement, The

Also known as 'The Suffrage Monument', this sculpture, which includes portrait heads of Susan B. ANTHONY, Lucretia MOTT and Elizabeth Cady STANTON, stands in the United States Capitol Building, the only national monument to the women's movement. It was sculpted by Adelaide JOHNSON from a seven-ton block of white Carrara marble, her work financed by the NATIONAL WOMAN'S PARTY who presented it to the nation on behalf of American women on 15 February 1921.

Woman Not Inferior to Man

An early feminist tract, by SOPHIA, a Person of Quality, subtitled *A short and modest Vindication of the natural Right of the Fair-Sex to a perfect Equality of Power, Dignity and*

Esteem, with the Men, published in London in 1739. It was reprinted in 1743 with the reply of an anonymous Gentleman, *Man Superior to Woman*, and Sophia's final word on the subject, *Woman's Superior Excellence Over Man*. Although she never claimed authorship, scholars generally identify 'Sophia' as Lady Mary Wortley MONTAGU.

Woman on the Edge of Time

Novel by Marge PIERCY first published in 1976 and already a classic of feminist SCIENCE FICTION. It tells the story of Connie Ramos, held against her will in a mental hospital in present-day New York, who discovers she can escape her intolerable present by mental time-travel to Mattapoisett, a non-sexist future UTOPIA. Mattapoisett is an ecologically aware, communal society which has abolished SEXISM at the root by use of reproductive technologies: women no longer have the privilege or the pain of physically bearing children. Instead, children are created by the genetic material of three 'co-mothers' – who may be male or female – in artificial, mechanical wombs. Once they are born, the babies are nurtured equally by all three mothers, the men having been given small but functional breasts. Rare among feminist utopian novelists, Piercy looks not only at sexual differences, but also at class and racial conflicts, bringing a sharp political awareness to focus on the grim realities of the present day as well as creating a desirable and believable alternative.

Woman Question, The

A phrase which reveals a pre-feminist consciousness. It was used widely in the nineteenth century. After the use of the term feminism became more established, it was chiefly Marxists who still referred to 'the Woman Question'. What is questioned is women's status and role in contemporary society, and how it developed historically, with a view towards a very different future. Although feminism can be seen to have originated through the committed exploration of the woman question, the question in itself does not imply a feminist answer, and not all of the thinkers who have applied themselves to the woman question have been feminists in even the widest sense.

Woman Who Did, The

Novel by Grant ALLEN, first published in England in 1895. Considered scandalous in its day, it relates the story of fictional high-minded feminist Herminia Barton who refuses to marry her lover, on the principle that marriage is slavery, even after bearing his child. In the end she kills herself to leave her daughter free to enjoy conventional married happiness.

woman-centredness

One of the major conceptual contributions of modern feminism is that of the woman-centred analysis. This is the idea that female experience should be the major focus of study for feminists, as well as the source of values for the new society they are trying to create. Although putting women first was a basic organizing principle of the WOMEN'S LIBERATION MOVEMENT from the beginning, the woman-centred perspective developed more slowly, from the theoretical writings of lesbian feminists in the early 1970s. In their 1970 position paper, 'The WOMAN-IDENTIFIED WOMAN', the RADICALESBIANS wrote of the necessity for women to refuse male definitions of themselves and find a new identity: 'Only women can give to each other a new sense of self. That identity we have to develop with reference to ourselves, and not in relation to men.'

Before the emergence of this view, most feminists felt that women must struggle to overcome their feminine social conditioning in order to be accepted as the equals of men; or they took the view that all GENDER distinctions and SEX-ROLES were wrong and must be abolished, to be replaced by ANDROGYNY.

The woman-centred analysis questioned the suitability of male-defined virtues and needs, not only for women, but for all humanity. Instead, it suggested that those qualities always considered feminine – even if they were the result of oppression – might be necessary and valuable characteristics. Rather than accepting patriarchal terms and considering women as lacking in any way, the woman-centred perspective is an attempt to redefine the world, and humanity, from the woman's point of view.

An example of this can be seen in the changing concept of WOMEN'S STUDIES. Scholars in almost every field, whether humanities or sciences, found it unsatisfactory simply to 'add women on' to a male-defined study, whether it was history or psychology. It was not enough just to focus on women – as if women were an exotic minority, or an exception to the rule – and look for women's place in a man's world. Instead, women had to be seen as human beings, and as the majority whose experiences and qualities were potentially normative for *all* human beings.

womanculture
Women's culture. Under PATRIARCHY, human culture has been male-defined, and where women's needs, interests and experiences have differed from the ANDROCENTRIC norm they have tended to be ignored, denied, or trivialized. Womanculture is the attempt to create a new society which will fulfil women's needs and reflect female and/or feminist values. Aspects of this culture,

which Robin MORGAN has called 'the new women's renaissance', can be seen in the development of SPIRITUAL FEMINISM, in the establishment of feminist PUBLISHING houses and other women-only businesses, in THEATRE, FILM, ART and literature, both within feminist communities and in the larger society. Although CULTURAL FEMINISM is often denounced as apolitical, woman-culture is also an aspect of radical feminism, in that it emphasizes the achievement of social change through the creation of alternative institutions, and shares the goal of 'living the revolution'.
(*See also* SEPARATISM; WOMAN-CENTRED)

Womanhouse

Art project created by twenty-one students from the Feminist Art Program at the California Institute of the Arts, under the direction of Judy CHICAGO and Miriam SCHAPIRO, in 1971–2. A dilapidated, seventeen-room mansion on Mariposa Street, Los Angeles, was transformed into an environment in which the artists worked from their own experiences to transform rooms into visions of female reality and fantasy such as the flesh-pink 'Nurturant Kitchen' by Vickie Hodgetts, Robin Weltsch and Susan Frazier, a gigantic 'Nursery' by Shawnee Wollenmann, and the 'Menstrual Bathroom' by Judy CHICAGO. It was open to the public for one month in 1972 and had about 10,000 visitors.

Woman-Identified Woman

This phrase describes the radical feminist or the lesbian feminist and sometimes, because it leaves unanswered the question of sexual orientation, appears to be a euphemism for lesbian. The term was first used in 'The Woman-Identified Woman', a position paper presented by LAVENDER MENACE (later called RADICALESBIANS) at the second CONGRESS TO UNITE WOMEN, May 1970, in New York City.

The paper declared: 'Lesbian is a label invented by the Man to throw at any woman who dares to be his equal, who dares to challenge his prerogative (including that of all women as part of the exchange medium among men), who dares to assert the primacy of her own needs.' To consider lesbianism only a 'sexual alternative' was both divisive and sexist, and revealed women who thought in such terms to still be male-identified.

The woman-identified woman does not define herself in relation to men, but focuses her attention and commitment on herself and other women, accepting the primacy of women – whether or not she chooses to express her sexuality with them. This new, WOMAN-CENTRED consciousness, according to the Radicalesbians, 'is the revolutionary force from which all else must follow', and without it, women's liberation will not be possible.
(*See also* POLITICAL LESBIAN)

womanism

1) Black feminism. This term is preferred by many black feminists because it is rooted in black culture, whereas the word feminism is perceived as coming out of the white woman's culture. Alice WALKER, who has done much to publicize the term, has said that although it is not 'better' than the word feminism, she prefers 'the sound, the feel, the fit of it' and believes that new words are important to help society recognize changes that old words cannot describe.

2) Term used before the word *feminism* gained widespread acceptance in the 1890s. It meant advocacy of women's rights; enthusiasm for women's achievements, abilities, and qualities; the belief in women's superiority to men; any positive, pro-woman stance.

womanist

Self-descriptive term used by black feminists and feminists of colour, the advantage being that it avoids the racism implicit in the term 'feminist', so long as only the non-white feminist requires a qualifying prefix (i.e. 'black feminism' implies that feminism is self-evidently part of the white woman's culture). As defined by Alice WALKER in 1979, womanist encompasses feminist and also refers to someone who is instinctively pro-woman. She traces its roots to the black folk expression 'womanish', used by mothers of female children who display wilful, courageous or outrageous behaviour.

Woman's Bible, The

Analysis and critique of the Bible from a feminist point of view, written by Elizabeth Cady STANTON with Lillie Devereux Blake, Frances Ellen Burr, Clara Bewick Colby, Ellen Battelle Dietrick, Ursula N. Gestefeld, the Revd Phebe Hanaford and Louisa Southworth, and published in two parts in 1895 and 1898. At the time, excuses for denying women equal rights with men were often found in religious teachings, so the motivating impulse behind this commentary was to discover what the scriptures really said about women, and to suggest reasons and alternative interpretations. For example, one of the favourite anti-suffrage arguments was found in God's statement to Eve: 'Thy desire shall be to thy husband, and he shall rule over thee.' The feminist interpretation, however, was that this, like the corresponding pronouncement to Adam that he should eat his bread in the sweat of his face, was not a command, but rather a prediction. If it were a command, it would be sacrilegious for man to invent machines to make his work easier; thus equal rights for women was linked with the theory of progress.

Publication of *The Woman's Bible* resulted in much controversy and criticism, most of it from people who had not read the book. The authors were denounced less for what they actually said than for their audacity, as women, in commenting on the Bible at all. Even many of the suffragists disapproved, believing it would alienate religious believers from the cause and, despite pleas for tolerance from the more liberal thinkers, the suffrage convention of 1896 passed a resolution disavowing any connection with *The Woman's Bible*.

Woman's Commonwealth

A commune established in 1866 in Belton, Texas, composed of between thirty-five and fifty women and their children. Religious revelation caused them to refuse sexual or economic intercourse with their husbands, so they supported themselves by selling butter, eggs and firewood and taking in laundry until they were able to buy a farm. In 1886, they began building the Central Hotel which became their residence and main economic enterprise until they moved to Washington, D.C., in 1899. The women continued to stay together – later on a farm in Maryland – until at least 1918.
(*See also* SEPARATISM)

Woman's Dreadnought

Weekly newspaper founded in March 1914 and edited by Sylvia PANKHURST for the East London Federation of Suffragettes, as a forum in which working women could express themselves and find their interests defended. In July 1917, the title was changed to *Worker's Dreadnought*, reflecting the change of emphasis and content which had been obvious for some time. It ceased publication in 1924.

womanspace

A place where women can be alone together, free from male intrusion; any physical space for women only which fosters the sense of community among women and allows them to lay the foundations for a new, woman-centred culture.
(*See also* SEPARATISM)

Womanspirit

1) Term for feminist, non-materialist philosophy which stresses that in addition to political and social action, there must also be a change in consciousness in order for women's liberation to be achieved. Womanspirit, also called feminist spirituality or SPIRITUAL FEMINISM, attempts to integrate spirituality into all aspects of life, refuting the traditional mind/body, material/spiritual dualisms of patriarchal RELIGION. The symbol of Womanspirit is the circle, implying that it is all-embracing, non-linear, and never-ending.

2) Title of a magazine founded in 1974, published quarterly by an editorial collective based in Oregon, which explores and expresses aspects of women's spirituality

through articles, letters, fiction, poetry and art. They have never attempted to limit or firmly define the meaning of spirituality, and in an early issue declared their intention 'to put women in touch – in communion – with each other and ourselves . . . we always want to look at the consciousness: it must be pro-woman, woman-proud, aware of the potential of women'.

Women Against Rape (WAR)

British group launched in 1976 to work for changes in the legal treatment of RAPE victims through a campaign of direct action in the courts, parliament, government offices and the media to create public awareness of rape as a serious crime. Since 1978 local WAR groups have fought also for the recognition that rape can take place within marriage, and for financial assistance for rape victims. They are part of a network connected with WAGES FOR HOUSEWORK, the English Collective of Prostitutes, and similar campaigns in the United States.

Women Against Violence Against Women (WAVAW)

A network of local groups throughout Britain who share the aim of revealing the link between men's sexual VIOLENCE and the continuation of male domination over women despite talk of equal rights. WAVAW draws specific connections between race, class and gender

in relation to male violence: for example, violence by white men against black women may be both racist in intention and aimed specifically at black women as women.

The first Women Against Violence Against Women conference took place in London in November 1981, with 1,000 women from all over the country meeting to discuss such issues as RAPE in marriage, the pressure to be heterosexual, feminist eroticism, language as violence, and the sexual abuse of girls. Papers from this and two other conferences were published by ONLYWOMEN PRESS in 1985 as *Women Against Violence Against Women*.

Women Against Violence Against Women groups have petitioned for women's safety in public and private life (for example, for better street lighting and laws against rape in marriage), established a feminist self-defence teachers' network, done research in an attempt to define the extent of male violence, held exhibitions to publicize the connection between PORNOGRAPHY and violence, and organized RECLAIM THE NIGHT marches. WAVAW advocates forms of direct action which include the picketing of sex shops, strip shows and sexually violent films, and defacing pornographic or insulting posters of women with stickers such as 'You call it Art, we call it violence against women'.

The name Women Against Violence Against Women was also used

by a feminist anti-pornography group in Los Angeles in the mid-1970s.

'women and . . .' syndrome

Identified by Liz Stanley and Sue Wise as a problem connected to WOMEN'S STUDIES: the emphasis on filling the gaps in established disciplines by focusing on 'women and crime', 'women and psychology', 'women and work', etc. In this way, women become an area of study and are merely added on to the male-centred tradition without challenging the original ANDRO-CENTRIC bias. By contrast, a feminist perspective would begin by presuming the centrality of women and question the applicability of male-determined traditions, attitudes and limitations.

Women and Madness

Book by Phyllis CHESLER published in 1972. An influential work, one of the cornerstones of contemporary feminist theory, it examines the connection between the concept of femininity and mental health. Drawing on many studies and interviews, Chesler showed how 'normal' female behaviour is precisely that considered sick and abnormal in a man. To follow society's prescription for feminine behaviour is to risk victimization, depression, and mental illness. Yet women who refused the weak and passive female role, by being independent, strong, ambitious, lesbian, etc. were labelled deviant or mad. The cure and punishment offered by psychologists were one and the same: to force her into the SEX-ROLE allowed to women, which usually meant driving her mad.

Women's Action Alliance

American organization conceived by Brenda Feigen Fasteau and Gloria STEINEM in 1971 as an information-referral service connected to and partially funded by MS. Magazine, with an office in New York. Its goals are to work for full equality for all persons, to educate the public on feminist issues, and to assist, support and sponsor feminist programmes, issues and actions. It provides technical assistance, including how-to workshops on fund-raising and communication; offers information services about women's issues and programmes; holds conferences, and has published such books as *A Practical Guide to the Women's Movement* (1975) and *Women's Action Almanac* (1980), a comprehensive guide to women's resources, issues, organizations and activities in the United States.

women's centres

One of the most visible aspects of the WOMEN'S LIBERATION MOVE-MENT, in many ways its backbone, are women's centres. For many women these centres provide their first contact with organized feminist activity. Developed locally, to serve local needs, the women's centre may be a meeting place, a refuge, a bookshop and information service, or it may provide counselling, pregnancy testing, self-defence classes and many other services. Physically, it may be an old house, an abandoned property, a converted shop, or a single room. These centres survive on donations, grants, and fund-raising events and are usually staffed by volunteers.

The first women's centre in Britain was the London Women's Liberation Workshop which opened in 1969. By 1973 there were five in Greater London, and others in Bristol, Lancaster, Cardiff and Edinburgh. In 1985 there were more than forty women's centres in cities and towns throughout Britain.

In a 1979 survey of over 300 women's centres in the United States, the Women's Action Alliance concluded that the average life-span of a women's centre was about two years. However, many did not close, but evolved into a more specialized function, becoming, for example, a RAPE CRISIS CENTRE, a battered women's refuge, a women's bookshop or café. At the same time, new women's centres are always opening to fulfil the community need.

Women's Christian
Temperance Union (WCTU)
Organized in 1874 in Cleveland, Ohio, as part of the crusade to pro-

hibit alcohol. Although not feminist in nature (it exalted woman's domestic role and supposed moral superiority), under the leadership of Frances WILLARD (1881–98) it became the largest and most influential organization of women in the nineteenth century, and brought many progressive, reform-minded women in contact with each other, as well as putting more money and organizers into the suffrage campaigns than any of the official suffrage organizations. Although it made the idea of women's suffrage 'respectable' and attractive to many conservatives, the WCTU support roused active antagonism from liquor interests against any proposed women's suffrage amendments. After Willard's death, the WCTU changed character and became a single-issue temperance organization.

women's culture
See WOMANCULTURE

Women's Equity Action League
(WEAL)
An American women's rights group founded in 1968 by Ohio lawyer Dr Elizabeth Boyer. Composed mostly of professional women (and some men), it cultivated a conservative image, calling itself 'the right wing of the women's movement'. In 1972 it opened a national office in Washington, D.C. Its goals are to work for the equal participation of

women in society and to improve the social, economic and legal status of women through education, legislation and litigation. To this end it established a fund to provide for research on patterns of discrimination, to publish information kits on laws and regulations concerning women, and to pay legal costs for selected sex discrimination cases. It also publishes a national newsletter and 'Washington Report' to keep members informed of recent Congressional action and legislation affecting women.

Women's Franchise League

Founded in 1889 by Emmeline and Richard PANKHURST and led by Lydia BECKER, it was the first British radical alternative to the suffrage movement. Considered impractical by the established campaigners, the League demanded equal rights for women not only in politics, but in divorce and inheritance laws. Besides the Pankhursts, the Council included Jacob Bright, Josephine BUTLER, Jane Cobden, Clementia Doughty Taylor and – representing American suffragists – Elizabeth Cady STANTON. The League was disbanded by 1893 due to lack of funds.

Women's Freedom League
(WFL)

British suffrage organization which developed in 1907 from a split in the WOMEN'S SOCIAL AND POLITICAL UNION between the loyal followers of Emmeline PANKHURST, and those with a greater commitment to working-class women, who believed that 'the members of the branches are the ultimate power in the Union'.

This latter group, led by Charlotte DESPARD, Edith HOWMARTYN, Teresa BILLINGTON-GRIEG, Caroline Hodgson and Irene Fenwick Miller, at first claimed to be the true WSPU but soon, in the interests of harmony, formed the League with perhaps 20 per cent of the WSPU's membership, and issued a newspaper called *The Vote*.

Charlotte Despard was elected president and, despite later accusations that she wielded too much power, the WFL remained a democratically-run society. Tactics were militant but, unlike those of the WSPU, were always aimed clearly at the government: ballot-boxes might be set on fire, but not private property. Other campaigns included a boycott of the 1911 census, and the organization of the Women's Tax Resistance League.

There were always strong ties between the WFL and the Labour Party and, in 1910, it passed a motion to support Labour candidates. Ultimately it remained politically independent, however, votes for women being its major, but not only, concern.

During World War I, it was the only major suffrage group to 'keep the Suffrage flag flying' as it argued that this war showed 'the supreme

357

necessity of women having a voice on the councils of the nation'. It formed the WOMEN'S SUFFRAGE NATIONAL AID CORPS, conducted many campaigns against the reintroduction of section 40d of the Defence of the Realm Act (under which women found to be suffering from venereal disease could be sentenced to six months hard labour), and, with Sylvia PANKHURST, established the League of Rights for Soldiers' and Sailors' Wives and Relations.

After the vote was granted in 1918, membership dropped dramatically, but the WFL declared that its work was not finished and adopted a wider-ranging programme including demands for equal pay, equal opportunities, better housing and child care, and a national minimum wage.

The WFL celebrated its Golden Jubilee in 1957 but, by that time, it had attracted no new members since before World War II, and local meetings were no longer held. In 1961, the last president, Marian Reeves, died and the remnants of the League disbanded.

women's health movement
See HEALTH MOVEMENT

Women's History
See HISTORY; WOMEN'S STUDIES

Women's Institute for Freedom of the Press
Voluntary organization based in Washington, D.C. founded in 1972 for research and educational purposes. The 700 women who are associates of the Institute constitute an international support network and communications system to work towards shared goals of constructive changes in the world's communications systems. They conduct and publish research on how freedom of the press can be expanded to include everyone, publish a monthly periodical titled *Media Report to Woman* and a yearly *Index/Directory of Women's Media*. In her introduction to the 1985 *Index*, editor Martha Leslie Allen wrote, 'We at the Women's Institute for Freedom of the Press believe that by building a strong women's communications system, women can prevent a return to the 1950s, when there were no women's media and our options were limited to what the male-owned media told us were acceptable roles for women.'
(*See also* JOURNALISM)

Women's International League for Peace and Freedom
(WILPF)
Pacifist organization founded during a women's peace congress at the Hague in 1915 attended by feminists from many countries, including Rosika SCHWIMMER, Lida HEYMANN and Anita AUGSPURG. Jane ADDAMS was elected the first president. The WILPF is still in existence today with the goal of uniting women of different political, social and national backgrounds to work

together for total disarmament, the abolition of violent means of coercion for the settlement of disputes, and the development of world organization for political, social and economic cooperation between peoples. Members believe in helping to bring about, by non-violent means, a social transformation which will provide social, economic and political equality for all.

(*See also* PACIFISM; PEACE MOVEMENT)

Women's Liberation Movement (WLM)

The modern feminist movement, sometimes called the new feminist movement, the radical women's movement, or simply the women's movement. Sometimes a distinction is made between the equal rights movement known as MAINSTREAM FEMINISM and typified by the NATIONAL ORGANIZATION FOR WOMEN, and the more radical social protest of women's liberation, but the term has been in widespread, general use since at least 1970.

The Women's Liberation Movement was born in America in the 1960s out of other movements of the political NEW LEFT, particularly the civil rights and antiwar movements. In 1964, Ruby Doris Robinson presented a paper protesting the inferior status of women in the Student Non-Violent Coordinating Committee (SNCC) which elicited Stokely Carmichael's notorious reply that 'The only position for women in SNCC is prone'. Feminists were also ridiculed for bringing up women's rights at the Students for a Democratic Society (SDS) conventions in 1965 and 1966. The final radicalizing experience took place at the National Conference for New Politics (NCNP) in Chicago in August 1967. This was a last attempt to pull together the various strands of the fragmented new left into a unified political movement. The major split at the conference was over race, and the men who dominated it felt that dividing representation and power by race was important, but that sexual discrimination was not. When a group of radical women led by Jo FREEMAN and Shulamith FIRESTONE attempted to present a resolution that women, who represented 51 per cent of the population, must receive 51 per cent of the convention votes, they were refused access to the microphones and told 'we have more important issues to talk about here than women's liberation'. In response, the women held a meeting in Chicago the following week, and wrote and circulated a paper, 'To the Women of the Left', calling on women to organize their own, autonomous movement for women's liberation.

Similar events in Canada at the founding meeting of the New Left Committee in September 1967 led to the first Canadian women's liberation collective, which was in close communication with the Chicago group from the beginning.

The idea of women's liberation spread rapidly through the networks established by political activism. The 'BURIAL OF TRADITIONAL WOMANHOOD' action in the midst of an anti-war demonstration in Washington, D.C., on 15 January 1968, brought together women from all over the country, and they organized groups in their own cities when they returned home.

The existence of the movement burst upon the general public in September 1968, during the Miss America pageant in Atlantic City, New Jersey, where demonstrations against SEXISM and the OBJECTIFICATION of women were given a great deal of media attention. This attention was almost uniformly hostile, with feminists represented as 'BRA-BURNERS', but all the publicity, no matter how negative, ensured that women everywhere, in all walks of life, became aware of the Women's Liberation Movement. Suddenly, what Betty FRIEDAN had called 'THE PROBLEM WITHOUT A NAME', had not only a name but a possible cure. With the exception of NOW, which was hardly prepared to lead a national mass movement, there was no organization to join. Women everywhere began to meet in small groups to discuss their problems, practise CONSCIOUSNESS-RAISING, or become involved in lobbying or direct action to change their circumstances. By 1970, the Women's Liberation Movement consisted of thousands of small groups and was growing and changing daily.

The term 'women's liberation' developed out of an identification by new left radical women with Third World and black liberation movements and because, in the late 1960s, 'liberation' was a concept much in favour. In the early days, some women preferred the term 'radical women's movement' or 'women's movement'. Jo Freeman who, as editor of VOICE OF THE WOMEN'S LIBERATION MOVEMENT, did more than anyone to popularize the term, explained the reasoning of those who advocated 'women's liberation' over 'women's movement': 'they wanted to define the terms of debate . . . The problem, they felt, was not one of women, but of women's liberation and the best way to get people to think of the problem in those terms was to label it as such from the very beginning.' (Freeman, 1975)

News of events in America, plus a growing awareness among women that they shared a similar oppression due to their sex, regardless of other circumstances, caused the WLM to spread to other Western countries.

In Britain, as in America, knowledge of radical politics combined with the experience of being excluded from meaningful action led many left-wing women towards feminism. Juliet MITCH-

ELL's essay 'THE LONGEST REVOLUTION' (1966) was an important step in reviving the 'woman question' on the left. When they interviewed women about how they came to feminism, Anna COOTE and Beatrix CAMPBELL (1982) found two things mentioned most frequently: the equal pay strike successfully staged by women sewing machinists at the Ford motor works in Dagenham in June 1968, and the arrival from America, in 1969, of Anne KOEDT's paper 'THE MYTH OF THE VAGINAL ORGANISM'. The first women's groups formed in 1968, and in 1969 several small groups banded together as a loose collective called the London Women's Liberation Workshop, and published a newsletter called SHREW. The first NATIONAL WOMEN'S LIBERATION CONFERENCE was held in 1970 at Ruskin College, Oxford.

Women's Liberation is now a worldwide movement, too diverse to summarize. Its originating concept, of women organizing around their own oppression and recognizing that the PERSONAL IS POLITICAL, retains its power, and although they may share the same ultimate goals women from different cultures and backgrounds will have different priorities, and will approach the struggle against sexist oppression from many different angles.

The WLM is not a club with membership requirements or lists of rules; it is not monolithic, but, rather, constantly changing.

Historically, social movements tend to become more centralized and bureaucratic as they grow older, yet the WLM continues to resist centralization and to mistrust leaders and hierarchies. Organization is still based around the small group, at the local level, with women's centres and specific, limited campaigns providing the impetus for activism. This lack of structure is sometimes considered a weakness, but it can also be seen as the movement's greatest strength, allowing it to continue to live and grow, in directions which cannot always be predicted.

(*See also* SEVEN DEMANDS; ZAP ACTIONS)

Women's Lib

A demeaning abbreviation for Women's Liberation. Although not always used with that intent, the shortening of 'liberation' to 'lib' is trivializing, and reflects male unwillingness to take women seriously.

women's movement

Vague, catch-all phrase which means different things to different people. It is more widely used, and more all-embracing, than either FEMINISM or WOMEN'S LIBERATION MOVEMENT, and can include any and all activities and organizations which have the aim of improving women's status and situation. The contemporary women's movement is usually considered to have started in the late 1960s, some forty years after the subsidence of what is called the FIRST WAVE OF FEMINISM, but many would agree with Mary Stott that 'There's always been a women's movement this century!'

women's music
See MUSIC AND MUSICIANS

Women's National Coordinating Committee

Short-lived British committee established at the first national women's liberation conference at RUSKIN COLLEGE in 1970 as a means of linking the autonomous women's liberation groups around the country. It was never meant to be a ruling body or to impose any formal structure on the local groups and, when political differences split the committee meetings, it was decided at Skegness in 1971 to dissolve the national committee and leave the movement to its natural diversity, its groups linked only by ideas and a common cause.

Women's Party, The

Name adopted by the WOMEN'S SOCIAL AND POLITICAL UNION on 2 November 1917, belatedly marking the change of direction the organization had taken at the outbreak of World War I from being militantly pro-suffrage to being extremely anti-German, with all other considerations submerged by the necessity of winning the war. Emmeline PANKHURST was Treasurer, Annie KENNEY was Secretary, Flora DRUMMOND was Chief Organizer, and Christabel PANKHURST continued to edit the party's official organ, *Britannia*. In addition to a fiercely xenophobic foreign policy, the party did have women's interests in mind, at least once the war was over. For the future they advocated equal pay for equal work, equal employment opportunities, and equal rights in marriage and divorce. 'Co-operative Housekeeping' was recommended as the means whereby all children would be equally well provided for by the community, and married women would be relieved of their customary double burden of paid job and unpaid housework. The Women's Party ended abruptly in 1919, when Christabel and Emmeline Pankhurst lost their faith in the power of the vote to change the world.

Women's Peace Party

American organization founded by Jane ADDAMS and Carrie Chapman CATT at a national conference held in Washington, D.C. in January 1915. Members included Anna Howard SHAW, Charlotte Perkins GILMAN and other prominent suffragists. Internal political frictions caused it to collapse within a few years, and it was absorbed by the WOMEN'S INTERNATIONAL LEAGUE FOR PEACE AND FREEDOM.

Women's Political Union
(first called the Equality League of Self-Supporting Women)

Organized in January 1907 by Harriot Stanton BLATCH in an attempt to recreate interest in the American women's movement, it began with a gathering of forty women in New York City, discussing how to put new life into the suffrage campaign. They decided that the time for discussion and education was past, and action must be taken, and they aimed to replace the leisured middle-class women, who made up other suffrage organizations, with working women in industry, business and the professions. By 1908 it had over 19,000 members and had succeeded in revitalizing the movement with political awareness, open-air suffrage meetings (the first in thirty years) and parades. In 1915 it merged with the CONGRESSIONAL UNION FOR WOMAN SUFFRAGE.

Women's Press, The

1) Founded in Toronto in 1970 by a socialist-feminist collective out of the desire to reflect the state of the women's movement in Canada at a time when most printed material about the women's liberation movement in North America was oriented around women in the United States. By 1985 they had published eighty-five books, most of them specifically Canadian in orientation, and including an annual thematic datebook titled *Everywoman's Almanac*.

2) Founded in London in 1977 'to publish work which reflects the goals of the WOMEN'S LIBERATION MOVEMENT, which is accessible in language and price, which looks good enough to compliment both the writer and the reader'. They publish original work, reprints and translations, non-fiction and fiction including feminist theory, philosophy, criticism, science fiction, novels, essays and short story collections.

(*See also* PUBLISHING)

Women's Review

London-based, monthly periodical founded in 1985 'out of the desire to create a free space where the voices of many women can be heard'. In the first issue the editors explained their aim: 'Because the creativity and culture of women has been trivialised, tokenised and plucked out of context in the mainstream press, much of women's work becomes a necessary part of defiance, self-defence and criticism of male structures. *Women's Review* will be a positive response to women's creativity, celebrating and affirming the richness of their work.' It received the 1985 Pandora Award from Women in Publishing in recognition of the magazine's positive contribution to the image of women in publishing.

Women's Review of Books, The

Monthly book review in newspaper form founded in 1983 by the Wellesley College Center for Research on Women (Wellesley, Massachusetts) covering current books in all fields by and/or about women. Its editorial policy is feminist but not defined specifically: 'We seek to represent the widest possible range of feminist perspectives both in the books reviewed and in the content of the reviews. We believe that no one of us, alone or in a group, can speak for feminism, or women, as such; all of our thinking and writing takes place in a specific political, social, ethnic and sexual context, and a responsible review periodical should reflect and further that diversity.'

Women's Revolutions per Minute (WRPM)

British feminist music distribution company based in Birmingham which combines politics, music and business. It was founded in 1977 by Nicolle Freni and Tierl Thompson to import women's music – mainly from OLIVIA RECORDS – from the United States. Caroline Hutton, who bought the business from them in 1979 and continues to run it, defines the aims of WRPM as being to provide positive images of women and communicate how women are changing themselves and the world, and to do this by making available women's music, promoting and encouraging women performers, playing an active role in the development of women's music in Britain, and to generate sufficient profit to employ women at a reasonable salary.
(*See also* MUSIC AND MUSICIANS)

women's rights movement

The aspect of feminism which considers women's emancipation to be chiefly or wholly a matter of legal changes, the winning of civil and property rights on a basis of equality with men. Although it is a part of the broader-based WOMEN'S LIBERATION MOVEMENT, it is different in that it is basically reformist in nature, accepting the male-defined status quo and seeking less to change it than to include more women within it. This term is sometimes used as a synonym for the women's suffrage movement.

Women's Room, The

Novel by Marilyn FRENCH published in 1977. Unrelentingly grim in its depiction of the ordinary lives of white, middle-class American women in the 1950s, '60s and early '70s, this book reveals in fictional form the failure of the FEMININE MYSTIQUE. A bestseller, it is probably the most widely-read novel to come out of the women's liberation movement. Although it may be criticized on literary grounds, it has more value as a work of sociology, and obviously filled a need for thousands of women who saw their own unhappiness echoed in this work of fiction. Fay Weldon called it 'the kind of book that changes lives'.

Women's Social and Political Union (WSPU)

The best known of the British women's suffrage organizations, it was started in Manchester in October 1903 by Emmeline PANKHURST and a small group of women who supported the Independent Labour Party, as a means of promoting the interests of working-class women. By 1906 it had moved away from the Labour Party, from Manchester, and into the middle class. When a London office was opened, Christabel PANKHURST became the chief organizer, aided by Sylvia PANKHURST as Secretary, Emmeline PETHICK-LAWRENCE as Treasurer, and Annie KENNEY as a paid organizer. A constitution was drafted by Teresa Billington which gave as the WSPU's objects:

'To secure for Women the Parliamentary Vote as it is or may be granted to men; to use the power thus obtained to establish equality of rights and opportunities between the sexes, and to promote the social and industrial well-being of the community.'

Methods for achieving these objects were listed:

'1. Action entirely independent of all political parties.

2. Opposition to whatever Government is in power until such time as the franchise is granted.

3. Participation in Parliamentary Elections in opposition to the Government candidate and independently of all other candidates.

4. Vigorous agitation upon lines justified by the position of outlawry to which women are at present condemned.

5. The organizing of women all over the country to enable them to give adequate expression to their desire for political freedom.

6. Education of public opinion by all the usual methods, such as public meetings, demonstrations, debates, distribution of literature, newspapers, correspondence, and deputations to public representatives.'

Membership was open to 'women of all shades of political opinion who approve the objects and methods of the Union, and who are prepared to act independently of party'.

The Union was never a democratically run organization, for it was dominated by the Pankhursts, who demanded unquestioning loyalty from their followers, and by the Pethick-Lawrences.

A campaign of militant feminism was started by Christabel Pankhurst: members of the WSPU, known commonly as SUFFRAGETTES, were encouraged to take actions which would cause them to be arrested and thus draw attention to their cause. It worked extremely well. As more and more suffragettes were arrested, refused to pay fines, and were sent to jail, the newspaper coverage attracted public sympathy and outrage, the WSPU grew and 'the woman question' had to be taken seriously by politicians.

By August 1907, the Union had expanded to seventy different branches around Britain. This led to a split between the followers of Emmeline and Christabel Pankhurst, and those who felt that local policies should be voted on by members of local branches. Emmeline Pankhurst announced a new committee composed of herself, Mabel Tuke, Emmeline Pethick-Lawrence, Christabel Pankhurst, Annie Kenney, Mary Gawthorpe, Mary Neal, Elizabeth ROBINS and Elizabeth WOLSTEN-HOLME-ELMY. All members were required to sign a pledge that they would not support the candidate of any political party until women had the vote.

Disturbed by these autocratic measures, some members broke away. Charlotte DESPARD, Caroline Hodgson, Teresa Billington, Irene Fenwick Miller and Edith HOW-MARTYN formed a committee and named the new group the WOMEN'S FREEDOM LEAGUE.

Despite the increasing visibility of the suffragettes, politicians, including the Prime Minister Herbert Asquith, expressed the opinion that most women did not want the vote. Hoping to prove him wrong, the WSPU held a mass meeting in Hyde Park on 21 June 1908. A march of some 30,000 – many of them wearing the WSPU colours of purple, green and white – was led by 'General' Flora DRUMMOND, and

between 250,000 and 500,000 gathered, although more apparently from curiosity than sympathy. At the end of the day a resolution was carried by acclamation: 'that this meeting calls upon the Government to grant votes to women without delay'. Asquith's response was negative, causing Christabel Pankhurst to declare that 'great meetings, although they are indispensable for rousing public interest, fail as a means of directly influencing the action of the government'. Emmeline Pethick-Lawrence wrote: 'It would be impossible to have a greater demonstration than we have held . . . Nothing but militant action is left to us now.'

In October 1912, Emmeline and Richard Pethick-Lawrence found themselves ousted from the Union by the Pankhursts. Unwilling to harm the cause to which they had devoted themselves for so many years, the Pethick-Lawrences did not complain and made no attempt to divide the Union. They continued to edit the journal *Votes for Women*, but it ceased to be the official WSPU organ and was replaced by the *Suffragette*, under the control of Christabel Pankhurst.

A violent new phase of militancy began in 1913 when Emmeline Pankhurst declared that suffragettes were 'guerrillists' who were warranted in employing methods of war. They held life sacred, so the damage they did was only to property, including window-breaking, stone-throwing, the burning of slogans onto putting greens, the cutting of telephone and telegraph lines, destruction of mail-boxes, and the burning and bombing of (empty) buildings, both public and private property. The reason for it all was 'to make the electors and the Government so uncomfortable that, in order to put an end to the nuisance, they will give women the vote.'

The militant campaign was ended not by the vote but by the outbreak of World War I in August 1914. Christabel Pankhurst wrote: 'All – everything – that we women have been fighting for and treasure would disappear in the event of a German victory.' WSPU meetings and speeches were devoted now to such subjects as 'The War Crisis' and 'The German Peril', and membership dropped off drastically. The total change in attitude can be illustrated by the drive, in 1915, led by the Pankhursts with Grace Roe and Annie Kenney, to recruit women to the munitions industry: the Ministry of Munitions awarded them a £2,000 grant to finance a celebration of 'women's right to serve'.

In 1916, two groups of former WSPU members still devoted to the cause of women's suffrage, formed 'The Suffragettes of the WSPU' and 'The Independent Women's Social and Political Union', but neither lasted long.

In 1917 the Pankhursts' WSPU changed its name to THE WOMEN'S PARTY, which lasted until 1919.

women's studies

In 1934, Mary Ritter BEARD wrote a 56-page syllabus for a course called 'A Changing Political Economy as it Affects Women', and although the syllabus was never used, she is now considered to have invented the concept of women's studies. Beard was ahead of her time as she struggled to change the study of HISTORY so that it included women's contributions. Not until the end of the 1960s, when the women's liberation movement had worked a change on public awareness, was there widespread recognition that women's experiences and achievements had been ignored or minimized in every academic discipline. Women began to demand to know more about women of the past and in other cultures, and American universities quickly responded with many courses, chiefly of the 'WOMEN AND . . .' variety, in history, literature, sociology, ANTHROPOLOGY and other departments. Within a few years, separate women's studies departments had been created, offering both undergraduate and graduate-level degrees.

In Britain, however, the universities – particularly the more traditional and prestigious ones – have been reluctant to acknowledge the existence of women's studies. The first M.A. in women's studies was offered by the University of Kent in 1980, and it was followed by Bradford in 1982 and Sheffield Polytechnic in 1983, but there are still no undergraduate degree courses. Feminists working in adult education in the late 1960s were the first to create women's studies courses, and directories of women's studies courses in the United Kingdom throughout the 1970s and 1980s have shown that the largest group of women's studies courses have been offered in the area of adult education.

Although women's studies emerged from the women's liberation movement, women's studies are not necessarily feminist. The National Women's Studies Association, founded in America in 1977, declared its aim to be that of promoting feminist EDUCATION, but there are those who feel politics – feminist or otherwise – should be kept out of academia. This point of view sees women's studies as an area of study like any other, with the subject 'women' to be examined within the context of traditional, male-defined fields. Women are merely added-on, and the male-centred perspective is not challenged.

To feminist scholars, however, women's studies is something new, with the potential to change the very nature of knowledge by refusing to accept an ANDROCENTRIC viewpoint, by reconsidering every-thing from a woman-centred perspective. Dale SPENDER has pointed out this revolutionary aspect by referring to women's studies as 'men's studies modified'.

According to Gloria Bowles and Renate Duelli Klein, the crucial debate on the subject of women's studies in the 1980s is between the integrationists who want to see feminist scholarship incorporated into existing disciplines, to change them from within, and those who consider women's studies a discipline of its own, necessarily kept separate as a centre for the development of radical feminist thought.

Women's Suffrage Journal, The

English periodical founded by Lydia BECKER in March 1870, and edited by her until her death in 1891. It was, for more than twenty years, a clear, careful and detailed record of every speech and event, in or out of Parliament, which seemed likely to favour the granting of votes to women.

Women's Suffrage Movement

Also called, in America, the woman suffrage movement, this long struggle to win the vote is the best-known part of the FIRST WAVE OF FEMINISM.

The beginning, in America, is usually considered to have been the SENECA FALLS convention of 1848, at which a resolution was passed 'That it is the duty of the women of this country to secure to themselves their sacred right to the elective franchise.' Many women felt this was too radical a demand, but others, who prevailed, felt that only the vote would enable women to secure their other rights. After the Civil War, the Fourteenth and Fifteenth Amendments, which conferred the rights and duties of citizens, including the vote, upon the newly freed slaves, seemed to offer a similar hope to women. But the word 'male' was introduced. Despite many ardent campaigns, white women were told they must wait, and not spoil 'the Negroes' hour', and black women were encouraged to consider the good of the whole race, and be patient a while longer. Although some, like Sojourner TRUTH, recognized that '. . . if colored men get their rights and not colored women theirs, you see the colored men will be masters over the women, and it will be just as bad as it was before', few were willing to risk leaving all power in the hands of white men.

For white feminists in particular, many of whom had been involved in the ABOLITION MOVEMENT, the passage of the Fifteenth Amendment in 1870 was a bitter disappointment. The women's movement split into two major factions, one represented by the 'respectable' AMERICAN WOMAN SUFFRAGE ASSOCIATION, which concentrated on the vote, and the other, the more revolutionary NATIONAL WOMAN SUFFRAGE ASSOCIATION which continued to emphasize the importance of other aims besides suffrage. By 1890, however, the conservatives were in the lead, and the women's movement had become effectively a single-issue movement. The American and the National merged to become the NATIONAL AMERICAN WOMAN SUFFRAGE ASSOCIATION. Despite their agreement and dedication, however, they had no clear ideas how to go about winning the vote, and the suffrage movement entered a stagnant period in which little was accomplished. In 1913, Alice PAUL revitalized the movement with tactics she had learned in England from the SUFFRAGETTES. Her CONGRESSIONAL UNION FOR WOMEN'S SUFFRAGE became the radical wing of the American movement. Then, in 1915, Carrie Chapman CATT brought new conviction to NAWSA with her 'Winning Plan'. Between the two forces – mass demonstrations and militant tactics on one side, diplomacy, charm and lobbying on the other – the woman suffrage amendment, known as the ANTHONY AMENDMENT, which had been introduced into every Congressional session from 1878, was finally ratified on 26 August 1920.

The starting date for the British women's suffrage movement might be said to be 7 June 1866 – the day Emily DAVIES and Elizabeth GARRETT, on behalf of the KENSINGTON SOCIETY and 1,499 women, gave a petition for women's enfranchisement to John Stuart MILL, who had agreed to present it to Parliament. In January 1867 Lydia BECKER formed the first suffrage society – the Manchester Women's Suffrage Committee. More petitions were presented to Parliament, and there was always a certain amount of support for limited suffrage – that is, for extending existing voting rights to property-owning women – but for the next thirty years women's suffrage was a minority interest rather than a movement, kept alive by the tireless activities of Lydia Becker and a few other dedicated women. After Becker's death in 1890, Millicent Garrett FAWCETT emerged as the new leader, but the movement was effectively reborn with the founding of the WOMEN'S SOCIAL AND POLITICAL UNION (WSPU) in 1903 by Emmeline PANKHURST.

Whereas Mrs Fawcett was always respectable and law-abiding in her pursuit of the vote, the charismatic Pankhursts led the WSPU into a campaign of militancy in which thousands of women broke the law and went to gaol to prove their determination to have the vote.

The Electoral Reform Bill, giving the vote to all women aged thirty and over, became law in January 1918. In 1928 the age limitation became the same as for men, twenty-one.

The vote took on such great symbolic significance during the long years in which men argued it was too important to entrust to women, and women insisted it was too important to leave in the hands of men alone, that the achievement of women's suffrage might have been expected to usher in utopia. In fact, little changed, either in the lives of individual women, or in the way laws were made. Until the discovery of a GENDER GAP in America in the 1980s, it seemed that sex had no noticeable effect on the way people voted. Although the women's movement was never only a movement for women's suffrage, that one issue had become so predominant that when the women's suffrage movement was ended, feminism, too, seemed to have achieved its goal. Although it never entirely disappeared, it went into a quiet phase, losing force as a social movement until the late 1960s.

The following chart shows when women in various countries gained the right to vote on an equal basis with men. (Information from *Sisterhood is Global*, edited by Robin MORGAN, 1984, and *Votes for Women* by Roger Fulford, 1957.)

1893 New Zealand
1902 Australia
1906 Finland
1913 Norway
1915 Denmark, Iceland
1917 USSR
1918 Canada
1919 Austria, Germany,
        the Netherlands, Poland,

	Sweden, Luxembourg, Czechoslovakia
1920	USA
1922	Ireland
1928	Great Britain
1929	Ecuador
1930	South Africa
1931	Spain, Sri Lanka, Portugal
1932	Thailand
1934	Brazil, Cuba
1936	Costa Rica
1937	Philippines
1941	Indonesia
1942	Dominican Republic, Uruguay
1945	France, Hungary, Italy, Japan, Vietnam, Yugoslavia, Bolivia
1946	Albania, Rumania, Panama
1947	Argentina, Venezuela
1948	Israel, Korea
1949	China, Chile
1950	El Salvador, Ghana, India
1951	Nepal
1952	Greece
1953	Mexico
1954	Columbia
1955	Nicaragua
1956	Egypt, Pakistan, Senegal
1957	Lebanon
1959	Morocco
1962	Algeria
1963	Iran, Kenya, Libya
1964	Sudan, Zambia
1965	Afghanistan, Guatemala
1977	Nigeria
1979	Peru, Zimbabwe

(See also ANTHONY, SUSAN B.; STANTON, ELIZABETH CADY; CHORLTON V. LINGS; CAT AND MOUSE ACT; BLACK FRIDAY; DRUMMOND, FLORA; PETHICK-LAWRENCE, EMMELINE; WOMEN'S FRANCHISE LEAGUE; WOMEN'S FREEDOM LEAGUE; HUNGER STRIKES)

Women's Suffrage National Aid Corps (WSNAC)

Organization established in London by the Women's Freedom League during World War I to provide for the women and children left with insufficient support when their men went to war. Free clinics and a distribution system for milk and children's clothes were established, as well as cheap cafés and at least one shop to provide more employment. At the same time, a sister group, the League of Rights for Soldiers' and Sailors' Wives and Relations, was pressing the government to provide them with better allowances and pensions.

Women's Theatre Group

The longest-running, professional all-woman theatre company in Britain, it was organized in 1973 after a season of women's plays at the Almost Free Theatre in London. Their aim is to explore social and political issues from a feminist standpoint, as well as to provide opportunities for women to work in every aspect of theatrical production. They are limited by funds to producing only two or three productions a year, and alternate between collectively created works, and commissioning new plays from women playwrights.

womon

New spelling of woman preferred by some feminists as a way of emphasizing that they are woman-identified and, quite literally and comprehensively, removing man from their self-proclaimed identity. The plural form is usually spelled wimmin or womyn.

Woodhull, Victoria (Claflin), 1838–1927

American. One of the most outrageous and colourful figures of the women's rights movement, she combined a belief in the full legal and moral equality of women and men with strong interests in spiritualism, free love, eugenics, and other unpopular causes of her day. With her sister, Tennessee CLAFLIN, she worked as a travelling mind-reader and public lecturer. They were the first women stockbrokers in America and published their own journal, *Woodhull and Claflin's Weekly*, from 1870–6. In 1871, she scored a great victory for the suffrage movement by convincing the Senate Judiciary Committee to hear her plea for a constitutional amendment; in the same year, however, she scandalized the more conservative suffragists by speaking in favour of free love, and was defeated in her bid for leadership of the NATIONAL WOMAN SUFFRAGE ASSOCIATION. Undeterred, she ran for President of the United States, the first woman ever to do so. In 1877, she moved to London where she became a society hostess and took part in the women's suffrage movement there.

Woolf, Virginia, 1882–1941

English writer. The study of Virginia Woolf and her writings amounts to a small industry in itself these days, due to the development and rapid growth of a feminist LITERARY CRITICISM. Prior to the raising of feminist consciousness, most of those who wrote about Woolf depicted her as an élitist, utterly non-political artist, but now her interest in and importance to women has been discovered, and she is recognized as an important feminist philosopher, as well as novelist and critic.

The most important of her feminist writings (although she did not like to call herself a feminist), A ROOM OF ONE'S OWN (1928) and *Three Guineas* (1938), anticipated and provided the basis for much that has been written since on such subjects as women and writing, women's relationship to male-defined culture, a specifically female literary tradition, and the importance to women of economic independence. Although it would be hard to define any of her novels as feminist, all of them contain strong feminist elements with as much interest for women today as when they were first published. *The Voyage Out* (1915) and *Night and Day* (1919) explore the problems of marriage and career faced by young women; *Mrs Dalloway* (1922) is a close examination of female consciousness; *To the Lighthouse* (1927) reveals the conflict between women and men, sympathy and egotism; *Orlando* (1928) plays with ANDROGYNY as it lightly investigates the nature of sexuality; *The Years* (1937) examines women's lives through changing times. Her style, too, has provided much material for those who argue that there are important differences between masculine and feminine writing.

work

There is a human need for work, and when Victorian society denied middle-class women most outlets to express it (even denying that they had such a need), the growth of a feminist movement was inevitable. The earliest campaigns for women's rights centred on EDUCATION (as a means to prepare women to work), on meaningful employment for unmarried women, and on alternatives to marriage as women's only 'career'. Women already in paid employment campaigned for better working conditions, for better pay, and – somewhat later – for EQUAL PAY FOR EQUAL WORK.

Women have always worked, whether or not they have been paid for it, and another important feminist goal is to have this work acknowledged. This includes not only the abolition of the concept of 'women's work', and equal pay-

ment for what men have defined as work, but also a redefinition of the concept of work which would break down the dichotomy between public and private.

(*See also* HOUSEWORK; REPRODUCTION; WAGES FOR HOUSEWORK)

World Plan of Action for Women

Plan for the worldwide improvement of the status of women adopted by delegates to the United Nations conference in Mexico City in 1975, endorsed later that same year by the U.N. General Assembly.

(*See also* INTERNATIONAL WOMEN'S YEAR)

World Woman's Party

Founded in November 1938 by Alice PAUL and the NATIONAL WOMAN'S PARTY 'to raise the status of women throughout the world'. Based in Geneva, with Emmeline PETHICK-LAWRENCE the honorary president, this organization was dedicated to the idea that to be effective, the women's movement must become international, and that through the solidarity of women across national boundaries, freedom and equality for all would eventually be achieved. The World Woman's Party had a notable effect on the United Nations, ensuring that declarations affirming the principle of 'the equal rights of men and women' were included throughout the United Nationals

Charter, and later helped establish a U.N. Commission on the Status of Women which presented a report, urging complete equality for women in all fields, to the General Assembly of the United Nations in New York in 1947. The World Woman's Party continued to promote the cause of equal suffrage, equal legal rights and equal power for women throughout the world well into the 1950s.

Wright, Frances (Fanny),
1795–1852
Scottish-American. Radical reformer, orator and world traveller, she founded Nashoba, an experimental settlement in Tennessee for the education and gradual emancipation of slaves. She lec-

tured widely in public at a time when this was almost unheard of for a woman, and edited the *New Harmony Gazette* with Robert Dale Owen. Despite her friendship with Lucretia MOTT, she had little sympathy with the largely middle-class women's movement of her day, preferring to devote her efforts to helping the working class. Yet she believed in, and spoke out for, women's rights to equality in law, better education, birth control and free love.

writing
See LANGUAGE; L'ÉCRITURE FÉMININE; LITERARY CRITICISM; NOVELS AND NOVELISTS; POETS AND POETRY.

Writing the Body
See L'ÉCRITURE FÉMININE

X

X

Name of the gender-free child in a story by Lois Gould, *X: A Fabulous Child's Story* (1972) which did much to demonstrate the impact sex-role stereotyping has upon individuals by showing what freedom from it might be like. The story, which was first published in *Ms.* and later reprinted by Daughters Publishing Co., was also influential in popularizing the concept of ANDROGYNY as a desirable feminist goal.

X, Laura

American. Born Laura Shaw Murra, she followed the example of Malcolm X and rejected her slave name because it symbolized patriarchal ownership. X, adopted in 1969, symbolizes the anonymity of women's HISTORY. Her work within the Women's Liberation Movement has been varied and influential. In 1968 she founded the Women's History Research Center in Berkeley, California, which also doubled as an emergency shelter for BATTERED WOMEN and their children. In 1969 she began her ultimately successful campaign to win national recognition for INTERNATIONAL WOMEN'S DAY by organizing the first public event in its honour in the United States in twenty-two years. In 1970 she co-founded, edited and published a feminist newspaper called *It Ain't Me Babe*, and her interest in women's music was reflected in the concerts she gave with Redstockings West, and her publication of *The Women's Songbook* in 1971. Since 1975 she has been researching and campaigning on the issue of marital RAPE. In 1979, largely due to her efforts, the Governor of California passed a bill making marital rape a crime. In 1980 she established the National Clearinghouse on Marital Rape in order to educate the public and to offer technical assistance to campaigns in other states.

Xiang Jingyu (Hsiang Ching-yu), 1895–1928

Chinese revolutionary. As a student, she was one of the leaders in the May 4th movement of 1915 and, after graduation, she worked as a teacher and led an anti-foot-binding campaign. Her decision to cut her hair short made it the fashion among other Chinese intellectuals and feminists. At the Chinese Communist Party's Second National Congress in 1922 she was elected a member of the Central Committee and made head of the Women's Department which she had established almost single-handed. The author of many articles on the position of women and the women's movement in China, she was critical of all non-SOCIALIST FEMINISTS, arguing that only radical change in the existing social system could improve women's position, and that the struggle for women's emancipation must be a part of the overall political movement to change China. She was arrested for her political activities and executed in May 1928.

Y

'Yellow Wallpaper, The'
Story by Charlotte Perkins GILMAN, first published in 1892 and probably the best known of her writings. Autobiographical, it tells of a young mother driven to madness by the care of her well-meaning doctor/husband. In real life, the author found that the forced idleness and dependency of a 'rest cure' drove her nearly to madness, and it was only a divorce and meaningful work which brought her out of depression. For many years considered one of the great American tales of horror, 'The Yellow Wallpaper' was rediscovered in the early 1970s and read from a feminist perspective.

Z

zap action
Form of protest and guerrilla theatre popular in late 1960s and early 1970s with some American feminist organizations including WITCH; a symbolic, public activity designed to attract attention to a specific issue and thereby raise the public consciousness about sexism in general. They included a mock ceremony in which a sheep was crowned outside the 1968 Miss America Contest and a funeral march mourning those who had died of self-induced abortions, held in March 1970, as the Michigan Legislature debated an abortion reform bill.

Zetkin, Clara (Eissner), 1854–1933
German. Her feminism was inspired by her mother, Josephine Vitale Eissner, and her teacher, Auguste SCHMIDT. Joining the German Social Democratic Party (SPD) in 1881, she soon became, after Friedrich ENGELS and August BEBEL, the principal socialist theoretician of the 'woman question'. She considered that women's economic dependence on men and lack of employment was at the root of their oppression. In her view, women and men were fundamentally different, but their different roles were of equal importance; it was for the good of all society that women should be able to fulfil their functions as mothers, wives and, like men, as social beings through meaningful work. Her analysis emphasized class over sex: women must have rights not for their own sakes, but for the good of the working class as a whole.

Refusing any alliance with BOURGEOIS FEMINISTS as impossible, Zetkin organized the first mass working-class women's emancipation movement in Europe during the 1890s, and edited the socialist women's magazine *Die Gleichheit* (Equality) from 1892–1917. In 1907, she created the Socialist Women's International and, in 1910, she proposed the recognition of INTERNATIONAL WOMEN'S DAY, which is still celebrated on 8 March.

Bibliography

Abbott, Sidney and Love, Barbara, *Sappho Was a Right-On Woman: A Liberated View of Lesbianism*. New York: Stein and Day, 1973.

Abel, Elizabeth and Abel, Emily K. (eds), *The Signs Reader: Women, Gender and Scholarship*. Chicago: University of Chicago Press, 1983.

Adams, Abigail, letter to John Adams, Braintree, 31 March 1776, in *The Feminist Papers*, edited by Alice S. Rossi, 1974.

Adler, Margot, *Drawing Down the Moon: Witches, Druids, Goddess-Worshippers and Other Pagans in America Today*. New York: Viking, 1979.

Alpert, Jane, *Growing Up Underground*. New York: William Morrow & Co., 1981.

Amos, Valerie and Parmar, Pratibha, 'Challenging Imperial Feminism', in *Feminist Review*, 17, Autumn 1984.

Ascher, Carol, DeSalvo, Louise and Ruddick, Sara (eds), *Between Women: Biographers, Novelists, Critics, Teachers and Artists Write About Their Work on Women*. Boston: Beacon Press, 1984.

Atkinson, Ti-Grace, 'Radical Feminism', in *Notes from the Second Year*, 1970.
'The Institution of Sexual Intercourse', in *Notes from the Second Year*, 1970.

Bachofen, J.J., *Myth, Religion and Mother Right*. Princeton University Press, Bollingen Series, 1973.

Banks, Olive, *Faces of Feminism*. Oxford: Martin Robertson, 1981.
The Biographical Dictionary of British Feminists: Vol. 1 1800–1930. Brighton: Harvester Press, 1985.

Barr, Marlene, S. (ed), *Future Females: A Critical Anthology*. Bowling Green State University Popular Press, 1981.

Barrett, Michèle, *Women's Oppression Today: Problems in Marxist Feminist Analysis*. London: Verso, 1980.
'Introduction' to *Women and Writing* by Virginia Woolf. 1979.

Barry, Kathleen, *Female Sexual Slavery*. New Jersey: Prentice-Hall, Inc., 1979.
'Beyond Pornography: From Defensive Politics to Creating a Vision', in *Take Back the Night*, edited by Laura Lederer. 1982.

Bartky, Sandra, 'Narcissism, Femininity and Alienation', in *Social Theory and Practice 8*, no. 2. Summer 1982.

Baum, Charlotte, Hyman, Paula and Michel, Sonya (eds), *The Jewish Woman in America*. New York: The Dial Press, 1976.

Beal, Frances M., 'Double Jeopardy: To Be Black and Female', in *Sisterhood is Powerful*, edited by Robin Morgan, 1970.

Beauvoir, Simone de, *The Second Sex*, translated and edited by H.M. Parshley. London: Jonathan Cape, 1953.

Becker, Susan D., *The Origins of the Equal Rights Amendment: American Feminism Between the Wars*. Westport & London: Greenwood Press, 1981.

Bell, Quentin, *Virginia Woolf: A Biography*. London: Hogarth Press, 1972.

Berg, Barbara J., *The Remembered Gate: Origins of American Feminism 1800–1860*. London: Oxford University Press, 1978.

Bernard, Jessie, 'The Paradox of the Happy Marriage' in *Woman in Sexist Society*, edited by Gornick and Moran, 1972.

Bernikow, Louise (ed), *The World Split Open: Women Poets 1552–1950*. New York: Vintage Books, 1974.

    Among Women. New York: Harmony Books, 1980.

Bird, Caroline, *The Spirit of Houston: The First National Women's Conference*. Washington, D.C.: U.S. Government Printing Office, 1978.

Blackwood, Caroline, *On the Perimeter*. London: Fontana, 1984.

Boston Women's Health Book Collective, *Our Bodies, Ourselves: A Health Book by and for Women*. British Edition by Angela Phillips and Jill Rakusen, Penguin Books, 1978.

Bouchier, David, *The Feminist Challenge: The Movement for Women's Liberation in Britain and the United States*. London: Macmillan Ltd., 1983.

Bowles, Gloria and Klein, Renate Duelli (eds), *Theories of Women's Studies*. London: Routledge and Kegan Paul, 1983.

Breaching the Peace. London: Onlywomen Press, 1983.

Briffault, Robert, *The Mothers*, abridged by Gordon Rattray Taylor. London: George Allen and Unwin, 1959.

Britten, Margaret, *The Single Woman in the Family of God*. London: Epworth Press, 1984.

Brown, Cheryl L. and Olson, Karen (eds), *Feminist Criticism: Essays on Theory, Poetry and Prose*. Metuchen, N.J. and London: The Scarecrow Press, Inc., 1978.

Brown, Janet, *Feminist Drama: Definition and Critical Analysis*. New Jersey and London: The Scarecrow Press, Inc., 1979.

Brownmiller, Susan, *Against Our Will: Men, Women and Rape*. New York: Simon & Schuster, 1975.

    'Let's Put Pornography Back in the Closet', in *Take Back the Night*, edited by Laura Lederer, 1982.

    Femininity. London: Hamish Hamilton, 1984.

Brownstein, Rachel M., *Becoming a Heroine: Reading About Women in Novels*. London: Penguin Books, 1984.

Buhle, Mari Jo and Paul (eds), *The Concise History of Woman Suffrage: Selections from the Classic Work of Stanton, Anthony, Gage and Harper*. Urbana: University of Illinois Press, 1978.

Building Feminist Theory: Essays from Quest, a feminist quarterly. New York and London; Longman, 1981.

Bullock, Alan and Stallybrass, Oliver, *The Fontana Dictionary of Modern Thought*. London: Fontana Books, 1977.

Bunch, Charlotte, 'Not for Lesbians Only', in *Building Feminist Theory: Essays From* Quest. New York and London: Longman, 1981.
    'Beyond Either/Or: Feminist Options'. New York: Longman, 1981.
    'The Reform Tool Kit'. New York: Longman, 1981.
    'Feminism in the 80s: Facing Down the Right', speech given at second Lesbians' Colorado conference, 23 November 1980; distributed by The Crossing Press, 1981.

Bunch, Charlotte and Pollack, Sandra (eds), *Learning Our Way: Essays in Feminist Education*. New York: The Crossing Press, 1983.

Burris, Barbara, 'The Fourth World Manifesto', in *Notes From the Third Year*, New York, 1971.

Cadman, Eileen, Chester, Gail, and Pivot, Agnes, *Rolling Our Own: Women as printers, publishers and distributors*. London: Minority Press Group, 1981.

Caesar, Ann, 'Italian Feminism and the Novel: Sibilla Aleramo's *A Woman*', in *Feminist Review* 5, 1980.

Cambridge Women's Peace Collective, *My Country is the Whole World: An Anthology of Women's Work on Peace and War*. London: Pandora Press, 1984.

Cameron, Deborah, *Feminism and Linguistic Theory*. London: Macmillan Ltd, 1985.

Campbell, Beatrix, *Wigan Pier Revisited: Poverty and Politics in the Eighties*. London: Virago, 1984.

Carden, Maren Lockwood, *The New Feminist Movement*. New York: Russell Sage Foundation, 1974.

Cartledge, Sue and Ryan, Joanna, *Sex and Love: New Thoughts on Old Contradictions*. London: The Women's Press, 1984.

Chapman, Jane Roberts and Gates, Margaret (eds), *Women Into Wives: The Legal and Economic Impact of Marriage*. Vol. 2, Sage Yearbooks in Women's Policy Studies. London: Sage Publications, 1977.

Charvet, John, *Feminism*. London: J.M. Dent & Sons, 1982.

Chesler, Phyllis, *Women and Madness*. New York: Doubleday, 1972.
    About Men. New York: Bantam Books, 1980.
    'Patient and Patriarch: Women in the Psychotherapeutic relationship', in *Women in Sexist Society*, edited by Gornick and Moran, 1972.

Chester, Laura and Barba, Sharon (eds), *Rising Tides: 20th Century American Women Poets*. New York: Washington Square Press, 1973.

Chew, Doris Nield, *The Life and Writings of Ada Nield Chew*. London: Virago Press, 1982.

Chicago, Judy, *Through the Flower: My Struggle as a Woman Artist*. New York: Doubleday, 1975. London: The Women's Press, 1982.

Chodorow, Nancy, *The Reproduction of Mothering: Psychoanalysis and the Socio-*

logy of Gender. Berkeley and London: The University of California Press, 1978.

Chopin, Kate, *The Awakening*. New York: Avon, 1972.

Cisler, Lucinda, 'On Abortion and Abortion Law', in *Notes from the Second Year*, 1970.

    'Unfinished Business: Birth Control and Women's Liberation'; in *Sisterhood is Powerful*, edited by Robin Morgan, 1970.

Cixous, Hélène, 'The Laugh of the Medusa', in *New French Feminisms*, edited by Marks and de Courtivron. 1981.

Clardy, Andrea Fleck, 'Bestsellers from Crone's Own, Light Cleaning, Down There, and Dozens of Other Feminist Presses' in *Ms*. Vol. XIV, No. 2, August 1985.

Clark, Gracia, 'The Beguines: A Medieval Women's Community', in *Building Feminist Theory: Essays from* Quest. New York and London: Longman, 1981.

Clausen, Jan, *A Movement of Poets: Thoughts on Poetry and Feminism*. New York: Long Haul Press, 1982.

Clements, Barbara Evans, *Bolshevik Feminist: The Life of Alexandra Kollontai* Bloomington and London: Indiana University Press, 1979.

Collins, Wendy, Friedman, Ellen and Pivot, Agnes, *Women: Vol. 3 of The Directory of Social Change*. London: Wildwood House, 1978.

Combahee River Collective, 'A Black Feminist Statement', in *Capitalist Patriarchy and the Case for Socialist Feminism* edited by Zillah Einstein. New York: Monthly Review Press, 1979.

Coote, Anna and Campbell, Beatrix, *Sweet Freedom: The Struggle for Women's Liberation*. London: Picador, 1982.

Costin, Lela B., 'Feminism, Pacifism, Internationalism and the 1915 International Congress of Women', in *Women's Studies International Forum*, Vol. 5, No. 3/4, 1982.

Coveney, L., Jackson, M., Jeffreys, S., Kaye, L., and Mahoney, P., *The Sexuality Papers: Male Sexuality and the Social Control of Women*. London: Hutchinson, 1984.

Coward, Rosalind, *Patriarchal Precedents: Sexuality and Social Relations*. London: Routledge and Kegan Paul, 1983.

    'Are Women's Novels Feminist Novels?' in *The New Feminist Criticism* edited by Elaine Showalter, 1985.

    'Socialism, Feminism and Socialist Feminism' in *No Turning Back* edited by Feminist Anthology Collective, 1981.

Croll, Elizabeth, *Feminism and Socialism in China*. London: Routledge and Kegan Paul, 1978.

    The Women's Movement in China: A Selection of Readings. London: Anglo-Chinese Educational Institute, Modern China Series No. 6, 1974.

Daly, Mary, *Beyond God the Father: Toward a Philosophy of Women's Liberation*. Boston: Beacon Press, 1977.

Gyn/Ecology: The Metaethics of Radical Feminism. London: The Women's Press, 1979.

Pure Lust: Elemental Feminist Philosophy. London: The Women's Press, 1984.

Damon, Gene, 'The Least of These: The Minority Whose Screams Haven't Yet Been Heard', in *Sisterhood is Powerful* edited by Robin Morgan. 1970.

Davis, Barbara Hillyer, 'Disabled Women: Speaking for Ourselves', in *The Women's Review of Books,* Vol. III, No. 2, November 1985.

Davis, Elizabeth Gould, *The First Sex.* Baltimore: Penguin, 1972.

Deckard, Barbara Sinclair, *The Women's Movement: Political, Socioeconomic and Psychological Issues.* New York: Harper & Row, 1983.

De Lauretis, Teresa, *Alice Doesn't: Feminism, Semiotics, Cinema.* London: Macmillan, 1984.

Delmar, Rosalind, 'What is feminism?' in *The Body Politic* edited by Michelene Wandor. 1978.

Delphy, Christine, *Close to Home: A Materialist Analysis of Women's Oppression* translated and edited by Diana Leonard. London: Hutchinson, 1984.

Densmore, Dana, 'Independence from the Sexual Revolution', in *Notes from the Third Year,* 1971.

Diner, Helen, *Mothers and Amazons: The First Feminine History of Culture,* translated and edited by John Philip Lundin. New York: Doubleday, 1973.

Dinnerstein, Dorothy, *The Mermaid and the Minotaur: Sexual Arrangements and Human Malaise.* New York: Harper & Row, 1976.

Dreifus, Claudia, *Seizing our Bodies: The Politics of Women's Health,* New York: Vintage Books, 1978.

   'The Selling of a Feminist' in *Notes from the Third Year,* 1971.

Dunbar, Roxanne, 'Female Liberation as the Basis for Social Revolution', in *Notes from the Second Year,* 1970.

Dworkin, Andrea, *Woman Hating.* New York: E.P. Dutton and Co., 1974.

   'Why So-Called Radical Men Love and Need Pornography', in *Take Back the Night,* edited by Laura Lederer. 1982.

   'For Men, Freedom of Speech; for Women, Silence Please', in *Take Back the Night,* edited by Laura Lederer. 1982.

   'Pornography and Grief', in *Take Back the Night,* edited by Laura Lederer. 1982.

   Right Wing Women: The Politics of Domesticated Females. London: The Women's Press, 1983.

Echols, Alice, 'The Taming of the Id: Feminist Sexual Politics, 1968–83', in *Pleasure and Danger: Exploring Female Sexuality,* edited by Carole S. Vance, 1984.

Edmondson, Linda Harriet, *Feminism in Russia 1900–1917.* London: Heinemann, 1984.

Egerton, Jayne, 'Prudes and Puritans', in *Women Against Violence Against Women*, edited by Rhodes and McNeil. 1985.

Ehrenreich, Barbara, *The Hearts of Men: American Dreams and the Flight From Commitment*. London: Pluto Press, 1983.

'The Real and Ever-Widening Gender Gap' in *Esquire*, June 1984.

Ehrenreich, Barbara and English, Deidre, *For Her Own Good: 150 Years of the Experts' Advice to Women*. London: Pluto Press, 1979.

Ehrlich, Carol, 'The Unhappy Marriage of Marxism and Feminism: Can It Be Saved' in *Women and Revolution*, edited by Lydia Sargent, 1981.

'Socialism, Anarchism and Feminism' in *Quiet Rumours*. London: Dark Star, no date.

Eisenstein, Hester, *Contemporary Feminist Thought*. London: Unwin, 1984.

Eisenstein, Zillah R., *The Radical Future of Liberal Feminism*. London: Longman, 1981.

Feminism and Sexual Equality: Crisis in Liberal America. New York: Monthly Review Press, 1984.

(ed) *Capitalist Patriarchy and the Case for Socialist Feminism*. New York & London: Monthly Review Press, 1979.

Elgin, Suzette Haden, *A First Dictionary and Grammar of Láadan*. Madison: The Society for the Furtherance and Study of Fantasy and Science Fiction, 1985.

Ellmann, Mary, *Thinking About Women*. London: Virago, 1979.

Ernst, Sheila and Goodison, Lucy, *In Our Own Hands: A Book of Self-Help Therapy*. London: The Women's Press, 1981.

Evans, Mari (ed), *Black Women Writers: Arguments and Interviews*. London: Pluto Press, 1985.

Evans, Mary (ed), *The Woman Question: Readings on the Subordination of Women*. London: Fontana, 1982.

Evans, Richard J., *The Feminists: Women's Emancipation Movements in Europe, America and Australasia 1840–1920*. London: Croom Helm, 1984.

Evans, Sara, *Personal Politics: The Roots of Women's Liberation in the Civil Rights Movement and the New Left*. New York: Vintage Books, 1980.

Faderman, Lillian, *Surpassing the Love of Men*. London: Junction Books, 1981.

Fairbairns, Zoë, *Benefits*. London: Virago, 1979.

Farrow, Lynne, 'Feminism as Anarchism'. 1974; reprinted in *Quiet Rumours*. London: Dark Star, no date.

Feminism and Nonviolence Study Group, *Piecing it Together: Feminism and Nonviolence*. Feminism and Nonviolence Study Group, 2 College Close, Buckleigh, Westwood Ho, Devon, 1983.

Feminist Anthology Collective, *No Turning Back: Writings from the Women's Liberation Movement, 1975–1980*. London: The Women's Press, 1981.

Ferguson, Mary Anne (ed), *Images of Women in Literature, Third Edition*. Boston: Houghton Mifflin, 1981.

Ferree, Myra Marx and Hess, Beth B., *Controversy and Coalition: The New Feminist Movement*. Boston: Twayne Publishers, 1985.

Figes, Eva, *Patriarchal Attitudes*. London: Faber and Faber, 1970. New York: Fawcett, 1971.

Firestone, Shulamith, *The Dialectic of Sex: The Case for Feminist Revolution*. New York: Bantam, 1971.
    'On American Feminism', in *Woman in Sexist Society,* edited by Gornick and Moran. 1972.

First, Ruth and Scott, Ann, *Olive Schreiner*. London: Andre Deutsch, 1980.

Fisher, Elizabeth, *Woman's Creation: Sexual Evolution and the Shaping of Society*. New York: McGraw-Hill, 1980.

Flexner, Eleanor, *Century of Struggle: The Woman's Rights Movement in the United States*. New York: Atheneum, 1974.

Foreman, Ann, *Femininity as Alienation: Women and the Family in Marxism and Psychoanalysis*. London: Pluto Press, 1977.

Francke, Linda Bird, *The Ambivalence of Abortion*. London: Allen Lane, 1979.

Frankfort, Ellen, *Vaginal Politics*. New York: Bantam, 1973.

Freeman, Jo, *The Politics of Women's Liberation*. New York & London: Longman, 1975.

French, Marilyn, *The Women's Room*. London: Sphere, 1978.
    Beyond Power: Women, Men and Morals. London: Jonathan Cape, 1985.

Friedan, Betty, *The Feminine Mystique*. London: Penguin, 1982.
    It Changed My Life. New York: Dell, 1977.
    The Second Stage. London: Abacus, 1983.

Friedman, Scarlet and Sarah, Elizabeth (eds), *On the Problem of Men: Two Feminist Conferences*. London: The Women's Press, 1982.

Fritz, Leah, *Thinking Like a Woman*. New York: WIN Books, 1975.
    Dreamers & Dealers: An Intimate Appraisal of the Women's Movement. Boston: Beacon Press, 1980.

Frye, Marilyn, 'Who Wants a Piece of the Pie?' in *Building Feminist Theory: Essays from* Quest. New York and London: Longman, 1981.

Fulford, Roger, *Votes for Women*. London: White Lion, 1976.

Fuller, Margaret, *Woman in the Nineteenth Century*. New York: W.W. Norton & Co., 1971, with an introduction by Bernard Rosenthal.
    'The Great Lawsuit. Man versus Men. Woman versus Women'. 1843. Reprinted in *The Feminist Papers*, edited by Alice Rossi. 1974.

Garner, Les, *Stepping Stones to Women's Liberty: Feminist Ideas in the Women's Suffrage Movement 1900–1918*. London: Heinemann, 1984.

Gearhart, Sally Miller, *The Wanderground: Stories of the Hill Women*. Watertown, Massachusetts: Persephone Press, 1978.
    'The Future – If There Is One – Is Female' in McAllister, Pam, *Reweaving the Web of Life: Feminism and Nonviolence*. Philadelphia: New Society Publishers, 1982.

Giddings, Paula, *When and Where I Enter: The Impact of Black Women on Race and Sex in America*. New York: Bantam Books, 1985.

Giffin, Frederick C. (ed), *Woman as Revolutionary*. New York: New American Library, 1973.

Gilbert, Sandra M., and Gubar, Susan, *The Madwoman in the Attic: The Woman Writer and the 19th Century Literary Imagination*. New Haven & London: Yale University Press, 1979.

Gilligan, Carol, *In a Different Voice: Psychological Theory and Women's Development*. Cambridge and London: Harvard University Press, 1982.

Gilman, Charlotte Perkins, *Herland*. New York: Pantheon, 1979, with an introduction by Ann J. Lane.
    The Living of Charlotte Perkins Gilman: An Autobiography. New York: Harper and Row, 1975.
    'The Yellow Wallpaper', in *The Charlotte Perkins Gilman Reader*, edited and introduced by Lane, Ann J. 1980.

Gordon, Linda, *Woman's Body, Woman's Right*. London: Penguin, 1977.

Gornick, Vivian and Moran, Barbara K.(eds), *Woman in Sexist Society: Studies in Power and Powerlessness*. New York: New American Library, 1972.

Gould, Lois, 'X: A Fabulous Child's Story', in *Ms.*, December 1972; reprinted New York: Daughters Publishing Co., 1978.

Goulianos, Joan (ed), *By a Woman Writt: Literature from Six Centuries By and About Women*. Baltimore: Penguin Books, 1974.

Graves, Robert, *The White Goddess: A Historical Grammar of Poetic Myth*. London: Faber and Faber, 1948.

Greenberg, Blu, *On Women and Judaism: A View from Tradition*. Philadelphia: The Jewish Publication Society of America, 1981.

Greer, Germaine, *The Female Eunuch*. London: MacGibbon & Kee, 1970.
    The Obstacle Race. London: Secker & Warburg, 1979.
    Sex and Destiny: The Politics of Human Fertility. London: Picador, 1985.

Griffin, Susan, *Woman and Nature: The Roaring Inside Her*. New York: Harper & Row, 1978. London: The Women's Press, 1984.
    Pornography and Silence. New York: Harper & Row, 1981. London: The Women's Press, 1981.

Grimstad, Kirsten and Rennie, Susan (eds), *The New Woman's Survival Catalog*. New York: Coward, McCann & Geoghegan, 1973.
    The New Woman's Survival Sourcebook. New York: Alfred A. Knopf, 1975.

Gurko, Miriam, *The Ladies of Seneca Falls: The Birth of the Woman's Rights Movement*. New York: Schocken Books, 1976.

Haber, Barbara, *Women in America: A Guide to Books 1963–1975*. University of Illinois Press, 1981.

Hacker, Marilyn, 'Science Fiction and Feminism: The Work of Joanna Russ', in *Chrysalis* No. 4, 1977.

Hamblin, Angela, 'Is a Feminist Heterosexuality Possible?' in *Sex and Love:*

New Thoughts on Old Contradictions, edited by Cartledge and Ryan. 1983.

Hanisch, Carol, 'The Personal is Political', in *Notes from the Second Year*, 1970.
    'The Liberal Takeover of Women's Liberation' in *Feminist Revolution*, edited by Redstockings. New York: Redstockings, 1975.

Harford, Barbara and Hopkins, Sarah (eds), *Greenham Common: Women at the Wire*. London: The Women's Press, 1984.

Hartmann, Heidi, 'The Unhappy Marriage of Marxism and Feminism', in *Women and Revolution*, edited by Lydia Sargent. 1981.

Hartsock, Nancy, 'Political Change: Two Perspectives on Power', in *Building Feminist Theory: Essays from Quest*. 1981.
    'Fundamental Feminism: Process and Perspective', in *Building Feminist Theory: Essays from Quest*. 1981.
    'Feminist Theory and the Development of Revolutionary Strategy', in *Capitalist Patriarchy and the Case for Socialist Feminism* edited by Zillah Eisenstein. 1979.

Haskell, Molly, *From Reverence to Rape: The Treatment of Women in the Movies*. London: Penguin Books, 1974.

Hawxhurst, Donna, and Morrow, Sue, *Living Our Visions: Building Feminist Community*. Tempe, Arizona: Fourth World, 1984.

Hedges, Elaine and Wendt, Ingrid, *In Her Own Image: Women Working in the Arts*. New York: The Feminist Press, 1980.

Heilbrun, Carolyn G., *Toward a Recognition of Androgyny*. New York: Harper and Row, 1974.

Henley, Nancy M., *Body Politics*. Englewood Cliffs, N.J. Prentice-Hall, 1977.

Herschberger, Ruth, *Adam's Rib*. New York: Harper & Row, 1970.

Hersh, Blanche Glassman, *The Slavery of Sex: Feminist-Abolitionists in America*. University of Illinois Press, 1978.

Heschel, Susannah (ed), *On Being a Jewish Feminist: A Reader*. New York: Schocken Books, 1983.

Hole, Judith, and Levine, Ellen, *Rebirth of Feminism*. New York: Quadrangle Books, 1973.

Holland, Barbara (ed), *Soviet Sisterhood: British Feminists on Women in the USSR*. London: Fourth Estate Ltd., 1985.

Holland, Joy (ed), *Feminist Action 1*. London: Battle Axe Books, 1984.

Hooks, Bell, *Ain't I a Woman: Black Women and Feminism*. Boston: South End Press, 1981.
    Feminist Theory: From Margin to Center. Boston: South End Press, 1984.

Hubbard, Ruth, Henifin, Mary Sue, and Fried, Barbara, *Women Look at Biology Looking at Women: A Collection of Feminist Critiques*. Cambridge, Mass.: Schenkman Publishing Co., 1979.

Hull, Gloria, T. and Smith, Barbara, 'The Politics of Black Women's Studies', in *Learning Our Way*, edited by Charlotte Bunch, and Sandra Pollack. 1983.

International Council of Women, *Women in a Changing World: The Dynamic*

Story of the International Council of Women since 1888. London: Routledge and Kegan Paul, 1966.

Irigaray, Luce, 'This Sex Which Is Not One', in *New French Feminisms*, edited by Marks and de Courtivron., 1981.

'When the Goods Get Together', in *New French Feminisms*, edited by Marks and de Courtivron. 1981.

Jacobus, Mary, *Women Writing and Writing About Women*. London: Croom Helm, 1979.

Jaggar, Alison M., *Feminist Politics and Human Nature*. Sussex: Harvester Press, 1983.

Jaggar, Alison M. and McBride, William L., ' "Reproduction" as Male Ideology', in *Women's Studies International Forum*, Vol. 8, Number 3, 1985.

Janeway, Elizabeth, *Man's World, Woman's Place: A Study in Social Mythology*. New York: Dell, 1971.

Jeffreys, Sheila, *The Spinster and Her Enemies: Feminism and Sexuality 1880–1930*. London: Pandora Press, 1986.

Jehlin, Myra, 'Archimedes and the Paradox of Feminist Criticism', in *Feminist Theory: A Critique of Ideology*, edited by Keohane, Rosaldo and Gelpi. 1982.

Joan, Polly and Chesman, Andrea, *Guide to Women's Publishing*. California: Dustbooks, 1978.

Johnston, Jill, *Lesbian Nation: The Feminist Solution*. New York: Simon and Schuster, 1973.

Jones, Ann Rosalind, 'Julia Kristeva on Femininity: The Limits of a Semiotic Politics', in *Feminist Review* 18, Winter 1984.

'Writing the Body: Toward an Understanding of *l'écriture féminine*', in *The New Feminist Criticism*, edited by Elaine Showalter. 1985.

Jones, Lynne (ed), *Keeping the Peace*. London: The Women's Press, 1983.

Jong, Erica, *Fear of Flying*. London: Granada, 1974.

Joreen, 'The BITCH Manifesto', in *Notes from the Second Year*. New York, 1970.

Joseph, Gloria, 'The Incompatible *Ménage à Trois*: Marxism, Feminism, and Racism', in *Women and Revolution*, edited by Lydia Sargent. 1981.

Juhasz, Suzanne, *Naked and Fiery Forms: Modern American Poetry by Women. A New Tradition*. New York: Harper & Row, 1976.

Kamm, Josephine, *Rapiers and Battleaxes: The Women's Movement and Its Aftermath*. London: George Allen & Unwin, 1966.

Kaplan, E. Ann, *Women and Film: Both Sides of the Camera*. London: Methuen, 1983.

Kaplan, Marion A., *The Jewish Feminist Movement in Germany: The Campaigns of the Judische Frauenbund, 1904–1938*. Westport, Conn.: The Greenwood Press, 1979.

Kelly, Joan, 'Early Feminist Theory and the *Querelle des Femmes*, 1400–1789', in *Signs: Journal of Women in Culture and Society*, vol. 8, no. 1, 1982.

Kenney, Annie, *Memories of a Militant*. London: Edward Arnold, 1924.

Keohane, Nannerl O., Rosaldo, Michelle, and Gelpi, Barbara C. (eds), *Feminist Theory: A Critique of Ideology*. Sussex: Harvester Press, 1982.

Kessler, Carol Farley (ed), *Daring to Dream: Utopian Stories by United States Women: 1836–1919*. London: Pandora Press, 1984.

Keyssar, Helene, *Feminist Theatre*. London: Macmillan, 1984.

Kimball, Gayle (ed), *Women's Culture: The Women's Renaissance of the Seventies*. Metuchen, N.J. and London: The Scarecrow Press, 1981.

Koedt, Anne, 'Lesbianism and Feminism', in *Notes From the Third Year*, 1971.

    'The Myth of the Vaginal Orgasm', in *Notes from the Second Year*, 1970.

Kolodny, Annette, 'Some Notes on Defining a "feminist literary criticism" ', in *Feminist Criticism*, edited by Brown and Olson, 1978.

    'Dancing Through the Mine-Field: Some Observations on the Theory, Practice, and Politics of a Feminist Literary Criticism', in *Men's Studies Modified*, edited by Dale Spender, 1981.

Koltun, Elizabeth, *The Jewish Woman: New Perspectives*. New York: Schocken Books, 1976.

Komisar, Lucy, *The New Feminism*. London: Franklin Watts, 1971.

Kornegger, Peggy, 'Anarchism: The Feminist Connection', 1975, reprinted in *Quiet Rumours*. London: Dark Star, no date.

Kraditor, Aileen S., *The Ideas of the Woman Suffrage Movement, 1890–1920*. New York: W.W. Norton & Co., 1981.

Kramarae, Cheris, *Women and Men Speaking: Frameworks for Analysis*. Rowley, Mass.: Newbury House, 1981.

Kramarae, Cheris and Treichler, Paula, *A Feminist Dictionary*. London: Pandora Press, 1985.

Kristeva, Julia, 'Woman Can Never Be Defined', in *New French Feminisms*, edited by Marks and de Courtivron, 1981.

    'Oscillation Between Power and Denial', edited by Marks and de Courtivron, 1981.

    'Chinese Women against the Tide' and 'About Chinese Women', edited by Marks and de Courtivron, 1981.

    Desire in Language: A Semiotic Approach to Literature and Art. Oxford: Basil Blackwell, 1981.

Kuhn, Annette, *Women's Pictures: Feminism and Cinema*. London: Routledge and Kegan Paul, 1982.

Lakoff, Robin. *Language and Woman's Place*. New York: Harper & Row, 1975.

Lane, Ann J. (ed), *The Charlotte Perkins Gilman Reader*. New York: Pantheon Books, 1980. London: The Women's Press, 1981.

Leavitt, Dinah Luise, *Feminist Theatre Groups*. Jefferson, N.C.: McFarland, 1980.

Lederer, Laura (ed), *Take Back the Night: Women on Pornography*. New York: Bantam, 1982.

LeGuin, Ursula K., *The Left Hand of Darkness*. London: Granada, 1973.
    The Language of the Night. edited by Susan Wood. New York: G.P. Putnam's Sons, 1979.

Lerner, Gerda, *The Majority Finds Its Past: Placing Women in History*. New York: Oxford University Press, 1979.

Lessing, Doris, *The Golden Notebook*. New York: Ballantine, 1962.
    A Small Personal Voice. New York: Vintage Books, 1975. Edited by Paul Schlueter.

Lidderdale, Jane and Nicholson, Mary, *Dear Miss Weaver: Harriet Shaw Weaver 1876–1961*. London: Faber and Faber, 1970.

Linklater, Andro, *An Unhusbanded Life: Charlotte Despard*. London: Hutchinson, 1980.

London Rape Action Group, 'Towards a Revolutionary Feminist Analysis of Rape', in *Women Against Violence Against Women*, edited by Rhodes and McNeil, 1985.

Lorde, Audre, 'Uses of the Erotic: The Erotic as Power', in *Take Back the Night*, edited by Laura Lederer, 1982.
    Sister Outsider. Trumansburg, N.Y.: The Crossing Press, 1984.

Love Your Enemy? The Debate Between Heterosexual Feminism and Political Lesbianism. London: Onlywomen Press, 1981.

Lutz, Alma, *Susan B. Anthony: Rebel, Crusader, Humanitarian*. Boston: Beacon Press, 1959.

McAllister, Pam (ed), *Reweaving the Web of Life: Feminism and Nonviolence*. Philadelphia: New Society Publishers, 1982.

McKluskie, Kate, 'Women's Language and Literature: A Problem in Women's Studies', in *Feminist Review* 14, Summer 1983.

Maitland, Sara, *A Map of the New Country: Women and Christianity*. London: Routledge and Kegan Paul, 1983.

Maitland, Sara and Garcia, Jo (eds), *Walking on the Water: Women Talk About Spirituality*. London: Virago, 1983.

Mamonova, Tatyana (ed), *Women and Russia: Feminist Writings from the Soviet Union*. Oxford: Basil Blackwell, 1984.

Marcus, Jane, 'Art and Anger', in *Feminist Studies*, February 1978.
    'The Divine Rage to be Didactic: Elizabeth Robins' *The Convert*,' introduction to *The Convert* by Elizabeth Robins. London: The Women's Press, 1980.

Margolis, Karen, 'The Long and Winding Roads (reflections on *Beyond the Fragments*)', in *Feminist Review* 5, 1980.

Marks, Elaine and de Courtivron, Isabelle (eds), *New French Feminisms: An Anthology*. Brighton: Harvester Press, 1981.

Martin, Angela, 'Chantal Ackerman's Films: a dossier', in *Feminist Review* 3, 1979.

Mainardi, Pat, 'The Politics of Housework', in *Sisterhood is Powerful*, edited by Robin Morgan. 1970.

Martyna, Wendy, 'Beyond the He/Man Approach: The Case for Nonsexist Language', in *Language, Gender and Society*, edited by Thorne, Kramarae and Henley, 1983.

Mayne, Judith, 'Feminist Film Theory and Criticism', in *Signs: Journal of Women in Culture and Society*, Vol. 11, No. 1, Autumn 1985.

Mernissi, Fatima, *Beyond the Veil: Male-Female Dynamics in Muslim Society*. London: Al Saqi Books, 1985.

Miller, Casey and Swift, Kate, *The Handbook of Non-Sexist Writing for Writers, Editors and Speakers*. London: The Women's Press, 1981.
    Words and Women. New York: Anchor Press/Doubleday, 1976.

Miller, Jean Baker, *Toward a New Psychology of Women*. Boston: Beacon Press, 1976. London: Penguin, 1978.

Millett, Kate, *Sexual Politics*. New York: Avon, 1971. London: Virago, 1977.
    'Sexual Politics: A Manifesto for Revolution,' in *Notes from the Second Year*, 1970.

Mitchell, David, *Queen Christabel*. London: Macdonald and Jane's, 1977.
    The Fighting Pankhursts. New York: Macmillan, 1980.

Mitchell, Juliet, *Woman's Estate*. London: Penguin, 1971.
    Psychoanalysis and Feminism. London: Penguin, 1982.
    Women: The Longest Revolution. London: Virago, 1984.

Mitchell, Juliet and Oakley, Ann (eds), *The Rights and Wrongs of Women*. London: Penguin, 1976.

Moers, Ellen, *Literary Women: The Great Writers*. New York: Doubleday, 1976. London: The Women's Press, 1978.

Mohin, Lilian (ed), *One Foot on the Mountain: An Anthology of British Feminist Poetry 1969–1979*. London: Onlywomen Press, 1982.

Mohr, James C., *Abortion in America: The Origins and Evolution of National Policy, 1800–1900*. Oxford University Press, 1978.

Moltmann-Wendall, Elizabeth, *The Women Around Jesus*. SCM Press, 1984.

Montefiore, Janet, 'Feminist Identity and the Poetic Tradition', in *Feminist Review* 13, Spring 1983.

Montgomery, Sarah, 'Women's Women's Films', in *Feminist Review* 18, Winter 1984.

Moore, Honor (ed), *The New Women's Theatre*. New York: Vintage, 1977.

Moraga, Cherríe and Anzaldúa, Gloria (eds), *This Bridge Called My Back: Writings by Radical Women of Color*. New York: Kitchen Table: Women of Color Press, 1983.

Morgan, Elaine, *The Descent of Woman*. New York: Bantam Books, 1973.

Morgan, Robin (ed), *Sisterhood is Powerful*. New York: Vintage Books, 1970.
   Monster. New York: Vintage Books, 1972.
   Going Too Far. New York: Vintage Books, 1978.
   The Anatomy of Freedom: Feminism, Physics and Global Politics. Oxford: Martin Robertson, 1983.
   (ed) *Sisterhood is Global*. New York: Anchor Books, 1984.

Morrison, Toni, 'What the Black Woman Thinks About Women's Lib' in The New York Times Magazine, 22 August 1971.

Mulvey, Laura, 'Visual Pleasure and Narrative Cinema', in *Screen* Vol. 16, No. 3, Autumn 1975.

Murray, Janet Horowitz, *Strong-Minded Women: And Other Lost Voices From 19th Century England*. London: Penguin, 1984.

Neumann, Erich, *The Great Mother: An Analysis of the Archetype*. Princeton University Press, 1974.

Newton, Judith L., Ryan, Mary and Walkowitz, Judith (eds), *Sex and Class in Women's History*. London: Routledge and Kegan Paul, 1983.

New York Radical Feminists, 'Politics of the Ego', 1969, reprinted in *Rebirth of Feminism* by Judith Hole, and Ellen Levine, 1973.

Nochlin, Linda, 'Why Are There No Great Women Artists?' in *Women in Sexist Society*, edited by Gornick and Moran, 1972.

Oakley, Ann, *Subject Women*. Oxford: Martin Robertson, 1981.
   Taking it Like a Woman. London: Jonathan Cape, 1984.

Oakley, Mary Ann B., *Elizabeth Cady Stanton*. New York: The Feminist Press, 1972.

O'Brien, Mary, *The Politics of Reproduction*. London: Routledge and Kegan Paul, 1981.

O'Hara, Maureen, 'Prostitution – Towards a feminist analysis and strategy', in *Women Against Violence Against Women*, edited by Rhodes and McNeil. 1985.

Olsen, Tillie, *Silences*. New York: Seymour Lawrence, Delacourt Press, 1978. London: Virago, 1980.

O'Neill, Lois Decker, *The Women's Book of World Records and Achievements*. New York: Anchor Press, 1979.

O'Neill, William L., *Everyone Was Brave: A History of Feminism in America*. New York: Quadrangle Books, 1976.

Ostriker, Alicia, *Writing Like a Woman*. Ann Arbor: The University of Michigan Press, 1983.

Palmer, A.W., *A Dictionary of Modern History 1789–1945*. London: Penguin, 1964.

Parker, Rozsika, 'Portrait of the Artist as Housewife' in *Spare Rib*, 60, July 1977.

Parker, Rozsika and Pollock, Griselda, *Old Mistresses: Women, Art and Ideology*. London: Routledge and Kegan Paul, 1981.

Petchesky, Rosalind, 'Dissolving the Hyphen: A Report on Marxist-Feminist

Groups 1–5', in *Capitalist Patriarchy and the Case for Socialist Feminism*, by Z. Eisenstein, 1979.

Peterson, Deena, *A Practical Guide to the Women's Movement*. New York: Women's Action Alliance, 1975.

Piercy, Marge, *Woman on the Edge of Time*. New York: Knopf, 1976. London: The Women's Press, 1979.

    Parti-Colored Blocks for a Quilt. Ann Arbor: University of Michigan Press, 1982.

Pizan, Christine de, *The Book of the City of Ladies*, translated by Earl Jeffrey Richards, with foreword by Marina Warner. London: Pan, 1983.

Pomeroy, Sarah B., *Goddesses, Whores, Wives and Slaves: Women in Classical Antiquity*. New York: Schocken Books, 1975.

Porter, Cathy, *Alexandra Kollontai*. London: Virago, 1980.

Raymond, Janice G., *The Transsexual Empire: The Making of the She-Male*. Boston: Beacon Press, 1979.

Redstockings of the Women's Liberation Movement (eds), *Feminist Revolution*. New York: Redstockings, 1975.

    Feminist Revolution (An Abridged Edition with Additional Writings). New York: Random House, 1978.

Reed, Evelyn, *Problems of Women's Liberation*. New York: Pathfinder Press, 1971.

    Woman's Evolution. New York: Pathfinder Press, 1975.

Reiter, Rayna (ed), *Toward an Anthropology of Women*. New York and London: Monthly Review Press, 1975.

Rhodes, Dusty and McNeill, Sandra (eds), *Women Against Violence Against Women*. London: Onlywomen Press, 1985.

Rich, Adrienne, *Of Woman Born: Motherhood as Experience and Institution*. New York: W.W. Norton, 1976. London: Virago, 1977.

    On Lies, Secrets and Silence: Selected Prose 1966–1978. New York: W.W. Norton, 1979. London: Virago, 1980.

    Compulsory Heterosexuality and Lesbian Existence. London: Onlywomen Press, 1981.

    Poems, Selected and New, 1950–1974. New York: W.W. Norton, 1974.

    The Dream of a Common Language: Poems 1974–1977. New York: W.W. Norton, 1978.

Richards, Janet Radcliffe, *The Sceptical Feminist: A Philosophical Inquiry*. London: Penguin Books, 1982.

Riencourt, Amaury de, *Sex and Power in History*. New York: Delta, 1974.

Roberts, Helen (ed), *Doing Feminist Research*. London: Routledge and Kegan Paul, 1981.

Robins, Elizabeth, *The Convert*. London: The Women's Press, 1980.

Rohrlich, Ruby and Baruch, Elaine Hoffman (eds), *Women in Search of Utopia: Mavericks and Mythmakers*. New York: Schocken Books, 1984.

Rosaldo, Michelle Zimbalist and Lamphere, Louise (eds), *Woman, Culture and Society*. Stanford: Stanford University Press, 1974.

Rosen, Andrew, *Rise Up Women! The Militant Campaign of the Women's Social and Political Union 1903–1914*. London: Routledge and Kegan Paul, 1974.

Rosen, Marjorie, *Popcorn Venus*. New York: Avon, 1974.

Rosenberg, Jan, *Women's Reflections: The Feminist Film Movement*. Ann Arbor: UMI Research Press, 1983.

Rosenberg, Rosalind, *Beyond Separate Spheres: Intellectual Roots of Modern Feminism*. New Haven and London: Yale University Press, 1982.

Rossi, Alice S. (ed), *The Feminist Papers: From Adams to de Beauvoir*. New York: Bantam Books, 1974.

Rover, Constance, *Women's Suffrage and Party Politics in Britain, 1866–1914*. London: Routledge and Kegan Paul, 1967.

Rowbotham, Sheila, *Women, Resistance and Revolution*. London: Penguin, 1972.
Hidden From History. London: Pluto Press, 1977.
Woman's Consciousness, Man's World. London: Penguin, 1976.
Dreams and Dilemmas. London: Virago, 1983.

Rowbotham, Sheila, Segal, Lynne and Wainwright, Hilary, *Beyond the Fragments: Feminism and the Making of Socialism*. London: Merlin Press, 1979.

Rowbotham, Sheila, 'The beginnings of Women's Liberation in Britain', in *The Body Politic* edited by Michelene Wandor, 1978.

Rowe, Marsha (ed), Spare Rib *Reader*. London: Penguin, 1982.

Rubin, Gayle, 'The Traffic in Women', from *Towards an Anthropology of Women* edited by Rayna R. Reiter, 1975.
'Thinking Sex: Notes for a Radical Theory of the Politics of Sexuality', in *Pleasure and Danger: Exploring Female Sexuality* edited by Carole S. Vance, 1984.

Ruddick, Sara and Daniels, Pamela (eds), *Working It Out: 23 Women Writers, Artists, Scientists and Scholars Talk About Their Lives and Work*. New York: Pantheon, 1977.

Rule, Jane, *Lesbian Images*. New York: Pocket Books, 1976.

Rumens, Carol (ed), *Making For the Open: The Chatto Book of Post-Feminist Poetry 1964–1984*. London: Chatto and Windus, 1985.

Russ, Joanna, *The Female Man*. New York: Bantam, 1975.
How to Suppress Women's Writings. London: The Women's Press, 1984.
Magic Mommas, Trembling Sisters, Puritans and Perverts: Feminist Essays. New York: The Crossing Press, 1985.

Russell, Diana E.H., 'Pornography and Violence: What Does the New Research Say?', in *Take Back the Night*, edited by Laura Lederer, 1982.

Ruthven, K.K., *Feminist Literary Studies: An Introduction*. Cambridge University Press, 1984.

Ruzek, Sheryl Burt, *The Women's Health Movement: Feminist Alternatives to Medical Control*. New York: Praeger, 1978.

Sarachild, Kathie, 'A Program for Feminist "Consciousness Raising"', in *Notes from the Second Year,* 1970.

Sargent, Lydia (ed), *Women and Revolution: A Discussion of the Unhappy Marriage of Marxism and Feminism.* London: Pluto Press, 1981.

Sayers, Janet, *Biological Politics: Feminist and Anti-Feminist Perspectives.* London: Tavistock, 1982.

Schneir, Miriam (ed), *Feminism: The Essential Historical Writings.* New York: Vintage Books, 1972.

Schreiner, Olive, *The Story of an African Farm.* First published 1886. London: Collins, 1965.

   Women and Labour. London: Virago, 1977.

Schwarz, Judith, *Radical Feminists of Heterodoxy: Greenwich Village 1912–1940.* Lebanon: N.H.: New Victoria Publishers, 1982.

Schwarzer, Alice, *Simone de Beauvoir Today: Conversations 1972–1982,* translated by Marianne Howarth. London: Chatto and Windus, 1984.

Scott, Anne Firor and Scott, Andrew M., *One Half the People: The Fight for Woman Suffrage.* University of Illinois Press, 1982.

Scovill, Ruth, 'Women's Music', in *Women's Culture: The Women's Renaissance of the Seventies,* edited by Gayle Kimball, 1981.

Scruton, Roger, *A Dictionary of Political Thought.* London: Pan, 1983.

Segal, Lynne (ed), *What is to be done about the Family?* London, Penguin, 1983.

Seyersted, Per, *Kate Chopin: A Critical Biography.* Baton Rouge and London: Louisiana State University Press, 1980.

Shaw, Evelyn and Darling, Joan, *Strategies of Being Female: Animal Patterns, Human Choices.* Brighton: Harvester Press, 1985.

Sherfey, Mary Jane, *The Nature and Evolution of Female Sexuality.* New York: Vintage, 1973.

Sherr, Lynn and Kazickas, Jurate, *The American Woman's Gazetteer.* New York: Bantam, 1976.

Showalter, Elaine, *A Literature of Their Own: British Women Novelists from Brontë to Lessing.* New Jersey: Princeton University Press, 1977.

   (ed), *The New Feminist Criticism: Essays on Women, Literature and Theory.* New York: Pantheon, 1985.

Shulman, Alix Kates, *Memoirs of an Ex-Prom Queen.* New York: Bantam, 1973.
   Burning Questions. New York: Knopf, 1978.
   'Sex and Power: Sexual Bases of Radical Feminism', in *Signs: Journal of Women in Culture and Society,* Summer 1980, Volume 5, Number 4.
   'Living Our Life', in *Between Women* edited by Ascher, DeSalvo and Ruddick. 1984.

Shuttle, Penelope and Redgrove, Peter, *The Wise Wound: Menstruation and Everywoman.* London: Penguin, 1980.

Sicherman, Barbara and Green, Carol Hurd, *Notable American Women: The Modern Period.* Cambridge, Mass. and London: Belknap Press, 1980.

Singer, June, *Androgyny: Toward a New Theory of Sexuality*. New York: Doubleday/Anchor, 1977.

Slaughter, Jane and Kern, Robert, *European Women on the Left: Socialism and Feminism, and the Problems Faced by Political Women, 1880 to the Present*. Westport and London: Greenwood Press, 1981.

Smeal, Eleanor, *Why and How Women Will Elect the Next President*. New York: Harper and Row, 1984.

Smedley, Agnes, *Daughter of Earth*, with afterword by Paul Lauter. New York: The Feminist Press, 1973. London: Virago, 1977.

    Portraits of Chinese Women in Revolution, edited and with an introduction by Jan MacKinnon and Steve MacKinnon; afterword by Florence Howe. New York: The Feminist Press, 1976.

Smith, Barbara, 'Notes for Yet Another Paper on Black Feminism, or Will the Real Enemy Please Stand Up?' in *Conditions Five*, 1979.

    'Toward a Black Feminist Criticism', in *The New Feminist Criticism*, edited by Elaine Showalter. 1985.

Smith-Rosenberg, Carroll, *Disorderly Conduct: Visions of Gender in Victorian America*. New York: Knopf, 1985.

Snitow, Ann, Stansell, Christine and Thompson, Sharon (eds), *Desire: The Politics of Sexuality*. London: Virago, 1984.

Snodgrass, Jon (ed), *For Men Against Sexism: A Book of Readings*. New York: Times Change Press, 1977.

Snyder-Ott, Joelynn, *Women and Creativity*. Millbrae, California: Les Femmes, 1978.

Solanas, Valerie, *SCUM Manifesto*. New York: Olympia Press, 1968.

Spacks, Patricia Meyer, *The Female Imagination*. New York: Avon Books, 1976.

Spender, Dale, 'The gatekeepers: a feminist critique of academic publishing', in *Doing Feminist Research*, edited by Helen Roberts. 1981.

    Man Made Language. London: Routledge and Kegan Paul, 1981.

    Men's Studies Modified: The Impact of Feminism on the Academic Disciplines. Oxford: Pergamon Press, 1981.

    Women of Ideas (And What Men Have Done to Them). London: Routledge and Kegan Paul, 1982.

    (ed), *Feminist Theorists*. London: The Women's Press, 1983.

    There's Always Been a Women's Movement This Century. London: Pandora Press, 1983.

    Time and Tide Wait for No Man. London: Pandora Press, 1984.

    For the Record: The Making and Meaning of Feminist Knowledge. London: The Women's Press, 1985.

Spender, Lynne, *Intruders on the Rights of Men: Women's Unpublished Heritage*. London: Pandora Press, 1983.

Spretnak, Charlene (ed), *The Politics of Women's Spirituality: Essays on the Rise of*

Spiritual Power Within the Feminist Movement. New York: Anchor Press, 1982.

Stambler, Sookie (ed.), *Women's Liberation: Blueprint for the Future*. New York: Ace Books, 1970.

Stanley, Liz, ' "Male Needs": The Problems and Problems of Working with Gay Men', in *On the Problem of Men* edited by Scarlet Friedman and Elizabeth Sarah. 1982.

Stanley, Liz and Wise, Sue, *Breaking Out: Feminist Consciousness and Feminist Research*. London: Routledge and Kegan Paul, 1983.

Star, Susan Leigh, 'The Politics of Right and Left: Sex Differences in Hemispheric Brain Asymmetry', in *Women Look at Biology Looking at Women*, edited by Hubbard, Henifin and Fried, 1979.

Steinem, Gloria, *Outrageous Acts and Everyday Rebellions*. London: Jonathan Cape, 1984.

'How Women Live, Vote, Think . . . Louis Harris National Survey' in *Ms.*, July 1984.

Sternburg, Janet (ed), *The Writer On Her Work*. New York: W.W. Norton, 1980.

Stevens, May, 'My Work and My Working-Class Father', in *Working It Out*, edited by Ruddick and Daniels. 1977.

Stites, Richard, *The Women's Liberation Movement in Russia: Feminism, Nihilism and Bolshevism 1860–1930*. Princeton University Press, 1978.

Stone, Merlin, *When God was a Woman*. New York: The Dial Press, 1976.

Ancient Mirrors of Womanhood: Our Goddess and Heroine Heritage. New York: New Sibylline Books, 1979.

Stott, Mary, *Forgetting's No Excuse*. London: Faber and Faber, 1973.

Strachey, Ray, *The Cause: A Short History of the Women's Movement in Great Britain*. London: Virago, 1978.

Strainchamps, Ethel, 'Our Sexist Language', in *Woman in Sexist Society*, edited by Gornick and Moran. 1972.

Stubbs, Patricia, *Women and Fiction: Feminism and the Novel 1880–1920*. London: Methuen, 1981.

Tanner, Leslie B. (ed), *Voices from Women's Liberation*. New York: Signet, 1971.

Tanner, Nancy, 'Matrifocality in Indonesia and Africa and Among Black Americans', in *Woman, Culture and Society* edited by Rosaldo and Lamphere. 1974.

Taylor, Barbara, *Eve and the New Jerusalem: Socialism and Feminism in the Nineteenth Century*. London: Virago, 1983.

Thompson, Dorothy (ed), *Over Our Dead Bodies: Women Against the Bomb*, London: Virago, 1983.

Thompson, William, *Appeal of One Half the Human Race, Women, Against the Pretensions of the Other Half, Men, to Retain Them in Political and Thence in Civil and Domestic Slavery*, with an introduction by Richard Pankhurst. London: Virago, 1983.

Tomalin, Claire, *The Life and Death of Mary Wollstonecraft*. London: Penguin, 1977.

Tristan, Flora, *The London Journal of Flora Tristan*, translated, annotated and introduced by Jean Hawkes. London: Virago, 1982.

Uglow, Jennifer S., *The Macmillan Dictionary of Women's Biography*. London: Macmillan, 1984.

Vance, Carole S. (ed), *Pleasure and Danger: Exploring Female Sexuality*. London: Routledge and Kegan Paul, 1984.

Vetterling-Braggin, Mary (ed), *Sexist Language: A Modern Philosophical Analysis*. New Jersey: Rowman and Littlefield, 1981.

Wallace, Michele, *Black Macho and the Myth of the Superwoman*. New York: Dial Press, 1979.

Wandor, Michelene (ed), *The Body Politic: Women's Liberation in Britain*. London: Stage One, 1978.

    Understudies: Theatre and Sexual Politics. London: Methuen, 1981.

    (ed) *Plays by Women, Volume Two*. London: Methuen, 1983.

    (ed) *On Gender and Writing*. London: Pandora Press, 1983.

Warren, Mary Anne, *The Nature of Woman: An Encyclopedia and Guide to the Literature*. California: Edgepress, 1980.

Weideger, Paula, *Menstruation and Menopause*. New York: Knopf, 1976. Published in UK as *Female Cycles*. London: The Women's Press, 1978.

Weisstein, Naomi, '*Kinder, Küche, Kirche* as Scientific Law: Psychology Constructs the Female', in *Sisterhood is Powerful* edited by Robin Morgan. 1970.

    ' "How can a little girl like you teach a great big class of men?" the Chairman Said, and Other Adventures of a Woman in Science,' in *Working it Out*, edited by Ruddick and Daniels. 1977.

Wilson, Elizabeth, *What is to be done about Violence Against Women?* London: Penguin, 1983.

Wittig, Monique, *Les Guérillères*. London: Peter Owen, 1971.

    'One is Not Born a Woman' in *Feminist Issues* 1:2, Winter 1981.

Wittig, Monique and Zeig, Sande, *Lesbian Peoples: Materials for a Dictionary*. London: Virago, 1980.

Wolgast, Elizabeth H., *Equality and the Rights of Women*. London: Cornell University Press, 1980.

Wollstonecraft, Mary, *Vindication of the Rights of Women*. London: Penguin, 1985.

Women's Action Alliance, *Women's Action Almanac*. New York: William Morrow and Co., 1979.

Women and Geography Study Group of the IBG, *Geography and Gender: An Introduction to Feminist Geography*. London: Hutchinson, 1984.

Women in Eastern Europe Group (ed), *Woman and Russia: First Feminist Samizdat*. London: Sheba, 1980.

Wood, Elizabeth, 'Women in Music', in *Signs: Journal of Women in Culture and Society* 1980, Vol. 6, No. 2.

Woolf, Virginia, *A Room of One's Own*. London: Hogarth Press, 1928.
    Three Guineas. London: Hogarth Press, 1938.
    Women and Writing, edited and introduced by Michèle Barrett. New York: Harcourt Brace Jovanovich, 1979. London: The Women's Press, 1979.

Yalom, Marilyn (ed), *Women Writers of the West Coast: Speaking of Their Lives and Careers*. Santa Barbara: Capra Press, 1983.

Yates, Gayle Graham, *What Women Want: The Ideas of the Movement*. Harvard University Press, 1975.

Young, Iris Marion, 'Humanism, Gynocentrism and Feminist Politics', in *Women's Studies International Forum*, Vol. 8, Number 3, 1985.